An Overview of the Menu Bar's Selections

Menu	Description
File	File-related commands that operate on your program file, such as loading a program from disk, saving a program you enter to disk, and printing the program.
Edit	Includes options that aid in adding, changing, searching for, and deleting text from the current program.
View	Options for moving around the editor and controlling the display.
Project	This menu includes the Build command, which runs the compiler and linker, and the Execute command, which enables you to test your program without leaving the workbench.
Browse	Used for examining C++ classes.
Debug	This pull-down menu includes the commands that enable you to examine the code as it runs to help you get errors out of your program.
Tools	Special features that can be added to the workbench (not available as installed).
Options	Options for setting up the workbench to better suit the way a programmer works.
Window	Standard Windows menu for selecting and arranging windows.
Help	Visual C++ provides a rich assortment of online help. Instead of having to look in a bulky Visual C++ reference manual, you can select from the various help-related topics to find anything you need about the workbench or Visual C++.

The Visual C++ Variable Data Types

Declaration Name	Data Type Description
char	Character
unsigned char	Unsigned character
signed char	Signed character (same as char)
int	Integer
unsigned int	Unsigned integer
signed int	Signed integer (same as int)
short int	Short integer
unsigned short int	Unsigned short integer
signed short int	Signed short integer (same as short int)
long	Long integer
long int	Long integer (same as long)
signed long int	Signed long integer (same as long int)
unsigned long int	Unsigned long integer
float	Floating-point (real)
double	Double floating-point (real)
long double	Long double floating-point (real)

Ranges of Visual C++ Variables

Type	Range
char	–128 to 127
unsigned char	0 to 255
signed	
in	
un	
sig	
short int	–32768 to 32767
unsigned short int	0 to 65535
signed short int	–32768 to 32767
long int	–2147483648 to 2147483647
signed long int	–2147483648 to 2147483647
unsigned long	0 to 4294967296
float	–3.4E38 to 3.4E+38
double	–1.7E308 to 1.7E+308
long double	–3.4E4932 to 1.1E+4932
float	–3.4E+38 to 3.4E+38
double	–1.7E+308 to 1.7E+308
long double	–3.4E+4932 to 1.1E+4932

Visual C++'s Special Escape Sequence Characters

Escape Sequence	Meaning
\a	Alarm (a beep from the speaker)
\b	Backspace
\f	Form feed (new page on printer)
\n	Newline (carriage return and line feed)
\r	Carriage return
\t	Tab
\v	Vertical tab
\\	Backslash (\)
\?	Question mark
\'	Single quotation mark
\"	Double quotation mark
\000	Octal number
\xhh	Hexadecimal number
\0	Terminator (or binary zero)

Visual C++'s Primary Math Operators

Math Operator	Description
*	Multiplication
/	Division or integer division
%	Modulus (also called remainder)
+	Unary: Specifies a positive amount (optional for positive values)
	Binary: Performs addition
-	Unary: Specifies a negative amount
	Binary: Performs subtraction

The Compound Operators and Their Equivalent Meanings

Compound Operator	Example	Equivalent Assignments
+=	a += 100;	a = a + 100;
-=	b -= 0.25;	b = b - 0.25;
*=	c *= 13;	c = c * 13;
/=	d /= 4;	d = d / 4;
%=	e %= 2;	e = e % 2;

The Relational Operators and Their Meanings

Relational Operator	Description
==	Equal to
>	Greater than
>=	Greater than or equal to
<	Less than
<=	Less than or equal to
!=	Not equal to

The Logical Operators

Logical Operator	Meaning	Description
&&	AND	Returns true if and only if both sides of the && are true.
¦¦	OR	Returns true if one or the other side of the ¦¦ is true (or if both sides are true).
!	NOT	Changes a true relation to false or a false relation to true.

The Automatic Data Type Promotions

Source Data Type	What It Promotes To
char	int or the largest data type if int is not the largest data type in the expression.
short	int or the largest data type if int is not the largest data type in the expression.
unsigned short	unsigned int or the largest data type if unsigned int is not the largest data type in the expression.
float	The larger of double or long double, depending on which appears in the expression.
double	long double if a long double appears in the expression.

The Structure Access Operators

Operator	Description
.	Accesses data in a member of an individual structure variable.
->	Accesses data in a member of a structure pointed to by a pointer.

Possible Origin Values

Visual C++ Name	Description
ios::beg	Beginning of file
ios::cur	Current file position
ios::end	End of file

Possible File Access Modes

Mode	Description
ios::app	Opens a file for appending (adding to).
ios::ate	Seeks to end of file on opening it.
ios::in	Opens a file for reading.
ios::out	Opens a file for writing.
ios::binary	Opens a file in binary mode.
ios::trunc	Discards the contents if the file exists.
ios::nocreate	If file does not exist, open fails.

ios::noreplace	If file exists, open fails unless appending or seeking to the end of file on opening.

Visual C++ Operator Precedence Table

Precedence Level	Symbol	Description	Associativity
1	::	C++ scope access/ resolution	Left to right
2	()	Function call	Left to right
	[]	Array subscript	
	->	Visual C++ indirect component selector	
	.	C++ direct component selector	
3 Unary	!	Logical negation	Right to left
	~	Bitwise (1's) complement	
	+	Unary plus	
	-	Unary minus	
	&	Address of	
	*	Indirection	
	sizeof	Returns size of operand in bytes	
	new	Dynamically allocates C++ storage	
	delete	Dynamically deallocates C++ storage	
	type	Typecast	
4 Member Access	.*	C++ dereference	Left to right
	->*	C++ dereference	
	()	Expression parentheses	
5 Multiplicative	*	Multiply	Left to right
	/	Divide	
	%	Remainder (modulus)	
6 Additive	+	Binary plus	Left to right
	-	Binary minus	
7 Shift	<<	Leftshift	Left to right
	>>	Rightshift	
8 Relational	<	Less than	Left to right
	<=	Less than or equal to	
	>	Greater than	
	>=	Greater than or equal to	
9 Equality	==	Equal to	Left to right
	!=	Not equal to	
10	&	Bitwise AND	Left to right
11	^	Bitwise XOR	Left to right
12	¦	Bitwise OR	Left to right
13	&&	Logical AND	Left to right
14	¦¦	Logical OR	Left to right
15 Ternary	?:	Conditional	Right to left
16 Assignment	=	Simple assignment	Right to left
	*=	Compound assign product	
	/=	Compound assign quotient	
	%=	Compound assign remainder	
	+=	Compound assign sum	
	-=	Compound assign difference	
	&=	Compound assign bitwise AND	
	^=	Compound assign bitwise XOR	
	¦=	Compound assign bitwise OR	
	<<=	Compound assign left shift	

The 12 Easy Elements

In 12 Easy Lessons

A *Concept* introduces you to a new topic and tells you what you'll learn.

Stop & Type lets you know it's time to fire up your compiler and try a sample.

Every sample program contains three sections: *input* (the code you enter), *output* (the results you get), and *analysis* (a complete explanation).

Each lesson has three parts—two *units* and a *review project*—designed to make learning Visual C++ easy.

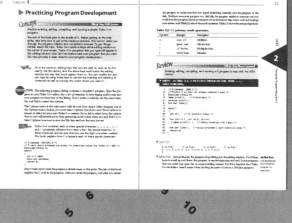

What did you just learn? Each section wraps up with a *Review*, introducing a sample program that applies to the lesson.

Learn from coding *tips*, *notes* about the language, and *warnings* about what to avoid.

Greg Perry makes Visual C++ fun and easy by providing *real-world analogies* and *examples*.

Each project contains a real-world code example, so you can apply your new Visual C++ knowledge.

If a line of code in the program confuses you, check the *line-by-line explanation*.

The far right column looks at *The Big Picture*, helping you understand coding strategies and techniques.

The enclosed CD-ROM contains answers to all the *Review Questions*, plus the Visual C++ compiler and all the code in the book.

The *full-color tear-out cheat sheet* at the beginning of the book details syntax and structure.

SAMS
PUBLISHING

Visual C++™
in **12**
Easy Lessons

Greg Perry and
Ian Spencer

SAMS
PUBLISHING

201 W. 103rd St.
Indianapolis, Indiana 46290

For Mary.

Copyright © 1995 by Sams Publishing

FIRST EDITION

International Standard Book Number: 0-672-30637-9

Library of Congress Catalog Card Number: 95-68846

98 97 96 95   4 3 2 1

Interpretation of the printing code: the rightmost double-digit number is the year of the book's printing; the rightmost single-digit, the number of the book's printing. For example, a printing code of 95-1 shows that the first printing of the book occurred in 1995.

Composed in Stone Serif and MCPdigital by Macmillan Computer Publishing

Printed in the United States of America

Publisher	*Richard K. Swadley*
Acquisitions Manager	*Greg Weigand*
Development Manager	*Dean Miller*
Managing Editor	*Cindy Morrow*
Marketing Manager	*Gregg Bushyeager*

Acquisitions Editor
Grace M. Buechlein

Development Editor
Dean Miller

Software Development Specialist
Wayne Blankenbeckler

Production Editor
Ryan Rader

Technical Reviewer
Vincent Mayfield

Editorial Coordinator
Bill Whitmer

Technical Edit Coordinator
Lynette Quinn

Formatter
Frank Sinclair

Editorial Assistant
Sharon Cox

Cover Designer
Tim Amrhein

Book Designer
Alyssa Yesh

Production Team Supervisor
Brad Chinn

Production
Mary Ann Abramson
Angela D. Bannan, Carol Bowers
Georgiana Briggs, Mona Brown
Michael Brumitt, Charlotte Clapp
Jeanne Clark, Terrie Deemer
Michael Dietsch, Judy Everly
Mike Henry, Louisa Klucznik
Ayanna Lacey, Kevin Laseau
Paula Lowell, Casey Price
Nancy Price, Brian-Kent Proffitt
Bobbi Satterfield, SA Springer
Susan Van Ness, Mark Walchle
Angelina Ward, Kelly Warner

Indexer
Cheryl Dietsch

Overview

Contents

Acknowledgments

I want to thank the editors at Sams Publishing, who somehow take my words and turn them into coherent readable text. Rosemarie Graham and Dean Miller have been behind me for years, and I thank them sincerely. I especially want to thank Grace Buechlein for her support before and during this book. My hat goes off also to Ian Spencer for his superior expertise that made this book possible.

About the Authors

Greg Perry is quickly becoming one of the most sought-after speakers and writers in the programming field. He is known for being able to take programming topics and bring them down to the beginner's level. Perry has been a programmer and trainer for the past 18 years. He received his first degree in computer science, and then he received a master's degree in corporate finance. Perry is the author of more than 35 other computer books, including *Teach Yourself Object-Oriented Programming with Visual C++*, *Moving from C to C++*, *QBasic Programming 101* (all from Sams Publishing), and *The Complete Idiot's Guide to Visual Basic* (from Alpha Books). In addition, he has published articles in several publications, including *Software Development*, *Access Advisor*, *PC World*, and *Data Training*. In his spare time, he wanders around Italy, eating the world's best ice cream and pasta.

Ian Spencer is a freelance consultant experienced in the diverse worlds of Windows application development and midrange systems development, especially with IBM systems. He has been in the computer industry since graduating in 1981 with a degree in Computer Science from Manchester University. His main business interests are in providing business solutions in the world of manufacturing companies and providing troubleshooting assistance on development projects. He has written a number of systems using C++ and class libraries, and he is well-respected as an authority on Windows programming. His other books include *Teach Yourself OWL Programming in 21 Days* (Sams Publishing). Ian lives in Walsall—somewhere near the middle of England—with his wife Mary, daughters Philippa and Suzanne, and their dog Ross.

Introduction

The book you hold offers something you might not have encountered before. Whereas other books teach you Visual C++, this book also includes a Visual C++ compiler. With this book, there is literally nothing else to buy (except, of course, the computer)! Microsoft's Visual C++ compiler turns your computer into a C++ programming powerhouse. The compiler included is the full Visual C++ 1.0 release including all the online help, source code, and libraries. The CD that comes with this book also includes all the code listings in the book, as well as answers to all the exercises at the end of each unit.

Despite the great CD included, this book would be worthless if it didn't teach C++. *Visual C++ in 12 Easy Lessons* starts at the beginning, assuming that you don't know Visual C++. By the time you're finished, you will have mastered the Visual C++ language. You'll be learning how to program, how to perform input and output, how to work with disk files, and how to achieve advanced memory management through Visual C++ programs.

If you've looked at the computer want ads lately, you've surely noticed the assortment of C++ programming positions. It seems as if there are always more jobs than C++ programmers. Why not join the ranks? This book will help get you there.

Who Should Use This Book

Visual C++ in 12 Easy Lessons is aimed primarily at beginning programmers who have never programmed or have never seen a C++ program. Text, questions, exercises, and numerous program listings are aimed at both beginning programmers and those new to Visual C++.

If you already program but have never had the time to tackle Visual C++, this book is right for you because it teaches more than just the language. This book attempts to teach you how to program correctly, concentrating on proper coding techniques in addition to the Visual C++ language.

This book does not attempt to cover the difficult topic of Windows programming because we believe you need to know the basics of programming first.

This Book's Philosophy

Visual C++ in 12 Easy Lessons extends the traditional programming textbook tutorial by offering all the text and language syntax needed for newcomers to C++. It also offers complete program examples, exercises, questions, tips, warnings, notes—and, of course, a full-featured Visual C++ compiler.

This book focuses on programming correctly in Visual C++ by teaching structured programming techniques and proper program design. Emphasis is placed on a program's readability rather than on "tricks of the trade" code examples. In this changing world, programs should be clear, properly structured, and well documented. This book doesn't waver from that philosophy.

A Note to the Instructor

If you're an instructor using this book for your class, you'll find that the inclusion of a Visual C++ compiler lets the entire class participate on the same level, using the same compiler for their programs. When you demonstrate the editing, compiling, linking, and running of Visual C++ programs, you'll know that your students will be using the same compiler that you use in class.

Each unit offers numerous questions and exercises that provide a foundation for classroom discussions. The answers to all the questions and exercises are on the enclosed CD. In addition, each unit contains one or more Extra Credit programming exercises that you can assign as homework. The answers to these exercises don't appear on the CD.

The typical semester class is divided into 15 or 16 weeks of study. A useful lesson plan that incorporates this book would spend one week on each lesson, with four exams (one every four weeks). Each lesson contains two units, and one unit can easily be covered in one classroom sitting.

Because *Visual C++ in 12 Easy Lessons* becomes a part-time teacher, questioning and guiding the student as he or she reads and learns, you can spend more classroom time looking at complete program examples and exploring the theory of Visual C++ instead of taking time to cover petty details.

Overview

Here is an overview of this book, giving you a bird's-eye view of where you're about to head:

Lesson 1: Programming with Visual C++

This lesson explains what Visual C++ is by giving a brief history of the C++ programming language and presenting an overview of C++'s advantages over other languages. You'll learn how to develop Visual C++ programs and the steps you follow to write and run programs. You'll dive right into working with the Visual C++ compiler in the second unit. The focus is on using the Visual Workbench to easily compile and run programs.

Lesson 2: Analyzing Visual C++ Programs

This lesson familiarizes you with the format of Visual C++ programs. After you master this lesson, you'll be able to recognize Visual C++ programs and write simple programs that output data.

Lesson 3: Data Basics

Visual C++ supports all kinds of data. This lesson teaches you about Visual C++ variables. You must understand the various data types possible in Visual C++ before you can work with data. You'll see how Visual C++ supports both numeric and character data.

Lesson 4: Simple Operators

This lesson introduces you to the rich assortment of Visual C++ operators. These operators make up for the fact that the Visual C++ programming language is very small. The operators and their order of precedence are more important in Visual C++ than in most other programming languages. Before you finish this lesson, you'll be using the relational operators to write programs that make decisions based on calculations and data that the user enters.

Lesson 5: Upgraded Operators

This lesson extends your knowledge of the Visual C++ operators by teaching you some of the more advanced data-manipulation operators and their nuances. Then it goes on to look at the special switch statement used to make complicated decisions more readable.

Lesson 6: Looping Back and Forth

Visual C++ data processing is powerful due to the looping and selection constructs it offers. This lesson shows you how to write programs that execute certain parts of the program over and over again. After learning about the loop control commands in the first unit, you'll be ready to control those loops with the commands taught in the second. You'll see how to exit a loop early.

Lesson 7: Break It Up with Functions

As you become more skilled in writing C++, your programs become bigger. This lesson explores the C++ function mechanism and shows how you can break code up into small, simple, understandable units. It explores the concept of scope and the unique C++ feature of allowing more than one function to share the same name.

Lesson 8: Lots of Data

Visual C++ offers arrays that hold multiple occurrences of repeating data but don't require much effort on your part to process. Unlike many other programming languages, Visual C++ also uses pointer variables a great deal. Pointer variables and arrays work together to give you flexible data storage.

Lesson 9: Consolidating Items

Variables, arrays, and pointers aren't enough to hold the types of data that your programs require. Structures allow for more powerful grouping of many different kinds of data into manageable units and prepare the ground for the C++ class concept of the next lesson. By the time you reach this lesson, you'll begin to see some limitations of regular variables. By mastering an advanced topic called *dynamic memory allocation*, you'll be writing advanced memory-management programs that utilize your system's resources better than most other programming languages allow.

Lesson 10: Object-Oriented Programming

In this lesson, you break away from the traditional programming and learn about the features of C++ that make it the special language it is. After a discussion on the meaning of object orientation, you look at the simple way that structures can become classes. You then look at features to make classes more usable by controlling their creation and deletion.

Lesson 11: Inheritance and Virtual Functions

Lesson 10 introduced the basic class mechanism. The first unit in this lesson builds on this and shows how to make new classes from old classes. The second unit introduces the real magic of C++ with the clever way C++ can decide which function to call by examining the objects being used.

Lesson 12: Using Disk Files

Visual C++ is not just a programming language. It is a means of accessing code written by other people, which you can then easily use as your own. In this lesson, you look at how you can use both built-in functions of Visual C++ and more powerful class libraries of code. Your computer would be too limiting if you couldn't store data to the disk and put that data back into your programs. Disk files are required by most real-world applications. The units in this lesson describe how Visual C++ processes sequential and random-access files, showing a class library in practice.

This Book's CD

This book contains a full-featured C++ compiler called Visual C++. Visual C++ is made by Microsoft, who need no introduction as the most important software company in the world today. The compiler comes with a Windows-based integrated editor, debugger, compiler, and linker, which compile both C and C++ programs professionally.

Note   Appendix A explains how to install the Visual C++ compiler on your computer.

The CD is an integral part of learning Visual C++ with *Visual C++ in 12 Easy Lessons*. It contains all the code from all of this book's programs. The first line of every program in this book contains a comment with the program's CD filename.

The CD also contains the answers to all review questions and exercises at the end of each lesson, except for the Extra Credit problems.

Conventions Used in This Book

This book uses the following typographic conventions:

▶ Code lines, variables, and any text you see on-screen appear in monospace.

▶ Placeholders in statement syntax explanations appear in *italic monospace*.

▶ New terms appear in *italic*.

▶ Filenames in regular text appear in uppercase, such as MYFILE.DAT.

▶ Optional parameters in statement syntax explanations are enclosed in flat brackets ([ ]). You don't type the brackets when you include these parameters.

▶ Menu commands appear like this: File | Open. This command means to select the Open option from the File menu.

The following items also appear throughout this book:

Note   When further thought is needed on a particular topic, the Note icon brings extra information to your attention.

Tip   A Tip shows you an extra shortcut or advantage possible with the command you just learned.

Warning   Sometimes you must take extra care when trying a particular command or function. Warnings point out the dangers before you encounter them yourself.

In addition, you'll find several sidebars with useful information that is related to the topic at hand.

Concept   What You Will Learn

The concept icon and text are located at the beginning of each major section in the book. The concept provides a succinct overview of the material in the section.

Review   What You Have Learned

A review section appears at the end of major sections and recaps the material you learned in that section.

STOP&TYPE Provides a description of a subsequent program listing.

▼ INPUT   LISTING

A program listing that teaches the major concepts from the section you just finished.

▼ OUTPUT

A typical output of the program.

▼ ANALYSIS

A detailed description of the program appearing at the end of the previous section in the book.

Definition—Definitions of new terms often appear in these definition notes, which are located near the paragraph in which the term first appears.

Lesson ▶ 1

Programming with Visual C++

Programming
and Visual C++

code

compiler

debugging

editor

programming

▶ **What You'll Learn**

- ▶ Introduction to programming
- ▶ C++ compared with other languages
- ▶ C++ and PCs

This book is all you need in order to learn the fundamentals of Visual C++, even if you have never programmed a computer. Writing computer programs is different from using them. Most of today's word processors are fairly easy to learn to use, but lots of work goes into creating them. Word processors are just an example of the results of programming efforts. Many programmers spend many hours, days, and weeks writing the programs that people use.

Visual C++ is Microsoft's version of the C++ programming language. Based on the C programming language, C++ is an improved version of C that takes the C language to the next level of evolution of programming languages—those that provide *object-oriented programming*.

This unit introduces you to the Visual C++ programming language and to programming concepts in general. You will step through the history of C++, see how C++ compares to the C programming language, and learn a little about what to expect when working with Microsoft's Visual C++.

▶ **Introduction to Programming**

Concept   **What You Will Learn**

The mystery of programming will quickly disappear when you see that programming is a process of reducing a problem into small steps that the computer can understand.

Definition—A *program* is a list of detailed instructions.

A program is simply a list of instructions that tells the computer what to do. Computers are only dumb machines. They cannot think; they can only execute your orders within the programs that you write. Without programs, computers are worthless.

A program is to a computer what a recipe is to a cook. A recipe is nothing more than a program (a list of instructions) that tells the cook exactly what to do. The recipe's end result is a finished dish, and the end result of a computer program is an application such as a word processor or a payroll program. By itself, your computer does not know how to be a word processor. By following a list of detailed programming instructions written by a programmer, however, the computer performs the actions necessary to do word processing.

If you want your computer to help you with your household budget, keep track of names and addresses, or play a game of solitaire, you have to supply a program so that it knows how to do those things. You can either buy the program or write one yourself.

There are several advantages to writing your own programs. When you write your own programs, they do exactly what you want them to (you hope!). Although it would be foolish to try to write every program that you need to use (there is not enough time, and there are many good programs on the market), some applications are so specific that you simply cannot find a program that does exactly what you want.

 Note   Some companies hire a staff of programmers to write the programs used within the company. When a company acquires a computer system, that company does not want to change the way it does business. Therefore, the programmers design and write programs that are exactly right for the company. Even when a company buys a set of programs, it often wants to write new programs or change the prewritten software to fit its business better.

Definition—Prewritten software is often called *packaged software*.

Tip   If you are brand new to the programming process and you want a more in-depth look at how individuals and companies' data processing departments write programs, check out *Absolute Beginner's Guide to Programming* (Sams Publishing, 1993).

The Programming Process

When you want to write a program, where do you begin? Before leaping to the keyboard and typing, a good programmer goes through several steps:

1. Decide what is to be done. Before writing a line of code, you need to understand what you are trying to do. Large organizations employ *systems analysts* to do nothing but understand the business processes and document them in a form that the programming team can understand.

2. Design the program. This is where the programmer decides how the program will work. There are two sides to this: First, how will the user of the program use it (for example, will it have menus to help the user, will it produce reports, what will they look like)? Second, what is the best way to write it? Again, in a large organization, there might be designers whose job it is simply to decide how the program should work and document this in a way that enables the programmer to easily turn the description into a working program.

3. The programmer then translates the design of how the program should work into step-by-step detailed instructions that the computer understands, which is sometimes called *coding*.

4. The programmer then tests the program thoroughly. The difference between a good program and a bad program is often the amount of effort put into this stage. Even good programmers will make mistakes in coding their programs. It is the programmer's job to find them all.

This book concentrates on the final two steps. Let's look at them in detail.

Definition—An *editor* lets you easily type and change programs.

To give Visual C++ programming instructions to *your* computer, all you need to do is install the copy of Visual C++ that comes with this book. Appendix A explains how to install the compiler. Your Visual C++ includes an editor and a compiler. An editor is similar to a word processor. It is a program that enables you to type a Visual C++ program into memory, make changes to the program (such as moving, copying, and inserting text), and save the program permanently to a disk file. After you use the editor to type the program, you must compile it with the Visual C++ compiler before you run the program.

Definition—A *compiler* converts your program to low-level machine instructions.

Visual C++ is a compiled language. A C++ compiler (the C++ programming language that is part of your Visual C++) takes your C++ language instructions and translates them into a form that your computer can read. A C++ compiler is a tool that your computer uses to understand the C++ language instructions in your programs. Microsoft's Visual C++ comes with its own editor and integrated programming environment that makes your programming easier to manage.

Definition—A program is also known as *code*.

After you write Visual C++ code, you run it through Visual C++, issue the proper compiling instructions, and run the program. The program's output is the result of the program. The user of the program is the person (sometimes the programmer) who uses the program but cares little (or not at all) about the underlying program that produces the output. Figure 1.1 shows a diagram of the steps necessary to write and execute a Visual C++ program.

Definition—A *preprocessor* reads a program's preprocessor directives to control the compilation.

Notice that your Visual C++ program must be routed through a preprocessor before it is compiled. The preprocessor reads special symbols in the code called *preprocessor directives* that you enter in the program to control the program's compilation. Visual C++ automatically performs the preprocessor step, so it requires no additional learning on your part except for the preprocessor directives that you put inside your programs. This book teaches you about the most important preprocessor directive, #include, in Unit 4, "Visual C++'s Program Structure."

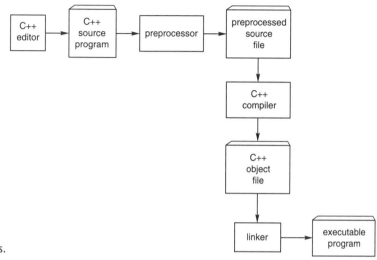

FIGURE 1.1.
The steps necessary to make a Visual C++ program produce results.

As Figure 1.1 shows, your program must go through one last stage after compiling and before running. It is called the linking, or the link editing, stage. When your program is linked, a program called the linker supplies needed runtime information to the compiled program. You also can combine several compiled programs into one executable program by linking them. Most of the time, however, Visual C++ does all the linking. You rarely have to concern yourself with the linking stage until you write advanced applications.

Exterminating Pests

Definition—A *syntax error* is usually a typing error.

Because you are typing instructions for a machine, you must be very accurate. If you misspell a word, leave out a quotation mark, or make another mistake, Visual C++ informs you with an error message. The most common error is a *syntax error*, which generally means that you misspelled a word.

When you compile your program and it has mistakes, your compiler tells you what it thinks those mistakes are. The compiler will not send your program through the linker if you made typing mistakes. Therefore, you must read the compiler's error message, figure out what the problem is, and correct the error by returning to the editor and fixing the mistake.

Definition—A program mistake is called a *bug*. When you correct a mistake, you debug the program.

A program error is commonly known as a *bug*. If you don't understand the error message, you might have to check your compiler's help text or scour your program's source code until you find the offending code line. The process of locating and correcting program errors is called *debugging*.

Note Visual C++ can't catch all program bugs. Sometimes *logic errors* creep into your code. Logic errors are more difficult to find than typing errors because your compiler does not tell you about them. For instance, if you write a program that prints payroll checks, but you tell the computer to print all checks for a negative amount, the computer will obey your instructions. Of course, the instructions themselves are incorrect because they are the result of an error in your logic.

Throughout this book, you are given a chance to find bugs in programs. One or two problems at the end of each unit show you an incorrect program statement or group of statements that lets you hone your debugging skills.

Review   **What You Have Learned**

The program that you write tells the computer exactly what to do and how to do it. You must learn how to write programs that contain no errors.

Note This unit does not contain Stop and Type sections due to its textual nature.

▶ C++ Compared with Other Languages

Concept   **What You Will Learn**

C++ is an efficient language that relies more than other languages on operators.

Note If you have not programmed before, do not concern yourself if you do not understand this section. Some of the discussion relates to ideas that are covered in detail in later units.

The really special thing about C++ is that it is an object-oriented programming language. Because this is a complicated concept, you will explore it later in the book, starting in Unit 20.

If you have programmed before, you should understand a little about how C++ differs from other programming languages. C++ is very efficient. It evolved from C, which was designed to allow technical programmers to write the fastest possible code. A C++ program will normally run much faster than a BASIC program.

C++ is a *structured language* that allows large programs to be built out of small, easy to understand pieces of code. Early languages, such as the original BASIC and FORTRAN, did not have this idea. To write large programs was difficult and the results of trying are described as *spaghetti code*. Many of the object-oriented features of C++ have been introduced to address this problem. C++ has many of the features of a high-level language (a programming language that uses commands that bear little relationship to the instructions a computer uses), but it also can handle the same programming detail as assembler language (code that directly represents machine instructions, which is a low-level language).

Definition—A *keyword* is a C++ language command.

Definition—An *operator* is a special character that performs a specific function, such as Multiply.

Visual C++ is a small programming language with only 44 commands (called keywords), plus a number more that are Visual C++-specific and not always available in other C++ language implementations. To compensate for its small vocabulary, C++ has one of the largest assortments of operators, such as +, -, and &&. The large number of operators in C++ might tempt programmers to write cryptic programs that have only a small amount of code. You will see throughout this book, however, that making the program more readable is more important than saving some lines of code. This book teaches you how to use the C++ operators to their fullest extent while maintaining readable programs.

C++'s large number of operators (almost equal to the number of keywords) requires an understanding of the order in which operators will be applied. Unlike most other languages, there are many levels of *precedence*, which helps C++ to decide what you were trying to write. Appendix C includes the complete C++ operator table. As you learn C++, you must learn how this table works. This is not as difficult as it sounds, but its importance can't be overstated.

C++ is a strongly typed language. This means that the language does not automatically change numbers into words and vice versa. Although this might seem inconvenient, it stops accidental mistakes. C was quite careless about this. Languages such as BASIC and PASCAL are very strict. C++ does provide a number of special ways to allow the programmer to easily convert from one type to another.

Definition—*I/O* stands for input/output and refers to data flowing to and from your PC.

C++ also has no input or output statements. (You might want to read that sentence again!) C++ has no commands that perform input or output. This is one of the most important reasons why C++ is available on so many different computers. The I/O statements of most languages tie those languages to specific hardware. BASIC, for instance, has almost 20 I/O commands, some of which write to the screen, some to the printer, some to a modem, and so forth. If you write a BASIC program for a personal computer, chances are good that it cannot run on a mainframe without considerable modification.

C++'s input and output is performed through the abundant use of operators and function calls. With every C++ compiler comes a library of standard I/O functions. I/O functions are hardware-independent, meaning that they work on any device and on any computer that conforms to the C++ standard.

C started out as a language for technical programmers. Although C++ is now considered a general-purpose language, it still carries the baggage of its C ancestry. To master C++ completely, you must be more aware of the way your computer works than most other languages require. You certainly do not have to be a hardware expert, but understanding the internal data representation makes C++ much more usable and meaningful. Other languages such as BASIC or PASCAL provide checks to ensure that you have not made a silly programming error when running your program. These checks slow the program down (and sometimes stop the programmer from deliberately doing something technical with the computer), so C++ decided it could do without them. Beware!

▶ C++ and Personal Computers

Concept   **What You Will Learn**

The small size of C made it a perfect candidate for personal computers. C++ built on this wide availability.

C was a relatively unknown language until it was placed on the personal computer. With the invention and growth of the personal computer, C blossomed into a worldwide computer language. C++ extends that use on smaller computers. C++ was developed by AT&T in the early 1980s. Most C++ programmers work on a personal computer-based C++ system.

Personal computers typically are called *PCs* from the widespread use of the original IBM PC. The early PCs did not have the memory capacity of the large computers used by government and big business. Nevertheless, PC owners still needed a way to program these machines. BASIC was the first programming language used for PCs. Over the years, many other languages were moved from larger computers to the PC. However, no language was as successful as C in becoming the worldwide standard programming language. C++ seems to be the next standard. C++ first appeared on PCs in 1988, and now C++ is one of the most popular programming languages in use.

Review
What You Have Learned

Visual C++ follows the AT&T standard closely. After you learn Visual C++, you'll be able to write C++ programs on virtually all computers. Different vendors provide their own tools for editing and compiling the programs, but the C++ language remains the same.

The *Visual* in *Visual C++* also refers to features of the product that are provided for Windows programming. This book does not seek to teach Windows programming. As a beginner, there are more than enough issues to cover. However, more than enough goodies are within the Visual toolset to help the novice programmer. Visual C++ takes advantage of the Windows environment to provide an easy to use programming environment. Among the helpful features are context-sensitive help, a Windows-based editor, and an integrated tool for building programs.

► Homework
General Knowledge

1. What is a program?
2. What does a computer do without programs?
3. What is a computer bug?
4. Name the two kinds of computer bugs.
5. What is the difference between the two kinds of computer bugs?
6. Instead of writing your own programs, why don't you purchase every program you need?
7. Why is C++ called a high-level low-level language?
8. How does an editor help you create C++ programs?
9. What does I/O mean?
10. Why does the C++ language contain no I/O commands?

Note   There are no What's the Output? or Find the Bug sections here due to this unit's conceptual nature.

Extra Credit

11. Technically, your computer cannot run the source code that you write, even though you supply this source code in the Visual C++ programming language. Describe what the computer does to your source code before you can run the programs that you write.

12. The advantages of writing your own programs include making programs that work just the way you want them to. What disadvantages can you think of to writing your own programs?

Overview of C++ Programs

dialog box

editing window

workbench

menu

▶ **What You'll Learn**

- ▶ Starting Visual C++
- ▶ The parts of the screen
- ▶ Entering a program
- ▶ Stopping Visual C++
- ▶ Get ready, get set, go!

The beginning programmer needs to master only the basics of the Visual C++ environment. Visual C++ includes the Visual Workbench, a full-screen editor, compiler, linker, and debugger that offers a standard interface from which you can do almost anything you will ever want to do in Visual C++.

This unit takes a quick look at how you start Visual C++ and use it to enter and run programs. You will enter a couple of short programs, compile them, fix their problems, run them, and save them to the disk drive. This unit is not about the Visual C++ language itself; that topic is left for the rest of the book. This unit's job is to get you comfortable with the mechanics of entering and editing programs, so that those tasks will be behind you and you can then concentrate on the most important thing—the Visual C++ programming language.

▶ **Starting Visual C++**

Concept   **What You Will Learn**

Learn to start the Visual C++ compiler.

Because of the wide assortment of computer configurations, there is no way to describe the start-up sequence of every person's Visual C++ programming environment. Nevertheless, you probably have installed Visual C++ (or had a system administrator, coworker, or friend do it for you) using Appendix A, so your Visual C++ should work exactly as described here.

Note   If you find that this section's Visual C++ start-up instructions do not work on your computer, you might have to ask someone familiar with Windows to help you. Getting Visual C++ to start properly does not require an understanding of C++, but it requires a working knowledge of Windows.

Most people who own Visual C++ should adhere to the following steps to start Visual C++.

If you are running Windows 3.1:

1. Turn on the PC if it is not already on.
2. If your PC does not automatically start Windows, type WIN at the DOS prompt.
3. Find the Microsoft Visual C++ program group in Program Manager.
4. Double-click on the Visual C++ icon. This will start the Visual Workbench. You should see the screen shown in Figure 2.1.

If you are running Windows 95:

1. Turn on the PC if it is not already on.
2. Press the Start button on the status bar.
3. Click Programs from the popup menu.
4. Click the Microsoft Visual C++ option, and a further menu will pop up.
5. Click the Visual C++ item. This will start the Visual Workbench. You will see the screen shown in Figure 2.1.

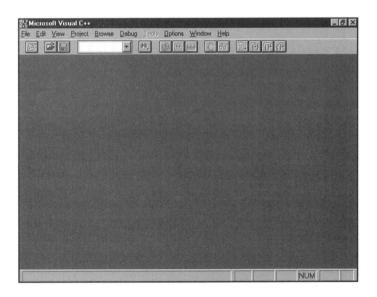

FIGURE 2.1.
The Visual C++ workbench.

Before going further, you should know that this book's Visual C++ compiler is limited in some respects when compared to other full-functioning C++ compilers available from Microsoft. None of these limitations will hamper your learning C++; the enclosed Visual C++ compiler is extremely powerful and contains a programming system unheard of just a decade ago. Nevertheless, the following items somewhat constrain the enclosed Visual C++ system:

1. The compiler supports only 16-bit programming. The programs you produce can run on both Windows 3.1 and Windows 95. They are not true Windows 95 programs.

2. This Visual C++ version is a Windows 3.1 program. It runs perfectly under Windows 95 and Windows NT.

3. The product comes without printed documentation. However, there are comprehensive help files accessible from the workbench help menu that cover all aspects of C++ programming.

The rest of this unit takes you through a guided tour of your new Visual C++ compiler.

Review   **What You Have Learned**

Learn to start your Visual C++ compiler so that you can begin writing programs as soon as possible.

► The Parts of the Screen

Concept   **What You Will Learn**

It's important to recognize your Visual C++ screen elements inside the workbench.

Definition—A *menu* is a list of operations displaying things you can do.

The workbench includes a menu bar across the top of the screen with menus such as File, Edit, and so on. You can select any menu in one of two ways:

► Press the Alt key, and then press the underscored letter of the menu you want to choose.

► If you have a mouse, move the mouse pointer over the name of the menu you want to select and click the left mouse button.

Either action displays a menu that falls down from the menu name you selected.

Note   The menu you see when you select from the menu bar is called a pull-down menu because it acts like a rolling window shade that you can pull down.

The list of items you see on the File menu relates to your program's file, which you eventually write and save to the disk.

To select from a pull-down menu after you have displayed it, move the mouse pointer over the menu option you want to select and click the left mouse button. You also can press the up-arrow and down-arrow keys to move the highlight to the option you want to select, and then press Enter to select that option.

Table 2.1 gives you an overview of the various Visual C++ menus on the menu bar. During the early part of your Visual C++ programming career, you will have little use for most of the menu options on the various pull-down menus.

Table 2.1. An overview of the menu bar's selections.

Menu	Description
File	File-related commands that operate on your program file, such as loading a program from disk, saving a program you enter to disk, and printing the program.
Edit	Includes options that aid in adding, changing, searching for, and deleting text from the current program.
View	Options for moving around the editor and controlling the display.
Project	This menu includes the Build command, which runs the compiler and linker, and the Execute command, which enables you to test your program without leaving the workbench.
Browse	Used for examining C++ classes.
Debug	This pull-down menu includes the commands that enable you to examine the code as it runs to help you get errors out of your program.
Tools	Special features that can be added to the workbench (not available as installed).
Options	Options for setting up the workbench to better suit the way a programmer works.
Window	Standard Windows menu for selecting and arranging windows.
Help	Visual C++ provides a rich assortment of online help. Instead of having to look in a bulky Visual C++ reference manual, you can select from the various help-related topics to find anything you need about the workbench or Visual C++.

Note   Not all of the pull-down menu options are available at all times. For instance, if you select the Edit pull-down menu, you'll notice that most of its options are grayed. Visual C++ is telling you that the grayed options are not active given your current environment. For example, if you've just started Visual C++ and have not yet entered a program, it makes no sense to copy or paste text because there is no text to work with.

Review
What You Have Learned

The menu lets you issue commands to Visual C++.

▶ Entering a Program

Concept
What You Will Learn

You'll do most of your work inside the editing window.

The large area in the middle of the Visual C++ workbench is the editing window in which you type and edit your C++ programs. If you just started Visual C++, chances are good that the large middle portion of the screen has nothing in it. To begin your first foray into the Visual C++ environment, select New from the File pull-down menu. This selection informs Visual C++ that you want to create a new program, and if a program is already in the editing area, you want to discard it (after making sure that the programmer does not want to save changes he or she made to this file).

After you select File | New, an editing window opens in the workbench. This editing window takes up only some of the screen. If you want the editing window to fill the screen (most programmers do), you can resize it by double-clicking the title bar or pressing the maximize button in the top right corner.

The resizing action is a standard part of Microsoft Windows. If you do not understand how Windows works, ask someone how to perform these tasks or refer to your Windows documentation.

Note   Visual C++ is a Multiple Document Interface (MDI) application. It follows the standard Windows rules for handling several windows at the same time. You can edit more than one file at the same time.

To get started with editing, enter the following program (EDIT.CPP) exactly as you see it. As you enter the program, you will notice that the Visual C++ editor works much like a simple word processor. Although Visual C++ includes many powerful editing commands such as copy, cut, paste, and multiple window editing, you need to remember only these basic editing tips to get started:

▶ Use the arrow keys to move the cursor (the blinking line) around the screen.

▶ The cursor for editing is different from the mouse pointer. You can click the mouse pointer to set the edit cursor to a place in the text, but it is always the cursor that gives the current text position.

▶ If you want to delete a character, position the cursor over the character to delete and press the Delete key. The character disappears, and the characters to the right shift to the left, filling in the hole left by the deleted character.

▶ If you want to insert a character, position the cursor where you want to insert and type the new text. The first time you do this, you will be in insert mode, meaning that the characters to the right of those you type will shift to the right and make room for new ones. If you press the Insert key, Visual C++ changes to overtype mode, meaning that the new characters you type replace those on the screen. The Insert key toggles you back and forth between the two modes. The OVR indicator on the status bar tells you what mode the editor is in currently.

```
// Filename: EDIT.CPP
#include <iostream.h>
void main()
{
    cout << "Visual C++ is easy!";
}
```

The Disk and Your Programs

As soon as you have typed a program into the editor, you should save it to the disk. Then you can load it back into the editor any time you need it, and it is also safely tucked away in case of power failure. Use options from the File pull-down menu to save and load programs.

To save the program you just typed, select Save from the File pull-down menu. When you do, you will see the dialog box shown in Figure 2.2. Dialog boxes are not menus, but they do offer choices of things you can do next. Visual C++ requires you to save the program to a filename. Visual C++ makes a guess as to what you want to name your file, but it is a lousy guess. Press the Backspace key to get rid of the name Visual C++ selects (UNTITLED.1) in the File Save As entry box.

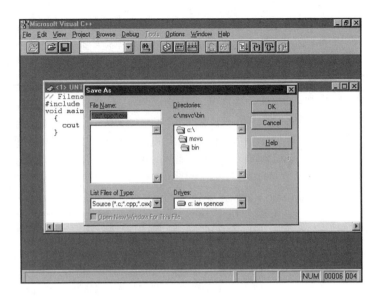

FIGURE 2.2.
Preparing to save
your program.

As with all programs in this book, the assumed filename is embedded at the top of each program after the word Filename:. This program's filename happens to be EDIT.CPP, but you can name it anything you want as long as you follow the naming conventions required by DOS. Using the File Save dialog box, you could select a different disk drive and directory if you wanted to save your program in a directory different from that chosen for you. For now, do nothing more than type EDIT.CPP into the top box where the cursor is sitting, and press Enter or click OK. Visual C++ then saves the program to disk. There is a deliberate error in the program, but Visual C++ won't notice it as you save the program. You have to ask Visual C++ to check the program by compiling it.

Note   This version of the compiler does not support the long filename convention used by Windows 95.

Whenever you want to start a new program and have saved the old one to disk, select File | New and Visual C++ gives you a clean slate to start another program. Use File | Close to remove a program from the screen that you no longer want to view. Visual C++ will ask you whether you want to save it if you have made changes.

If you want to load a program from the disk, you can select File | Open and type the filename of the program you want to run. Visual C++ loads the program, and you are on your way.

Running the Program

In the early days of computing, you had to compile, link, and execute your program to run it. Visual C++ makes these steps a snap by automating them with a couple of keystrokes. To run the program, select Execute from the Project pull-down menu (Ctrl+F5 is the shortcut for running the program). When you do this, Visual C++ inspects the program file and the program it should build to decide what it needs to do to build the program. In this case, it decides that the program does not exist and asks you whether you want to build it (which you do, of course). When you answer yes to its question, Visual C++ compiles your program—that is, it attempts to. After a brief pause, Visual C++ displays its output window (like the one in Figure 2.3) with several messages. The last message is displayed in the status bar too. It says

```
EDIT.EXE - 1 error(s), 0 warning(s)
```

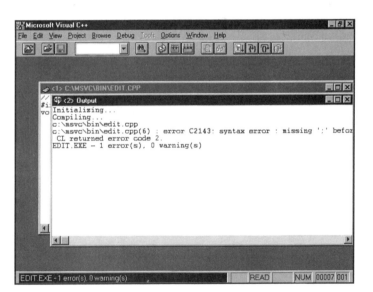

FIGURE 2.3.
Finding a problem.

Visual C++ found an error with the program, and until you fix the error, Visual C++ will not be able to run it. When it finds an error, Visual C++ notes where it found the error. When you double-click the actual error message or press the F4 key, it tries to highlight the offending line. In this case, it almost did so (it highlighted the line below the actual problem).

The statement beginning with cout does not have a semicolon at the end of it as Visual C++ requires. You can fix the error by moving the cursor to the end of the line and typing a semicolon.

After you add the semicolon, run the program again by pressing Ctrl+F5 or by selecting Execute from the Project pull-down menu. When you do, Visual C++ compiles and links your program. Now press Ctrl+F5 again; this time, a window pops up with your program's message, Visual C++ is easy!.

So that it can interact well with Windows, Visual C++ builds a little home for your program to run in. Windows programming is very complicated. To enable the beginner to get the benefits of working in the Windows environment without the complications of writing programs, Microsoft provides a feature called *QuickWin*, which allows simple programs to run under Windows. After inspecting the output of your program, you can remove the results by using the standard Windows actions to close a window, or by pressing Ctrl+C. QuickWin is a piece of code that is added into your program automatically by the linker.

All of these keystrokes—Ctrl+F5, F4, and so forth—seem to be a lot to remember. The good news is that you don't have to remember them. They are always available on the pull-down menus. While you are getting comfortable with Visual C++, rely on the menus as much as possible. As time goes by, you will pick up the shortcut keys. Even better news is that Visual C++ also gives you a toolbar—the row of buttons just under the menu. The pictures are meant to tell you what the buttons mean, but Visual C++ explains the option if you click the mouse button (without releasing it) on the button you are interested in. You can avoid running a toolbar command by moving the mouse off the button before releasing the left mouse button.

Review   **What You Have Learned**

The workbench's editing menus and shortcut keys give you power that's easy to master.

▶ **Stopping Visual C++**

Concept   **What You Will Learn**

Always exit the Visual C++ environment *and* Windows before turning off your computer.

When you are finished with your Visual C++ session, you can close the workbench by selecting File I Exit or double-clicking the system menu button (or clicking the X for exit button in Windows 95). If you have not saved your program to the disk, Visual C++ gives you one last chance to do so with a dialog box. You must then stop Windows before switching off your PC. Under Windows 3.1, you close the program manager; under Windows 95, you press the Open button and choose Shutdown. Of course, you do not have to stop and start your computer after each session.

 Tip Always return to DOS under Windows 3.1 or run Shutdown under Windows 95 before turning off your PC. You can lose programs that you worked long and hard on if you don't.

Review   **What You Have Learned**

The File | Exit selection terminates Visual C++ and returns to Windows.

► **Get Ready, Get Set, Go!**

Concept   **What You Will Learn**

You're ready to program!

Learning Visual C++'s entire programming environment, including all the ins and outs of the editor and compiler's options, is not as critical as learning the Visual C++ language. The compiler is just a way to transform your program from a source program (the Visual C++ instructions you write) to an executable file.

Nevertheless, you will add to your editing skills over time, picking up shortcut keys and editing techniques to improve your programming experience. Even though you do not know the entire range of editing commands (very few veteran Visual C++ users do either), you have seen that entering and running a program is as easy as using a word processor.

The most important part of using Visual C++ is not the editor but the programming language itself. Now that you have the basic editing skills down, it is time to start the first step on your journey toward programming. Turn the page and enter the ranks of Visual C++ programmers.

Review   **What You Have Learned**

Now that you've mastered the workbench, it's time to move to the specifics of the Visual C++ language.

▶ Homework
General Knowledge

1. What does *workbench* stand for and what is the workbench?

2. What are the two ways to select from a menu?

3. What command prepares the workbench for a new program file?

4. What is the difference between insert mode and overtype mode?

5. When you run a Visual C++ program, the resulting output doesn't appear on the workbench's screen. Where do you see the results?

6. What is a keyword?

7. What is an operator?

8. What are shortcut keys?

9. How do you start Visual C++?

10. What command do you type to stop Visual C++?

11. True or false: You must install Visual C++ before you can compile programs with Visual C++.

12. True or false: You must save your program to the disk if you want to edit the program in a subsequent session.

13. True or false: You should exit Visual C++ before turning off your computer.

14. True or false: Not all of Visual C++'s menu options are available at all times.

Note   There is no What's the Output? section here due to this unit's conceptual nature.

Find the Bug

15. Figure 2.4 contains an image of the workbench screen with an error showing. What kind of bug did the workbench find, a syntax error or a logic error?

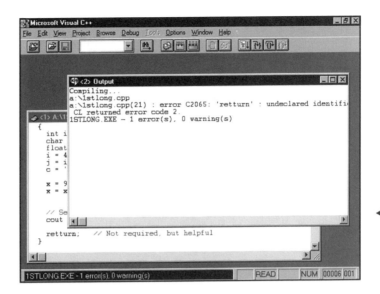

FIGURE 2.4.
An error just occurred.

Extra Credit

16. Just for practice, type the following program in the workbench and compile it. There will be an error, but the error will not show up until you run the program. Even though main() is incorrectly spelled as mane() on the sixth line, your compiler cannot catch all syntax errors, only many of them. Run the program to see what happens, and then correct the error and test the program again.

```
// Filename: PROBLRM.CPP
#include <iostream.h>
void mane()
  {
    // Something's wrong here!
    cout << "This won't display.";
    return;
  }
```

Progamming
with Visual
C++

STOP&TYPE In this lesson, you learned about the fundamentals of the Visual C++ compiler and how to enter and edit programs using Visual C++'s workbench. You saw the following:

▶ Introduction to programming concepts

▶ How C++ compares to other languages

▶ Starting Visual C++

▶ Using Visual C++'s menus

▶ How to enter and edit Visual C++ programs

▶ How to compile Visual C++ programs

▶ Stopping Visual C++

Note This project reviews entering and editing a Visual C++ program using the workbench. You are not expected to understand how the program works. The format of future projects will concentrate much more on Visual C++'s language specifics using a different project format.

Step 1: Start Visual C++.

Before using Visual C++, you must start the workbench. Follow these steps:

1. Turn on your computer.

2. Start Windows by typing WIN (if it does not automatically start Windows).

3. For Windows 3.1, choose the program group Microsoft Visual C++. Double-click on the icon titled Visual C++.

For Windows 95, click on the Open button, choose Programs from the popup menu, and select Microsoft Visual C++. Click on Visual C++.

Step 2: Open a program window.

1. The Visual C++ workbench is known as an MDI application. You enter and edit programs in one or more windows that appear in the workbench. Before typing a new program, you must open a new file in a new window. Type Alt+F,N (File New) to open a new file in an editing window.

Note Although I describe keystrokes to issue the commands, feel free to use the mouse to select menu options. Neither is a better way to use Windows; just use the way that is easiest for you.

2. Type the following program. When typing the program, be sure to press Enter at the end of each line (including the very last line). Type as accurately as possible so that no mistakes appear later. The program takes more lines than will fit in the workbench editing window, so you'll see the workbench scroll downward when you fill the open window.

Project 1 Listing. The Visual C++ project program.

```cpp
// Filename: PROJECT1.CPP

// Prints the first 20 odd, then even, numbers.

// Once done, it prints them in reverse order.

#include <iostream.h>


void main()

  {

    int num;    // The for loop control variable


    cout << "The first 20 odd numbers:\n";

    for (num = 1; num < 40; num += 2)

      { cout << num << ' '; }


    cout << "\n\nThe first 20 even numbers:\n";

    for (num = 2; num <= 40; num += 2)
```

continues

Project 1 Listing. continued

```
    { cout << num << ' '; }
```

```
cout << "\n\nThe first 20 odd numbers in reverse:\n";
```

```
for (num = 39; num >= 1; num -= 2)
```

```
    { cout << num << ' '; }
```

```
cout << "\n\nThe first 20 even numbers in reverse:\n";
```

```
for (num = 40; num >= 2; num -= 2)
```

```
    { cout << num << ' '; }
```

```
return;
```

```
}
```

3. When you finish typing the complete program, you can use PageUp, PageDown, and the arrow keys to scroll the top of the program back into view.

Step 3: Compile and run the program.

1. Before running the program, you must compile it. Choose Project | Build (Shift+F8), which is an alternative to Project | Execute when you know the program needs to be made.

2. If errors appear, the status bar will display an error count. Pressing F4 guides you through the code and leaves you near where the errors are. You can fix any errors that might appear. Recompile the program when you type it exactly as the listing shows.

3. If no errors appear, the error count will be zero and you can then press Ctrl+F5 to execute the program. Here is what you'll see in the QuickWin window:

```
The first 20 odd numbers:
1 3 5 7 9 11 13 15 17 19 21 23 25 27 29 31 33 35 37 39
The first 20 even numbers:
2 4 6 8 10 12 14 16 18 20 22 24 26 28 30 32 34 36 38 40
The first 20 odd numbers in reverse:
39 37 35 33 31 29 27 25 23 21 19 17 15 13 11 9 7 5 3 1
The first 20 even numbers in reverse:
40 38 36 34 32 30 28 26 24 22 20 18 16 14 12 10 8 6 4 2
```

4. Close the output window and return to the workbench's editing window (use Alt+Tab or click on the workbench window if you do not directly return to the workbench).

Step 4: Save your work.

If you exit Visual C++ without saving your program, you'll lose the program and have to reenter it in order to see the results again. Therefore, you'll want to save your programs to a disk file.

> **Note**   All of the programs in this book, including the one shown in Listing 1, are stored on the enclosed program disk. You don't have to save this listing unless you want the practice, because it is already on the disk.

1. To save a program, select Alt+F,S (for File Save). You'll see the File Save dialog box appear on the screen.

2. Type a program name along with a path name if you want to store the program in a subdirectory. All Visual C++ programs should end with the .CPP filename extension.

Step 5: Exit Visual C++.

1. Select Alt+F4 (for File Exit) to close Visual C++. If you did not save your program, Visual C++ tells you with a final dialog box that gives you one last chance to save the program.

2. After saving the program, you can exit Visual C++ and switch off your PC. You should always return to DOS with Windows 3.1 or shut down your PC under Windows 95 before powering off your computer.

Lesson ▶

Analyzing Visual C++ Programs

Unit 3:   **Style Issues**

Unit 4:   **Visual C++'s Program Structure**

Lesson 2 Project

3

Style Issues

- **comments**
- **freeform**
- **language syntax**
- **reserved words**
- **whitespace**

▶ What You'll Learn

- ▶ Entering a simple Visual C++ program
- ▶ Visual C++ special characters
- ▶ Freeform style
- ▶ Uppercase and lowercase
- ▶ Longer programs
- ▶ The importance of comments
- ▶ The syntax of Visual C++ comments
- ▶ Comments are for you, too
- ▶ C-style comments

This unit shows you a few Visual C++ programs. You will learn to familiarize yourself with the look and feel of simple Visual C++ programs. Do not be too concerned about understanding every line in every program. As a matter of fact, the less you worry about each program's specifics, the better off you will be for this unit.

▶ Entering a Simple Visual C++ Program

Concept   **What You Will Learn**

Enter and run a simple Visual C++ program and discuss the code and results.

STOP&TYPE   Here is a Visual C++ program. Although it is extremely simple, it contains all the elements necessary to be a valid Visual C++ program.

```
// Filename: CFIRST.CPP
// Program displays a message on-screen
#include <iostream.h>
void main()
  {
    cout << "I will be a C++ expert!";
  }
```

Even a simple Visual C++ program might intimidate a beginning programmer. Do not let it intimidate you! C++ has a bark that is often worse than its bite. If you were to type this program into your Visual C++ compiler's editor, compile it, and run it, you would see the following output on your screen:

```
I will be a C++ expert!
```

At this point, do not concern yourself with the specifics of the code in this program. The rest of this book explains things like that. Only one line in the entire seven-line program does anything noticeable (the one that begins with cout), and the rest of the program is simply there because C++ needs it to be there. You will find out why as you work through the unit.

Note The preceding program contains a total of seven lines, and only one really produces something you can see. More advanced Visual C++ programs might consist of 500 lines or more. That 7-to-1 setup-to-work ratio does not exist for every Visual C++ program. That would cause too much work on your part! The amount of code that sets up the program diminishes as a program grows.

Review **What You Have Learned**

C++ programs sometimes look cryptic, but when you learn the fundamentals of the language, you'll see that program formats are often similar. A simple program might contain several lines of code.

Note There are no more Stop and Type parts in this unit due to the textual nature of the material.

UNIT **3** Style Issues

▶ **Visual C++ Special Characters**

Concept **What You Will Learn**

C++ is a language rich in special characters.

Visual C++ is one of the few programming languages that uses almost every key on your keyboard. Visual C++ is picky about the keys you press. Notice that the program in the preceding section contains a left and a right brace, { and }. If you were to use parentheses, (and), or square brackets, [and], in place of the braces, Visual C++ would complain. Make sure that you also distinguish between left and right angled brackets, < and >, as well as the forward slash, /, and the backslash, \.

Be extremely careful to use the characters you are supposed to use. Computers are precise machines without as much tolerance for typing ambiguities as people have. Throughout *Visual C++ in 12 Easy Lessons*, you will learn when to use each of the characters and what they mean. Until then, be very careful to type the correct characters.

Visual C++ distinguishes between a capital letter *O* and a number *0* (zero). Also, a lower-case letter *l* will not substitute for a number *1*. Because you're dealing with a machine, you should type numbers when C++ wants numbers, letters when C++ wants letters, and exact special characters (characters that are neither letters nor numbers, such as brackets and the plus sign) when C++ wants them.

Review   **What You Have Learned**

Be extremely careful when typing C++ programs. When one special character such as a left brace is needed, a left parenthesis will not do!

▶ Freeform Style

Concept   **What You Will Learn**

C++'s freeform style lets you insert spacing and blank lines throughout your code to help make the program more readable.

Definition—*Whitespace* consists of the blank lines and indentations you add to code.

Most of the time, you can put lots of spacing in a Visual C++ program and C++ will not complain. You can put whitespace between symbols and the words that make up the C++ language (but you can't split up words with spaces). C++ programmers often put extra spaces and blank lines in programs to make the programs more readable. With whitespace, C++ programmers make C++ programs more readable to people, not to the Visual C++ compiler.

To your Visual C++ compiler, the following program is exactly the same program as the previous one you saw:

```
//Filename:CFIRST.CPP//Program displays a message on-screen
#include <iostream.h>
void main(){cout<<"I will be a C++ expert!";}
```

Definition—*Freeform* means that C++ lets you insert as many spaces and lines as you want.

Which is easier for you to read, the first or the second version of the program? Obviously, the first version is. Visual C++ is called a freeform compiler. You can indent lines of the program, or leave all the lines flush left.

Because your computer is a machine, it does not require extra whitespace to understand a program. As long as you follow all the coding rules of Visual C++, the compiler will be happy with the code you supply. In spite of the Visual C++ compiler's lack of concern for how nice a program looks, you should be concerned about the program's look. Add extra whitespace to group similar lines of code together and make the program easier to understand for people who read the program.

Note   As you see other programs throughout this book, you will begin to pick up some C++ whitespace conventions and develop some of your own.

PROGRAMS ALWAYS CHANGE

While you write Visual C++ programs, consider that someday you might have to change those programs or somebody you work with will have to. You could squeeze as much space out of a program as possible, but you will gain nothing from doing so. (You might save a few characters of computer memory, but not enough to make up for a messy program.)

If you add extra whitespace to make the program more readable to people, the program will be easy to modify in the future. In this ever-changing world, programs have to be modified to reflect those changes, and the person who writes more readable code gets hired for programming jobs faster than one who does not care about program readability. Updating and changing programs is called maintaining programs. A maintainable program is a readable program.

If you are confused now, you are right on track! You still do not have to understand any specifics about the two program listings seen so far. This unit is getting you used to the look and feel of Visual C++ programs, not their particulars. If you understand that Visual C++ is picky about the characters you type, and if you realize that a program should be readable to people, you deserve an A+ for the unit so far.

Review   **What You Have Learned**

The C++ freeform language allows for as much whitespace as you want to add.

UNIT **3** Style Issues

▶ **Uppercase and Lowercase**

What You Will Learn

C++ is extremely picky about your Caps Lock key. Most of a C++ program appears in lowercase letters.

Although Visual C++ cares little about whitespace, it does know the difference between uppercase and lowercase letters. Most of the time, Visual C++ prefers lowercase letters. Visual C++'s preference for lowercase letters sets it apart from most other programming languages. To many programming languages, the following statements are identical:

```
if (netpay > grosspay)

If (NetPay > GrossPay)

IF (NETPAY > GROSSPAY)
```

To Visual C++, the three lines are extremely different. As you learn the C++ language, you will see when to use lowercase and when to use uppercase. Again, most of the time, you will program in lowercase letters.

Visual C++ contains a fixed vocabulary of keyword commands (also referred to as reserved words). Appendix D contains a complete list of Visual C++ commands. A command is part of the limited vocabulary that Visual C++ recognizes. For example, the command that transmits a value from one place in the program to another is return. You must use lowercase letters for return, as well as for all the other commands in Visual C++.

 Tip Refer to Appendix D, "Visual C++ Command Reference," often as you learn the commands of Visual C++, especially the specific commands beginning in Lesson 3, "Data Basics."

If you want to print messages to the screen or to your printer, you can use uppercase, lowercase, or a mixture of both for the message itself. For example, recall that the program shown earlier printed this message to the screen:

```
I will be a C++ expert!
```

Because this is a message for the user of the program to read, you would want Visual C++ to print it using regular uppercase and lowercase characters. Because the message is not a keyword, it does not have to be all lowercase.

Note Before you go any further, a short review of the previous sections is warranted. Visual C++ is picky about lowercase commands and about making sure that you type special characters exactly right. Whitespace, however, is another thing entirely. Visual C++ does not care how much whitespace you add to a program for readability.

Review **What You Have Learned**

For and for are two different words to C++. Be sure to maintain consistency with uppercase and lowercase letters. C++'s preference is usually lowercase letters.

▶ **Longer Programs**

Concept **What You Will Learn**

Even long C++ programs are fairly easy to follow when you use whitespace and break long programs into a series of smaller functions.

The sample program shown earlier is extremely simple. Some Visual C++ programs require several hundred thousand lines of code. Budding authors would not tackle a sequel to *War and Peace*; likewise, brand-new Visual C++ programmers should stay away from huge programming projects. Most of the programs you write for a while will be relatively small, maybe only 10 to 100 lines of code.

Even a large program usually is not one big program stored in one file on the disk. Programmers often break up large programs into a set of smaller programs. The smaller programs work like building blocks, fitting together as needed to handle some kind of programming application.

Just to give you another early view of a Visual C++ program, here is a program longer than the one you saw earlier. Don't sweat the specifics yet. Glance over the program and start getting used to the variety of special characters that Visual C++ understands.

```
// Filename: 1STLONG.CPP
// Longer C++ program that demonstrates comments,
// variables, constants, and simple input/output
#include <iostream.h>
void main()
```

```
{
  int i, j;     // These three lines declare four variables
  char c;
  float x;
  i = 4;        // i is assigned an integer literal
  j = i + 7;    // j is assigned the result of a computation
  c = 'A';      // Enclose all character literals
                // in single quotation marks
  x = 9.087;    // x is a floating-point value
  x = x * 12.3;// Overwrites what was in x
                // with something else

  // Sends the values of the four variables to the screen
  cout << i << ", " << j << ", " << c << ", " << x << "\n";

  return;       // Not required, but helpful
}
```

The next few lessons discuss the commands in this program in depth. Again, just to give you an idea of the importance of readability, here is the same program as seen by the Visual C++ compiler, but a very different program indeed to someone who must maintain it later:

```
//Filename: 1STLONG.CPP//Longer C++ program that demonstrates
//comments, variables, constants, and simple input/output
#include <iostream.h>
void main(){int i,j;//These three lines declare four variables
char c;float x;i=4;// i is assigned an integer literal
j=i+7;//j is assigned the result of a computation
c='A';//Enclose all character literals//in single quotation marks
x=9.087;//x is a floating-point value
x=x*12.3;//Overwrites what was in x with something else
//Sends the values of the four variables to the screen
cout<<i<<", "<<j<<", "<<c<<", "<<x<<"\n";return;
//Not required, but helpful
}
```

Review   What You Have Learned

Longer programs don't have to be harder to read than shorter ones.

▶ The Importance of Comments

Concept   What You Will Learn

Provide readable comments that explain in plain language (non-C++) what's going on.

Suppose that your car breaks down in the middle of nowhere with no other cars in sight. The problem is not tools or parts; they are in the trunk. The problem is that you know absolutely nothing about the car, and when you open the trunk, you have no clue as to where the parts go or how to fix the problem.

Just about to despair, you glance down and see two car repair books in the trunk. You pick up the first one and realize that it is a book written by advanced, expert mechanics for advanced, expert mechanics. The book uses technical jargon you've never heard. You toss the worthless repair book over your shoulder and pick up the next book. The title is *Car Repair for the Un-Mechanic*. Glancing through the opening pages, you begin to smile. The second book assumes that you don't know a rotor widget #4 from a tactile stem #3B-7. The second book explains, in uncluttered and nonmechanical language and with a friendly style, exactly how to fix your problem.

You find that the second book contains the very same facts that the first one does. Of course, the first book does not help your plight one bit. It teaches you nothing and explains nothing. It assumes that you know enough to write the book yourself. The second book explains every concept in easy-to-understand language, and in 10 minutes, you fix the car just in time to drive to the cafe across the street for dinner. (You thought you were in the middle of a desert or something?)

Which of the following is true of this car story:

1. It has a point to it.
2. It mistakenly got mixed in with this book at the printer.
3. It proves that this book's author cannot focus on one subject for very long.

Obviously, the story has a point (and also hints at number 3). The point is that people react much better to material that is not technically above their heads. Of course, any subject is easy if it is explained well enough. If thermonuclear space transportation were explained in a simple manner, you could understand it.

By their very nature, Visual C++ programs are cryptic, even to established C++ programmers. As the previous lesson explained, programs rarely remain in one form. The life of a programmer includes not only writing new programs, but updating programs written earlier. As you write a Visual C++ program, add whitespace so that the program is easier to read. Even more important, add comments as well.

Comments are not Visual C++ commands. As a matter of fact, Visual C++ ignores any and all comments in your programs. Comments are nothing more than messages that explain what the program does. Comments are for people, not for the computer.

UNIT

3

Style Issues

Note If your Visual C++ programs contain only Visual C++ code and no comments, they will be virtually impossible to figure out later. Remember that Visual C++ is cryptic and extremely difficult to read. Many companies that employ programmers require that their programmers put comments throughout every program they write. Why do you think these companies require comments? It is because people change, jobs change, and companies must ensure that a program written by one person can be understood by the next person.

► The Syntax of Visual C++ Comments

Concept   **What You Will Learn**

Begin all comments with two slashes, //.

In computer lingo, language syntax refers to the spelling of commands, the ordering of special characters, and the placing of the language elements. When you learn the syntax for a Visual C++ command or operation, you learn the exact format required so that Visual C++ knows what you want it to do.

Comments are so important that you are now going to learn the syntax of comments (how to write comments so that Visual C++ knows that they are comments) before you learn any Visual C++ commands. Use comments abundantly so that someone reading your program later has a clear guide to the program's contents. A Visual C++ programmer might be able to trace through your Visual C++ code and figure out what the program does, but comments speed the process. The faster someone understands your code, the faster he or she can make any needed changes and move on to other projects.

A comment begins with two forward slashes, sometimes called a double slash. Comments extend to the end of the line. In other words, you cannot have a command, a comment, and then another command all on the same line. Here is an example of a Visual C++ line with a comment:

```
return ((a > b)?a:b);  // Grabs the larger of two values
```

Here is the same line without the comment:

```
return ((a > b)?a:b);
```

With a comment, you don't even have to know Visual C++ in order to know what the statement is doing. Without a comment, as you can see, the statement looks like garbage characters that make no sense.

The double slash is vital: without it, Visual C++ would refuse to accept the line. Even though `return ((a > b)?a:b);` is a valid Visual C++ command, if you left out the double slash comment signal, Visual C++ would see the words `Grabs the larger of two values` and not know what to do with them. After all, Visual C++ does not know English; it knows only C++. The comment is there not for Visual C++ but for a person looking through your program.

Comments can reside on lines all by themselves. Sometimes you use comments for more than one program statement. Comments are useful for describing a section of several lines in a program and for putting in program notes about the programmer and the program. For example, the following small Visual C++ program contains two lines of comments that extend the entire line length, as well as three additional comments to the right of Visual C++ code.

```
// Filename: COMAVGE.CPP
// Program to compute the average of three values
#include <iostream.h>
void main()
   {
     double g1, g2, g3;   // Variables to hold student grades

     cout << "What grade did the first student get? ";
     cin >> g1;

     cout << "What grade did the second student get? ";
     cin >> g2;

     cout << "What grade did the third student get? ";
     cin >> g3;

     double avg = (g1 + g2 + g3) / 3.0;   // Computes average

     cout << "The student average is " << avg;  // Prints average
     return;
   }
```

All of the programs on this book's program disk are stored under a separate filename. You must tell your Visual C++ compiler the program's filename before it can load the program into memory and run it. To help you quickly try the examples throughout this book, a comment on the first line of every program contains the name of the program as it is stored on the disk. For instance, you can load the preceding program from the book's program disk by retrieving the file named COMAVGE.CPP.

Many companies require their programmers to put their names in comments at the top of programs they write. If someone later has a question about the program, the original programmer can be traced. If several people make changes to a program, they often put their names too, with a brief comment about the changes they made. Because all these types of lines are commented, Visual C++ skips over them, as it should. Often, they also put at the beginning a brief description of what the program is supposed to do.

Scatter comments throughout a program as well. If you write some tricky code that needs explanation, spend a few lines of comments, if needed, explaining what the next few lines of code do.

Note   Be proud of yourself! You do not yet know one bit of Visual C++ code, but you understand exactly what the preceding program does. That's the purpose of comments! They document a program so that you don't have to go through tedious code to learn what parts of the program are doing.

A Visual C++ programmer usually can understand what a simple Visual C++ program is supposed to do, even if the program has no comments at all. As soon as you learn the Visual C++ language, you will be able to look through straight Visual C++ code, with no comments, and make changes that need to be made. The comments simply help describe what the program is doing.

Review   **What You Have Learned**

Comments begin with // and extend to the end of the line. You can put comments on lines by themselves or at the end of other C++ code.

▶ Comments Are for You, Too

Concept   **What You Will Learn**

Even if you write programs that you will maintain yourself, you'll need comments.

Suppose that you write programs for your own use and amusement. Nobody but you will ever see the Visual C++ code you write. Can you think of why you should take the time to add comments to your own programs? There are plenty of reasons.

Suppose that you write a Visual C++ program to track your bank records. A year later, your bank allows for automatic transfers of utility bill payments straight from your savings account. Your old program no longer suffices for the new banking system, so you get the Visual C++ code out and begin making changes. However, you can't remember what you did before, and the code is so succinct that it is difficult to follow. Luckily, you put comments in the code, so you read through the program until you get to the place you need to change. As soon as you are there, you know what is going on in the code, and you quickly make the changes.

Get into the habit of commenting as you write programs. Many people write programs without commenting as they go, thinking that they will add comments later. More often than not, the comments never get added. When program maintenance is required, it takes twice as long to change the code as it would if the programmer had added comments during the original programming phase.

As important as comments are, you can over-comment a program. Add comments to lines only when the program's code warrants it. You see many more comments in the first few programs in this book than you see later. As you learn the simple commands, this book attempts to clarify them through extra comments in the program listings.

Nevertheless, redundant comments are as bad as no comments at all. For example, even though you know nothing about Visual C++ commands, you might agree that the following code contains worthless comments:

```
totalsales = oldsales + newsales;    // Adds the old sales and
                                     // the new sales to get
                                     // total sales

cout << "Happy Birthday";    // Sends the Happy Birthday
                             // message to the cout
return;    // Return
```

Each of these comments is redundant, and they really do not explain what is going on any more than the Visual C++ code itself. However, consider this statement:

```
for (int ctr = 10; ctr > 0; ctr) // Prints the numbers
  {                              // from 10 to 1
    cout << ctr << endl;         // on-screen

  }
```

Although you don't know Visual C++ (and even if you did), you can see that the purpose of these two lines of code is hidden in the cryptic Visual C++ language. A Visual C++ programmer could figure out this code, but the comment makes it effortless. As you saw in the previous three code fragments, comments often span more than one line. Continue a comment on the next line (remembering to use a double slash) if it is too long to place on a single line.

It is also useful to describe in your comments why your program is doing something. In the previous snippet, it would be obvious to a C++ programmer that the program was putting the numbers on the screen. If this was part of a graph drawing program, it might be more helpful to comment it like this:

```
//
//  Display the range of the graph on the screen
//
for (int ctr = 10; ctr > 0; ctr)
  {
    cout << ctr << endl;
  }
```

Now you understand why the program has a piece of code in it.

Review   **What You Have Learned**

After writing a program, you'll need comments even if you maintain the program yourself. Use comments only when they help explain what is going on in the code.

▶ **C-Style Comments**

Concept   **What You Will Learn**

Visual C++ supports your use of the old C-style comments that begin with /* and end with */.

Visual C++ supports another kind of comment that you might see occasionally. Visual C++ is based on the C language, but Visual C++'s comment syntax differs from C's. The designers of Visual C++ decided to keep the old C-style comment syntax so that C programs would work, with little or no change, with Visual C++ compilers. Nevertheless, the double slash comments are considered superior. You should learn C comments just in case you see them.

A comment in C begins with the characters /* and ends with the characters */. Unlike with Visual C++ comments, you must end a C comment. If you do not put the ending */, C assumes that the next line (or the next hundred lines) is still a comment until it finally finds another */. The following line contains a C-style comment:

```
char name[25];   /* Reserves space for a 25-character name */
```

Because a C comment ends only when the */ is reached, the following three lines make up a single comment:

```
/* The following program calculates stock statistics
using the most modern technical analysis techniques
available. */
```

Of course, the three lines could also be commented like this:

```
/* The following program calculates stock statistics */
/* using the most modern technical analysis techniques */
/* available. */
```

Although you should become familiar with C comments, true Visual C++ programmers tend to avoid using them. The double slash is easier because you don't have to remember to end the comment. The C-style comments can be error-prone as well. If you embed one C-style comment within another, Visual C++ gets confused. Stay with Visual C++ comments as much as possible, and both you and your Visual C++ compiler will lead healthier and more productive lives.

Review　**What You Have Learned**

C comments can be dangerous if you accidentally embed one within another. Stick to C++'s // comment style. There might be times, however, when you run across C comments in a C++ program and you should understand their format.

UNIT
3
Style Issues

▶ # Homework
General Knowledge

1. What is whitespace?

2. What is meant by freeform?

3. What does it mean to maintain programs?

4. What does C++ prefer most, uppercase or lowercase letters in programs?

5. What are comments?

6. Why are comments necessary?

7. What does the compiler do when it sees a comment?

8. What do all C++ comments begin with?

9. What is the difference between a C-style comment and a C++-style comment?

10. What happens when you nest C-style comments?

11. True or false: Longer programs are more difficult to understand than shorter ones.

12. True or false: You can substitute parentheses for braces if you feel that the parentheses are more readable.

13. True or false: Comments are not Visual C++ commands.

14. True or false: You can nest one C++ comment inside another.

15. Match the special character on the left with that special character's description on the right.

Special Character	Description
[	Backslash
<	Left bracket
}	Right-angled bracket
¦	Right parenthesis
\	Forward slash (or just *slash*)
]	Left-angled bracket
{	Left parenthesis
)	Right brace
(	Vertical line
>	Left brace
/	Right bracket

Note   There is no What's the Output? section in this unit.

Find the Bug

16. Here is a comment and a C++ command (the `return` statement). Where is the problem?

```
// Go back to the IDE    return;
```

17. The following program contains three comment bugs. See whether you can determine what is wrong.

```
// This program computes taxes
#include <iostream.h>
void main()
```

```
{
  The next few lines calculate payroll taxes
  // Computes the gross pay    float gross = 40 * 5.25;

  float taxes = gross * .40;    / Just computed the taxes
  cout "The taxes are " << taxes;
  return;
}
```

Write Code That...

18. Tim Peterson wants to put his name at the top of his program using a comment. Write a comment that contains Tim's name using both the C++-style and the C-style approach.

19. Here is the same program you saw earlier, with one difference: The programmer forgot to precede the comments with double slashes. After trying to compile the program, the programmer looked at the 20 or so error messages and realized what was left out. See if you can help the programmer correct the program by inserting the proper commenting symbols everywhere they go.

```
Filename: 1STLONG.CPP
Longer C++ program that demonstrates comments,
variables, constants, and simple input/output
#include <iostream.h>
void main()
  {
    int i, j;        These three lines declare four variables
    char c;
    float x;

    i = 4;           i is assigned an integer literal
    j = i + 7;       j is assigned the result of a computation
    c = 'A';         Enclose all character literals
                     in single quotation marks

    x = 9.087;       x is a floating-point value

    x = x * 12.3;    Overwrites what was in x with something else

   Sends the values of the four variables to the screen
    cout << i << ", " << j << ", " << c << ", " << x << "\n";

    return;          Not required, but helpful
  }
```

Hint: Count the number of double slashes you put in this program. If you did not add 18 double slashes (or if you added more than 18), try again.

Extra Credit

20. Of the following eight lines, which contain useful comments and which contain redundant ones?

```
clog << '\n';                      // Sends an end-of-line to the error
                                   // log
radius3 = radius1 + radius2;       // Calculates radius3
                                   // The following code contains a C++
                                   // program
                                   // The following code tracks your
                                   // investments
clog << '\n';                      // Sends '\n' to clog
```

Visual C++'s Program Structure

header files

main()

preprocessor directives

variable

constant

▶ **What You'll Learn**

- ▶ The Visual C++ program
- ▶ Dissecting a program

C++ programs can be very different from one another, but they all share a similar structure. As the previous unit explained, part of a C++ program only sets up the rest of the program. Whether you write a checkbook program, a payroll program, or a chemical analysis program, you need to understand the overall structure of Visual C++ programs. This unit provides some explanation of a Visual C++ program's pieces so that you will be comfortable with the format of a program before getting to the specifics in Lesson 3, "Data Basics."

▶ **The Visual C++ Program**

Concept   **What You Will Learn**

You'll always find main(), #, and braces in DOS-based C++ programs.

The starting point for C++ programs is the main() function. The previous units showed you some Visual C++ programs. If you look them over, you will see the word main() in every one of them. Looking further still, you will see an opening brace after main() and a closing brace a little later. You never find an opening brace (a left brace) without a closing brace (a right brace).

Visual C++ programs also share another trait: Almost all of them have one or more lines that begin with the # (pound sign) character, followed by include. Figure 4.1 shows a simple outline of a Visual C++ program.

```
preprocessor ———————[ #include <iostream.h>
directive                main()
                         {
function main()              // C++ programming
block of C++ ————[           // commands go here.
code                     }
```

FIGURE 4.1.
An Outline of a simple
C++ program

Note   Notice that there is a closing brace for every opening brace? There is also a closing parenthesis for every opening parenthesis and a closing bracket for every opening bracket that appears in a program. The parentheses, braces, and brackets enclose language elements within the Visual C++ program. As with parentheses in written languages, these Visual C++

symbols enclose pieces of a program, and you must indicate with the closing character where the piece ends. Unlike a written document, the meaning of parentheses, braces, and brackets are quite distinct in C++ and each must be used in the correct way.

Before you know it, you will be comfortable with main(), #include, braces, and all the other parts of a Visual C++ program. The next section looks at a longer Visual C++ program and dissects pieces of it to ease you into Visual C++.

Review
What You Have Learned

Being able to understand main(), #, and braces is your first step in understanding Visual C++.

Note   There is no Stop and Type part here due to the textual nature of this section.

► Dissecting a Program

Concept
What You Will Learn

Look at the specific parts of a typical Visual C++ program to acquaint yourself with the code.

The next few pages provide a closer examination of the program in Listing 4.1. The idea is to give you a look at the big picture before getting into the specific language elements starting in Lesson 3.

▼ INPUT   LISTING 4.1. A SAMPLE VISUAL C++ PROGRAM.

```
// Filename: DISSECT.CPP
// Simple program for you to analyze

#include <iostream.h>

void main()
  {
    int age, weight;    // These lines define four variables
    char initial;
    double salary;
```

continues

UNIT

4

Visual C++'s Program Structure

```
    age = 13;          // Assigns an integer literal to age
    weight = age * 6;  // Assigns a weight based on a formula
    initial = 'D';     // All character literals are
                       // enclosed in single quotes
    salary = 200.50;   // salary requires a floating-point
                       // value because it was defined to
                       // be a floating-point
    salary = salary * 2.5; // Changes what was in salary

// Next line sends the values of the variables to the screen
    cout << age << ", " << weight << ", " << initial
         << ", " << salary;

    return;            // Good habit to end programs
                       // and functions with return
}
```

Keep in mind that this program is simple and does not actually perform a lot of valuable work. Despite its simplicity, you might not fully understand it all even after the explanation that comes next, but it is a good place to begin.

While looking through the program, see whether you can understand any or all of it. If you are new to programming, you should know that the computer reads each line of the program, starting with the first line and working its way down, until it has completed all the instructions (the statements on each line) in the program. (Of course, you first have to compile and link the program, as described in Lesson 1, before seeing the output from the program on your computer.)

Here is the output that results when you run this program:

```
13, 78, D, 501.25
```

The Program

After the previous unit, you know all about the first two lines in the program. They contain comments that describe the filename and a little about the program. Comments also are scattered throughout the code to explain what happens along the way.

The next line is called a preprocessor directive. It is repeated here:

```
#include <iostream.h>
```

This strange-looking statement is not actually a Visual C++ command, but it is a directive to the Visual C++ compiler. The directive directs the compiler (that is easy to remember). #include tells Visual C++ to take the filename located inside the angled brackets and load that file into the Visual C++ program at that point. In principle, the preprocessor first reads all the code looking for any lines beginning with a # symbol and acts upon them before compilation takes place. In the case of an `#include`, the compiler will view the program as if you had typed the contents of the file directly into the program file. In other words, the program grows to become the size of DISSECT.CPP (the program shown in the preceding section) plus IOSTREAM.H. Most files included with `#include` end in the .H filename extension because these files are header files.

The header file named IOSTREAM.H comes with your Visual C++ compiler. Header files are a way of telling your program about pieces of code that it needs that are extra to the C++ language. Recall that `cout` was not part of the C++ language. The header file contains the information that lets the compiler know that `cout` is a function and not just a made up word. The `include` files are located in your Visual C++ directory in a subdirectory called INCLUDE. If you want to include a file you wrote (all `#include` files must be text, such as those created with the Visual C++ editor), you have to put the included filename in quotation marks, like this:

```
#include "d:\myFiles\mine.h"
```

Note You might see other header files included, either in addition to IOSTREAM.H or in place of it. Sometimes, Visual C++ programmers use a C program that includes the header file named STDIO.H instead of IOSTREAM.H. Notice in Appendix D, "Visual C++ Command Reference," that `#include` is not listed with all the other Visual C++ commands. `#include` is not a Visual C++ command; it is simply a pre-command (hence its name, preprocessor directive) that directs the compiler to do something before it compiles the actual commands. In this case, `#include` tells Visual C++ to include a file from disk at that point in the program.

Braces and *main()*

You see these two lines in all of the Visual C++ programs in this book:

```
void main()
{
```

Note The `void` always goes with `main()`. Treat the following text as saying `void main()`. We'll worry about what `void` means much later on.

`main()` does not always appear toward the top of the program, as it does here. Sometimes `main()` appears farther down into the code. Wherever `main()` is, however, it begins the most critical section of any Visual C++ program. When you run the program, the program always begins executing at `main()`. No matter where `main()` is located in the program, it is the starting point for the program's execution. Therefore, it makes sense to put `main()` toward the top of a program. Sometimes, however, a lot of other stuff has to go before `main()`. No matter what appears before `main()`, `main()` begins the program's execution when you run the program.

> ***Note***   Not all programs written in C++ use `main()` as the starting point. You will not find a `main()` in a Windows program. Windows programs use `WinMain()` because Windows programs work in a way very different from ordinary programs.

`main()` is called a function. A function is not a command. It is a named section of a program, and its name always ends with a pair of parentheses. A program can have one function or many functions, but every program contains the `main()` function because the program has to begin somewhere. You can always tell where a function begins because functions always have names that end with parentheses. The parentheses tell Visual C++ that `main()` is a function and not a command or something else.

> ***Note***   None of the commands in Appendix D contain parentheses. Parentheses are part of function names, but they are never part of command names.

Because an opening brace follows `main()`, you can look for the matching closing brace (they always appear in pairs) and find out where `main()` ends. Every pair of braces in a Visual C++ program encloses something known as a compound statement. In this case, the compound statement is almost as long as the `main()` function. The next function—if there were one—could go after `main()`'s closing brace. You can never define a function inside another one. `main()` must finish before another function can begin being listed in the program.

> ***Note***   A statement ends in a semicolon. A compound statement is made up of a sequence of statements and can be used anywhere that a single statement can be used. A compound statement does not need a semicolon following it. A compound statement is often called a block.

Before you get too sidetracked, you are going to become extremely comfortable with the fact that `main()` is a function and that braces enclose blocks in a program. Read on to learn more about the rest of this sample program named DISSECT.CPP. There are more important aspects to the program at this stage in the game than fully understanding `main()`.

> ***Note***   The `void` before `main()` is required in simple Visual C++ programs that do not return values to the operating system. You will learn more about `void` in Lesson 7, "Break it Up with Functions."

Data

Here are the three lines that follow `main()`'s opening brace:

```
int age, weight;    // These lines define four variables
char initial;
float salary;
```

Definition—A *variable* is a named value that holds data that can be changed.

These three lines define four variables. A variable definition tells Visual C++ exactly what variables will be used in the lines that follow. This variable definition tells the compiler to make room in memory for four values, label them with names, and get ready to use them. Later in the program, values will be stored in those variables.

Definition—A *constant* is a value that cannot be changed but can be named.

Definition—A *literal* is an actual constant value stated in the program.

All Visual C++ programs contain both commands and data. The data is always made up of one or more variables, one or more literals, or a combination of both. A literal is sometimes called a constant, but in Visual C++, the word *constant* actually has another meaning (in most languages, literal and constant are synonymous).

> ***Note*** As the name implies, a variable is data that can change (become variable) as the program runs. A constant remains the same. In real life, a variable might be your salary. It increases over time (you hope). A constant is something that does not change, such as the number of days in July or the fact that Pi is 3.14159.

A variable is like a box inside your computer that holds something. That something might be a number or a character, a value of another variable, or the result of a calculation. Every variable within the same block is distinguished from others by its unique name. No two variables within the same block can have the same name. You can have as many variables as needed to hold changing data. After you define a variable and give it a value, the variable keeps its value until you change the value or define the variable with something else by putting some other data value into it. The next lesson more fully explains these concepts.

The three lines of code that follow the opening brace define four variables. The variable definition informs the rest of the program that two integer variables named `age` and `weight`, as well as a character variable named `initial` and a floating-point variable named `salary`, appear throughout the program. The terms *integer*, *character*, and *floating-point* basically refer to different types of data. Integers are whole numbers, and floating-point numbers contain decimal places.

Just as there are different types of variables, there are different types of constants. The first form of constant you should know is a *literal*. For now, you simply have to understand that a Visual C++ literal is any number, character, word, or phrase whose value is explicitly written when it is used and does not change as the program runs. The following are all valid Visual C++ literals:

```
5.6
-34
'W'
"Mary"
18.293345
0.0
```

As you can see, some literals are numeric and some are character-based. The single and double quotation marks around two of the literals, however, are not part of the actual literals. A single-character literal requires single quotation marks around it, and a string of characters such as "Mary" requires double quotation marks (often called just quotation marks).

The body of the DISSECT.CPP program (repeated next) assigns values to the defined variables.

```
age = 13;              // Assigns an integer literal to age
weight = age * 6;      // Assigns a weight based on a formula
initial = 'D';         // All character literals are
                       // enclosed in single quotes
salary = 200.50;       // salary requires a floating-point
                       // value because it was defined to
                       // be a floating-point
salary = salary * 2.5; // Changes what was in salary
```

The first line puts 13 in the integer variable, age. The second line multiplies 6 by the variable age's value to produce the value 78, which is stored in weight. The multiplication sign (*) in Visual C++ works just as an x does in mathematics. The other primary math operators are shown in Table 4.1.

Table 4.1. The primary math operators.

Operator	Meaning	Example
+	Addition	4 + 5
-	Subtraction	7 - 2
*	Multiplication	12 * 6
/	Division	48 / 12

Tip   Use an asterisk (*) for multiplication and not a lowercase x. The computer would confuse the variable name x with the multiplication symbol x if both were allowed.

When mathematical operators appear on the right side of an equal sign, the program completes the math before assigning the result to a variable. In the statement

```
salary = salary * 2.5;   // Changes what was in salary
```

the multiplication of `salary` and `2.5` is performed, and then the result is stored in `salary`.

 Note   Visual C++ follows math rules by calculating multiplication and division before it calculates any addition and subtraction if a combination appears within the same expression. Therefore, the following produces a result of 8, not 10, because C++ multiplies first, even though addition appears to the left. Lesson 4, "Simple Operators," explains math ordering further.

```
result = 2 + 3 * 2;   // Stores an 8 in result
```

Assigning Values to Variables

Use an equal sign (=), called the assignment operator, to put values into variables. The statement

```
age = 13;   // Assigns an integer literal to age
```

puts the literal `13` into the variable named `age`.

 Tip   Think of an equal sign as working exactly as a left-pointing arrow would. The value on the right of the equal sign moves left into the variable on the left of the equal sign. If there is a formula on the right, Visual C++ computes the answer and moves the answer into the variable on the left side of the equal sign.

In Listing 4.1, you find the following variables:

```
age
weight
initial
salary
```

Because `age` is an integer, you should put only integers into it.

 Note   A variable must hold a value that matches the variable's type.

Output to the Screen

The line that begins with cout (pronounced "see-out") at first looks very confusing:

```
cout << age << ", " << weight << ", " << initial
<< ", " << salary;
```

When the program reaches this line, it prints the contents of the four variables on-screen.

The output from the line is

```
13, 78, D, 501.25
```

Because there are no other output statements in the program, this line is the only line that produces something you can see when you run the program. The rest of the program either sets up the code (such as main() and the braces) or performs internal data manipulations (such as assigning values to variables).

cout is not a Visual C++ command, but it acts a lot like one. You will not see cout in Appendix D. cout has no built-in input or output commands. cout is a C++ class, described in the header file IOSTREAM.H. You will learn about classes much later on, but you'll make use of this class earlier because it is so easy to use. cout sends output to an output device, which is usually the screen. There is a special value you can send to cout called endl, which will send a command to start a new line to the screen.

> **Note**   You can guess at cout's purpose just by looking at the line with cout. The data values are being sent via the double angled brackets (<<) to the cout device. The values following cout go to the screen in the left-to-right order in which they appear. The opposite of cout is cin. cin gets keystrokes from the keyboard. Can you see that the following statement gets a number from the keyboard and stores it in the location called amount?
>
> ```
> cin >> amount;
> ```

You have seen that there are two parts to a program: the commands that the program executes, and the data that a program works on. Commands come in two forms: the C++ keywords that the compiler understands implicitly, and extra commands that the compiler can be made to understand with the use of header files.

Returning to the Operating System

As soon as your Visual C++ program finishes executing, it should return to the operating system so that another program can be run. The return statement at the end of main() ensures that the program returns to the operating system. return is optional when the function is preceded by void, so you do not have to use it for simple returns from functions such as main().

The closing brace after the `return` does two things in this program. It signals the end of a block (begun earlier with the opening brace), which is the end of the `main()` function, and it signals the end of the program.

Figure 4.2 repeats the entire program listing with some callouts that label the various parts of the program.

```
comments ──────────┌─ // Filename: DISSECT.CPP
                    └─ // Simple program for you to analyze

preprocessor ──────┌─ #include <iostream.h>
directive

function name ─────┌─ void main()
                   {
variable ──────────┌─   int age, weight;      // These lines define four variables
definition         │    char initial;
                   └─   float salary;

                        age = 13;             // Assign an integer literal to age
                        weight = age * 6;     // Assign a weight based on a formula
                        initial = 'D';        // All character literals are
                                              // enclosed in single quotes
                        salary = 200.50;      // salary requires a floating-point value
                                              // because it was defined to be a floating
                        salary = salary * 2.5;  // Change what was in salary

                        // The next line sends the values of the variables to the scr
                        cout << age << "," << weight << "," << initial << "," << s

                        return;               // Good habit to end programs
                                              // and functions with return
end of main() ──────┌─ }
                                                          comments
```

FIGURE 4.2.

The structure of the simple C++ program.

Familiarize yourself with the overall look and feel of this program. It helps to see an overview before diving straight into the specifics of the commands. Now that you have a general understanding of the format of Visual C++ programs, you are ready to tackle the language elements. Good luck with your venture into the world of the Visual C++ language particulars, beginning in the next lesson, "Data Basics."

Note Until now, there was no way to present you with an end-of-section Stop and Type analysis because you did not know enough about Visual C++ to see one. From now on, you'll see Stop and Type, Review, Input, Output, and Analysis parts at the end of most sections in each unit. You should ignore the line numbers (the numbers followed by colons at the start of the lines). These are not part of the code and are provided simply to allow easy reference to parts of the code.

STOP & TYPE Listing 4.2 contains another Visual C++ program that you can study in order to find the common elements mentioned in this unit.

UNIT

4

Visual C++'s Program Structure

Review

All C++ programs have similarities. Their structure is the same even though they often do very different work.

▼ **INPUT   LISTING 4.2. A VISUAL C++ PROGRAM FOR REVIEW.**

```
 1: // Filename: VARS.CPP
 2: // All programs share common traits
 3:
 4: #include <iostream.h>
 5:
 6: void main()
 7: {
 8:   char c;              // Define all variables before
 9:   int i;               // you use them
10:    float f;
11:
12:    // The next few lines store literal values
13:    // in the three variables just defined
14:    c = 'W';
15:    i = 64;
16:    f = 12.57;
17:
18:    // Print the values
19:    cout << "c is " << c << ", i is " << i << ", f is "
20:        << f;
21:
22:    return;   // Good habit to end programs
23:              // and functions with return
24: }
```

▼ **OUTPUT**

```
c is W, i is 64, f is 12.57
```

▼ **ANALYSIS**

Lines 1 and 2 are comments that describe the program's filename and a one-line statement about the program. Line 4 is a preprocessor directive that includes a file needed by the rest of the program. For the time being, include this file in all your Visual C++ programs. Later lessons will explain it in more detail.

You'll find several blank lines scattered throughout the code, such as lines 3, 5, and 11. Visual C++ ignores the blank lines, but the whitespace helps you read the program.

All programs have a main() function. You can always tell when a word in a C++ program is a function because of the parentheses that follow the name. All functions open with an opening left brace as shown in line 7. The matching right brace, and therefore the main() function, does not end until line 24.

> **Note**   Not all programs in this book will begin with void preceding main(). Until Lesson 7 explains how and when to use void, follow this book's lead: Use it when you see it, and don't use it when you write your own programs until you understand what void is all about.

Lines 8, 9, and 10 define three variables of three data types. The next lesson explains variables and data types in lots of detail. The important thing to note here is that you must define all variables before you use them. When you define the variables as done in lines 8 through 10, you tell C++ that you want those variables created.

Lines 14 through 16 put values in the three variables defined earlier. Until you put values in variables, you should not use those variables. Unlike some other programming languages, C++ does not place zeros in variables before you use them. Therefore, they will contain garbage or random values.

Lines 19 and 20 are actually one single C++ statement that takes two lines. The cout produces the output shown after the program listing.

You will understand all of these program details as you progress in this book. For now, try to get familiar with these concepts and see whether you can learn to spot common elements across C++ programs.

▶ **Homework**
General Knowledge

1. What preprocessor directive do C++ programmers almost always use to include header files?
2. What are the characters that enclose a Visual C++ block?
3. What kind of data must be enclosed in single quotation marks?
4. What kind of data must be enclosed in double quotation marks?
5. What sends output to the screen in Visual C++?
6. What kind of numeric data contains no decimal points?
7. What kind of numeric data contains decimal points?

8. Write the four arithmetic symbols.

9. Is `return` ever optional? If so, why is it a good idea to learn to always use `return`?

10. What are the literals in Listing 4.1? Hint: There are eight if you count the ones embedded in the `cout` statement.

11. Which of the following are variables and which are literals? Hint: A variable name cannot have quotation marks around it. If it did, Visual C++ would think it was a character literal (if single quotations were used) or a string literal (if double quotation marks were used).

```
'1.2'
Payroll
4543.23
name
47
"Diane"
```

12. True or false: `cout` is a Visual C++ command.

13. True or false: All lines in a Visual C++ program must end with semicolons.

14. True or false: A left brace is always followed later in the program with a right brace.

Find the Bug

15. What is missing from this short program? Add the missing line of code.

```
// Program to calculate swimming pool floor area
main()
{
  int width, length, area;
  width = 16;
  length = 32;
  area = width * length;
  cout << "The area is " << area;
```

16. Fred just entered his first C++ program, but the compiler gave him fits. See if you can tell Fred what's wrong with this simple program:

```
/* My first program
   /* At least I'm trying! */
   This program will print a simple message */
#include <Iostream.h>
void Main()
{
  Cout << "A simple program";
  Return;
}
```

Write Code That...

17. Glance through Listing 4.1 again. See whether you can figure out where `main()` ends. In other words, if there were more functions in this program, where would the next one go?

18. Write a preprocessor directive that includes the header file named STRING.H.

19. Write a comment that includes your name and date. Use C's style of comments. On the next line, use a C++ comment to do the very same thing.

Extra Credit

20. Write the statement that stores the result of a `sales` variable multiplied by a `profit` variable into a third variable named `netsales`.

21. Write the statement that outputs your name to the screen. Hint: Because your name is a string of more than one character, enclose it in double quotation marks.

22. Enter the corrected code from question number 17 in your Visual C++ compiler. Compile the program using Project | Build (Shift+F8) and run it with Project | Execute (Ctrl+F5). View the results in the QuickWin output window.

Analyzing
Visual C++
Programs

STOP&TYPE In this lesson, you learned about the fundamental format of all C++ programs. You saw the following:

▶ Visual C++ programs contain a `main()` function.

▶ Braces determine where the `main()` function begins and ends.

▶ Preprocessor directives direct the way Visual C++ compiles your program. Preprocessor directives always begin with a pound sign, `#`. The `#include` directive includes files needed by library functions.

Project 2 Listing. Introduction to Visual C++ programs.

```
1:  // Filename: PROJECT2.CPP

2:  // Introduces the format of Visual C++ programs and demonstrates

3:  // how to write Visual C++ comments, the #include preprocessor

4:  // directive, and the cout command that outputs data to the

5:  // screen.

6:

7:  #include <iostream.h>

8:

9:  void main()

10: {
```

▶ Visual C++ comments begin with // and end at the end of the line. Comments are for people, not for Visual C++.

▶ The cout command outputs data to your screen.

▶ All characters are important in Visual C++ programs.

Description

1: A Visual C++ comment that includes the program's filename.

2: A comment that begins the introduction of the program's description.

3: The program's description continues.

4: The program's description continues.

5: The program's description continues.

6: Extra blanks make your program more readable.

7: The cout command needs information in the IOSTREAM.H header file.

7: The compiler inserts a helpful file here.

8: Extra blanks make your program more readable.

9: All functions have names and the first function in all Visual C++ programs is main().

10: All functions begin with a left brace.

10: void means that main() does not return a value to the operating system.

continues

Project 2 Listing. continued

```
11:    cout << "I have a ";

12:    cout << "Sleekster";          // Continues the output line

13:    cout << " automobile.";

14:    cout << endl << endl;         // Prints 2 blank lines

15:

16:    cout << "I want to sell my car for $4800 (cheap!)." << endl;

17:    cout << "I have had the car for " << 5 << " years." << endl;

18:    cout << "It's really a grade-" << 'A' << " deal!"

19:         << endl << endl;

20:

21:    return;  // End the program

22:  }
```

Description

11: The screen output begins.

12: The car's model name prints. No new line occurs.

13: Finish the output.

14: Move the cursor down two lines.

14: endl sends a new line command to the screen.

15: Extra blanks make your program more readable.

16: Another message prints.

17: cout prints all kinds of data. Strings and an integer output here.

18: This cout outputs strings and a character literal.

19: Statements can be more than one line.

20: Extra blanks make your program more readable.

21: The final return; in main() always returns control back to Visual C++'s QuickWin window.

22: A closing brace always terminates the main() function.

▼ OUTPUT

```
I have a Sleekster automobile.
I want to sell my car for $4800 (cheap!).
I have had the car for 5 years.
It's really a grade-A deal!
```

Lesson ▶

Data Basics

Unit 5: **Numbers and Characters**

Unit 6: **String Data and I/O**

Lesson 3 Project

Numbers and Characters

▶ What You'll Learn

- ▶ Data and information
- ▶ Data in a Visual C++ program
- ▶ Characteristics of variables
- ▶ Literals
- ▶ Constant variables

Computers can store data in many different formats. Visual C++ works with that data and, through programs you write, processes it into information the user needs. In Lesson 2, "Analyzing Visual C++ Programs," you learned that programs consist of data and commands. You must learn to store that data properly so that your programs can manage it properly. Visual C++ uses constants and variables to hold data your programs need.

The term *data* is the plural of *datum*. As is common in many texts these days, this book uses the word *data* to mean both the plural and the singular. Accuracy in English is almost as important as accuracy in programming, but moving between the terms *datum* and *data* often results in more confusion than clarity.

▶ Data and Information

Concept   **What You Will Learn**

Although the terms are often used interchangeably, *data* and *information* have two different meanings.

Is there a difference between data and information? Maybe you have not thought too much about the two words and their meanings. Although most people think they have a good idea of what data and information mean, when asked to define them, people often use one to define the other, saying "Data is information" or "Information is data." As this section points out, there is a difference.

Definition—*Data processing* (DP) is simply the processing of data into meaningful information.

You might have heard the term *data processing*. At its simplest level, that's what the computer does best and does quickly. Figure 5.1 shows the basic model of every computer program ever written. The computer takes data as input, processes the data, and produces meaningful information as output.

FIGURE 5.1.
The basic input-process-output model.

Think of a corporate president's information needs. Does the president want to get a daily list of the salaries of each of the company's 5,000 employees, down to the lowest-paid part-time clerk? Of course not. A list of every employee would be just raw facts and figures that the president does not have time to deal with. To the president, the list would be a waste of time.

The president certainly is concerned with payroll, but he or she needs meaningful information, not a bunch of raw facts and figures (data). The president might prefer a computerized graphic that shows such things as the payroll trends over the past year, how the company's payroll figures match those of the competitors, and how one department's payroll compares to another's. Data organized in such a fashion is information for the president—something he or she can use to make a decision. Computers are the perfect tools for processing all the data and producing meaningful information used by people who make decisions based on that information.

Note   What is data to one person might be information to another. Would the part-time clerk care about the detailed payroll figure for his or her job? If so, wouldn't the salary for part-time clerks be important information to the clerk?

Review   **What You Have Learned**

Data is made up of raw facts and figures. Information is processed data that provides meaning for people.

Note   There is no Stop and Type part here due to this section's textual nature.

▶ **Data in a Visual C++ Program**

Concept   **What You Will Learn**

Learn about the numeric and character data capabilities of C++.

Definition—*GIGO* means garbage in, garbage out. You can't get good results from bad data.

Representing data properly should be the goal of every Visual C++ programmer. If the data is bad, GIGO results in bad output. A computer is not magic. It simply follows your program instructions and processes data with the commands you give it. If you give it bad data, it will produce bad results.

A Visual C++ program can process many kinds of data, but all Visual C++ data falls into these two broad categories:

▶ numeric data

▶ character data

This unit explains the numeric data types. The next unit, "String Data and I/O," explains the character data types. You do not have to be a mathematician to understand numeric data in a Visual C++ program. Let the computer do all the math! You want meaningful results, and it is the computer's job to take your data and produce meaningful results based on the instructions you supply.

In the second lesson, you learned about variables. You also saw programs that contained several literals (sometimes called constants). A variable is a storage location that holds a value. The contents of variables can change. Literals are numbers or character data that do not change.

Review   **What You Have Learned**

C++ supports numeric and character data. The more effort that your programs spend checking data values for accuracy, the better assured you can be of the program's resulting output.

Note   There is no Stop and Type part here due to this section's textual nature.

▶ Characteristics of Variables

Concept   **What You Will Learn**

All variables share common characteristics. To use variables, you must first learn how to specify the variable's characteristics.

Whenever your program needs to store some data temporarily, you store that data in a variable. You also can store data in a file for long-term storage, but during a program's execution, variables are the primary place you put data until you are ready to use it. You, the programmer, are responsible for telling the program when it needs a variable. Before you use a variable, you must define it. When you define a variable, you tell Visual C++ to reserve some storage for that variable and give it a name. Any time after a variable is defined, you can place values into that variable.

In Visual C++, you can place variable definitions anywhere in the program, as long as the program does not use the variables until after they are defined. To define a variable, you must understand these characteristics that all variables share:

▶ All variables have names.

▶ All variables have data types.

▶ All variables hold values.

Naming Rules for Variables

You must assign and use variable names in a program to distinguish the variables from each other. Variable names must be unique; you cannot have two variables with the same name in the same program. (Actually, you will learn about an exception to this rule in Lesson 7, "Break It Up with Functions." For now, assume that all variable names in the same program must be unique.) Here are the naming rules for variables:

▶ Variable names can range from 1 to 247(!) characters.

▶ All variable names must begin with a letter of the alphabet.

▶ After the first initial letter, variable names can contain letters, numbers, and the underscore (_) character.

Warning The Visual C++ compiler lets you start variable names with a leading underscore, but this practice is not recommended. Some of Visual C++'s built-in variable names begin with an underscore, and you might accidentally use Visual C++'s variable names for your own variables.

Tip Some Visual C++ programmers use underscore characters in variable names to separate parts of the name, such as `Sales_div1`. Others prefer a hump notation, such as `salesDiv1`. The term *hump notation* is perfect for describing the uppercase letter (the hump) in the middle of the variable name that resembles a camel's hump.

The following variable names are valid names because they follow the naming rules:

```
sales    x_211    d    ageLimit    Amount95
```

Visual C++ programmers generally use lowercase letters for variable names, saving uppercase for the secondary words within a variable's name. When a variable name is a combination of two or more words, such as numOfEmps, it is common to uppercase the first letter of each word. Never uppercase every letter in a variable name, because some Visual C++ programmers reserve uppercase names for constant data that does not change or an old-style C programming feature called macros. (You will read about constants later in this unit.) Programmers also use the case of the first letter to help distinguish between function names, which by convention start with an uppercase letter (but remember C++ itself is not aware of this convention).

Some programs have variables on 95 percent of their code lines. Because of the importance and abundance of variables, take the time to learn what makes a valid variable name and what makes an invalid variable name. You must know the naming rules of a variable before moving on.

 Warning   You do not have to follow the uppercase/lowercase tradition, but you should know that uppercase letters in variable names are different from lowercase letters. For example, each of the following four variables is viewed differently by your Visual C++ compiler:

```
amount    Amount    AMOUNT    aMOUNT
```

Never give a variable the same name as a Visual C++ command. Appendix D, "Visual C++ Command Reference," is a list of all the Visual C++ command names. If you inadvertently give a variable the same name as a command, such as while, the Visual C++ compiler will become confused and will not compile your program correctly. However, a variable name can contain a command without getting confused (so waitwhileprocessing would be a valid name).

Always use meaningful variable names. Give your variables names that help describe the values that they hold. For example, keeping track of chemistry weights in a variable called chemWeights is much more descriptive than using the variable name XYZ34. Even though both names are valid, chemWeights is easier to remember, and you get a good idea of what the variable holds by looking at its name.

Although you can and should use meaningful names, using names that are too long means too much typing and difficult to follow formulas.

Data Types

There are many different types of data, and you need different types of variables to hold them. Table 5.1 lists all the different types of Visual C++ variables. For instance, if a variable holds an integer, Visual C++ assumes that no decimal point or fractional part (the part to the right of the decimal point) exists for the variable's value.

Table 5.1. The Visual C++ variable data types.

Declaration Name	Data Type Description
char	Character
unsigned char	Unsigned character
signed char	Signed character (same as char)
int	Integer
unsigned int	Unsigned integer
signed int	Signed integer (same as int)
short int	Short integer
unsigned short int	Unsigned short integer
signed short int	Signed short integer (same as short int)
long	Long integer
long int	Long integer (same as long)
signed long int	Signed long integer (same as long int)
unsigned long int	Unsigned long integer
float	Floating-point (real)
double	Double floating-point (real)
long double	Long double floating-point (real)

The data type of the variable you use depends on the data you store in it. The following sections more fully describe these types. Concentrate on how to define variables before worrying about how to use variables for data storage.

Defining Variables

Definition—A *local variable* is a variable that belongs to the function with which it is declared.

When you define a variable, you place your order for Visual C++ to create a named space for that variable. Visual C++ does not care where you define a variable in a program, as long as you define it somewhere before the code that uses it. Local variables are by far the most common types of variables in Visual C++ programs, and they are the only kinds of variables you will see for much of this book. You can define variables either within the curly braces that mark the start and end of functions (remember that `main()` is what we called a function) or outside the braces.

Definition—A *global variable* is a variable that you define outside any function, which can be seen and used by all following functions.

Variables are easy to define. To define a variable, you must state its type, followed by its name. In Lesson 2, you saw a program that defined four variables in the following way:

```
void main()
  {
    int age, weight;    // These lines define four variables
    char initial;
    float salary;
    // Rest of program follows
```

These lines define two local integer variables named `age` and `weight`, a character variable named `initial`, and a floating-point variable named `salary`. You have no idea what is inside these variables, however. Generally, you cannot assume that a variable holds zero, or any other number, until you assign it a value. Unlike most other languages, C++ does not automatically initialize variables (BASIC sets new numbers to zero). Values of variables are never remembered from one execution of the program to another.

The code also defines a character variable called `initial`. Put only single characters in character variables. Next, a floating-point variable called `salary` is defined.

After these four variable definitions, Visual C++ reserves storage in memory, assigns the variable names to the four reserved locations, and waits for you to put data in the variables. Until you place data in the variables, you do not know what their values are, so do not use them for anything initially except to store data in them.

Many Data Types

There are many different types of data, and Visual C++ wants to have a data type available to hold any data you might need to store. Visual C++ has more data types than almost any other programming language. When you need to store data, you need to pick the right variable data type. Numeric variables hold numbers and character variables hold single characters.

Definition—An *array* is an aggregate data type that's a collection of individual data types.

Note You can't hold more than a single character in a Visual C++ character variable. To store a string of characters, you must use an array. The next unit describes how to represent string data.

Integers can hold only numbers that have no decimal point. These are sometimes called whole numbers. All of the following values are numeric integers:

```
33      -1     0      1     -83421
```

Store real numbers (numbers with decimal points) in floating-point variables. Any time you have to store a salary, a temperature, or any other number that might have a fractional part (a decimal portion), you must store it in a floating-point variable. All of the following expressions are floating-point numbers, and any floating-point variable can hold them:

```
145.7722   0.00    -2344.5    4.00004
```

Each of the types of variables holds a different range of variables. Table 5.2 shows a list of typical ranges that each Visual C++ variable type can hold.

Table 5.2. Ranges of Visual C++ variables.

Type	Range
char	–128 to 127
unsigned char	0 to 255
signed char	–128 to 127
int	–32768 to 32767
unsigned int	0 to 65535
signed int	–32768 to 32767
short int	–32768 to 32767
unsigned short int	0 to 65535
signed short int	–32768 to 32767
long int	–2147483648 to 2147483647
signed long int	–2147483648 to 2147483647
unsigned long	0 to 4294967296
float	–3.4E38 to 3.4E+38
double	–1.7E308 to 1.7E+308
long double	–3.4E4932 to 1.1E+4932
float	–3.4E+38 to 3.4E+38
double	–1.7E+308 to 1.7E+308
long double	–3.4E+4932 to 1.1E+4932

ote The unsigned variable types can hold only positive numbers, but they can hold larger positive values than the signed ones.

Table 5.2 holds true for Visual C++ with this book, but it might not hold true for other kinds of C++ compilers, even the latest Microsoft C++ compiler for the latest version of Windows. In Visual C++, integers and character variables frequently can be used interchangeably. As shown in Appendix B, "The ASCII Table," each ASCII table character has a unique number that corresponds to its location in the table. If you store a number in a character variable, Visual C++ treats the data as if it were the ASCII character that matches that number in the table. Conversely, you can store character data in an integer variable. Visual C++ finds that character's ASCII number and stores that number rather than the character. Examples that help illustrate this point appear later in this unit.

Definition—*Scientific notation* is a shortcut method for representing extremely large or small values.

You might think that some of the floating-point ranges from Table 5.2 look strange with their *E* notation. The *E* represents scientific notation. To determine what value each number represents, take the number before the *E* (meaning Exponent) and multiply it by 10 raised to the power after the plus sign. For instance, a floating-point number (type float) can contain a number as small as –3.4E+38.

Long integers and long doubles can hold larger numbers (and therefore, have a higher precision) than regular integers and regular double floating-point variables. This is due to the larger number of memory locations used by Visual C++ for these data types.

 ote Every time your computer has to access more storage for a single variable (as is usually the case for long variables), it takes the computer much longer to access it, perform calculations, and store it. Use the long variables only if you suspect your data might overflow the typical data type ranges. Although the ranges differ between computers, you should have an idea of whether your numbers might exceed the computer's storage ranges. If you are working with extremely large (or extremely small and fractional) numbers, you should consider using the long and double variables.

Most numeric variables should be signed unless you know for certain that your data contains only positive numbers. (Some values, such as age and distances, are always positive.) By making a variable unsigned, you gain a little extra storage range. That range of values, however, must always be positive. Obviously, you must be aware of what kinds of data your variables hold. You certainly do not always know exactly what each variable is holding, but you can have a general idea. For example, in storing a person's age, you should realize that a long integer variable would be a waste of space, because nobody can yet live longer than the largest value a regular integer can hold. These two variable definitions are exactly the same:

```
int i = 7;
```

and

```
signed int i = -7;
```

But they are not the same as this:

```
unsigned int i = -7;   // Unsigned variables can't hold negatives
```

Note C++ does not check whether the values you assign into a number will fit and will not produce an error if you exceed the maximum value that a field can hold.

STOP&TYPE Listing 5.1 contains a fragment of a Visual C++ program that defines four variables.

Review   **What You Have Learned**

When you define variables, use meaningful variable names and assign a data type that matches the data you store in the variable.

▼ INPUT   LISTING 5.1. DEFINING VARIABLES.

```
1:   void main()
2:   {
3:     char regionCode;
4:     int numEmployees;
5:     long int numCustomers;
6:     double yearlySales;
```

▼ OUTPUT

There is no output from this fragment of code.

▼ ANALYSIS

The four variables defined in Listing 5.1 are local variables because they are all defined after an opening brace. Line 3 defines a character variable that will hold one character. A character variable can always hold one character at most. The character might be a letter, digit, or special character such as & or #.

The listing defines two integer variables. The first integer named numEmployees is defined on line 4. numEmployees is a regular integer variable. Line 5's numCustomers is a long integer value because it can hold a number larger than 32767 (the maximum value that a regular integer can hold as pointed out in Table 5.2).

The yearlySales variable, defined on line 6, is large enough to hold a huge floating-point number.

▶ Literals

	What You Will Learn

You specify literals in different ways depending on their data type.

Definition—*Literals* are text representations in the program that do not change. They are used as values by the program.

There are several types of Visual C++ literals. Literals do not change. Integer literals are whole numbers that do not contain decimal points. Floating-point literals are numbers that contain a fractional portion (a decimal point with an optional value to the right of the decimal point).

Integer Literals

Visual C++ enables you to assign integer literals to variables, use integer literals for calculations, and print integer literals using the cout operator. All of the following numbers are integer literals:

1   34   -56

 Note   In most programming languages, literals are sometimes called constants. In C++, however, the term *constant* has a specific meaning as you'll see at the end of this unit. Therefore, this book sticks to using *literal* for nonvariable values that represent numeric, character, and string data.

Never precede an integer with a leading 0 unless you want Visual C++ to interpret the number as base-16 or base-8.

Hexadecimal (base-16) is a numbering system used for internal data. To represent a hexadecimal integer literal, add the 0x prefix to it. The following numbers are hexadecimal numbers:

0x13   0xF6C9   0x401   0XFFFFF

The x and hexadecimal letters can be any mixture of lowercase and uppercase.

A leading 0 before a number, without the x, indicates that the literal is an octal (base-8) number. Base-8 is not used much today. The following literals are base-8 literals because they begin with a leading 0:

```
044     05     01     076     004
```

If you write business-application programs in Visual C++, you might think that you will never have the need for hexadecimals, and you might be correct.

You can begin floating-point literals with a leading zero, for example, 0.9. They are properly interpreted by Visual C++. You can't have hexadecimal or octal floating-point literals, so the leading zero is sometimes used to specify precision in floating-point literals.

Long, Unsigned, and Floating-Point Literals

When you use a literal integer in a program, Visual C++ interprets its data type as the smallest type that can hold that number. For example, if you type 13, Visual C++ knows that this number fits into a signed integer memory location. It does not treat the number as a long integer, because 13 is not large enough to warrant a long integer literal size.

You can append a suffix character to numeric literals to override the default type. If you put an L at the end of an integer, Visual C++ interprets that integer as a long integer. The number 13 is an integer literal, but the number 13L is a long integer literal. For example, you might want to add the L if you were adding a number to a long integer variable.

Assign the U suffix to designate an unsigned integer literal. The number 13 is, by default, a signed integer literal. If you type 13U, Visual C++ treats it as an unsigned integer. The suffix UL indicates an unsigned long literal.

Visual C++ interprets all floating-point literals (numbers that contain decimal points) as double floating-point literals (double floating-point literals hold larger numbers than floating-point literals). This process ensures the maximum accuracy for such numbers. If you use the literal 32.05, Visual C++ treats it as a double floating-point data type, even though it would fit in a regular float. You can append the floating-point suffix (F) or the long double floating-point suffix (L) to literals that contain decimal points to represent a floating-point literal or a long double floating-point literal.

You might not use these suffixes often, but if you have to assign a literal value to an extended or unsigned variable, your literals might be a little more accurate if you append a U, L, UL, or F (their lowercase equivalents also work).

Putting Data in Variables

It is easy to fill variables with data. The equal sign (=) is used for assigning values to variables. The format of an assignment is

```
variable = expression;
```

The `variable` is a variable name that you defined earlier in the program. The `expression` is any variable, literal, expression, or combination that produces a resulting data type that is the same as the `variable`'s data type.

 Tip   Putting spaces around the equal sign makes it more readable, but the C++ compiler does not require them.

 Note   The equal sign means that you want to take the number, variable, or expression on the right side of the equal sign and put it into the variable on the left.

Consider a program that tracks your company's Top 100 ranking, monthly sales, and years in business. You could store these values in three Visual C++ variables. First you would define the variables by deciding on correct types and choosing descriptive names for them. You would then assign them values. Later in the program, these values might change (for example, if the program were to calculate a new pay increase for you).

Here is the code that defines these variables:

```
void main()
  {
    int ranking, years;
    float sales;
```

The next three statements assign values to the variables:

```
    ranking = 79;
    sales = 65750.93;
    years = 14;
// Rest of program would follow
```

Note   Never put commas in values that you assign to variables. The following statement is invalid:

```
    sales = 65,750.93;  // Don't do this!
```

Any expression can go to the right of the equal sign as long as it matches the type of variable on the left. Suppose that, earlier in a program, you stored your tax rate in a variable called `taxRate`, and then decided to use your tax rate for your spouse's rate as well. At the proper point in the program, you would code the following:

```
spouseTaxRate = taxRate;
```

At this point in the program, the value in `taxRate` is copied to a new variable named `spouseTaxRate`. The value in `taxRate` is still there after this line finishes. The variables were declared earlier in the program.

If your spouse's tax rate is 32 percent of yours, you can assign an expression to the spouse's variable, like so:

```
spouseTaxRate = taxRate * .32;   // Compute 32% of a tax rate
```

You must enclose character literals in single quotation marks if you want to assign character data to character variables. The following section of a program declares three variables, and then assigns three initials to them:

```
char first, middle, last;
first = 'F';
middle = 'I';
last = 'Q';
```

Visual C++ allows a shortcut for defining variables and then placing values in them. The following program both defines and initializes three variables at the same time.

```
char initial = 'G';   // Defines and initializes
// at the same time
int books = 230;
float price = 23.95;
```

Note Remember that a C++ variable is not initialized; it will contain random garbage. Good practice is to always initialize a variable as soon as it is declared.

Tip Visual C++ prefers that you store matching data values in the proper variables. Although you can assign a character literal to a floating-point variable, you should not do so. Sometimes Visual C++ will not allow it. There are ways that you can safely mix types, and this book explains when you can.

 STOP&TYPE Listing 5.2 contains the variable definitions for a character and one floating-point value.

Review

Store data values in variables using the assignment operator, =. You can assign initial values to variables when you define the variables or later in the program.

▼ **INPUT   LISTING 5.2. PUTTING DATA IN VARIABLES.**

```
1:   void main()
2:   {
3:     int i;
4:     char c = 'P';
5:     // Some program code goes here
6:     i = 35 * 14;
```

▼ **OUTPUT**

Lines 3 and 4 define an integer and a character variable. Line 3 defines the integer named i without storing an initial value in i. Later, on line 6, i is assigned the result of a calculation.

Line 4 defines a character variable named c and, at the same time, the literal value of P is stored in the variable. You must enclose all character literals inside single quotation marks.

 Note   The single quotation marks are not part of the data stored in character variables. The single quotation marks serve only to specify character literals.

▶ **Constant Variables**

Concept

Using const, you can define variables whose values never change.

You might think that the term *constant variable* sounds like a contradiction. After all, a constant never changes, and a variable holds values that change. Visual C++ constant variables, often called just constants, are different from what is termed a *constant* in other programming languages. In most programming languages, a constant is the same thing as a literal. Although some Visual C++ programmers use the words interchangeably, a literal is, technically speaking, reserved for data values that are typed directly into a program and do not change. Constants are the special variables described as follows.

In Visual C++ terminology, you can declare variables to be constants with the `const` keyword. Throughout your program, the constants act like variables; you can use a constant variable anywhere you can use a variable, but you cannot change constant variables. To declare a constant, put the keyword `const` in front of the variable declaration, like so:

```
const int ageLimit = 21;
```

 Warning You must put an initial value into the constant variable. If you don't, Visual C++ will never let you assign it a value later because you cannot do anything to change the value of a constant.

Any type of variable can be made a constant. Visual C++ offers the `const` keyword as an improvement of the `#define` preprocessor directive that C uses. A `#define` directive specifies that whenever a character string is found in the code, it should be replaced by another character string. This makes it a quick and easy way to substitute the same value throughout the code without retyping the literal. Although Visual C++ supports `#define` as well, `const` enables you to specify constant values with specific data types.

 Tip If you omit the data type of a constant variable, Visual C++ assumes that it is an integer. Therefore, the following two lines are equivalent:

```
const int ageLimit = 21;
```

and

```
const ageLimit = 21;
```

Use `const` when you have data that does not change but to which you want to assign a name. For example, a minimum sales level would be a good candidate for a constant. If you accidentally attempt to change a constant, Visual C++ will let you know.

Another advantage to named constant variables is that, if your program's environment changes and you must change the value initially assigned to the constant, you make the change in one place. If, instead, you typed the value throughout the program, you would have to change that value everywhere it appeared, as well as place a comment about the meaning of the literal at each use.

STOP&TYPE Listing 5.3 contains a program fragment, which contains two statements that define constant variables.

Review

Use const when you want to name a value that does not change.

▼ INPUT   LISTING 5.3. DEFINING TWO CONSTANT VARIABLES.

```
1:  const int bonusLevel = 3000;
2:  const float e = 2.718282;
```

▼ OUTPUT

Line 1 defines and initializes a constant integer variable named bonusLevel. Nowhere in the rest of the program can a new value be assigned to bonusLevel.

Line 2 defines a floating-point constant variable. In mathematics, e has a special meaning and its value is approximately equal to 2.718282.

Enumerated Constants

Concept

Visual C++ lets you define your own types for constants.

It is common to want to set a variable to particular values that mean something. For example, you might want a variable in which 0 means dog, 1 means cat, 2 means arachnid, and so on. You can do this if you like, but C++ has a way of letting you define the only allowable values, using the enum. An enum is an integer type for which each valid value is titled and listed (or *enumerated*). You can use an enumerated value in place of a literal. You can give an enumeration a name if you like. Here's an example:

```
enum Pet{dog,cat,arachnid};
```

You can declare a variable of the enumerated type:

```
Pet pet;
```

You can then assign enumerated values into the variable:

```
pet = cat;
```

As you can see, this makes the code much more readable, which makes enums great for variables with a limited number of correct values. You can assign enums into numeric types, typically ints. Then you can use them as a number. You can't assign a number into an enum, as in this example:

```
int i;

i = 2;  // OK

i = cat;// OK

Pet pet;

pet = 2;// Wrong!
```

By default, each value listed is one greater than the previous value. However, you can explicitly set a new value:

```
enum Pet{dog = 1, cat = 5, arachnid}; // arachnid is 6
```

You'll see examples of enumeration in later units.

▶ Homework
General Knowledge

1. What are the two general types of data?
2. What is another name for a literal?
3. What are the numeric literal suffixes and what do they mean?
4. What does Visual C++ do when you define a variable?
5. What is the Visual C++ difference between a variable and a constant?
6. What is the Visual C++ difference between a constant and a literal?
7. What is the Visual C++ difference between a variable and a literal?
8. What must you enclose character literals in?
9. Why can you not specify an integer literal with a leading zero?
10. Why can you never assign a value to a constant variable after you define it?
11. Why should you use the smallest variable data type available that holds the data you need to hold?
12. Which of the following are floating-point values?

    -0   -12   34.   34.0   34.4444444   -0.00001

13. Which of the following integers are decimal, which are hexadecimal, and which are octal?

    0   05   0x15   250   0250   0x250

14. What are the data types of each of these numbers?

```
5      5.55      5L      5.55L
```

15. If you were writing a program that tracked your financial records, which of the following generally are variable and which generally are constant?

```
Your social security number
Your age
Your salary
Your first name
Your date of birth
```

16. True or false: The following are identical:

```
const int ageLimit = 21;
```

and

```
const ageLimit = 21;
```

17. True or false: A variable can be a literal.

18. True or false: You cannot begin a floating-point literal with a leading zero.

Find the Bug

19. What are the valid variable names from the following list?

```
95Sales      sales#95     Sales95      _Sales_95    SALES_95
sales(95)    95_Sales     Sales95Qtr   Sales()
```

20. What is wrong with the following program fragment?

```
// Program that stores values in variables
void main()
{
  int age;
  char letter = 45.43;
  age = 12.5;
  // Rest of program follows
```

21. There are two errors in the first few lines of this program. What are they?

```
// Program that uses a constant variable
void main()
{
  const SALARY = 234.54;
  const int age;
  AGE = 21;
  // Rest of program follows
```

Write Code That...

22. Rewrite the following lines of variable definitions so that the data types are grouped in a more orderly fashion:

```
void main()
{
  float height;
  int num1;
  char answer;
  float salary;
  int num2;
  // Rest of program follows
```

23. Suppose that you are taking three classes at a local community college and you want to write a program to keep track of your letter grade and your numeric average in each class. To the following code fragment, add the variable definition lines that define the six variable names and their types.

```
void main()
{
```

24. Rewrite the following three numbers so that they do not use scientific notation:

```
2.3221E+4      2.3221E-4      -1.789E+2
```

25. Suppose that you are to write a program for a driver's license agency and need to store the driving age limit of 16 in a constant integer variable. How will you define it?

Extra Credit

26. Write a constant variable definition that defines the mathematical value of Pi. Pi is approximately equal to 3.14159 and never changes.

String Data and I/O

▶ **What You'll Learn**

▶ Character literals and variables

▶ String literals

▶ Special characters: escape sequences

▶ Integers and characters

▶ Storing strings in arrays

▶ Comparing `cout` and `cin`

Visual C++ differs from many other programming languages in that there is no such thing as a character string variable. There are character variables, but they hold only a single character of data. There are character string literals, but no character string variables. A string is simply a list of characters such as a word, phrase, sentence, or any set of characters strung together. If you have never programmed before, you will not miss string variables. If you have programmed in other languages, you might question Visual C++'s usefulness because it does not support string variables.

The designers of the C++ language decided against using string variables, but C++ offers alternatives to them that are almost as easy to use and much more efficient. After all, Visual C++ must offer a way for you to store people's names and addresses. This unit shows you how to designate string literals and how to store them in memory.

Performing input and output (often referred to as just I/O) is extremely easy with Visual C++. You need a way to get data and results of calculations to the screen and to get input from the user at the keyboard. This book has already used `cout` and `cin` for simple input and output.

After you learn about storing character and string data, you will have mastered all the fundamental data types in Visual C++. You will then need some way to output that data. This unit reviews `cout` and `cin`, and then explains how to make them work exactly the way you want.

*N*ote   Lesson 2's second unit gave a brief overview of character and string data as well as Visual C++'s I/O capabilities. This unit explains all the details that were skipped then. This unit also begins showing you full-length programs again now that you'll finally understand what all the statements do.

Character Literals and Variables

Concept

What You Will Learn

Character literals always appear inside single quotation marks. Define `char` variables for character data.

All character literals must appear between two single quotation marks. All of the following are character literals:

`'A'`   `'x'`   `' '`   `'*'`   `'&'`   `'1'`

As you can see, a character is any character—whether a letter, number, space, or special character—enclosed in single quotes. Never put single quotation marks around something other than a single character of data.

> **Note** Remember that C++ is extremely fussy about the characters you type to give it instructions. `'` and `"` have two very different meanings and cannot be used interchangeably.

In the previous unit, you learned how to define a character variable with the `char` keyword. The following statement defines a character variable:

```
char MyGrade;    // Defines a character variable
```

Your program can store a character inside `MyGrade` using the assignment operator, `=`. The following assignment statement stores an `A` in `MyGrade`:

```
MyGrade = 'A';    // Store character data in the character variable
```

Later in the program, another assignment might store a different value in `MyGrade`, either by assigning another character literal to the variable or by assigning another variable to `MyGrade`, such as this:

```
MyGrade = oldGrade;    // Replace the contents of MyGrade
```

> **Tip** If you know a character variable's initial value at the time that you define the variable, you can assign the variable a value at the same time you define the variable, like this:
>
> ```
> char MyGrade = 'A';  // Define and initialize
> ```

STOP&TYPE Listing 6.1 contains the beginnings of a Visual C++ program that defines and initializes three character variables.

Review   **What You Have Learned**

Define character variables with `char` and specify character literals by enclosing them inside single quotation marks.

▼ INPUT   LISTING 6.1. DEFINING AND STORING VALUES IN THREE CHARACTER VARIABLES.

```
1:  void main()
2:  {
3:    char first, middle, last;
4:    first = 'G';
5:    middle = 'M';
6:    last = 'P';
7:    // Rest of program would follow
```

▼ OUTPUT

There is no output from Listing 6.1 because the program is not complete.

▼ ANALYSIS

Definition—A *delimiter* is a character used to signal or enclose data.

The code declares three variables, and then assigns three initials to them. The initials are character literals because they are enclosed in single quotation marks. Visual C++ does not store the quotation marks in the three variables, only the characters. The single quotation marks serve only to delimit the character literals.

What if the character literals in this partial program did not have single quotation marks? What would Visual C++ do with the G, M, and P? Visual C++ would think that G, M, and P were three variables! Because it would not have seen any definition for those variables, Visual C++ would issue an error message. The quotation marks are vital to let Visual C++ know that you are assigning character literals and not other variables.

► String Literals

Concept

Enclose string literals inside quotation marks. All string literals end with a special string-terminating zero. Even though you cannot see this string-terminating zero, Visual C++ uses the string-terminating zero to detect the end of all strings.

One type of Visual C++ literal, called the string literal, does not have a matching variable to hold it. A string literal is always enclosed in double quotation marks (which are often called just quotation marks). The following are examples of string literals:

```
"C++ Programming"   "123"   " "   "4323 E. Oak Road"   "x"
```

Any string of characters between double quotation marks—even a single character—is considered to be a string literal. A single space, a word, or a group of words between double quotation marks are all C++ string literals.

Warning

If the string literal contains only numeric digits, it is still not a number; it is a string of numeric digits that cannot be used to perform mathematical calculations. You can perform calculations on numeric data only, not on string literals.

A string literal is any character, digit, or group of characters enclosed in double quotation marks. A character literal is any character enclosed in single quotation marks. That is how you determine whether a literal is a character or a string. If the literal has no quotation marks, it is a numeric constant.

The quotation marks are never considered part of the string. The quotation marks surround the string and simply inform the Visual C++ compiler that the code is a string literal and not another type of literal.

It is easy to print string literals. Simply put the string literals in a `cout` statement. The following code prints a string literal to the screen:

```
cout << "Visual C++ Programming in 12 Easy Lessons";
```

You can just as easily print character literals like this:

```
cout << 'A' << 'B' << 'C';
```

Later in this unit, you'll read more details on using `cout`, but as you can see, printing string and character data with `cout` is extremely easy.

String-Literal Endings

One additional aspect of string literals sometimes confuses beginning C++ programmers. All string literals end with a special string-terminating zero. You do not see the string-terminating zero, but C++ stores it at the end of the string in memory. Figure 6.1 shows what the string "C++ Lesson" looks like in memory.

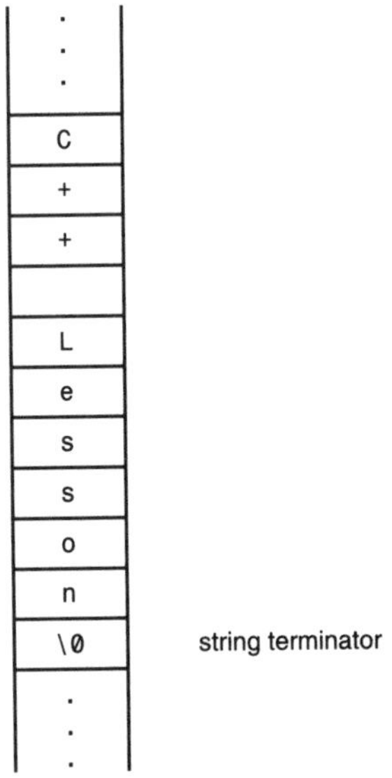

FIGURE 6.1.

In memory, a string literal always ends with 0.

You do not have to worry about putting the string-terminating zero at the end of a string literal. Visual C++ does it for you every time it stores a string. If your program contained the string "C++ Lesson", for example, the compiler would recognize it as a string literal (from the double quotation marks) and store the string-terminating zero at the end.

The string-terminating zero is important to C++. It is rarely called just a zero because zero is normally reserved for the number 0. Visual C++ uses the string terminator to know where the string literal ends in memory. (Remember that the double quotation marks are not stored as part of the string, so Visual C++ cannot use the quotation marks to determine where strings end.)

Definition—The first entry in the ASCII table is called the *null zero*.

Not only is the string-terminator different from the number zero, but the string-terminator is not the same as the character zero either. If you look in Appendix B's ASCII Table, you see that the first entry is the null-zero character. The null-zero character, ASCII value 0, is what strings end with. This string-delimiting zero is different from the character '0', which has an ASCII value of 48.

Note The string-terminator is called by all of the following names: ASCII 0, null 0, string-terminating 0, binary 0, and even '\0'. That last one is strange due to the backslash. Figure 6.1 used this '\0' to end its string. The backslash in a character value means that the following literal character will be treated in a special way, which will be shown later in the section "Special Characters: Escape Sequences."

Definition—A *bit* is an on or off switch inside your computer represented by 1s and 0s.

Computers do not really store characters. They store bit patterns of 1s and 0s and each combination of those patterns represents individual characters. These 1s and 0s are called binary numbers. If you've never learned about binary before, you might want to review *Assembly Language: For Real Programmers Only* from Sams Publishing. All memory locations in your computer actually hold bit patterns of characters. If the letter *A* is stored in memory, an *A* is not actually there; the binary bit pattern for the ASCII *A* (01000001) is stored there. Because the binary bit pattern for the null zero is 00000000, the string-delimiting zero is sometimes called a binary zero.

To illustrate these bit patterns further, Figure 6.2 shows the bit patterns for the following string literal when stored in memory:

```
"I am 30"
```

Figure 6.2 shows how a string is stored in your computer's memory at the bit level. It is important for you to recognize that the character 0 inside the number 30 is not the same 0 (at the bit level) as the string-terminator. If it were, Visual C++ would think that this string ended after the 3, which is incorrect.

I	01001001
	00100000
a	01100001
m	01101101
	00100000
3	00110011
0	00110000
	00000000 string terminator

FIGURE 6.2.
The bit pattern showing that a string terminator and a character zero are different.

String Lengths

Your program often has to know the length of a string. This becomes critical when you learn how to accept string input from the keyboard. The length of a string is the number of characters up to, but not including, the string terminator. Do not include the string terminator in the count, even though you know that C++ adds it to the end of the string.

Table 6.1 shows some string literals and their corresponding string lengths.

Table 6.1. String literals and their lengths.

String	Length
"X"	1
"0"	1
"Sam"	3
" "	0
"The Computer"	12

All character literals have a length of one, with no exception. There is no string terminator for character literals. The double quotation marks signal to Visual C++ that a string terminator is needed, so C++ adds one to the end of every string inside double quotes.

You should know that the following are different to Visual C++:

'R' and "R"

'R' is not a string. It could be a string only if it were enclosed within regular (not single) quotation marks. 'R' is a single character literal. 'R' does not have a terminating zero because it is not a string literal. 'R' is one character long, because all character literals (and variables) are one character long. "R" is a string literal because it is delimited by double quotation marks. Its length is also one, but it includes a terminator in memory so that Visual C++ knows where the string ends. Due to this difference, you cannot mix character literals and character strings. Figure 6.3 shows how 'R' and "R" are stored in memory.

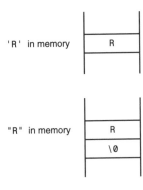

'R' in memory

"R" in memory

FIGURE 6.3.
'R' is a character literal
and "R" is a string literal.

STOP&**TYPE** Listing 6.2 contains a simple program that prints a string literal.

Review **What You Have Learned**

All strings end with terminators inside memory. The terminator tells Visual C++ where the string ends. The length of a string is the number of characters up to, but not including, the terminator.

▼ **INPUT   LISTING 6.2. PRINTING A STRING LITERAL.**

```
1:  // Filename: STLITPR.CPP
2:  // Printing string literals is easy
3:  #include <iostream.h>
4:
5:  void main()
6:  {
7:     cout << "This is a string literal.";
8:     return;
9:  }
```

▼ **OUTPUT**

```
This is a string literal.
```

▼ **ANALYSIS**

Line 7 prints a string on the screen using cout and the << operator. The string printed happens to be 25 characters long, but in memory, the string consumes 26 bytes due to the terminator at the end of the string.

Line 8's return sends control back to Visual C++'s QuickWin environment.

▶ # Special Characters: Escape Sequences

Concept **What You Will Learn**

There are several escape sequences that control output.

All the alphabetic, numeric, and special characters on your keyboard can be character literals. Some characters, however, cannot be represented by using your keyboard. They include some of the higher ASCII characters (such as the Spanish Ñ). Because you do not have keys for every character in the ASCII table, C++ enables you to represent these characters by typing their ASCII hexadecimal number inside single quotation marks.

You can still use all the ASCII characters, even if they are not on your computer's keyboard. To store the Spanish Ñ in a variable, look up its hexadecimal ASCII number in Appendix B. You find that it is A5. Add the prefix \x to it and enclose it in single quotation marks:

```
char sn='\xA5';    // Puts the Spanish Ñ into
                   // a variable called sn
```

Looking at the '\xA5', you might wonder how a single character can reside between those quotes. Earlier it was stated that single quotes always enclose a single character. Even though '\xA5' contains four characters inside the quotation marks, those four characters represent a single character, not a character string. If you were to include those four characters inside a string literal, C++ would treat \xA5 as a single character in the string. The string literal

```
"An accented a is \xA0"
```

is a C++ string that is 18 characters, not 21 characters. C++ interprets the \xA0 character as the á, just as it should. The backslash (\) signals to C++ that it should treat the next characters in a special way, not as a three-character string.

In addition to the hexadecimal ASCII codes you just read about, Visual C++ defines several escape sequences shown in Table 6.2.

Definition—An *escape sequence* represents special control characters.

Table 6.2. Visual C++'s special escape sequence characters.

Escape Sequence	Meaning
\a	Alarm (a beep from the speaker)
\b	Backspace
\f	Form feed (new page on printer)
\n	Newline (carriage return and line feed)
\r	Carriage return
\t	Tab
\v	Vertical tab
\\	Backslash (\)
\?	Question mark
\'	Single quotation mark
\"	Double quotation mark
\000	Octal number
\xhh	Hexadecimal number
\0	Terminator (or binary zero)

Tip From the table, you might realize that the way to create a string with quotes in it is to use an escape character, as in this example:

```
"\"This string is in quotes\""
```

Concept   **What You Will Learn**

Characters and integers are often interchangeable.

Visual C++ associates characters very closely with their ASCII numbers. Therefore, you can perform arithmetic on character data. This is one of the few places where it is okay to mix data types. Visual C++ integers and characters work well together thanks to the ASCII table in Appendix B. The section of code

```
char c;
c = 'A' + 7;    // Adds 7 to the ASCII character
```

actually stores an H in the character variable c. The ASCII value of the letter A is 65. Adding 7 to 65 produces 72. Because the variable c is not an integer variable but a character variable, Visual C++ uses the ASCII character value for H, not a 72, as the resulting value of c.

You also can store character literals in integer variables. If you do, Visual C++ stores the matching ASCII number for that character. The section of code

```
int i = 'A';
```

does not put a letter A in i because i is not a character variable. Visual C++ assigns the number 65 in the variable because 65 is the ASCII number for the letter A.

 Warning Integers and characters are about the only data types that Visual C++ safely mixes without a problem. You'll learn in Lesson 5, "Upgraded Operators," how to mix other data types safely.

Fortunately, you rarely need to use escape sequences unless you are writing a technical program or wanting to write strings with quote marks in them. One common pitfall is trying to write a DOS filename in a string, and then wondering why a program cannot find the file. What file does the following represent?

```
cout << "C:\temp\newfile.txt";
```

To correctly write a DOS filename, you need to use the double backslash escape sequence:

```
cout << "C:\\temp\\newfile.txt";
```

STOP&TYPE Listing 6.3 contains a program that defines three integer variables and three character variables but stores the opposite data type in each.

Review   **What You Have Learned**

You can store integers in character variables and characters in integer variables. In Lesson 6, "Looping Back and Forth," you'll learn how to set up repeating code that produces a series of characters while incrementing integers.

▼ INPUT   LISTING 6.3. MIXING INTEGERS AND CHARACTERS.

```
 1: // Filename: INTCHAR.CPP
 2: // Mixing integers and characters
 3: #include <iostream.h>
 4: void main()
 5: {
 6:   int i, j, k;   // Define 3 integers
 7:   char c, d, e;  // Define 3 characters
 8:
 9:   // Mix the data
10:   i = 'A';   // Stores 65 in i
11:   j = 'B';   // Stores 66 in j
12:    k = 'C';   // Stores 67 in k
13:
14:    c = 88;    // Stores 'X' in c
15:    d = 89;    // Stores 'Y' in d
16:    e = 90;    // Stores 'Z' in e
17:
18:    cout << i << ", " << j << ", " << k << '\n';
19:    cout << c << ", " << d << ", " << e << '\n';
20:    return;
21: }
```

▼ OUTPUT

```
65, 66, 67
X, Y, Z
```

▼ ANALYSIS

Even though lines 10 through 12 store the characters A, B, and C in variables, the numbers 65, 66, and 67 appear in the output because the variables are integer variables. Also, even though lines 14 through 16 store 88, 89, and 90, the output is X, Y, and Z due to the fact that the variables are character variables. The ASCII table's mapping of characters to integer values produces these results.

▶ Storing Strings in Arrays

Concept

There are no string variables, but you can store strings in character arrays.

Although Visual C++ has no string variables, character arrays work well for holding strings. The concept of an array might be new to you. As you will see in the rest of this unit, arrays are not difficult to understand. There are several kinds of arrays—integer arrays, floating-point arrays, and so on. As soon as you have mastered character arrays, the remaining array types (discussed in Lesson 8, "Lots of Data,") will be easy for you.

An array is a list (sometimes called a table) of variables. Most programming languages allow the use of such lists. Suppose that you have to keep track of the sales records of 100 salespeople. You could make up 100 variable names and assign a different salesperson's sales record to each one.

All those different variable names, however, are difficult to track. If you were to put the sales records in an array of floating-point variables, you would have to keep track of only a single name (the array name) and reference each of the 100 values by an index, normally called a *subscript*.

Later lessons in this book cover array processing in more detail. Because a string is simply a list of one or more characters, a character array is the perfect place to hold strings of information. Suppose that you want to keep track of a person's full name in a variable. There is no way, given what you have learned so far about variables, to store a string of characters in a single variable. Visual C++ supports an array of characters in which you can store multiple characters. A character array holds one or more character variables in a row in memory. This line defines such an array:

```
char fullName[10];   // fullName can hold a string
```

Definition—A *character array* is the C++ aggregate variable that holds multiple characters.

`fullName` is a character array. Always include brackets (`[]`) after an array name that you declare. This array is 10 characters long, and its name is `fullName`. You also can assign a value to the character array at the time you define the array. The following definition statement not only defines the character array but also assigns the name `"Ted Jones"` at the same time:

```
char fullName[10] = "Ted Jones";
```

All characters in an array are stored contiguously in memory. Figure 6.4 shows what `fullName` looks like in memory. Each of the 10 boxes of the array is called an *element*. Notice the terminator (the string-terminating character) at the end of the string. Notice also that the last character of the array contains no data. You filled only the first nine elements of the array with the data and the data's terminator. The tenth element does have a value in it, but whatever follows the string's terminator is not a concern.

Definition—*Contiguous* means that each item is next to each other with no space in between.

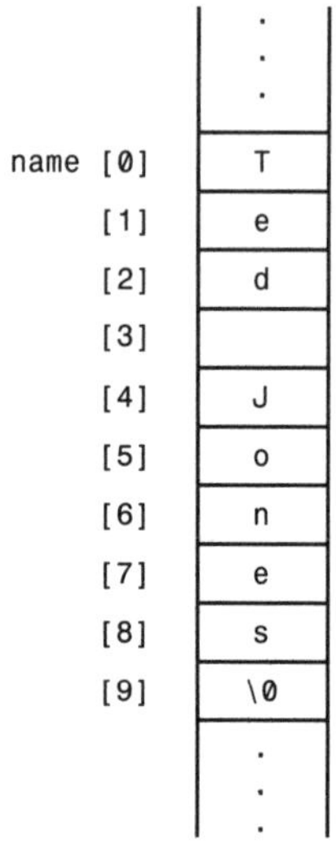

FIGURE 6.4.
Defining a character array
that holds a string.

The parts of an array are available, as is the array as a whole. This is the primary advantage of using an array rather than using many differently named variables. You can assign values to the individual array elements by putting the elements' location (called a subscript) in brackets, as follows:

```
name[1] = 'a';
```

This overwrites the e in the name Ted with an a. The character array now holds "Tad Jones".

All C++ array subscripts start at zero. Therefore, to overwrite the first element, you must use 0 as the subscript. Assigning name[1] (as done earlier) changes the value of the second element in the array, not the first.

You can print individual elements of an array as well. The statement

```
cout << name[0] << ". " << name[4] << ".";
```

prints this:

```
T. J.
```

You can print the entire string—or, more accurately, the entire array—with a single cout statement, as follows:

```
cout << name;
```

Notice that when you print an array, you do not include brackets after the array name. You must be sure to reserve enough characters in the array to hold the entire string. The line

```
char name[5]="Ted Jones";
```

is incorrect because it reserves only five characters for the array, whereas the name and its terminator require 10 characters. Visual C++ issues the error message array bounds overflow if you do not reserve enough characters.

Note Always reserve enough array elements to hold the string and its null-terminating character. It is easy to forget the extra place for the null character, but don't!

If your string contains 12 characters, it also must have a thirteenth location for the terminator or it will never be treated like a string. To help eliminate this error, C++ gives you a shortcut. The following two character array statements are the same:

```
char horse[13] = "Conservative";
```

and

```
char horse[] = "Conservative";
```

You can specify empty brackets only when you assign a value to the character array at the same time you declare the array. C++ counts the string's length, adds one for the terminator, and reserves the array space for you. If you do not assign a value to an array at the time it is declared, you cannot declare it with empty brackets. The statement

```
char initials[];    // Do not do this!
```

does not reserve any space for the array called initials. Because you did not assign a value to the array when you declared it, C++ assumes that this array contains zero elements. Therefore, you have no room to put values in this array later. Visual C++ generates an error if you attempt this.

An array is not a single variable but a list of variables. A character variable holds a single character, and a character array holds a bunch of character variables. Instead of that bunch of variables having different names, they all have the same name (the name of the array).

Arrays Versus Strings

Strings can exist in Visual C++ only as string literals, or as data residing in character arrays. Strings must be stored in character arrays, but not all character arrays contain strings.

Look at the two arrays shown in Figure 6.5. The first one, called first, is a character array, but it does not contain a string. Rather than a string, it contains a list of several characters. The second array, called second, contains a string because it has a terminator at its end.

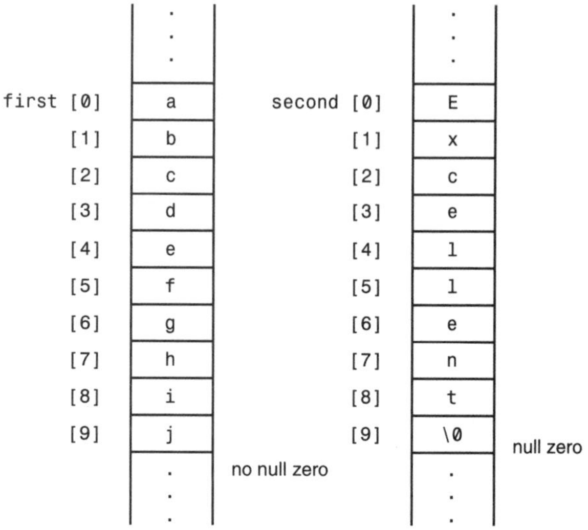

FIGURE 6.5.

first contains characters, and second contains a character string terminated by a terminator.

There are two ways to initialize these arrays. Here is an example of filling them with assignment statements at the point where they are defined:

```
char first[10]={'a', 'b', 'c', 'd', 'e', 'f', 'g', 'h',
'i', 'j'};
char second[10]="Excellent";
```

You must enclose the list of characters in braces as shown in Figure 6.5 if you want to put only individual characters in an array. You could initialize first later in the program, using assignment statements as the following code section does.

```
char first[10];
first[0]='a';
first[1]='b';
first[2]='c';
first[3]='d';
first[4]='e';
first[5]='f';
first[6]='g';
first[7]='h';
first[8]='i';
first[9]='j';    // 9 is the highest subscript
```

Because first does not contain a terminator, it does not contain a string of characters. It does contain characters that can be stored in the array (and used individually), but they can't be treated in a program as if they were a string.

Warning Never try to assign string values to character arrays using a regular assignment statement, except when you first define the character arrays.

Character arrays are not string variables (arrays can be used only to hold a string of characters), and they cannot go on the left side of an equal (=) sign. This program issues an error:

```
// Filename: ARAEQUAL.CPP
#include <iostream.h>
void main()
  {
    char dogName[20];    //  Reserves space for the dog's name
    dogName = "Ross";    //  INVALID!
    cout << dogName;     //  The program will never get here
    return;
  }
```

Because the dog's name was not assigned at the time the character array was declared, it cannot be assigned a value later. The following assignments are allowed if you replace the previous program's assignment with them:

```
dogName[0]='R';    // Assigns values one element at a time
dogName[1]='o';
dogName[2]='s';
dogName[3]='s';
dogName[4]='\0';   // Needed to ensure that this is a string!}
```

The dogName character array now holds a string because the last character is a terminator.

The length of the string is always the number of characters in the character array up to, but not including, the string-terminating null. The number of elements reserved for an array can be (and usually is) different from the string length. The character array in the preceding code contains 20 elements. This remains true whether those elements contain a string or just some character data.

You can't assign more than 20 characters to dogName because its reserved space is only 20 characters. However, you can store any string of 19 (leaving one for the terminator) or fewer characters to the array. If you assign the "Ross" string in the array as shown, and then assign a terminator to dogName[3] as in

```
dogName[3] = '\0';
```

the string in dogName is now only three characters long. You have, in effect, shortened the string. There are still 20 characters reserved for dogName, but the data inside it is the string "Ros" ending with a terminator.

Visual C++ does give you ways to assign values to strings. You can use the strcpy() function, for example. This is a built-in function that enables you to copy a string literal in a string. To copy the "Benji" pet name into the dogName array, type the following:

```
strcpy(dogName, "Benji");   // Copies Benji into the array
```

The strcpy() (*string copy*) function assumes that the first value in the parentheses is a character array name and that the second value is a valid string literal or another character array that holds a string. You must be sure that the first character array in the parentheses is long enough (in number of reserved elements) to hold whatever string you copy into it.

 Note   All programs that use strcpy() must have the following line inserted at the top of the program with the other #define preprocessor directives:

```
#include <string.h>
```

Visual C++ supplies the STRING.H file to help the strcpy() function work properly. The #include files such as IOSTREAM.H and STRING.H are explained in more detail in later lessons.

It is worth explaining how C++ uses the terminator character. C++ does not keep track of the length of a string, so functions such as strcpy simply look along the character array until they find a terminator. They cannot tell the length of the character array (C++ does not store that information internally either), so they keep looking until they find one, even if this is beyond the size of array you declared. Eventually, the function will come across a zero in memory somewhere and stop looking. If strcpy came across an unterminated string, it could copy hundreds of "characters" into the target character array before it found a zero—normally overwriting memory that does not belong to the target string. The results are usually catastrophic.

Getting Strings from the User

You can ask the user for a string. Using cin, you can get a single word (cin stops reading keyboard input after the first space) from the user and store it in a character array. Suppose that you defined a character array like this:

```
char input[80];
```

Using cin, the user can enter a string up to 79 characters (the extra character will hold the terminator) like this:

```
cout << "Please type the answer: ";  // Ask a question
cin >> input;   // Get a string from the user
```

The cout prompts the user to type something. Please remember that cin can get only one word at a time.

Warning Visual C++ does not protect your string lengths! If you enter a string longer than 80 characters, you will not get an error, but important areas of memory might be overwritten and your computer can freeze up!

With user input, it is especially important to *validate* the input before using the data in your program. You might write a program that stores a user's name in a 20 character array; if a user types in a longer name, your program might receive more than 19 characters. You can use other string functions such as strlen to find out how long the string is, and first store the name in a very big character array before copying the name to your 20 character array (only if the name is less than 19 characters long). Although this might seem tedious, if you do not do it, the effect on your program will be disastrous.

STOP&TYPE Listing 6.4 contains a program that stores strings in four character arrays using the following methods:

▶ Assignment at definition time

▶ Assignment one element at a time

▶ strcpy()

▶ Input by the user

Review **What You Have Learned**

Store strings in character arrays. Be sure to leave enough room for the terminator. There are several ways to store strings in arrays.

▼ INPUT LISTING 6.4. STORING STRINGS IN CHARACTER ARRAYS.

```
1: // Filename: STR.CPP
2: // Stores and initializes four character
3: // arrays for three friends first names
4:
5: #include <iostream.h>
6: #include <string.h>
7: void main()
8: {
9:     // Declares all arrays and initializes the first one
10:    char friend1[20]="Lucy";
11:    char friend2[20];
12:    char friend3[20];
13:    char friend4[20];
14:
15:    // Uses a function to initialize the second array
16:    strcpy(friend2, "James");
17:
```

continues

```
18:    friend3[0] = 'T';   // Initializes the third array
19:    friend3[1] = 'o';   // an element at a time
20:    friend3[2] = 'n';
21:    friend3[3] = 'y';
22:    friend3[4] = '\0';  // Without this, friend3 wouldn't
23:                        // hold a string
24:
25:    // Get a name from the user
26:    cout << "What is one of your friend's first name? ";
27:    cin >> friend4;
28:
29:    // Prints the names
30:    cout << friend1 << endl;
31:    cout << friend2 << endl;
32:    cout << friend3 << endl;
33:    cout << friend4 << endl;
34:    return;
35: }
```

▼ OUTPUT

```
What is one of your friend's first name? Marcia
Lucy
James
Tony
Marcia
```

▼ ANALYSIS

This program takes four character arrays and assigns them string values by using the four methods shown in this unit. Notice the extra #include file used with the string function strcpy().

Isn't the assignment of friend3, one element at a time, tedious? It is not used as often as the other methods of array initialization. strcpy() and other built-in string functions (all built-in string functions require #include <string.h>) are better to use. You will see many ways to initialize character arrays throughout this book.

▶ Comparing *cout* and *cin*

Concept   **What You Will Learn**

cout and cin work to input and output data. You can format the output if you wish using I/O manipulators.

cout and cin are defined in IOSTREAM.H. As long as you include this header file, you can perform I/O with cout and cin. cout and cin are called objects. In Visual C++ terminology, an object is like a variable; in this case the data type is a file instead of an integer or character. You never treat cin and cout as variables, however. As far as you are concerned, you can think of cin as being the keyboard and cout as being the screen.

Use cout with the << operator and use cin with the >> operator. << is called the inserter operator because you are inserting to the screen (putting data there). >> is called the extractor operator because you are extracting from the keyboard (getting data from it).

As you've seen already in this unit, you often see cout and cin in pairs. For example, before asking the user for a value, you should prompt the user with a cout description of what you want. The following two lines tell the user what he or she is expected to type, and then wait for the user to type a number:

```
cout << "How much do you make? ";
cin >> Salary;   // Waits for the user to type a number
```

Note Can you see the flow of data in the >> and << operators? The direction of the arrows tells you which way the data is flowing: either to the screen or from the keyboard.

Output Options

The cout operator guesses how you want data printed. Sometimes, Visual C++ makes an incorrect guess as to how cout should produce a value, but most of the time cout suffices for any output you require, as shown here:

```
// cout can output integers:
cout << 45;   // Prints a 45
// cout can output floating-point values:
cout << 1.234567;   // Prints 1.234567
// cout can output string values:
cout << "I am learning C++";   // Prints I am learning C++
```

Definition—An *I/O manipulator* modifies the way cout works.

Because Visual C++ can't always guess properly at how you want your data printed, you should learn a few of the I/O manipulators. Most of the time, you need a manipulator when you output numeric values. For instance, a float variable always contains six digits of precision. Therefore, when you print a float value, whether it is a literal or a floating-point variable, Visual C++ prints six digits. When you print a 4.5 like

```
cout << 4.5;
```

Visual C++ prints a 4.500000. The extra digits of precision often get in your way. You need a way to tell Visual C++ that you want only two digits of precision if you are printing a dollar value.

An output manipulator called precision() limits the precision of output printed with cout. Inside the precision() parentheses, you specify by integer literal or variable how many digits of precision you want to see in the output. To ensure trailing zeros, you must also set a cout flag. For instance, the cout

```
cout.setf(ios::fixed);       // Sets the cout flag for fixed-point
                             // non-scientific notation trailing zeros
cout.setf(ios::showpoint);   // Always shows decimal point
cout.precision(2);     // Two decimal places
cout << 4.5;
```

prints 4.50 on the screen. The cout.setf() is a strange-looking statement, and you will not fully understand the use of the periods and semicolons until later lessons on C++ objects. In the meantime, use the cout.setf() as described here and don't worry about the details at this point.

 Tip   All subsequent couts retain the precision set with the last precision(). Think of precision() as being "sticky." Whatever precision you set sticks with the cout device until you change it with a subsequent precision() later in the program.

Perhaps, due to a user's bad answer, you want to get rid of anything else the user might have typed after the variable you have checked. (Recall that whitespace divides variables, but the input will not be read until the user presses the enter key.) Also, the user's carriage return might still be left in the input and you want to get rid of it. The following statement erases up to a maximum of 80 characters (more than enough in most instances) of input, up to and including the first newline encountered:

```
cin.ignore(80, '\n');  // Flush the input
```

The syntax for this statement is not the clearest in the world, but you'll only rarely need to use the ignore() function in this way. \n is the escape sequence for newline. Because there isn't a character on the keyboard that you can use for newline (pressing Enter actually puts a newline in your code), C++ uses the backslash character to note that the following character is special, as you saw in the earlier section on escape code special characters.

If you have changed the precision with precision() and want to revert the precision to its default number of six places, either of the following statements works:

```
cout.precision(0);   // Resets to the default six places
```

or

```
cout.precision(6);   // Sets to the default six places
```

Visual C++ uses as much space as needed to print your numbers. For instance, it uses two output spaces to print a two-digit number, three output spaces for a three-digit number, and so on. You can use the () manipulator to add spacing to your output. The following cout statements show you what is possible with width():

```
cout.setf(ios::fixed);
cout.setf(ios::showpoint);
cout << 4.56  << endl;
cout.width(12);
cout << 4.56 << endl;
cout.width(8);
cout << "xyz" << endl;
cout.width(6);
cout << 12 << endl;
```

These four output commands produce the following output:

```
4.560000
    4.560000
     xyz
    12
```

Notice that each value prints within the width you specified.

Note The width() is the only manipulator that does not stick from one command to the next. Therefore, if you want to right-justify three numbers with a 10-space output width, you have to repeat width(), like this:

```
cout.width(10);
cout << 123 << endl;
cout.width(10);
cout << 12345 << endl;
cout.width(10);
cout << 1234567 << endl;
```

These three couts produce the following:

```
       123
     12345
   1234567
```

The width() is nice for aligning output. You can print data in tables in which all rows line up even if the data takes varying widths. This program prints a table of wins from the season of a local kids' soccer team. The numbers fall nicely beneath each team's name.

```
// Filename: TEAMMD.CPP
// Prints a table of team names and wins for three weeks
// using width-modifying conversion characters

#include <iostream.h>
void main()
{
```

```
cout.width(10);    cout << "Parrots";
cout.width(10);    cout << "Rams";
cout.width(10);    cout << "Kings";
cout.width(10);    cout << "Titans";
cout.width(10);    cout << "Chargers" << endl;
cout.width(10);    cout << 3;
cout.width(10);    cout << 5;
cout.width(10);    cout << 2;
cout.width(10);    cout << 1;
cout.width(10);    cout << 0 << endl;
cout.width(10);    cout << 2;
cout.width(10);    cout << 5;
cout.width(10);    cout << 1;
cout.width(10);    cout << 0;
cout.width(10);    cout << 1 << endl;
cout.width(10);    cout << 2;
cout.width(10);    cout << 6;
cout.width(10);    cout << 4;
cout.width(10);    cout << 3;
cout.width(10);    cout << 0 << endl;
return;
}
```

Here is the program's output:

```
   Parrots      Rams     Kings    Titans  Chargers
         3         5         2         1         0
         2         5         1         0         1
         2         6         4         3         0
```

 Tip   If you are an advanced programmer and you want to print a number in hexadecimal or octal, insert the hex or oct manipulator in the cout output. The result will appear in base-16 or base-8, respectively. To revert to decimal, insert the dec manipulator in the output before the decimal value prints.

Input Options

The cin acts like your keyboard, and combined with the >> operator, cin pauses your program and waits for the user at the keyboard to enter data. With a single cin, you can get one or more values (just as with cout you can display one or more values), as long as you separate the values in the cin with extra >> operators.

The following statement gets input from the user into a variable named Result:

```
cin >> Result;    // Lets the user type a value into Result
```

THE USER MAKES MISTAKES!

Will the user always type exactly what he or she is supposed to type? Think of the times you have visited an automatic teller. Did you ever press the wrong button? Most people do at one time or another. Usually, you can correct your mistake or cancel the operation and start over. When you write programs that require user input, you must be aware that the user—either intentionally or unintentionally—might not follow directions.

When you want an integer, the user might type a floating-point value. With simple `cin` statements, there is little you can do except check the data that the user entered to see whether it is reasonable and whether it falls within certain expected ranges.

The problem of getting multiple values with `cin` is further hindered by the fact that the user must type a whitespace character between the values. In Visual C++ terminology, a whitespace character is any space, Tab keystroke, or Enter keystroke. Therefore, in response to the statement

```
cin >> a >> b >> c;   // Gets three values from the keyboard
```

the user can enter three values separated by a space:

```
5 7 9
```

Or the user can press the Tab key:

```
5    7    9
```

Or the user can press Enter at the end of each value:

```
5
7
9
```

In all three cases, the program will store a 5 in a, a 7 in b, and a 9 in c.

It might seem that with all those choices, the user has freedom to do whatever seems most comfortable. The only problem is that there are many typing choices that the user might make that do not work. For example, what do you think will happen if the user types the following line?

```
5, 7, 9
```

The Visual C++ program does not consider a comma to be a whitespace character. Therefore, only the 5 is correctly put in a, and the other two variables will have garbage in them.

There is little you can do to control the user, but you can tell the user exactly what you want to see as input with a prompt message before each `cin`:

```
cout << "Please type three numbers.  Separate the three" << endl;
cout << "values with a space and do not use a period in ";
cout << "the numbers." << endl;

cin >> a >> b >> c;
```

It is even safer to stay away from multiple variables with `cin`. Instead of getting all three in one input, it might be better to get them one at a time, prompting the user along the way:

```
cout << "What is the first value?  (Please, no decimal ";
cout << "points)" << endl;
cin >> a;
cout << "What is the second value? ";
cin >> b;
cout << "What is the last value? ";
cin >> c;
```

In typical programming, you would be asking for input that the user understands, such as "What is your result?" or "How old are you?"

Getting Lines of Data

If you need to get a line of input, the `getline()` function is the right choice. `getline()` is useful when you want the user to enter a string of data into a character array. Whereas `cin` stops reading input when it gets to the first space, `getline()` ends only after the user presses the Enter key. Whatever the user typed up to that point goes to the character array.

There are several forms of `getline()`, but the most common one looks like this:

```
cin.getline(chararray, num);
```

The `chararray` is any character array you defined earlier that holds the input string. The `num` is the maximum number of characters you want to read with `getline()`. The `cin.` in front of `getline()` might look strange to you. `cin.` is not part of the `getline()` name. Rather, you are telling the `cin` object to go get a line from the keyboard. You do not have to understand object-oriented programming to understand `getline()`, but as soon as you have learned object-oriented concepts (explained in the last lessons in this book), you will see why `cin` and `getline()` are separated by a period.

`getline()` always stops reading the user's input when the maximum number of characters is entered. `getline()` also ensures that there is always room for a string-terminating zero. Therefore, if the user types exactly the same number of characters as the maximum number `getline()` allows, Visual C++ replaces the last character with a string terminator, thereby ensuring that the input is made into a string. (The newline keystroke is never stored in the string.)

If you want to correctly validate the input, `getline()` is more powerful than using the `cin` inserter. In later lessons, you will learn programming techniques that enable you to examine what the user has typed and handle the user's errors in a more professional way.

In the following program, the user can enter a two-word city name in response to the `cout` prompt:

```
// Filename: GETL.CPP
#include <iostream.h>
void main()
  {
    char city[15];
    cout << "Where are you from? ";
    cin.getline(city, 15);
    cout << "So you are from " << city << endl;
    return;
  }
```

Here is the output:

```
Where are you from? Los Angeles
So you are from Los Angeles
```

Performing input and output is extremely easy with Visual C++. You need a way to get data and results of calculations to the screen and to get input from the user at the keyboard. This book has already used `cout` and `cin` for simple input and output. This unit reviewed `cout` and `cin`, and then explained how to make them work exactly the way you want them to.

STOP&TYPE Listing 6.5 contains a program that gets and prints a floating-point variable and a character array.

Review   **What You Have Learned**

Use `getline()` to get strings from the user. `cin` without the `getline()` does not get more than one word at a time.

▼ INPUT   LISTING 6.5. GETTING AN INVENTORY ITEM'S PRICE AND DESCRIPTION.

```
1:   // Filename: INVENT2V.CPP
2:   #include <iostream.h>
3:
4:   void main()
5:   {
6:
7:     // Define the two inventory variables
8:     float price;
9:     char descrip[25];
```

continues

```
10:
11:    cout << "What is the item's description? ";
12:    cin.getline(descrip, 25);
13:
14:    cout << "What is the item's price? ";
15:    cin >> price;
16:
17:    cout << endl << endl "Here is the item:" << endl
18:    cout << "  Description: " << descrip;
19:
20:    cout.precision(2);
21:    cout.setf(ios::fixed);
22:    cout.setf(ios::showpoint);
23:    cout << "  Price: " << price << endl
24:    return;
25:  }
```

▼ OUTPUT

```
What is the item's description? Large Widgets
What is the item's price? 3.44

Here is the item:
Description: Large Widgets
Price: 3.44
```

▼ ANALYSIS

A 25-character array is defined in line 9, and the getline() in line 12 gets the value of the array from the user. After the price is entered in line 15, the data is printed back again in lines 17 through 23.

Lines 20, 21, and 22 ensure that two decimal places, no more and no fewer, will print for the price. Without these I/O manipulators, the price would print with six decimal places.

▶ Homework
General Knowledge

1. Which of the following are string literals, which are character literals, which are numeric literals, and which could be variable names?

```
Hi
'H'
"56"
'2'
"hi"
'1'
1
```

2. What is another name for a string terminator?

3. Where is the string terminator in this string?

```
"000000000"
```

4. What symbol is the extractor operator, and does `cin` or `cout` go with it?

5. What symbol is the inserter operator, and does `cin` or `cout` go with it?

6. What is the advantage of using `getline()` rather than `cin` when getting strings of user input?

7. What does the number in `getline()` do?

8. Using the ASCII table in Appendix B, write the decimal ASCII numbers for each of the characters in the following string.

```
"I'll take 10."
```

9. What is the length of this string? Hint: There is a difference between a character 0 and the string-terminating zero.

```
"That costs 50"
```

10. Using the ASCII table in Appendix B, write a line that assigns an upside-down question mark to a character variable named q.

11. How many elements are reserved in the following character array?

```
char MyAddress[25];   // Defines room for an address
```

12. How many characters will C++ reserve in the following array definition?

```
char movie[] = "Cinema Fantastico";
```

13. Which I/O manipulator limits the number of decimal places printing when you output floating-point data?

14. What header file must you include when you use the I/O manipulators?

15. Does a character array always hold a string? Why or why not?

16. True or false: `cout` is useful for inputting lines of input, such as a user's street address.

17. True or false: These are exactly the same thing in Visual C++:

```
"C" and 'C'
```

What's the Output?

18. What will the following four `cout`s print?

```
cout << 4.5 << " ";
cout.precision(1);
cout << 4.5 << " ";
cout << 4.5 << endl;
```

19. What does the following print, assuming that `name` holds "Jane Larson"?

```
cout << name[3] << name[5] << name[6]
    << name[7] << name[8] << "." << endl;
```

20. What is the output of the following program? (Assume that the user enters `The Italian Riviera` for the title.)

```
#include <iostream.h>
void main()
{
    char title[19];
    cin.getline(title, 19);
    cout << title << endl;
}
```

21. What value is in `c` when these two lines finish executing?

```
int c;
c = 'A' + 5;    // Adds 5 to the ASCII character
```

Find the Bug

22. The following `cout` has a problem. What is it?

```
cout << 'ABC';    // Almost works
```

23. The following `cout` statement attempts to send a single quotation mark to the screen. It tries to specify the single quotation mark as a character literal, but Visual C++ balks at `'''`. What is another way to designate and output a single quotation mark?

```
cout << '''; // Attempts to output a single quotation mark
```

24. What is wrong with the following program?

```
#include <iostream.h>
void main()
{
  char addr[25];
  strcpy(addr, "35 W. Hazelnut");
  cout << "My address is " << addr;
}
```

25. The following program is supposed to ask for a user's age and then display that age in dog years (to make the user feel younger). Something is wrong. Can you spot it?

```
#include <iostream.h>
void main()
{
  int age, dogage;

  cout >> "How old are you? ";
  cin << age;
```

```
    dogage = age / 7;   // Converts to a dog's age
    cout >> "In dog years, you are " >> dogage >> "years old.";
}
```

26. Using `cout`, a programmer wants to print three people's names, each stored in character array variables. The programmer wants the names to start printing every 15 columns. The following `cout` will not do it. Why?

```
cout.width(15);
cout << name1 << name2 << name3;   // Invalid
```

Write Code That...

27. How would you define and initialize a character array that is 20 characters long and holds the company name "Widgets, Inc."?

28. Write a program that asks the user for his or her first and last name. Print the names as they would appear in a phone book. In other words, if the user enters `Mary Freeman` for the first and last name, finish the program so that it prints this:

```
In a phone book, your name would look like this: Freeman, Mary
```

Extra Credit

29. Nancy Foster, a computer sales representative for HAL Computers, Inc., wants to know her average monthly sales for the previous 12 months. Write a program that asks her for each of the sales values and prints an average of them on the screen.

Project

Lesson ▶

Data Basics

STOP&TYPE In this lesson, you learned about the fundamental data variables found in most C++ programs. You learned the following:

▶ Variables are either numeric or character-based.

▶ There are several types of numeric variables, but all are basically short and long versions of integers and floating-point values.

▶ Visual C++ includes character variables that hold single characters.

Project 3 Listing. Introduction to data and I/O.

```cpp
1:  // Filename: PROJECT3.CPP

2:  // This program defines different kinds of variables and

3:  // lets the user's keyboard input fill the variables with

4:  // values. Subsequent couts print the data in the variables.

5:  #include <iostream.h>

6:  #include <iomanip.h>

7:

8:  void main()

9:  {

10:     char prodName[12];

11:     int count;

12:     float price;

13:     float totalInv;
```

▶ If you want to store a string of characters, you must use a character array to hold the string.

▶ cout sends data to the screen.

▶ cin gets data from the user at the keyboard.

Description

1: A Visual C++ comment that includes the program's filename.

2: A C++ comment that begins the program's description.

3: The program's description continues.

4: The program's description continues.

5: cout needs information in the IOSTREAM.H header file.

6: You need to include iomanip.h.

7: Extra blank lines make your program more readable.

8: All functions have names, and the first function in all C++ programs is main().

9: All functions begin with a left brace.

10: Defines a character array that can hold a string as long as 11 characters plus a terminator.

11: Defines an integer variable that will hold an inventory count.

12: Defines a floating-point variable that will hold a floating-point price per inventory item.

13: Defines a floating-point variable that will hold a floating-point total price of all the items.

5: Add ample comments at the top of your programs that give a brief description of the code.

continues

Project 3 Listing. continued

```
14:     cout << "Inventory Calculation" << endl;

15:     cout << "— — — — — — — — — —" << endl << endl;

16:

17:     cout << "This program calculates an inventory's cost."

18:           << endl << endl;

19:     cout << "What is the product name? ";

20:     cin >> prodName;

21:     cout << "How many " << prodName << "s are there? ";

22:     cin >> count;

23:     cout << "How much does each " << prodName << " cost? ";

24:     cin >> price;

25:     // Ready to extend the inventory cost

26:     totalInv = count * price;

27:     cout.precision(2);

28:     cout.setf(ios::showpoint);

29:     cout.setf(ios::fixed);

30:     cout << endl << "The total valuation for " << prodName
```

Description

14:	The first line of a title is printed.
15:	The title appears underlined on the screen due to the well-placed hyphens.
16:	Extra blank lines make your program more readable.
17:	A printed message to describe the program's goal.
18:	Two newlines that are a continuation of the previous line.
19:	A prompt for the item name.
20:	Takes the user's input and stores the item name in a character array.
21:	A prompt for the item's inventory count.
22:	The item's count is entered.
23:	The cost of each item is requested.
24:	The user enters the floating-point price per item.
25:	A comment describing the upcoming program section.
26:	The total inventory price for the item is calculated and stored in `totalInv`.
27:	The dollar values require two decimal places to be printed.
28:	An I/O manipulator that ensures a decimal point.
29:	An I/O manipulator that ensures fixed-point (as opposed to scientific notation) displays.
30:	You can continue couts on more than one line, as done here, as long as you break the line at a <<.

22: Notice how the item name, obtained in line 20, is embedded in the prompt.

continues

Project 3 Listing. continued

```
31:          << " is $" << totalInv << endl;

32:      return;

33:  }
```

Description

31: The cout continues.

32: The program returns to QuickWin.

33: All program functions (`main()` here) end with a closing brace.

▼ OUTPUT

```
Inventory Calculation
-------------------

This program calculates an inventory's cost.
What is the product name? Widget
How many Widgets are there? 3
How much does each Widget cost? 3.30
The total valuation for Widget is $9.90
```

Lesson ▶

Simple Operators

Unit 7: **Fundamental Math Operators**

Unit 8: **Relational and Logical Operators**

Lesson 4 Project

Fundamental Math Operators

associativity

math operators

overloaded operators

operator precedence

unary operators

▶ What You'll Learn

▶ Reviewing the basics

▶ Order of operators

▶ Advanced assignments

Although you've seen the four primary math operators (+, -, *, and /), there are several more. Appendix C, "Visual C++ Operator Precedence Table," lists all of Visual C++'s operators. C++ is a language rich in operators. Not all of them are math-related, but many are.

In this unit, you'll learn about several of the math operators and become more acquainted with the operator precedence that is so important in Visual C++. Appendix C's operator table not only describes each of the operators, but it also lists each operator in order of its precedence over other operators. As you might recall from Lesson 2, some operators execute before others, such as division before addition.

Although Visual C++ computes all your math results for you, you still must understand how to set up your calculations to achieve correct results. If you never thought math was fun, that's okay. There's a lot more to Visual C++ programming than math. However, programs are extremely useful for computing sales figures, inventory totals, and much more, relieving you from those tedious burdens. Knowing how to use Visual C++'s operators will let you set up your programs so that you can toss that pocket calculator out the window.

▶ Reviewing the Basics

Concept   **What You Will Learn**

> The primary math operators do what you expect them to. When you need simple arithmetic, the primary math operators will compute many of your needed answers.

Although you understand basic addition, subtraction, multiplication, and division, Visual C++ presents a few extra considerations that you need to understand. The following sections explore the primary math operators, shown in Table 7.1.

Table 7.1. Visual C++'s primary math operators.

Math Operator	Description
*	Multiplication
/	Division or integer division
%	Modulus (also called remainder)
+	Unary: Specifies a positive amount (optional for positive values)
	Binary: Performs addition
-	Unary: Specifies a negative amount
	Binary: Performs subtraction

Definition—An *overloaded* operator performs more than one operation depending on how you use it.

Notice that some of the operators are overloaded. For example, the division operator either performs regular division as you know it (sometimes called floating-point division) or computes integer division under certain circumstances. The following sections describe the dual operations of +, -, and /.

The Unary Operators

Definition—A *unary* operator operates on a single value.

The unary operators, + and -, are almost too obvious to discuss because they're so easy to understand. However, they do appear in different locations in the precedence table than their binary counterparts, so they warrant their own discussions.

 Warning The term *binary operator* has nothing to do with binary numbers. Whereas a unary operator operates on single values, binary operators operate on two values (*bi* is a prefix meaning two).

Anytime you put a plus sign in front of a single numeric literal or variable, the plus sign operates as a unary plus sign. The plus sign is optional. Both of the following statements are equivalent:

```
ageLimit = 18;    // Put a positive 18 in a variable
```

and

```
ageLimit = +18;    // Put a positive 18 in a variable
```

You can place the unary plus in front of variables:

```
newLimit = +ageLimit + 3;  // Raise the old age limit
```

Be careful when putting plus signs together. If you rearrange the previous assignment to be

```
newLimit = 3 + +ageLimit;  // Raise the old age limit
```

Visual C++ won't care and everything will work fine, but the space between the two plus signs is critical. Without the space, C++ will complain via a compile error. The ++ (two plus signs without a space between them) is another C++ operator that you'll learn about in the next lesson.

Again, the unary plus sign is very obvious and is one of the easiest operators to understand. The unary plus sign is also optional because if you omit it, C++ assumes that the literal or variable is a positive value.

If you want to negate a variable or specify a negative numeric literal, use the unary minus sign. The following statement stores a negative value in a variable:

```
rateOfGrowth = -.23;
```

You can negate (take the negative of) a variable's value like this:

```
factor = amount * -value;
```

value does not change in this statement. value is one of the rvalues, and only lvalues (factor in this case) change as a result of assignment statements. This statement tells Visual C++ the following:

> "Multiply the value in amount by the negative of the number in value and store that computed result in factor. Don't change either amount or value from their old values; change only factor."

Note   C++ distinguishes between variables that are on the left and right sides of the equal sign. All values can be rvalues, which is a variable on the right side of the equal sign. An rvalue only needs to provide a value. Not all values can be lvalues—numbers on the left side of the equals sign—because not all values can have new values assigned into them. Generally, you don't need to worry about the rvalue and lvalue concept, but you will see it in error messages.

Feel free to negate any mathematical expression such as the following:

```
a = -(b * c);
```

The quantity b multiplied by c is computed, and then the negative of that quantity is stored in a. Again, neither b nor c changes due to the assignment.

As with the unary plus sign, be sure to put a space before the unary minus sign:

```
a = b - -c;    // Without the space, strange things would happen!
```

> **Note**   In the preceding statement, the first negative sign is a binary subtraction and the second (the minus before c) is a unary minus. See the difference? As stated before, binary operators operate on two values, while a unary operator operates on only one value.

Two Divisions and Remainder

The division operator, /, performs mathematical division, with the value before the operator being divided by the value following the operator. The operation of division works in a different way depending on whether all the values are integers or not. If both values are integers, the result of the division will be an integer value too. If either operand is a real value (remember a real value is one that holds decimal places), the result will be a real value. It is important to note that it is not the type of the answer variable that determines the type of the result. Let's look at an example to see how this works in practice.

The program in Listing 7.1 contains an integer division operator. It's an integer division operator because an integer appears on both sides of the /. The programmer was hoping to get a more accurate value. Unit 9, "Special Operations," explains how you can change an integer value into a real value to force a real division.

▼ **INPUT   LISTING 7.1. PERFORMING INTEGER DIVISION.**

```
// Filename: INTDIV.CPP
// Computes integer division
#include <iostream.h>
void main()
  {
    int people, events;
    float avgEv;

    cout << "How many people will attend? ";
    cin >> people;
    cout << "How many events are scheduled? ";
    cin >> events;

    // Compute the average number of people per event
    avgEv = people / events;    // The integer division ensures
                                // that the fractional part of
                                // the answer is discarded
```

continues

UNIT 7 Fundamental Math Operators

```
    cout << "There will be an average of " << avgEv
         << " people per event." << endl;
    return;
}
```

Here is a sample run of the program:

```
How many people will attend? 14
How many events are scheduled? 3

There will be an average of 4 people per event.
```

Note If an integer variable, literal, or a combination of the two appears on both sides of the /, the / always computes integer division.

If a noninteger appears on one or both sides of the division operator, Visual C++ computes normal fractional division. For example, the following statement stores 10.5 in a float variable named ans:

```
ans = 21.0 / 2;   // Stores 10.5 in ans
```

Each of the following assignment statements also stores 10.5 in ans (notice the different decimal-point placements):

```
ans = 21 / 2.0;   // Stores 10.5 in ans
```

and

```
ans = 21.0 / 2.0;  // Stores 10.5 in ans
```

 Tip Do the division operator and the comment slashes confuse you because of their similarity? Of course, you can tell them apart, but perhaps in these statements the regular C-style comments would be a little less confusing:

```
ans = 21.0 / 2.0;   /* Stores 10.5 in ans */
```

Table 7.1 showed the modulus (or remainder) operator, %. The modulus operator performs the opposite of the integer division operator: Instead of returning the integer answer and discarding the remainder, the modulus operator returns the remainder and discards the integer division answer.

Warning Don't use % on floating-point values. % returns the remainder of integer division only.

The following statement stores 1 in ans:

```
ans = 21 % 2;   /* Stores a 1 in ans */
```

If you divide the integer 21 by 2, you will get 10 with a remainder of 1. % discards the integer answer and keeps the remainder (the opposite of what the integer division operator would do).

STOP&TYPE In Listing 7.1, you saw how the integer division operator worked. Listing 7.2 expands on that program by also showing modulus division and regular fractional division.

Review **What You Have Learned**

There are two kinds of division operators, plus a modulus operator. Between these three operators, you can compute both answers and remainders.

▼ **INPUT   LISTING 7.2. COMPUTING DIVISIONAL RESULTS.**

```
 1: // Filename: MOREDIV.CPP
 2: // Computes two kinds of divisions and the modulus
 3: #include <iostream.h>
 4: void main()
 5: {
 6:    int people, events, avgEv;
 7:    int leftOver;         // Will hold modulus
 8:    float floatPeople;    // Needed to force regular division
 9:    float exact;          // Will hold exact average
10:
11:    cout << "How many people will attend? ";
12:    cin >> people;
13:    cout << "How many events are scheduled? ";
14:    cin >> events;
15:
16:    // Compute the integer average number of people per event
17:    avgEv = people / events;   // The integer division ensures
18:                               // that the fractional part of
19:                               // the answer is discarded
20:    cout << endl << "There will be an average of " << avgEv
21:        << " people per event." << endl;
22:    leftOver = people % events;
23:    cout << "There will be " << leftOver
24:        << " without an event at any one time." << endl;
25:    floatPeople = people;  // Converts the integer to a floating-point
26:    exact = floatPeople / events;
27:    cout << "The exact average number of people per event is "
28:        << exact;
29:    return;
30: }
```

▼ OUTPUT

```
How many people will attend? 21
How many events are scheduled? 2

There will be an average of 10 people per event.
There will be 1 without an event at any one time.
The exact average number of people per event is 10.5.
```

▼ ANALYSIS

Line 7 defines an integer variable to hold the integer remainder calculated on line 22. Given the user's data-entry values shown in the output, one person will be left without an event.

Line 8 defines a floating-point variable for the sole purpose of assigning the integer number of people entered in line 12 to line 8's floating-point variable, as done in line 25. After you learn about a Visual C++ feature named *typecasting* in Lesson 5, you won't need to define such an intermediate variable. When line 25 assigns the integer variable named people to the floating-point variable named floatPeople, the integer becomes a floating-point value. The conversion of the number of people to floating-point lets line 26 perform exact fractional division instead of integer division only.

Another issue to beware of with division in C++ is what happens when you divide by zero. The answer to a mathematician is infinity; to a computer, the answer is a headache. You must never divide by zero, because this causes a severe error in your program. In later lessons, you will learn techniques to test the values in your program so that you can handle such an error gracefully.

▶ **Order of Operators**

Concept   **What You Will Learn**

Visual C++ computes operators based on the order of operator precedence, found in Appendix C.

Definition—*Hierarchy* is another name for operator precedence.

Just like the math that your high school algebra teacher taught (you do remember high school algebra, don't you?), Visual C++ follows a certain order when evaluating expressions. Visual C++ doesn't compute all expressions from left to right. Instead, Visual C++ computes expressions based on the hierarchy in the order of operators table, shown in Appendix C. The higher the operators are in the table, the higher their precedence. Therefore, a unary minus operator is said to have higher precedence than the regular binary subtraction operator.

The following assignment stores 10 in priority, not 18 as would be the case if Visual C++ calculated the expression from left to right:

```
priority = 4 + 2 * 3;
```

Appendix C's precedence table shows that multiplication has a higher precedence than addition; therefore, Visual C++ computes 2 * 3, getting 6, and then adds the 4 to the 6 to get the final answer of 10 to store in priority.

You'll notice in the operator precedence table that multiplication and division both appear on the same level, as do addition and subtraction. When two operators of the same level appear in the same expression, as in

```
another = 10 - 8 + 3;
```

Visual C++ calculates the expression from left to right. 10 - 8 produces 2, and the 2 is added to the 3 to get 5.

Parentheses override most operators because of their high level in the precedence table. If you were to put parentheses in the preceding expression, you could force Visual C++ to compute the expression differently. The expression

```
another = 10 - (8 + 3);
```

stores -1 in another because the 8 is added to the 3, producing 11, before the 11 is sub-tracted from 10, which gives you the -1 answer.

 Tip Clarify your code as much as possible by using extra parentheses even if they're unnecessary. For example, parentheses aren't really needed in the expression

```
another = (10 - 8) + 3;
```

because Visual C++ calculates the subtraction first due to its position left of the addition in the expression. However, the parentheses show your intent and help you keep straight the order you meant to take place. Also, if you happen to misread the operator precedence table, the extra parentheses force the expression's evaluation to match your desired order, just in case Visual C++ wouldn't have calculated that order auto-matically.

Perhaps a few more examples of combined operators will help clarify operator precedence even more. Study how Figure 7.1 illustrates the order of expression evaluation.

Definition—To *nest* operations means to put one calculation inside another.

Sometimes, you might need to nest parentheses inside one another. The innermost pa-rentheses calculate first. Figure 7.2 shows how nested parentheses compute.

$$2 * 3 + 3 * 2$$
$$6 + 3 * 2$$
$$6 + 6$$
$$12$$

$$20 + 20 / (5 + 5) \% 2$$
$$20 + 20 / 10 \% 2$$
$$20 + 10 \% 2$$
$$20 + 0$$
$$20$$

Figure 7.1.
Watch that order of
precedence!

$$((2 + 3) + 6 * (3 + (4 - 2))) + 3$$
$$(5 + 6 * (3 + (4 - 2))) + 3$$
$$(5 + 6 * (3 + 2)) + 3$$
$$(5 + 6 * 5) + 3$$
$$(5 + 30) + 3$$
$$35 + 3$$
$$38$$
Whew!

Figure 7.2.
Visual C++ calculates the
innermost parentheses
first.

Warning Be sure that your expressions have an equal number of opening and
closing parentheses.

Tip These examples are great for learning Visual C++, but when you write
your own Visual C++ programs, try to keep your expressions simple. Break
a long expression into two or more expressions, even if doing so means
defining an intermediate variable. The assignment

```
netPay = grossPay - taxRate * grossPay + bonus;
```

is easier to understand when you break it up like this:

```
taxes = taxRate * grossPay;
netPay = grossPay - taxes + bonus;
```

 STOP&TYPE Listing 7.3 contains a program that computes each of the three expressions il-
lustrated in the previous two figures, proving beyond a shadow of a doubt how the order
of precedence works. (You never doubted the figures, did you?)

Review
What You Have Learned

Visual C++ follows the order of operators when computing expressions. You can use parentheses to override many of the expressions' default order.

▼ INPUT   LISTING 7.3. CALCULATING LONG EXPRESSIONS IN VISUAL C++.

```cpp
// Filename: EXPRESS.CPP
// Computing expressions with C++
#include <iostream.h>

void main()
  {
    int ans1, ans2, ans3;

    ans1 = 2 * 3 + 3 * 2;
    cout << "The first answer is " << ans1 << endl;
    ans2 = 20 + 20 / (5 + 5) % 2;
    cout << "The second answer is " << ans2 << endl;
    ans3 = ((2 + 3) + 6 * (3 + (4 - 2))) + 3;
    cout << "The third answer is " << ans3 << endl;
    return;
  }
```

▼ OUTPUT

```
The first answer is 12
The second answer is 20
The third answer is 38
```

▼ ANALYSIS

As shown here, Visual C++ computes mathematical results as described in this section and as dictated by the operator precedence table.

In your regular Visual C++ programming, your programs will calculate using more variables than numeric literals, but you must understand how the calculating order works by practicing with simple integer literals as shown here.

If you're ever unsure how Visual C++ will order an expression, use parentheses. If you're still unsure, write a simple program to test a sample expression using numeric literals so that you can practice with the expression.

Definition—A *debugger* is a special tool that allows you to look at variables as your code executes step by step.

If you are performing complicated calculations, there is another good reason for breaking up your calculation into several steps: It allows you to inspect the progress of the calculation with the Visual C++ integrated debugger. This useful tool lets you look

UNIT
7
Fundamental Math Operators

inside the program as it works so that you can easily find errors that you cannot spot by just looking at the code. By running your program with the Debug | Go or Debug | Step Into command, you can step through your program a line at a time. The online help for the Visual Workbench explains how to do this under the section "Debugger: General Information." If you are having difficulty visualizing how Visual C++ does its math, now is the time to watch how it works with the debugger.

► Advanced Assignments

Concept   **What You Will Learn**

Learn other ways to use the equal sign.

The assignment operator has more power in Visual C++ than in other programming languages. The next two sections explain how the Visual C++ assignment operator combines with other operators to improve your power and decrease your programming effort.

Multiple Assignments

If you want to assign the same value to more than one expression, Visual C++ lets you string together multiple assignment statements. For example, if you wanted to put zero in several initial total variables, you could do this:

```
total1 = 0;
total2 = 0;
total3 = 0;
```

But multiple assignments like these make your work easier:

```
total1 = total2 = total3 = 0;   // Put 0 in three variables
```

Look at Appendix C's operator table and you'll see a column labeled Associativity. This column tells you whether an expression works from right to left or left to right. The assignment operator associates from right to left. Figure 7.3 illustrates what a right-to-left associativity means.

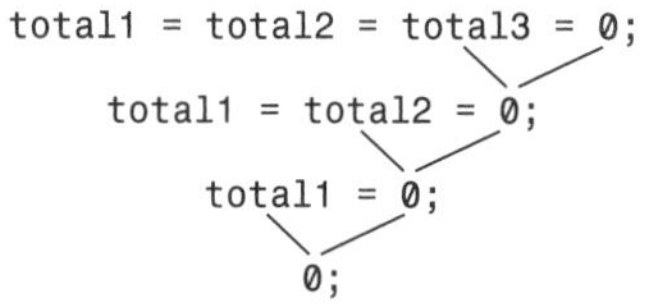

Figure 7.3.
Operator associativity describes in which direction to operate.

```
total1 = total2 = total3 = 0;
     total1 = total2 = 0;
          total1 = 0;
               0;
```

As Visual C++ assigns the zero to each variable on the right, that variable gets the zero and the entire expression becomes zero as well. That expression's zero is then available for the next variable to the left, and so on. Eventually, Visual C++ assigns the zero to `total1` and the result of that expression is zero. There's nothing to do with that final zero, so Visual C++ discards it and continues execution at the next statement in the program.

All expressions have values. The assignment statement not only assigns values, but it also creates a value while performing the assignment. Therefore, that value is available for subsequent assignment statements if there are any more assignments to be made to the left of that line. The value produced by the assignment lets you combine two statements such as

```
monthAvg = dailyAvg * 30;
yearAvg = 12 * monthAvg;
```

into a single statement such as this:

```
yearAvg = 12 * (monthAvg = dailyAvg * 30);
```

Visual C++ first computes the monthly average and stores that average in `monthAvg`. The entire assignment expression in parentheses becomes a value that is then multiplied by `12` and assigned to `yearAvg`.

Which of the two statement groups do you think is better? The second is (probably) more efficient, but too many Visual C++ programmers go overboard in trying to squeeze efficiency out of their programs. Although the first pair of statements isn't as efficient, it's much easier to read, maintain, and change later if needed.

 Tip Although C++ provides many of these clever features, code is more understandable and maintainable if you avoid multiple assignments and mixing assignments in the middle of expressions.

Note Associativity will come into play more as you learn about more powerful operators.

IS A RULE NOW BROKEN?

Any astute reader (that's you, right?) will see right away that right-to-left associativity seems to violate a rule stated earlier in this unit. Earlier, you read that two or more operators in the same expression that appear on the same level in the operator precedence table compute from left to right.

Well, now that you understand associativity, that "rule" can be set in stone with the following definition: "The associativity of operators determines the order in

UNIT

7

Fundamental Math Operators

which they compute if two or more operators from the same precedence level appear in the same expression."

All of the fundamental math operators (+, -, *, /, and %) have left-to-right associativity, so they do indeed compute from left to right when they appear on the same level in an expression. Stick to simple expressions and you will not need to worry about associativity.

Compound Operators

There are several operations that commonly put the same variable on both sides of the equal sign. Here are some examples:

```
count = count + 1;          // Add 1 to count
salary = salary * bonusFactor;  // Adjust the salary
monthly = monthly + daily;  // Add to daily sales
```

When you see the same variable on both sides of an operator, the variable is being updated in some way. count is being increased by one, salary is being changed to reflect a bonus factor, and monthly is being updated with the current day's total sales (thus keeping a running monthly total).

Such updating of variable values is so common that the designers of Visual C++ added several compound operators to Visual C++ that don't exist in other programming languages. If you want to update the value of a variable, why should you have to go to the trouble of repeating the variable name on both sides of the equal sign? (At least, that was the designers' thinking.)

Definition—The compound operators are sometimes called *compound assignment operators*.

Table 7.2 lists each of the compound operators and describes the equivalent assignment statements through examples. As you can see, the compound operators provide you with easier but equivalent updating capabilities.

Table 7.2. The compound operators and their equivalent meanings.

Compound Operator	Example	Equivalent Assignments
+=	a += 100;	a = a + 100;
-=	b -= 0.25;	b = b - 0.25;
*=	c *= 13;	c = c * 13;
/=	d /= 4;	d = d / 4;
%=	e %= 2;	e = e % 2;

Be very careful when using the compound assignment operators! Before going any further, find the compound assignment operator precedence level in Appendix C's precedence table. You'll see that all the compound operators have lower precedence than the regular math operators. In other words, `*=` appears several levels down from the multiplication operator, `*`.

Such precedence can cause you agony when you combine the compound assignment operators with other expressions that use the regular operators. For example, given the variable definitions

```
int value = 5;
int x = 3;
```

how do you think you would change the following expression to use a compound subtraction operator?

```
value = value - x + 2;     // Be careful!
```

At first, you might be tempted to rewrite such an expression as

```
value -= x + 2;
```

Doing so, however, does not yield the same results because the `-=` operator has much lower precedence than the plus sign and the regular minus sign. In the first assignment, the `x` is first subtracted from `value`, and then the `2` is added to that result before the final computed `4` is put in `value`.

In the compound version, Visual C++ computes the `-=` only after adding the `2` and the `x`. Therefore, Visual C++ stores a `0` in `value`! The compound operator, due to its precedence, is actually equivalent to this statement:

```
value = value - (x + 2);   // Equivalent to value -= x + 2
```

As you're beginning to see, precedence can affect everything you compute in Visual C++. Earlier, this unit suggested that you enclose as much as you can in parentheses to clarify everything you do, even if normal precedence handles your calculation perfectly. The compound operators and their low precedence really make the use of ample parentheses vital. Instead of writing statements such as

```
value -= x + 2;
```

perhaps it would be safer to include parentheses so that both you and Visual C++ are on the same precedence wavelength:

```
value -= (x + 2);
```

Tip So as not to confuse other programmers who might have to read your programs, it is safer not to use the compound operators in complicated expressions.

UNIT
7
Fundamental Math Operators

STOP&TYPE Listing 7.4 contains a program that computes interest at the end of five compounding periods.

Review
What You Have Learned

Whenever you need to add to a total or update a variable in some way, the compound assignment operators give you lots of power—as long as you keep the operator precedence in mind.

▼ INPUT   LISTING 7.4. COMPUTING INTEREST FOR FIVE PERIODS.

```
 1: // Filename: INTFIVE.CPP
 2: // Compute five periods of interest
 3: #include <iostream.h>
 4: #include <iomanip.h>
 5: void main()
 6: {
 7:   float intRate;      // Interest rate per period
 8:   float principal;    // Loan amount
 9:
10:     cout << "Welcome to loan central!" << endl;  // Title
11:     cout << "-----------------------" << endl << endl;
12:
13:     cout << "How much was the loan for? ";
14:     cin >> principal;
15:
16:     cout << "What is the period interest rate (i.e., .03 for 3%)? ";
17:     cin >> intRate;
18:
19:     cout << "Here is the total owed after five periods" << endl;
20:     cout << "(Assuming no payment is made)"  << endl;
21:
22:     principal *= (1 + intRate);    // First period interest
23:     principal *= (1 + intRate);
24:     principal *= (1 + intRate);
25:     principal *= (1 + intRate);
26:     principal *= (1 + intRate);    // Fifth period interest
27:
28:     cout << setprecision(2);
29:     cout.setf(ios::fixed);         // Ensure two decimal places
30:     cout.setf(ios::showpoint);
31:     cout << "$" << principal
32:         << " total amount owed after five periods." << endl;
33:     return;
34: }
```

▼ **OUTPUT**

```
Welcome to loan central!
-----------------------

How much was the loan for? 1000.00
What is the period interest rate (i.e., .03 for 3%)? .10
Here is the total owed after five periods
 (Assuming no payment is made)
$1610.51 total amount owed after five periods.
```

▼ **ANALYSIS**

The heart of this program lies in the computations on lines 22 through 26. Each line increases the loan principal by the interest rate for that period. If you were to need the original principal for a printed loan invoice or for an additional kind of calculation you add later, you would first have to save the original principal in another variable. Each compound assignment operator updates whatever value appears on the left side of the compound assignment, just as the regular assignment changes its lvalue.

Tip In Lesson 6, "Looping Back and Forth," you'll learn how to write programs using loops that eliminate some of the tedious repetition in Listing 7.4.

If you are not confident with math, you might be concerned that computing is always about doing complicated calculations. In fact, the opposite is true. In even the most complicated programs, the majority of calculations are very simple. In commercial programming, the programmer's job is not to work out the complicated formula—for example, mortgage repayments—but to translate the formula that an analyst will provide into computer code.

▶ # Homework
General Knowledge

1. What's the difference between a unary operator and a binary operator?

2. Suppose that you stored a -6 in the variable named amount. How could you then store the negative of amount in a variable called negAmount?

3. What is meant by overloaded operator?

4. How many kinds of division can / perform? What are they called?

5. Which operator finds the remainder of integer division?

UNIT **7**

Fundamental Math Operators

6. What's another name for the remainder operator?

7. Why does an assignment statement produce a value as well as an assignment?

8. What is the associativity of the assignment operator?

9. What is the associativity of the multiplication operator?

10. What value would Visual C++ compute in the following expression?

    ```
    ((7 + 3) + 2)
    ```

11. Why are the parentheses in question 10 not needed?

12. What value would Visual C++ compute in the following expression?

    ```
    (1 + 2) * 3 / 4
    ```

13. What value would Visual C++ compute in the following expression?

    ```
    (1 + (10 - (2 + 2)))
    ```

14. What value would Visual C++ compute in the following expression?

    ```
    22 * 2 - 8 % (3 - 1)
    ```

15. True or false: The unary plus sign is optional.

16. True or false: The unary minus sign is optional.

17. True or false: You can apply the unary minus sign to variables and expressions but not to integer literals.

18. True or false: Binary operators work best for binary values.

What's the Output?

19. Here is a tricky multiline computational program! See if you can determine the output.

    ```cpp
    // Filename: TRCKMATH.CPP
    // Computes several layers of expressions
    #include <iostream.h>
    void main()
    {
      int x;
      x = 2 + 5 * 2 - 1 % 2;
      x += 14;
      x -= 5;
      x *= 2 - 7;
      cout << "The value of x is " << x ;
      return;}
    ```

Find the Bug

20. What's wrong with the following assignment?

```
netSales = sales — adjustedSales;
```

Write Code That...

21. Write the assignment statement that performs the same math as the following formula:

$$a = \frac{(9 - 5)}{(3 * 12)}$$

22. Write the assignment statement that performs the same math as the following formula:

$$b = \frac{y2}{(2 - q)}$$

23. Rewrite the following assignment statement so that it takes three separate assignments instead of one:

```
a = (b = x * 12) * (c = 34 + w);
```

24. Oops! You make so much writing Visual C++ programs that your taxes just went up eight percent! Write a statement that takes your current tax rate, stored in a variable named `taxRate`, and increases that rate by eight percent. (Hint: To increase a variable by eight percent, you can multiply the variable by `(1 + .08)`.) Write the statement using a regular assignment and multiplication operator, and then write the statement with a compound assignment operator.

25. Rewrite Listing 7.4 to print the principal after each period so that the user can see the loan amount building each period.

26. Write a program to calculate the area of a circle whose radius is 2.4. The formula for a circle's area is

```
area = PI * (radius²)
```

Pi is approximately 3.14159. Hint: Pi is an excellent value to define as a constant using `const`.

27. Rewrite question 26 so that the program asks the user for a radius and then computes the area of a circle that has the radius that the user specified.

UNIT

7

Fundamental Math Operators

Extra Credit

28. Write a program that computes the first five powers of 3 (3^1, 3^2, 3^3, 3^4, and 3^5). Print descriptions before each power. The first two lines of output would look like this:

```
3 raised to the power of 1 is 3
3 raised to the power of 2 is 9
```

29. William the Worker always works 52 hours a week. He earns $5.65 for the first 40 hours he works. He gets time and a half (1.5 times his regular hourly pay) for the first 10 hours over 40. He gets double time for all hours over 50. He is in the 32 percent tax bracket. Write a program with appropriate titles that prints William's gross pay, net pay, and taxes.

Relational and Logical Operators

▶ **What You'll Learn**

▶ Making decisions with relational operators

▶ The `if` command tests for relations

▶ Otherwise, there's `else`

▶ Logical operators

Not all Visual C++ operators do math. This unit teaches you all about operators that test data. Computers are great not only for making speedy calculations but also for testing data. You might need a program to test data to find the answers to questions such as these:

▶ Are our current sales on target with our projected sales?

▶ Did we run out of inventory for any items?

▶ Which region generated the highest costs last year?

▶ Did the user enter a value within an expected range?

▶ Which employees will reach retirement age within the next three years?

▶ Which salesperson sold the most goods?

The relational and logic operators give your programs the power to answer questions such as these. Now that you understand user input with `cin`, you can write programs that manipulate different data values every time someone runs the program, in case the user enters different values for each run. Customers don't always buy the same number of products, salespeople don't always sell the same items, and your employees don't always work the same hours.

Definition—A *data-driven program* is a program whose data dictates the order of execution.

By being able to test data and act accordingly, your programs can take one of several logic paths. For the first time in this book, you will see data-driven programs that don't necessarily execute sequentially, line-by-line. From now on, many programs that you write will contain code that might or might not execute, depending on the data that is entered.

 Tip Think of data-driven programs as programs that take different paths, just as you do when you drive your car. You rarely drive to the same place each time you get in your car. You might leave your neighborhood using the same path but then turn into the grocer, get gas, take the freeway, or take a detour around construction. Your current needs determine the path you take, just as the data determines the path taken by the statements in your programs.

▶ Making Decisions with Relational Operators

Concept

Learn how the six relational operators produce true or false results.

Table 8.1 lists the six relational operators that you'll learn about in this section. Unlike the math operators you learned about in Unit 3, the relational operators don't calculate numbers. Instead, relational operators test one data value against another, letting you determine how the values compare.

Note The relational operators are binary operators. Therefore, they work between two values, just as the * does.

Definition—A *relational operator* tests data values against one another.

Table 8.1. The relational operators and their meanings.

Relational Operator	Description
==	Equal to
>	Greater than
>=	Greater than or equal to
<	Less than
<=	Less than or equal to
!=	Not equal to

 Warning Be sure that you compare similar data. For example, you would never compare a character variable to a floating-point variable. Make sure that the value on one side of a relational operator matches the data type on the other side.

As you read through the table's descriptions of the relational operators, perhaps you can begin to get a glimpse of their use. There are many times when you'll want to know if two values are the same, if one is less than another, if one is more than another, or if two values are different.

UNIT

8

Relational and Logical Operators

In everyday life, you compare data just as you will do in Visual C++ programs. For example, here is a list of six statements. Each statement, when spoken, matches the operation of each of the six relational operators shown in Table 8.1.

1. My overcoat sales last month were *equal* to $50,000.

2. Cable television provides fewer channels than satellite television. (The number of cable stations is *less than* the number of satellite stations.)

3. A first-class ticket from New York to Los Angeles is *greater than or equal to* the price of a coach ticket around the world.

4. It rained as much as, or perhaps less than, yesterday. (The amount of rain today was *less than or equal to* yesterday.)

5. Shelly is older than Michael. (Shelly's age is *greater than* Michael's.)

6. The color of your belt is not the same as the color of your shoes. (The belt's color is *not equal to* the shoes' color.)

Note   All relational operators return either a true value, which is represented as a 1 in Visual C++, or a false value, which is represented as a 0 in Visual C++.

The relational operations are assumed to be true or false. In other words, the overcoat sales in statement 1 were equal to $50,000 or they were not, cable either provides fewer channels or it provides more, and so on. Whenever you compare any two values, either in real life or in a program, there is always a question of whether the comparison is true or not. You'll use the relational operators to test for a true or false result and act accordingly.

Definition—*Pseudocode* is a written description of a program in plain speech, not in Visual C++ code.

Look at Figure 8.1; it acquaints you with relational logic in a program. The pseudocode in the program checks to see whether the daily sales were more than yesterday's sales. If the sales were more, one section of the program takes over. If the sales were less, a different section of the program takes over. In either case, only one of the two program sections executes.

See how the data drives this program outline? One and only one section of the program (in addition to the initial testing of the data) executes, and the data dictates which of those sections executes. Eventually, whatever section took over finishes, the end of the program executes (perhaps to print a sales report), and the program terminates.

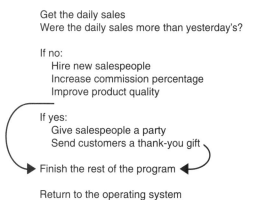

Get the daily sales
Were the daily sales more than yesterday's?

If no:
    Hire new salespeople
    Increase commission percentage
    Improve product quality

If yes:
    Give salespeople a party
    Send customers a thank-you gift

Finish the rest of the program

Return to the operating system

FIGURE 8.1.

The test determines which
of the two sections to
execute.

Let's move to a more Visual C++-like representation of the relational operators. Using the integer variables defined here, can you see that all of the following sentences are true?

```
int a = 1;
int b = 2;
int c = 3;
int d = 1;
```

1. a == d because they contain the same value.

2. c > b because 3 is greater than 2.

3. c >= b because 3 is greater than or equal to 2. (The *or* implies that c can be greater than b or equal to b.)

4. a < c because 1 is less than 3.

5. a <= d because 1 is less than or equal to 1.

6. b != d because 2 is not equal to 1.

All of the preceding sentences about the variables are true. See whether you can spot which of the following are false:

1. a >= d

2. b != c

3. a == c

4. c <= a

The third and fourth statements are false. Working with simple variables such as these seems like little more than an easy mental exercise, and testing meaningful values such as sales figures in your Visual C++ programs isn't much more difficult.

UNIT

8

Relational and Logical Operators

Be sure that you use the double equal sign (==) when testing for equality, and reserve the use of the single equal sign (=) for assignment only. (Some programming languages, such as BASIC, use the single equal sign for both assignment and relational testing.) This is very important because, unlike most other languages, C++ will accept that assignment as valid, and then test the *result* of the assignment for being true or false. This version of Visual C++ will not warn you of this mistake. We will review this problem carefully later in this section.

STOP&TYPE I want to drive home a final point before you get to official Visual C++ code that uses relational operators for actual work. You saw earlier that Visual C++ evaluates true relational expressions as 1 and false relational expressions as 0. Listing 8.1 assigns the answers to several relational operators to variables and prints the results. Try to predict the program's output before looking at the answer.

Review

What You Have Learned

The relational operators compare values against other values and determine whether those values compare as true or false based on the specified relational operation. Visual C++ prints only a 1 or a 0 in Listing 8.1 because 1 and 0 represent true and false relations.

▼ INPUT   LISTING 8.1. PRINTING THE RESULTS OF RELATIONAL OPERATORS.

```
 1: // Filename: RELAT1ST.CPP
 2: // Prints the results of several relational operations
 3: #include <iostream.h>
 4: void main()
 5: {
 6:   int high = 45;
 7:   int low = 10;
 8:   int middle = 25;
 9:   int answer;
10:
11:   answer = high > low;
12:   cout << "High > low is " << answer << endl;
13:
14:   answer = low > high;
15:   cout << "Low > high is " << answer << endl;
16:
17:   answer = middle == middle;
18:   cout << "Middle == middle is " << answer << endl;
19:
20:   answer = high >= middle;
```

```
21:    cout << "High >= middle is " << answer << endl;
22:
23:    answer = middle <= low;
24:    cout << "Middle <= low is " << answer << endl;
25:
26:    answer = 0 == 0;
27:    cout << "Bonus relation: 0 == 0 is " << answer << endl;
28:
29:    return;
30:  }
```

▼ OUTPUT

```
High > low is 1
Low > high is 0
Middle == middle is 1
High >= middle is 1
Middle <= low is 0
Bonus relation: 0 == 0 is 1
```

▼ ANALYSIS

The 1s and 0s in the output show whether the relational tests performed were true or false. Most of this program's relational testing should now be obvious to you. The high value is certainly greater than the low value; hence, line 11 stores a 1 (true) in answer. The low value is not greater than the high value, so the second assignment, line 14, stores a 0 (false) in answer.

The only possibly tricky assignment occurs in line 26. Although 0 is equal to 0, you might be tempted to think that the zero means false. You must remember that the six relational operators return either 1 or 0 based on how two values compare. 0 compares exactly to 0 in line 26. It is because 0 is equal to 0 that == is true. The true result is always 1.

HOW CAN THIS 1 OR 0 BUSINESS HELP ME?

At this point, you might be wondering how a return of 1 or 0 can help you when you write Visual C++ programs. Have patience, because the next section shows you how to incorporate the six relational operators into useful Visual C++ code using a new command named if.

To get a taste of 1's and 0's advantages, consider the following section of code:

```
cout << "How many tickets were sold? ";
cin >> num;
salePay = num * 1.45+(num > 500)*25;  // Maybe pay a bonus
```

UNIT 8

Relational and Logical Operators

The pay for the salesperson, stored in `salePay`, will always be at least $1.45 per ticket. The trick comes in the statement's second half. If more than 500 tickets are sold, the relation (`num > 500`) is true (or 1) and the `1 * 25` adds an additional $25 to the pay. If, however, the tickets did not total more than 500, (`num > 500`) is false (or 0) and `0 * 25` is $0, so no bonus is paid.

```
cout << "How many tickets were sold? ";
cin >> num;
salePay = num * 1.45+(num > 500)*25;   // Maybe pay a bonus
```

Warning   Before you continue, be sure that you understand the code in the preceding sidebar. Some newcomers to Visual C++ must take a few extra moments to figure out what's going on. Although such relational statements are efficient, some Visual C++ programmers overuse them. If your code is hard to read and maintain, you don't gain anything with tricks. If you think it's clearer to separate the preceding code's last line into more than one statement, do so for your sake as well as for those who must maintain your program later. The next section's `if` statement gives you a much better way to break the preceding assignment into two more-readable statements.

Note   Obviously, not all relational logic requires that you work with sales figures, but sales totals and bonuses make for great illustrations of relational logic. That's why you're seeing so many such examples here.

▶ The *if* Command Tests for Relations

Concept   **What You Will Learn**

The `if` statement uses the relational operators to determine which lines of a program to execute.

Every programming language has some form of an `if` statement. The `if` statement tests the relational operators and decides exactly which sections of a program to execute and which to ignore. It is the `if` statement that determines whether a program should detour or go straight.

Definition—A *keyword* is a command's trigger word, such as `if` or `return`.

Although you now have several units of this book under your belt, you don't know a lot of Visual C++ commands (also called statements). You've seen the `return` statement at the end of `main()`. `return` sends control back to QuickWin after your program completes its execution. The assignment statement is a command, but no keyword is associated with the assignment, only an equal sign.

> **Note** The `if` statement lets your programs make decisions at runtime based on data values.

The `if` statement is one of the most important statements in Visual C++. Without `if`, Visual C++ could only sequentially execute statements, limiting the amount of decision-making your programs could do. Now that you understand the relational operators, it's time to see how `if` can use the true and false relations to take action based on those relations.

The `if` statement is a multiline programming statement. Unlike `return`, `if` almost always takes more than one line of code. Here is the format of the `if` statement:

```
if (relationalTest)
  { A block of one or more Visual C++ statements }
```

From the italics, you can tell that `if` uses a relational test that you must supply inside parentheses. The parentheses are required; without them, Visual C++ won't compile your program. `relationalTest` can be the comparison of any two variables, literals, or a combination of both, as shown in the following sample `if` lines:

```
if (sales < 50000)

if (initial > 'M')

if (amount <= value)
```

> **Warning** Never put a semicolon after the closing parenthesis! Visual C++ will think that the `if` statement is finished and will begin executing the block of statements that follow the `if`, whether or not the relational test was true or false.

> **Tip** Semicolons terminate only complete Visual C++ statements and functions. The `if` doesn't end after the closing parenthesis; therefore, no semicolon follows the parenthesis. Put semicolons at the end of all statements inside the `if`'s block.

The block of statements that follows the `if` can contain any valid Visual C++ statements, including `cout`s, `cin`s, assignments, and even additional `if` statements (meaning that you can nest `if` statements). If the block of code contains only a single statement, you don't need the enclosing braces. However, good Visual C++ programmers develop the habit early of including `if`'s braces around even a block of just one statement. If you later add more to the body of the `if`, you could too easily forget to add the braces, and program logic errors would appear that can be difficult to trace.

Visual C++'s `if` reads exactly like you use *if* in real life. Consider the following statement:

"If I learn Visual C++, I'll be able to write Visual C++ programs."

What if you don't learn Visual C++? You'll never write a Visual C++ program. The body of that `if` statement, therefore, will never happen. What if you do learn Visual C++? You'll be able to write Visual C++ programs. The truth of the `if` relational test, *if I learn Visual C++* or *if I don't learn Visual C++*, determines the next course of action.

Note   `if` needs no header file. Only library functions such as `strcpy()` require header files.

Figure 8.2 illustrates how `if` works. It shows how the body of the `if` statement might or might not execute, depending on the relation.

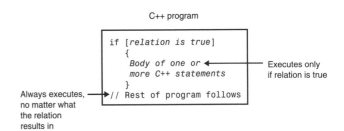

FIGURE 8.2.
The body executes only if
the relational test is true.

In the following code, a special message might or might not print:

```
cout << "What is your IQ? ";
cin >> iq;    // Assume that iq is a defined integer
if (iq >= 140)
  { cout << "How brilliant you are!" << endl; }
cout << "Have a nice day.";
```

The program will print either

```
How brilliant you are!
Have a nice day.
```

or

```
Have a nice day.
```

Do you see how the data drives the program? There is a line in the program, the second cout, that might never execute. The cout's execution is based solely on the value of the variable iq and how that value compares to the number 140. If and only if iq holds a value greater than or equal to 140 will the second cout execute.

The preceding code sample's if body contained only a single statement to keep things simple initially. The braces aren't required, but they're still recommended. The following if statement's body contains four statements:

```
cout << "What is your IQ? ";
cin >> iq;   // Assume that iq is a defined integer
if (iq >= 140)
  {
    cout << "How brilliant you are!" << endl;
    cout << "Perhaps you should consider learning Visual C++" << endl;
    cout << "in order to put your talents and that %d IQ " << iq;
    cout << "to good use!" << endl;
  }
cout << "Have a nice day." << endl;
```

> **Tip** The indentation of the if's code body is not required. As you learned in Lesson 2, Visual C++ is a free-form language, so such spacing is optional. The indentation helps to show you where the if's body begins and ends. Therefore, by indenting the code body, you help to improve your program's readability.

Do you remember the following line from an earlier sidebar?

```
salePay = num * 1.45 + (num > 500) * 25;   // Maybe pay a bonus
```

You now know enough to break that tricky line into two more-readable but equivalent statements:

```
salePay = num * 1.45;
if (num > 500)
  { salePay += 25; }   // Pay a bonus if sold enough
```

STOP&TYPE You're writing a billing program for a small hotel. The hotel charges a high rate (called the rack rate) and a discount rate. First-time customers are charged the rack rate and repeat customers get the discount. Listing 8.2 contains a program that calculates the cost of a room according to the customer's history with the hotel.

Review   **What You Have Learned**

The if statement chooses whether or not to execute a section of a Visual C++ program.

▼ **INPUT   LISTING 8.2. COMPUTING A HOTEL RATE.**

```
 1:  // Filename: HOTELIF.CPP
 2:  // Determines a hotel price
 3:  #include <iostream.h>
 4:  #include <iomanip.h>
 5:  void main()
 6:  {
 7:    char ans;
 8:    int numNights;
 9:    float rackRate = 67.50;
10:    float discRate = 57.65;
11:    float totalCost = 0.0;
12:
13:    cout << "How many nights did the customer stay? ";
14:    cin >> numNights;
15:
16:    cout << "Has the customer stayed here before (Y/N)? ";
17:    cin >> ans;
18:
19:    if (ans == 'Y')
20:      { totalCost = discRate * numNights; }
21:
22:    if (ans == 'N')
23:      { totalCost = rackRate * numNights; }
24:
25:    cout.setf(ios::showpoint);
26:    cout.setf(ios::fixed);
27:    cout << setprecision(2);
28:    cout << "The total cost is $" << totalCost << endl;
29:
30:    return;
31:  }
```

Note   There are two possible outputs, depending on whether the customer has stayed at the hotel before. Therefore, two different runs of the program follow.

▼ OUTPUT

```
How many nights did the customer stay? 2
Has the customer stayed here before (Y/N)? Y
The total cost is $115.30

How many nights did the customer stay? 2
Has the customer stayed here before (Y/N)? N
The total cost is $135.00
```

▼ ANALYSIS

The customer's number of nights is multiplied by either the rack rate, stored in `rackRate`, or the discount rate, stored in `discRate`. These two possibilities require that two `if` statements be made. If the first `if` on line 19 is true, the discount rate is computed. If the second `if` on line 22 tests for a true relation, the rack rate is computed.

This program assumes that the user will enter an uppercase Y or an uppercase N. The initial zero assigned to `totalCost` keeps garbage out of the variable, just in case the user doesn't enter an uppercase Y or N. If you ran the program and got a total cost of `$0.00`, you would know that you must enter an uppercase answer to the question. Later in this unit, you will learn how to ensure that the user enters exactly what is expected (such as an uppercase Y or N) through a process known as *input validation*. In Lesson 8, you will learn how to test for either uppercase or lowercase answers. Of course, you could use four sets of `if` statements—testing for Y, y, N, and n—but there are almost always better ways to program instead of duplicating effort.

Notice that the `if` statements test a character variable. Therefore, the `ifs'` relational operators must compare against a character. In this case, the characters tested are the Y and N character literals. The order of the comparison is unimportant; line 19's `if`, for example, could read like this with the same effect:

```
if ('Y' == ans)    // Reverse the comparison order
```

 Warning Never compare floating-point or double floating-point values for equality. It's difficult to represent exact floating-point quantities inside a computer. Therefore, use >= and <= to compare within a small range of values if you ever want to compare two floating-point values for equality.

There are several ways to improve upon this program. You'll learn how in the sections that follow.

▶ **Otherwise, There's** *else*

Concept   **What You Will Learn**

`else` determines what happens if the relation is false.

The `if` statement determines whether a block of statements does or doesn't execute. Whatever happens, the statements that follow the `if`'s closing brace execute after the `if` completes its test and possible body of code.

The `if` as you currently know it determines whether or not a block executes, but it's possible to extend the action of `if` so that it executes one block of code or another. To make `if` decide between one of two possible blocks of code, add the `else` statement after the `if`'s closing brace. Here is the format of the `if-else` statement:

```
if (relationalTest)
  { A block of one or more Visual C++ statements }
else
  { A block of one or more Visual C++ statements }
```

Figure 8.3 shows the action of the `if-else` statement. Notice that either block executes and that the true or false relation determines which block executes. No matter which of the blocks executes, the statements following the `if` execute, and the program continues as usual after the `if-else` does its job.

With the simple `if` statement, the block executes if the relation is true. If you add an `else` block, that block of statements executes if the relation is false.

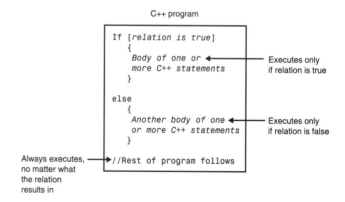

FIGURE 8.3.
The body of the `if` or the body of the `else` executes, but never both.

Warning The `if` can execute only one optional block of code, or one of two blocks if you use `else`. There's no way to make `if` decide between one of three or more blocks of code unless you nest one `if` inside another. In Lesson 5, you'll learn about the `switch` statement, which lets your program choose from among more than two possible courses of action.

STOP&TYPE `else` improves the hotel billing computation program in Listing 8.2. `else` eliminates the need for two `if` statements, as Listing 8.3 shows.

Review **What You Have Learned**

When your program must select between one of two possible actions, `if`-`else` handles the job well.

▼ INPUT   LISTING 8.3. ONLY ONE `if` IS NOW NEEDED FOR THE HOTEL BILLING.

```
 1:   // Filename: HOTLELSE.CPP
 2:   // Determines a hotel price by choosing
 3:   // between one of two possible options
 4:   #include <iostream.h>
 5:
 6:   void main()
 7:   {
 8:     char ans;
 9:     int numNights;
10:     float rackRate = 67.50;
11:     float discRate = 57.65;
12:     float totalCost;
13:
14:     cout << "How many nights did the customer stay? ";
15:     cin >> numNights;
16:
17:     cout << "Has the customer stayed here before (Y/N)? ";
18:     cin >> ans;
19:
20:     if (ans == 'Y')
21:       { totalCost = discRate * numNights; }
22:     else
23:       { totalCost = rackRate * numNights; }// Only one if needed
24:
25:     cout.precision(2);
26:     cout.setf(ios::showpoint);
27:     cout.setf(ios::fixed);
28:     cout << "The total cost is $" << totalCost << endl;
29:
30:     return;
31:   }
```

UNIT **8**

Relational and Logical Operators

▼ **OUTPUT**

```
How many nights did the customer stay? 2
Has the customer stayed here before (Y/N)? Y
The total cost is $115.30

How many nights did the customer stay? 2
Has the customer stayed here before (Y/N)? N
The total cost is $135.00
```

▼ **ANALYSIS**

As you can see, the program got simpler with the else. Two ifs, each testing for an opposite relation, are no longer needed. Basically, lines 20 through 23 say this:

"If the user typed a Y, use the discount rate; otherwise (else), use the rack rate."

▶ **Logical Operators**

| | **What You Will Learn** |

You can combine relational operators to add power to if statements.

Definition—A *logical operator* extends the action of relational if tests.

There is another group of operators called the logical operators. They let you combine two or more relational tests into a single statement or change the value returned from a relation. Table 8.2 lists Visual C++'s logical operators. The first two logical operators are binary operators, because they work on two values. The last logical operator, !, is a unary operator. The values that the logical operators work on are always relational tests.

Table 8.2. The logical operators.

Logical Operator	Meaning	Description
&&	AND	Returns true if and only if both sides of the && are true.
¦¦	OR	Returns true if one or the other side of the ¦¦ is true (or if both sides are true).
!	NOT	Changes a true relation to false or a false relation to true.

Note The logical operators are sometimes called *the compound relational operators* because they combine the action of two or more relations.

Definition—*Input validation* ensures that the user entered an appropriate value.

Assume that the user was supposed to enter a value between 1 and 5 that represented his or her department number. How can you ensure that the user enters a value within the range of 1 to 5? You can perform input validation before moving on. Consider the following `if`:

```
cout << "What is your department number? ";
cin >> dept;    // Get a department number
if (dept < 1 || dept > 5)
  {
    cout << "You did not enter a correct department number!" << endl;
    return;    // Return to QuickWin
  }
else
  {
    // Put the correct department code here
  }
```

The `||` inside the `if` statement tells Visual C++ to check that the user's input falls within the range of 1 to 5. If the user enters a value less than 1 or more than 5, the error message prints and the program terminates early. If the user's value falls within the proper range, the user doesn't see the error message and the appropriate department code executes.

WATCH OPERATOR PRECEDENCE

The logical operators as well as the relational operators appear in the operator precedence table. Visual C++ interprets the `if` in the preceding code like so

```
if ( (dept < 1) || (dept > 5) )
```

because relational operators have higher precedence than logical operators. For clarity, include the extra parentheses as shown here.

Often, there are several ways to write the same program. The preceding code used an `||` (OR) operator to make sure that the user's entered value fell within the expected range. You can use an `&&` (AND) logical operator to perform a test with the same results. Look at this difference:

```
cout << "What is your department number? ";
cin >> dept;    // Get a department number
if ((dept >= 1) && (dept <= 5))
  {    // Put the correct department code here }
else
```

```
{ cout << "You did not enter a correct department number!" << endl;
return;    // Return to QuickWin early
}
```

This if tells Visual C++ the following:

> "If the user's value is greater than or equal to 1 and if the user's value is less than or equal to 5, accept the input. Otherwise, print an error message and exit the program."

Without the logical operators, you would have to use a nested if to perform the same check, and a nested if isn't as easy to read. Here's the same code with a nested if:

```
cout << "What is your department number? ";
cin >> dept;    // Get a department number
if (dept >= 1)
   {
      if (dept <= 5)
         {
            // Put the correct department code here
         }
      else
         {
            cout << "You did not enter a correct department number!" << endl;}
            return;    // Return to the IDE early
         }
   }
else
   {
      cout << "You did not enter a correct department number!" << endl; }
   }
```

 Tip   Note carefully the indentation of the braces and statements. There are various styles of indentation in C++. The style in this example is the easiest to follow and allows you to quickly see that you have put in all the matching levels of braces correctly.

The nested if requires that both of the first two ifs be true before the first block of code executes. An else is required for both ifs in this code because if either the user's value is less than 1 or the user's value is more than 5, the error should print. As you can see here, a simple logical operator keeps your programming clearer.

The ! (NOT) operator isn't used much because logic is easier to write and maintain if you keep it positive. Virtually any relational test that uses a ! operator is easier to understand if you reverse the logic and remove the !. For example, the if

```
if (!(c >= b))
```

is identical to

```
if (c < b)
```

The second statement is easier to read and write. There is at least one good use for the ! operator, and you'll read about it in Lesson 9.

Visual C++ contains a short-circuiting feature that sometimes hurts more than it helps. If the left side of an ¦¦ test is true, Visual C++ doesn't bother evaluating the right side in order to save run time. In other words, if the following if's amt is more than 70

```
if ((amt > 70) ¦¦ (amt < 100))
```

Visual C++ doesn't bother to check whether amt is less than 100. There's no need to. The ¦¦ requests that Visual C++ evaluate the if as true if either side of the ¦¦ is true. If the left side is true, the if is true no matter what the right side evaluates to.

Visual C++ also short-circuits && operators if the left side is false. Therefore, a statement such as

```
if ((value <= 10) && (value >= 0))
```

takes a shortcut if value is more than 10. There's no need for Visual C++ to spend the execution time looking at the right side of the && if the left side is false; && requires that both sides be true before the if expression can be true. If the left side is false, the if is false no matter how the right side evaluates.

The short-circuiting feature is fine for efficiency, but make sure that you don't write tricky code that relies on both sides of the logical operator to execute. Consider the following statement:

```
if ((sales > 1000) && (inventoryFlag = 1))
```

If you were to code such an if statement (obviously, the bodies of some of these sample if statements are missing), Visual C++ would allow this as valid, but it is probably not what was intended. Do you see it? An assignment appears to the right of the &&, not an equality relational operator, ==, as was probably intended. Visual C++ goes ahead and compiles your program.

What you are seeing is the result of C++ being derived from C. In C, the language was designed to allow very efficient code, related to processor instructions. Because processors often have an instruction to "assign and test the result," the idea of a C if statement allowing both testing and assignment seems very sensible. However, compiler technology has moved forward from the days when C was designed, and the C++ compiler will often "rewrite" the simple code the programmer writes into *optimized* code without the need for the programmer to be aware of the best instructions to use. Modern programmers recognize that the costs of unreadable and error-prone code outweigh the advantages of small efficiency gains. You will find that C++ allows very complicated single statements. However, most C++ programmers do not take advantage of the flexibility because it makes the code too hard to understand.

To bring the point home, let's look closely at how Visual C++ handles the statement. If you leave this statement in your program, and if the sales are more than 1,000, Visual C++ will go ahead and look at the right side of the &&. Visual C++ then stores a 1 in the variable named inventoryFlag because of the assignment. The result of the assignment is 1, and 1 is true (any nonzero value in Visual C++ is considered to be true).

Let us assume that the intention is to test the value. If the inventoryFlag is zero and the sales are greater than 1,000, the program both assigns 1 into inventoryFlag and then finds the value to be true. This statement always executes the body of the if statement when sales are greater than 1,000, regardless of the status of the flag.

If the programmer really wants the assignment to work when the sales are greater than 1,000, the following code is much clearer:

```
if (sales > 1000)
  {
    inventoryFlag = 1;
    // Rest of if's body goes here
  }
```

STOP&TYPE The program in Listing 8.4 contains a regular if, an if with an else, and an if with logical operators.

Review   What You Have Learned

Use if for a simple decision, if-else if you need to determine one of two courses of action, and logical operators if you need to combine two or more relational operators.

▼ **INPUT   LISTING 8.4. THERE ARE DIFFERENT WAYS TO HANDLE DATA COMBINATIONS.**

```
 1:   // Filename: LOGICALS.CPP
 2:   // A program with an if, an if-else,
 3:   // and a logical operator
 4:   #include <iostream.h>
 5:   void main()
 6:   {
 7:     int numCusts;
 8:     float totalSales;
 9:
10:     cout << "How many customers were in yesterday? ";
11:     cin >> numCusts;
12:
13:     cout << "What were the total sales? ";
14:     cin >> totalSales;
15:
16:     // A simple if
17:     if (numCusts > 25)
```

```
18:          { cout << "Order more snacks for tomorrow." << endl; }
19:
20:      // An if-else
21:      if (totalSales >= 2000.00)
22:        {
23:          cout << "Reorder stock." << endl;
24:          cout << "Give sales staff a raise." << endl;
25:        }
26:      else
27:       { cout << "Replace the sales staff." << endl; }
28:
29:      // An if with a logical test
30:      if ((numCusts >= 50) && (totalSales >= 5000.00))
31:        {
32:          cout << "Take a day off!" << endl;
33:          cout << "Remodel the store." << endl;
34:        }
35:      return;
36:  }
```

▼ OUTPUT

```
How many customers were in yesterday? 13
What were the total sales? 675.45
Replace the sales staff.

How many customers were in yesterday? 43
What were the total sales? 1982.34
Order more snacks for tomorrow.
Replace the sales staff.

How many customers were in yesterday? 54
What were the total sales? 9045.67
Order more snacks for tomorrow.
Reorder stock.
Give sales staff a raise.
Take a day off!
Remodel the store.
```

▼ ANALYSIS

As you can see from the three runs shown in the output, very different messages print depending on the combination of the user's input. The if and the logical operators help ensure that every possible option is covered. The if on line 17 prints a message only if the number of customers exceeds 25. Whether that message prints or not, line 21 contains the first line of an if-else that prints a message based on the quantity of the total sales. Line 31 controls the printing that prints a message only if both the number of customers and the total sales exceed certain limits.

▶ Homework
General Knowledge

1. Why don't the relational operators do any math?

2. What values do the relational operators return?

3. Would the following assignment store a 1 (true) or a 0 (false) in `answer`? (This is trickier than it first appears!)

```
answer = (4 == 4 == 4);
```

4. What is input validation?

5. What's the difference between an `if` and an `if-else` statement?

6. Which logical operator works on a single relational value?

7. Why are braces suggested around all `if` bodies, even if the body of the `if` contains only a single statement?

8. How do the logical operators differ from the relational operators?

9. Determine which of the following tests are true and which are false based on the following variable definitions:

```
int a = 0;
int b = 1;
```

A. (a < b ¦¦ b < a)

B. !b

C. !a

D. (!(a == b))

E. (a != b)

F. (a && b)

G. (a ¦¦ b)

10. What is the short-circuiting feature of the logical operators?

11. Does the word `Hi` appear always or sometimes given the following `if` statement?

```
if (9 > 3);
  { cout << "Hi" << endl; }
```

12. True or false: You should use the `!` operator as often as possible.

13. True or false: `if-else` lets your program choose from among many possible actions.

14. True or false: A nested `if` statement lets your program choose from among many possible actions.

15. True or false: The short-circuiting feature helps improve your program's efficiency.

What's the Output?

16. This uses that tricky ! you were told to stay away from. (You'll understand why when you see this problem.) Will the following cout execute?

```
if (!1)
   { cout << "This is tricky!" << endl; }
```

Find the Bug

17. What's wrong with the following if statement?

```
if age == 18
   { cout << "You can vote" << endl;  }
```

18. What's wrong with the following if statement?

```
if (amt < 2);
   { flag = 1;
     cout << "Everything is not all well..." << endl;
   }
```

Write Code That...

19. Rewrite the following code to remove the ! but keep the same if logic:

```
if (!(sales != oldSales))
```

20. Write a program that computes pay and overtime pay based on the following conditions:

    A. Pay $5.65 for each hour up to and including 40 hours worked.

    B. Pay time and a half for any hours worked from over 40 to 50.

    C. Pay double time for any hours worked over 50.

Extra Credit

21. Rewrite question 20 so that a special tax of $.02 per hour is deducted from all employees working fewer than 40 hours to help pay for their added training needs.

22. Write a program for a health food store that calculates price from the following table based on the number of vitamins sold:

Number Sold	Cost Per Vitamin
25 or fewer	$.05 per vitamin
26 to 49	$.04 per vitamin over 25
50 or more	$.03 per vitamin over 49

Simple
Operators

STOP&TYPE In this lesson, you learned about many of Visual C++'s operators. You saw the following:

▶ The fundamental math operators perform addition, subtraction, multiplication, and division.

▶ There are two kinds of division: integer division and regular fractional division.

▶ The modulus operator (%) computes a remainder from integer division.

▶ The precedence of operators affects the order of calculations.

Project 4 Listing. An introduction to operators and `if` testing.

```
1:// Filename: PROJECT4.CPP

2:// Computes a tax amount for the tax preparer's client

3:#include <iostream.h>

4:#include <iomanip.h>

5:void main()

6:{

7:  float earnings;

8:  float taxOwed = 0.00;    // Stays zero unless changed

9:                           // in computations

10:

11:  cout << "Tax Time!" << endl;    // Title

12:  cout << "--------" << endl << endl;

13:
```

▶ The relational operators let you test data against other data and follow an execution path accordingly.

▶ The logical operators let you combine relational operators to test for a wider range of conditions and perform user input validation.

Description

1: A C++ comment that includes the program's filename.

2: A C++ comment that describes the program.

3: Include the definitions for using `cin` and `cout`.

4: You need to include `iomanip.h`.

5: All functions have names, and the first function in all C++ programs is `main()`.

6: All functions begin with a left brace.

7: Defines a floating-point variable that will hold the client's earnings.

8: Defines a floating-point variable that will hold the client's computed tax.

8: The initial value is zero and remains zero only if the earnings are less than $5,000.

9: When continuing a comment on a second line, you need to use the comment symbol again.

10: Extra blank lines make your program more readable.

11: A printed title helps describe the program to the user.

11: Put a title at the top of your screens so that the user knows exactly what the program is about to do.

12: Dashes underline the title.

13: Extra blank lines make your program more readable.

continues

Project 4 Listing. continued

```
14:  cout << "How much did the client earn? ";

15:  cin >> earnings;

16:

17:  if ((earnings < 0.0) || (earnings > 999999.99))

18:  {

19:     cout << "I believe that you made a mistake. Try again."

20:        << endl;

21:     return;   // Return early to QuickWin

22:  }

23:

24:  if (earnings > 20000.00)

25:  {

26:     taxOwed = (earnings - 20000.00F) * .28F;

27:     taxOwed += (9999.99F * .20F);   // 20% for $10K to 19.9K

28:     taxOwed += (4999.99F * .10F);   // 10% for $5K to 9.9K

29:  }

30:
```

Description

14:	A prompt for the client's total earnings amount.
15:	Gets the earnings from the user and stores them in earnings.
16:	Extra blank lines make your program more readable.
17:	Checks whether the user entered an earnings value between `$0.01` and `$999,999.99`.
18:	Opening brace starts the if processing.
19:	Prints an error message.
20:	A new line to tidy the output.
21:	Returns to QuickWin to finish.
22:	The closing brace terminates the body of the `if` block.
23:	Extra blank lines make your program more readable.
24:	Checks whether the earnings are more than $20,000.
25:	Opening brace starts the `if` processing.
26:	Computes a 28% rate on all earnings over $20,000.
27:	Computes a 20% rate on earnings from $10,000 to $19,999.99.
28:	Computes a 10% rate on earnings from $5,000 to $9,999.99.
29:	The closing brace terminates the `if`'s body.
30:	Extra blank lines make your program more readable.

17: If the earnings don't fall between $0.01 and $999,999.99, the program assumes that there's a problem with the user's input.

continues

Project 4 Listing. continued

```
31:  if ((earnings >= 10000.00) && (earnings < 20000.00))

32:    {

33:      taxOwed = (earnings - 10000.00F) * .20F;

34:      taxOwed += (4999.99F * .10F);    // 10% for $5K to 9.9K

35:    }

36:

37:  if ((earnings >= 4999.99) && (earnings < 10000.00))

38:    {

39:      taxOwed = (earnings - 4999.99F) * .10F;

40:    }

41:

42:  cout.precision(2);

43:  cout.setf(ios::fixed);

44:  cout.setf(ios::showpoint);

45:  cout << endl << "The client owes a total of " << taxOwed

46:      << " in taxes.";

47:
```

Description

31: Checks whether the earnings are between $10,000 and $19,999.99.

31: Both sides of the && must be true before the body of the if executes.

32: Opening brace starts the if processing.

33: Computes a 20% rate on earnings from $10,000 to $19,999.99.

34: Computes a 10% rate on earnings from $5,000 to $9,999.99.

35: The closing brace terminates the if's body.

36: Extra blank lines make your program more readable.

37: Checks whether the earnings fall between $5,000 and $9,999.00.

38: Opening brace starts the if processing.

39: Computes a tax rate of 10% on all earnings of $5,000.00 or more.

40: The closing brace terminates the if's body.

41: Extra blank lines make your program more readable.

42: Sets the precision for output to two decimal places.

42: Take care to present your program output neatly to the user.

43: Sets the output format to fixed format rather than exponent.

44: Makes sure the decimal point is always shown.

45: Prints the amount of tax computed. A zero remains in earnings if all of the if tests were false.

46: Divide very long statements over several lines to make them more readable.

47: Extra blank lines make your program more readable.

continues

Project 4 Listing. continued

```
48:    return;
```

```
49:}
```

Description

48: Return to QuickWin.

49: main()'s closing brace terminates the program.

▼ OUTPUT

```
Tax Time!
--------
How much did the client earn? 13443.50
The client owes a total of $1188.70 in taxes.
Tax Time!
--------
How much did the client earn? 28734.99
The client owes a total of $4945.79 in taxes.
```

Lesson ▶

Upgraded Operators

Unit 9: Special Operations

Unit 10: Power with *switch*

Lesson 5 Project

Special Operations

data promotion

decrement

increment

sizeof

typecasting

What You'll Learn

▶ Combining data types

▶ The sizeof operator

▶ Using the conditional operator

▶ Adding and subtracting one

Although you now understand a large number of Visual C++ operators, there are a few left to cover. You won't learn about all the remaining operators in this unit because some of them work only when you write advanced programs (which you will do in this book, but not until Lesson 8 and beyond).

This unit explores several operators that help you change data from one data type to another. Visual C++ prefers to work with similar data types, but you can't always ensure that your data will have the same type. Hence, you must use the type-changing operators discussed here to convert between types.

The remainder of this unit shows you how to use some shortcut operators. In Lesson 4, you saw how the compound assignment operators ease your programming burden. Visual C++ is the only major programming language with compound assignment operators. Visual C++ also provides you with additional operators that—although you could write programs without having them—do save you a lot of time. You'll want to use them as much as possible.

Combining Data Types

What You Will Learn

> If you must mix data types, you can first convert all the data to the same type so that your expressions operate on similar values.

There's no way to write a program that does much work without mixing data types in some way. Data values come in all shapes, sizes, and forms, and you must be able to work with combinations of data. Visual C++ converts from one data type to another in the following two ways:

▶ Automatic promotion

▶ Using the typecast operator

The following sections explain how each method works.

Automatic Promotion

Definition—The *promotion* of one data type to another occurs automatically when you mix types in an expression.

Visual C++ does its best to help you when you mix one data type with another, such as when you add a floating-point to an integer. Much of the time, Visual C++ assumes that you want the smaller data type converted to the larger one before it evaluates any expression. This automatic promotion of data means that you don't always have to be on guard, watching each and every constant and variable in each and every expression that you write.

Visual C++ often converts one data type to another. Given the variable definitions

```
int i=7;
float f=12.3;
```

you can add, subtract, or combine the data types in virtually any order without worrying about the results. Visual C++ automatically promotes the integer to a floating-point value before carrying out the evaluation. Therefore, the expression

```
ans = f + i;   // Visual C++ converts both to float
```

adds 12.3 to 7.0 (notice the decimal), resulting in 19.3, which is stored in ans. For now, assume that ans is a floating-point variable that you've defined.

Note   i is changed to a floating-point only for that single expression. In reality, the compiler doesn't change i. Instead, it grabs the integer value out of i and then converts that value to a float before doing the math. i never changes from an integer variable that holds a 7.

The promotion of the smaller data type to the larger one provides for as much accuracy as possible. Although you're about to learn a way to promote down—for example, from a floating-point to an integer—you almost always want as much precision retained as possible.

Look at Table 9.1 to see how Visual C++ promotes from each of the smaller data types to the larger ones.

Table 9.1. The automatic data-type promotions.

Source Data Type	What It Promotes To
char	int or the largest data type if int is not the largest data type in the expression
short	int or the largest data type if int is not the largest data type in the expression

continues

Table 9.1. continued

Source Data Type	What It Promotes To
unsigned short	unsigned int or the largest data type if unsigned int is not the largest data type in the expression
float	The larger of double or long double, depending on which appears in the expression
double	long double if a long double appears in the expression

In Lesson 3, you saw how to use the data-type suffix characters such as L and U to specify numeric literals that you want Visual C++ to treat as specific data types. Visual C++ treats all numeric literals such as 2, -0.00002, and 123.45 as floating-point literals, except in these two cases:

▶ When you specify a suffix character to override the default data type.

▶ When the numeric literal is too big to fit within the range of floating-point precision, such as 839495605.5677654323 (floats only handle up to six digits of precision), Visual C++ treats the literal as if it were a double floating-point value.

Definition—To *truncate* means to cut off or eliminate part of a number, such as the decimal portion.

The only problem that can arise is when you attempt to store a higher precision value in a smaller precision variable. For example, if you want to put a double floating-point value that contains fractional digits in an integer variable, you already know that the integer can't hold the fractional portion. Therefore, Visual C++ truncates the decimal portion, converting the number to an integer.

In the following code, three variables are defined—two integers and a floating-point value. When Visual C++ multiplies the integer by the floating-point value, it converts the integer to a floating-point by changing the value of i to 8.000000. Visual C++ then multiplies the 8.000000 by f to get 55.2. However, the variable that is to hold the resulting 55.2 is an integer variable, and an integer variable can't hold the .2. Therefore, Visual C++ truncates the fractional portion and stores 55 in result. 55 is approximately equal to the correct answer, but .2 is a large enough truncation to be aware of.

```
int i = 8;
int result;
float f = 6.9;
result = i * f;   // Oops! Puts only 55 in result
```

Warning   The order of promotion does affect calculated results!

Would `result` have held a different result if Visual C++ had first converted `f` to an integer before multiplying? Think this through. You will see that `result` would have held an entirely different value. Visual C++ would have multiplied 8 by 6 and stored only a 48 in `result`. As you can see, it's vital that you understand Visual C++'s promotion so that you can mix and match expressions and be able to predict how Visual C++ will handle the math.

Mixing data types is fairly common. You might need to multiply the number of products sold by a price to get a total price. As a matter of fact, several programs so far in this book have mixed integers and floating-point values, such as multiplying the hours worked times a pay rate. The next section explains an important operator in Visual C++ that helps with type changes—the typecast operator.

The Typecast Operator

Definition—A *typecast* changes one data type to another.

The typecast operator is one of the strangest-looking operators in Visual C++. Unlike most of the other operators, the typecast operator doesn't use a traditional symbol such as `*` or `%`. Here are some of the typecast operators:

```
(char)
(int)
(float)
(double)
```

As you can see, there is a different typecast operator for every kind of data type in Visual C++. The data type must appear in parentheses. By using typecasting, you can specify exactly when and where you want one data type converted to another.

> *Note* In Visual C++, you can define your own data types. You'll see how in Lesson 9. You can typecast using your own data types as well as the built-in data types.

To typecast one value's data type to another data type, place the typecast operator right before the value (either a variable, literal, or expression). In the previous expression, you saw how Visual C++ combined an integer and a floating-point value. If you would like to convert the floating-point value to an integer, you can place an integer typecast operator right before the floating-point variable:

```
int i = 8;
int result;
float f = 6.9;
result = i * (int)f;   // Convert f before multiplying
```

f becomes the integer 6. Without the typecast, Visual C++ multiplies 8.0 by 6.9 to get a result of 55.2 before storing 55 in the integer variable. With the typecast, Visual C++ multiplies 8 by 6 to get 48 and then stores 48 in the variable named result.

 Warning   Notice that Visual C++ doesn't round floating-points to the closest integer. It merely truncates the fractional portion when converting from a floating-point value to an integer. If you want to round a floating-point to an integer, you can use a built-in operator, which you'll learn about in Lesson 12.

Recall the problem of integer division giving a whole number answer even if a fractional answer was required. You might now see that the solution to force a real division is to use a typecast:

```
int people,events;
float avgEv;
avgEv = (float)people / events;
```

Now C++ will provide a floating-point division, and as long as the result can hold the precision, a more accurate result will be given.

Can you see that the following typecast is redundant and adds nothing to what Visual C++ would do without the typecast?

```
result = (float)i * f;   // Visual C++ first converts i to float anyway
```

 Note   A typecast doesn't change a value's data type permanently. The value is changed for the location of the typecast only.

If you need to, you also can typecast the result of an entire expression:

```
ans = a + b * (long int)(e / y * 2);
```

In this assignment statement, Visual C++ computes the result of e / y * 2 and then converts that result to a long integer. Most of the time, you can let Visual C++ handle the automatic typecasting for you through its promotion rules, which you read about earlier. However, typecasting gives you exact control over data-type changes when you need those changes. There are specific times in Visual C++ when you will have to typecast. One of the most important times is when you dynamically allocate data in Lesson 10.

The designers of C++ wanted to base C++ on the C language. In C++, you can write your typecasts using function-call notation. Instead of putting the data type in parentheses, you can put the converted value in parentheses. Therefore, you can write the statements

```
result = i * (int)f;     // Convert f before multiplying
result = (float)i * f;   // Visual C++ first converts i to float anyway
ans = a + b * (long int)(e / y * 2);
```

like this:

```
result = i * int(f);      // Convert f before multiplying
result = float(i * f);    // Visual C++ first converts i to float anyway
ans = a + b * long int(e / y * 2);
```

The new C++-only notation makes the typecasts look a little less strange. Also, when you move to advanced Visual C++ using object-oriented programming, the new notation is required to change the behavior of objects to related types.

STOP&TYPE The program in Listing 9.1 contains one expression that is typecast several times in different ways. As you will see from the output, the location of the typecast, Visual C++'s automatic promotion of data types, and the resulting variable's data type all play parts in how Visual C++ evaluates expressions.

Review

What You Have Learned

Use typecasting operators when you want to control exactly where one type changes to another type.

▼ **INPUT   LISTING 9.1. USING TYPECAST OPERATORS.**

```
 1:// Filename: TYPECAST.CPP
 2:// Applies the typecast operator to a single expression
 3:// in several different ways to show the different results
 4:#include <iostream.h>
 5:void main()
 6: {
 7:    double answer;    // Make variable large to hold any precision
 8:    int i = 9;
 9:    float f = 7.8;
10:    double d = 16.4;
11:
12:    // Apply the typecast in several ways
13:    answer = (i * f * d);
14:    cout << "The answer after (i * f * d) is "
15:        << answer << endl;
16:
17:    answer = float(i * f * d);    // The typecast
18:    cout << "The answer after float(i * f * d) is "
19:        << answer << endl;
20:
21:    answer = (i * int(f) * int(d));
22:    cout << "The answer after (i * int(f) * int(d)) is "
23:        << answer << endl;
24:
25:    answer = int(i * f * d);
26:    cout << "The answer after int(i * f * d) is "
27:        << answer << endl;
28:
```

continues

```
29:    answer = float(i * f * d);
30:    cout << "The answer after float(i * f * d) is "
31:         << answer << endl;
32:
33:    return;
34: }
```

▼ OUTPUT

```
The answer after (i * f * d) is 1151.280028
The answer after ((float)i * f * d) is 1151.280028
The answer after (i * (int)f * (int)d) is 1008
The answer after (int)(i * f * d) is 1151
The answer after float(i * f * d) is 1151.280028
```

▼ ANALYSIS

The movement of the typecast sometimes changes the answer a little (as shown in the loss of precision in the fourth line of the output, which results from the calculation in line 25) or a lot (as shown in the third line of the output, which results from the calculation in line 21).

When Visual C++ calculates the expression without any typecasting on your part (line 13), that answer actually is the most accurate. However, the answer Visual C++ produces might not always be the most accurate, especially if you store the answer in an integer variable. When storing a double floating-point calculation in an integer variable (which you might need to do in some mathematical computations or financial interest rate period calculations), you'll want to control exactly where the precision gets lost.

Be sure that you understand the difference between the third and fourth lines of output. At first, it appears that both calculations are the same because all the multiplied values are converted to integers before being stored in the double floating-point variable. The difference lies in when they are converted to integer values. In the fourth line of the output, the parentheses contain a double floating-point calculation because Visual C++ promotes the integer and the floating-point value inside the parentheses to double floating-point. This is done because double floating-point is the highest precision inside the parentheses. Only after the double floating-point calculation finishes does the typecast change the result to integer, which means truncating only the fractional portion from the result.

In the third line of the output, the floating-point and the double floating-point variables are first typecast to integers. Only after all three values are integers does the multiplication occur. The integer multiplication produces a much smaller result than the same multiplication when three double floating-point values let the fractional portions of f and d stay in the calculation.

Having fun? Typecasting and data-type conversions aren't always the most exciting components of Visual C++, but your current understanding is worth the time that you spent. As you progress in Visual C++, you'll see why typecasting can become very important as you write longer programs.

THE FRACTIONAL PORTION

By using typecasts, you can store only the fractional portion of a floating-point value if you need to. It's easy to find the whole-number portion of a floating-point number, because you only have to store the value in an integer or long integer variable or typecast the value to an integer.

A simple subtraction does the trick of storing only the fractional portion. Suppose you want to store the fractional part of fract in a variable named rightSide. Here is how to do just that:

```
rightSide = fract - int(fract);
```

Suppose fract holds 33.456. Subtracting 33 (the integer portion on the right of the minus sign) from 33.456 (the value on the left of the minus sign) results in the fraction 0.456, which goes into rightSide.

Warning Remember that despite its powerful operator capabilities, Visual C++ isn't great at storing large precision values with extreme accuracy (very few programming languages are, except for those dedicated to such purposes). Therefore, if you think that 0.456 is going into a variable, don't be surprised if Visual C++ stores 0.045601 in the variable. You don't have to print the full precision, and besides, 0.000001 is not very big at all. (However, a little 0.000001 here and a little 0.000001 there, and you'll wind up with 0.000002 in no time!)

▶ **The *sizeof* Operator**

Concept   **What You Will Learn**

The sizeof operator determines how much memory is needed to hold a value.

Visual C++ has a second operator that looks a lot like the typecast operator. Instead of using a symbol, as most of the other operators do, the sizeof operator uses parentheses.

Here is the general format of `sizeof`:

```
sizeof(dataValue)
```

`sizeof()` looks a lot like a function call because of the parentheses. However, `sizeof` is an operator because it works on built-in data-type names as well as data that you define. Here are some sample `sizeof` expressions:

```
numBytes = sizeof(int);    // Store the number of bytes an integer takes

storage1 = sizeof(myName);    // The amount of memory taken by a string

storage2 = "A string";    // Put 9 in storage2
```

`sizeof()` always returns the total amount of memory it takes to hold whatever value you put in the `sizeof` parentheses.

Note   Actually, the parentheses are optional if you pass a variable and not a built-in data type to `sizeof`, but `sizeof` is easier to read when you include the parentheses. All examples in this book that use `sizeof()` include the parentheses.

Warning   Don't use `sizeof` to find the length of a string. Use the `strlen()` function if you need to find the length of a string. (You will learn more about how functions work in Lesson 7.) By definition, `sizeof` returns the number of bytes it takes to hold whatever value you pass it. You'll remember from Lesson 3 that Visual C++ always needs a terminator byte to hold any string.

`sizeof` does not work with arrays in all circumstances. The main exception will be highlighted in Lesson 8 when we look at functions.

Different Visual C++ compilers store data in different ways. Visual C++'s `sizeof` operator might very well return values that differ from those of other Visual C++ compilers, depending on the data type and the type of machine running the program at the time.

STOP&TYPE   Listing 9.2 contains a program that prints the amount of storage it takes to store several built-in data types, variables, and literals in memory using Visual C++.

Review   **What You Have Learned**

The `sizeof` operator lets you find the storage requirements of your program's target machine. `sizeof` returns the number of bytes of storage needed to hold the value that you pass to it.

▼ **INPUT   LISTING 9.2. USE** sizeof **TO RETURN SEVERAL VALUES.**

```
 1: // Filename: SIZEOF.CPP
 2: // The sizeof operator always returns the amount of memory
 3: // (the number of bytes) that it takes to store a value
 4: #include <iostream.h>
 5: void main()
 6: {
 7:    char c = 'x';
 8:    char name[] = "Italy";
 9:    int i = 29;
10:    float f = 6.7643;
11:    double d = 9493945.6656543;
12:
13:    // Print the sizes of the data
14:    // Typecast sizeof to an integer because sizeof returns its
15:    // value as a long integer and this program prints with %d only
16:    cout << "The sizes of variables:" << endl;
17:    cout << "The size of c is " << int(sizeof(c)) << endl;
18:    cout << "The size of name is " << int(sizeof(name)) << endl;
19:    cout << "(See, that was not the length of the string!)" << endl;
20:    cout << "The size of i is " << int(sizeof(i)) << endl;
21:    cout << "The size of f is " << int(sizeof(f)) << endl;
22:    cout << "The size of d is " << int(sizeof(d)) << endl;
23:    cout << endl << "The sizes of literals:" << endl;
24:    cout << "The size of 4.3445 is " << int(sizeof(4.3445))
25:         << endl;
26:    cout << "The size of Hello is " << int(sizeof("Hello"))
27:         << endl;
28:    cout << "The sizes of data types:" << endl;
29:    cout << "The size of a long double is "
30:         << int(sizeof(long double)) << endl;
31:    cout << "The size of a float is " << int(sizeof(float));
32:    return;
33: }
```

▼ **OUTPUT**

```
The sizes of variables:
The size of c is 1
The size of name is 6
 (See, that was not the length of the string!)
The size of i is 2
The size of f is 4
The size of d is 8

The sizes of literals:
The size of 4.3445 is 8
The size of Hello is 6

The sizes of data types:
The size of a long double is 10
The size of a float is 4
```

▼ **ANALYSIS**

This program is divided into three sections that print these values:

▶ Variable sizes (lines 16 through 22)

▶ Literal sizes (lines 23 through 27)

▶ Data-type sizes (lines 28 through 31)

If `sizeof` were a function instead of a built-in operator, it couldn't return the sizes of data types. Notice that each `cout` typecasts the `sizeof` operator to an integer because `sizeof` normally returns a special internally defined data type named `size_t` unless you type-cast its return value.

`sizeof` returns the number of bytes that it takes to hold data. `name`'s string has a size of five but `sizeof` returns six in line 18 because `name` requires six bytes with the terminator.

> **Note**   When you learn how to create your own data types in Lesson 9, you'll see that `sizeof` works with those data types as well. (`sizeof` is really smart!)

▶ Using the Conditional Operator

Concept

What You Will Learn

You can exchange simple multiline `if`-`else` code for a single operator—the conditional operator.

Definition—A *ternary* operator works on three values (called *operands*).

The conditional operator does a lot of work. In fact, it's the only ternary operator in the Visual C++ language. The other operators are either unary or binary and work on either single values or two values at a time, as you've seen.

When discussing the conditional operator in general, this book shows it like this: `?:`. However, in programs, there is always a value between the `?` and the `:`. Before looking at an example of the conditional operator, you should see its format:

```
relationalTest ? trueCode : falseCode;
```

 Tip   Often, Visual C++ programmers put parentheses around each of the conditional operator's values, as you'll see in a moment.

The relational test is any Visual C++ expression that uses a relational operator—for example, any relational expression that might appear in an `if` statement. The relational test can include one or more logical operators as well if you want to combine several relational tests into a single test. If and only if the relational test evaluates to a true (non-zero) condition, the trueCode executes. If the relational test evaluates to a false (zero) condition, the falseCode executes.

Use the conditional operator in place of simple if-else statements such as the following:

```
if (a > b)
  { c = 17; }
else
  { c = 23; }
```

In this if, the relational test is a > b, the trueCode is c = 17;, and the falseCode is c = 23;. Here is the very same logic expressed as a single conditional statement:

```
(a > b) ? (c = 17) : (c = 23);
```

Notice how the parentheses help distinguish the three parts of the conditional operator. The question mark helps the statement read as follows:

"Is a greater than b? If so, put 17 in c. Otherwise, put 23 in c."

Figure 9.1 shows when the conditional operator's true and false conditions execute. The individual parts (operands) of the conditional don't require semicolons at the end of their statements. Notice, however, that the conditional operator includes a colon, not a semi-colon, before the third argument.

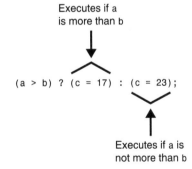

Figure 9.1.
Either the *trueCode* or the *falseCode* executes, but never both.

If both the true and false expressions assign values to the same variable, as done here, you can improve the efficiency by assigning the variable one time to the right of the conditional operator. In other words, the line

```
(a > b) ? (c = 17) : (c = 23);
```

becomes this:

```
c = (a > b) ? 17 : 23;
```

You can put parentheses around the 17 and 23 if doing so improves the code's readability for you. You don't have to put assignment statements in the conditional. Any statement, even a cout or a cin, will work in the trueCode and falseCode parts of the conditional operator.

READABILITY AND THE CONDITIONAL

At first, most Visual C++ programmers feel that multiline if-else logic is easier to read than an equivalent conditional operator. Although they're correct, after you accustom yourself to the conditional operator, it becomes just as easy to follow as a multiline if-else because you can read the entire statement on one line without having to scan four or more lines. In addition, the conditional is slightly more efficient than if.

You can do some very tricky things with the conditional, such as writing a single statement that performs nested if-else logic. Such tricks are best left alone, however. A complicated conditional is too difficult to maintain later.

STOP&TYPE Listing 9.3 is a program that prints the minimum and maximum values entered by the user. First the program uses if-else logic, and then it uses conditional operators.

Review   **What You Have Learned**

The conditional operator replaces if-else logic and is more efficient as well.

▼ INPUT   LISTING 9.3. USING THE CONDITIONAL OPERATOR.

```
 1: // Filename: CONDIT.CPP
 2: // Finds the minimum and maximum values
 3: // from the user's entered values
 4: #include <iostream.h>
 5: void main()
 6: {
 7:    int val1, val2, min, max;
 8:
 9:    cout << "Enter a value: ";
10:    cin >> val1;
11:
12:    cout << "Enter another value: ";
13:    cin >> val2;
14:
15:    if (val1 < val2)
16:       { min = val1;
```

```
17:          max = val2; }
18:    else
19:       { max = val1;
20:          min = val2; }
21:
22:    cout << endl << "Using if-else, the minimum is "
23:          << min << " and the maximum is " << max << endl;
24:
25:    min = (val1 < val2) ? val1 : val2;
26:    max = (val2 > val1) ? val2 : val1;
27:
28:    cout << endl << "Using ?:, the minimum is "
29:          << min << " and the maximum is " << max << endl;
30:    return;
31: }
```

▼ OUTPUT

```
Enter a value: 45
Enter another value: 67

Using if-else, the minimum is 45 and the maximum is 67

Using ?:, the minimum is 45 and the maximum is 67
```

▼ ANALYSIS

Lines 25 and 26 are the focus of this program. The if-else statement group from lines 15 to 20 performs the very same logic as the two lines starting at 25. The user's smaller value is either val1 or val2. The conditional operator in line 25 stores the smaller of the two values in min, and the conditional operator in line 26 stores the larger of the two values in max.

You also can squeeze the same logic into a single line using the comma operator, also known as the sequence point. It ensures that the statements on either side of the comma execute from left to right. Here is the statement that will assign both values to min and max using a single conditional:

```
(val1 < val2) ? (min = val1, max = val2) : (min = val2, max = val1);
```

Obviously, such code is cumbersome and the individual conditional statements are much easier to write. Semicolons wouldn't work between the inner assignments because the first semicolon would signal the end of the conditional operator, and the remaining part of the statement would be in error as soon as Visual C++ spotted the colon.

 Tip   Don't use the comma operator for day-to-day coding in C++. It leads to code that is difficult to follow. You might come across it in other people's code, so be aware of it.

▶ **Adding and Subtracting One**

Concept   **What You Will Learn**

The increment and decrement operators add and subtract one from variables.

Definition—To *increment* means to add one and to *decrement* means to subtract one.

The increment and decrement operators, ++ and -- respectively, are two of the most distinguishing operators in Visual C++. In fact, the ++ in C++ came from C's original important increment operator. These operators aren't necessary for Visual C++ programs; you can use an assignment statement to add one to or subtract one from any value whenever you need to. However, the increment and decrement operators are simple. You can use them in places where an assignment statement could be awkward.

 Tip   Use the increment and decrement operators for readability and efficiency. Efficiency becomes especially important when you need to increment or decrement a variable several hundred or thousand times in a program, as you will do in Lesson 6.

Table 9.2 describes the actions of the ++ and -- operators. It shows equivalent assignment statements. There are actually two sets of increment and decrement operators. One pair is called the prefix operators, and the other pair is called the postfix operators. The difference lies in where you put the ++ and --, either before or after the variable being incremented or decremented.

Table 9.2. Visual C++'s increment and decrement operators.

Operator	Example	Order	Equivalent Assignments
++	++i;	Prefix	i = i + 1; or i += 1;
--	--i;	Prefix	i = i - 1; or i -= 1;
++	i++;	Postfix	i = i + 1; or i += 1;
--	i--;	Postfix	i = i - 1; or i -= 1;

There are times when you should use prefix and times when you should use postfix. However, as you can see from Table 9.2's Equivalent Assignments column, their actions appear to be exactly the same. The difference between prefix and postfix appears when you combine the ++ and -- with other variables inside larger expressions. When you use the ++ and -- on single variables, as done in Table 9.2's Example column, the postfix and prefix notations are identical.

Warning Use the increment and decrement operators only on integer variables, not on floating-point variables. Also, never use these operators on literal values. The ++ and -- increment only integer variables.

After the variable definitions

```
int i = 10;
int j = 20;
```

the following statements add one to and subtract one from i and j respectively:

```
i++;    // i now holds 11
j--;    // j now holds 19
```

If the ++ and -- were expressed as prefix, the results would be the same. Now, after the statements

```
--i;
++j;
```

i and j hold their original values.

Being able to increment gives you the advantage of changing a variable without dedicating an entire statement to the change. The statements

```
cout << "The age is now " << age << endl;
age += 1;
```

can become this statement:

```
cout << "The age is now " << age++ << endl;
```

In this cout, the use of postfix is required. This leads us to the reason that there is a difference between the two categories of increment and decrement operators. In effect, if you specify prefix increment and decrement, Visual C++ performs the increment and decrement before any other operator in the expression. If, however, you specify postfix, Visual C++ computes the entire expression, including any assignment, and then performs the increment or decrement. In the previous cout, if you had incremented age using prefix (++age), Visual C++ would have incremented age before printing the age:

```
age += 1;   // Increment the age before the cout
cout << "The age is now " << age << endl;
```

The operator precedence table in Appendix C lists the prefix operators first and the postfix operators last to illustrate their precedence relative to the other operators. Technically speaking, the table is incorrect because the prefix operators actually should appear on the topmost level, with the postfix operators immediately following on the next level, to translate such confusing expressions as this:

```
a = +i+++j++;
```

By now, you know that such confusing statements aren't worth the trouble of maintaining later. Practically speaking, the prefix operators execute first in an expression and the postfix operators execute last.

Prefix and postfix differences become extremely important when you combine the operators with other operators in an expression such as this:

```
int a;
int i = 12;
int j = 6;
a = i++ - j;
```

When the last line finishes executing, you know that i will be 13. There's no doubt about the ++. It adds one to i. However, the timing of that addition is in question. Does the increment occur before or after the assignment to a?

i increments after a is assigned its value. Therefore, a is assigned the value of 6 (12-6), and then Visual C++ increments i to 13. If prefix is used, like so

```
int a;
int i = 12;
int j = 6;
a = ++i - j;
```

i is incremented before a gets its value. Therefore, a is assigned a 7 (13-6). Again, i is 13 whether or not prefix or postfix is used, but the surrounding expression differs depending on the prefix or postfix notation.

 Warning   The execution of prefix and postfix is under Visual C++'s control. Nothing you can do will change the execution of prefix before postfix in your expressions. The following statement wastes a lot of parentheses. They do nothing to force an early execution of the postfix decrement:

```
a = (((i--))) * value;    // Still decrements i LAST
```

Another common trap is using the ++ or -- operators twice in one expression on the same variable. What is the value of the following code?

```
int j = 0;
int k = ++j + ++j + ++j;
```

Visual C++ will give you an answer, but different compiler versions will give different answers. The official answer is that the result is undefined. The compiler will not warn you, but you should avoid such statements. (Visual C++ gives the answer 6, which is what you might expect.)

Be extremely careful when combining increment and decrement operators inside expressions with logical operators. To be safe, don't use increment and decrement at the same time that you use logical operators. For example, don't do this:

```
if ( (i == 10) || (j != ++k) )
```

A problem occurs if i is equal to 10. You might recall from Lesson 4 that Visual C++ short-circuits the ¦¦ logical operator if the left side evaluates to true. Visual C++ never looks at the right side if i is indeed 10. Therefore, k isn't incremented if the short-circuit happens. Even though k is incremented using prefix, Visual C++ still doesn't increment k because of the short-circuiting feature. However, k does increment if i is not equal to 10, because Visual C++ has to evaluate the right side of the ¦¦ to see whether the right side is true or false. This "maybe/maybe not" execution provides fertile soil for program bugs. If you want k incremented, pull it out of the if ahead of time like this:

```
++k;   // This can be either prefix or postfix
if ( (i == 10) ¦¦ (j != k))
```

STOP&TYPE Listing 9.4 contains a program that prints the values of integer variables being incremented and decremented. You will see the increment and decrement used much more frequently when you learn in Lesson 6 how Visual C++ performs loops.

Review
What You Have Learned

++ adds one to integer variables and -- subtracts one. The prefix and postfix differences determine how the increment and decrement operators affect surrounding operators.

▼ INPUT   LISTING 9.4. USING INCREMENT AND DECREMENT OPERATORS TO CHANGE VARIABLES.

```
 1:  // Filename: INCDEC.CPP
 2:  // Uses increment and decrement
 3:  #include <iostream.h>
 4:  void main()
 5:  {
 6:    int age;
 7:    int lastYear, nextYear;
 8:
 9:    cout << "How old are you? ";
10:    cin >> age;
11:
12:    lastYear = age;
13:    nextYear = age;
14:
15:    cout << "Wow, you're a year older than last year ("
16:        << —lastYear << ")" << endl;
17:    cout << "and you'll be " << ++nextYear
18:        << " next year."  << endl;
19:
20:    return;
21:  }
```

▼ OUTPUT

```
How old are you? 32
Wow, you're a year older than last year (31)
and you'll be 33 next year.
```

▼ ANALYSIS

The increment and decrement occur inside each of the couts in lines 15 through 18. The program wouldn't work correctly if postfix were used because Visual C++ would print the statements before decrementing and incrementing the age as needed. The age is assigned to lastYear and nextYear in lines 12 and 13 without using the increment there. Consider what would happen if you attempted to replace the middle of the program with this:

```
lastYear = --age;
nextYear = ++age;

cout << "Wow, you're a year older than last year ("
     << lastYear << ")" << endl;
cout << "and you'll be " << nextYear
     << " next year."  << endl;
```

The printed results wouldn't be correct! The first statement assigns a correct age - 1 value, but then the age variable is off by one. Therefore, nextYear would be assigned the current age of the user.

▶ **Homework**
General Knowledge

1. If you were to multiply an integer by a floating point and store the result in a floating-point variable, would you get a correct value? If so, why? If not, why not?

2. What is meant by promotion of data types?

3. Given the following variable definitions

```
int a;
long b;
float c;
double d;
```

what is the resulting data type for the following expressions?

    A. a + b

    B. a + c

    C. d + c

    D. a * d

    E. a + b + c + d

4. Which of the following is most efficient?

```
i++;
i+=1;
i = i + 1;
```

5. Which operator replaces simple `if-else` statements?

6. Why is `?:` called a ternary operator?

7. True or false: You don't actually need typecasts because of Visual C++'s automatic data-type promotion.

8. True or false: Visual C++ will automatically convert the smallest data type in an expression to the data type of the largest value in the expression unless you override the smallest data type with a typecast.

9. True or false: A typecast changes a variable's data type for the rest of the program.

10. True or false: Postfix and prefix mean the same thing when incrementing or decrementing a single variable and when no other computations are being made in the same expression.

11. True or false: You should nest conditional operators to eliminate nested `if-else` logic.

What's the Output?

12. What value resides in a after the following?

```
int a = 6;
b = ++a - 1;
```

13. What value resides in b after the code in question 12 finishes?

14. What value resides in a after the following?

```
int a = 6;
b = a++ - 1;
```

15. What value resides in b after the code in question 14 finishes?

Find the Bug

16. What's wrong with the following conditional statement?

```
r = (u < 100) ? (r = 12) : (r = 13);
```

17. What's wrong with the following conditional statement?

```
(9 > i || u <= 8) ? (p = 12) ; (p = 13);
```

Write Code That...

18. Given the variable definitions

```
char c;
int i;
float f;
double d;
```

rewrite each of the following expressions using typecasts that match the automatic promotion that Visual C++ would perform without the typecasts. The first one is done for you. (Hint: One or more expressions might require two typecasts to match the automatic promotion that Visual C++ will perform.)

```
answer = i * 4.5; becomes answer = float(i) * 4.5;
```

    A. `answer = i * d;`

    B. `answer = c + i + f;`

    C. `answer = d + f;`

    D. `answer = c + i + 2;`

19. Rewrite the following conditional statement using parentheses to help make the three parts of the conditional statement clearer:

```
age <= 18 ? adultCode = 0: adultCode = 1;
```

20. Eliminate the following `if-else` to use only a conditional operator:

```
if (price > 21.00)
   { salePercent = .12; }
else
   { salePercent = .08; }
```

21. Write a program that asks the user for the number of years, from 1 to 40, that he or she has worked. If the user enters a value that doesn't fall in that range, print an error and terminate the program early. Otherwise, print a message that says the following (assuming that the user enters 13):

```
You have worked 13 years
```

If the user enters 1, print the singular of the message, like this:

```
You have worked 1 year
```

Use a conditional to print the singular or plural of year. (Hint: Store an s or a null character in a character variable.)

Extra Credit

22. Write a program that prints the final price of purchases at a store where everything costs exactly one dollar. Ask for the number of items purchased. Compute a sales tax of 8 percent if the user's purchase is less than $100 and 7.5 percent if the purchase is greater than or equal to $100. Also, if the purchase is over $500, give the customer an additional 10 percent after-tax discount. Print the purchase price, the amount of the tax, the amount of the discount ($0.00 if no discount applies), and the total price. Don't use an `if` statement in the program. Use only the conditional operator when your program must make a choice. Typecast all operations so that Visual C++ doesn't have to promote anything to floating-point.

10

Power with *switch*

▶ **What You'll Learn**

▶ Multiple choice with nested `ifs`

▶ Making the `switch`

▶ `break` up that `switch`

▶ Using `switch` for menus

This unit teaches you about the `switch` statement. The `switch` statement is useful for selecting from among many different actions. You've already learned about these two ways that your Visual C++ program can choose between different courses of action:

▶ The `if-else` statement

▶ The `?:` conditional operator

The conditional is just an efficient shortcut for implementing simple `if-else` logic. Both the `if-else` statement and the conditional operator are perfect for choosing from between two courses of action, but there are times when your program must select from more than two alternative courses. The `switch` statement provides you with an easy way to set up multiple-choice selection logic from within your program.

▶ **Multiple Choice with Nested *ifs***

Concept   **What You Will Learn**

You can nest `if-else` statements to perform multiple-choice actions.

You'll better understand the advantages of the `switch` statement if you first see how to implement `switch` logic using the `if-else` statement that you already know. Until now, you learned how the `if-else` statement selects from between two courses of action. Surprisingly, the majority of the time, your programs will choose from between only two actions at a time, so `if-else` (or the simplified conditional operator in many cases) is a statement you'll use a lot. However, when your program must select from among many possible courses of action, you have to stack `if-else` logic, nesting the statements, to achieve a multiple-choice selection.

Suppose that a program you write for a credit-reporting agency needs to charge a different customer-loan percentage based on the current customer's credit rating of A (good) or B (fair). Only two courses of action are necessary, so this simple `if-else` statement works fine:

```
if (rating == 'A')
  { loanRate = .11; }   // Good rating
```

```
else
  { loanRate = .13; }    // Fair rating
// Rest of loan program logic would follow
```

Using pseudocode, here is what the preceding `if-else` states:

If the customer's rating is A,
   the customer's loan rate should be 11%.
Otherwise,
   the customer's loan rate should be 13%.

 Tip It's a good idea to use pseudocode to explain program logic. The specific syntax of the programming language doesn't get in the way. Seeing pseudocode with the `if-else` statement that you already know will make it that much easier for you to understand later pseudocode that explains the `switch` statement.

There are two (and only two) options in this logic. Either the customer's rating is A, or the rating is not A, which means that the rating has to be B. No explicit test for the B has to be made, because there are only two options. If the test for A fails, the rating has to be B.

Let's introduce a third option, a rating of C for a poor credit history. The program must now choose from among three options: A, B, or C. A simple `if-else` won't work. The third option requires a nested `if` like this one:

```
if (rating == 'A')
  { loanRate = .11; }    // Good rating
else
  if (rating == 'B')         // Must test explicitly
    { loanRate = .13; }    // for the fair rating
  else
    { loanRate = .15; }    // Poor rating
// Rest of loan program logic would follow
```

As soon as you add a nested `if`, the logic gets more convoluted. However, one or even two levels of nesting don't complicate the logic too much for understanding. Here is the pseudocode for this nested `if`:

If the customer's rating is A,
   the customer's loan rate should be 11%.
Otherwise,
   if the customer's rating is B,
   the customer's loan rate should be 13%.
Otherwise,
   the customer's loan rate should be 15%.

Do you see why no explicit test was needed to see whether the rating was C? It was assumed that there were only three choices—A, B, or C. (Perhaps input validation performed
earlier in the program ensured that only these three valid values were entered.) If the
rating wasn't A, and if the rating wasn't B, the rating had to be C, and the appropriate
loan rate was computed accordingly.

The problem with nested `if-else` logic is that too many levels of nesting introduce dif-
ficult-to-follow logic. Although one or even two nested `if` statements aren't impossible
to follow, there has to be a better way to represent multiple-choice logic. There is a better way, as you'll see in the next section.

To see how such embedded `if`s can really confuse, what if there are six different credit
ratings to deal with? Here is a way to represent such a large number of options:

```
if (rating == 'A')
  { loanRate = .11; }
else
  if (rating == 'B')
    { loanRate = .13; }
  else
    if (rating == 'C')
      { loanRate = .15; }
    else
      if (rating == 'D')
        { loanRate = .17; }
      else
        if (rating == 'E')
          { loanRate = .19; }
        else
          {loanRate = .21; }
// Rest of loan program logic would follow
```

Some credit agencies have many more kinds of credit ratings than the six shown here, so
the problem of selecting from multiple-choice logic, with its many possible outcomes,
gets to be a real burden for programmers. Some programmers opt to code only `if` statements without embedded `if-else` logic, like this:

```
if (rating == 'A')
  { loanRate = .11; }
if (rating == 'B')
  { loanRate = .13; }
if (rating == 'C')
  { loanRate = .15; }
if (rating == 'D')
  { loanRate = .17; }
if (rating == 'E')
  { loanRate = .19; }
if (rating == 'F')
  { loanRate = .21; }
// Rest of loan program logic would follow
```

Such simple sequential `if` logic might be slightly easier to follow than the previous embedded `if-else` logic, but the code isn't as efficient. You should agree that readability is more important than efficiency, but this code is extremely less efficient than the nested `ifs`, and it only gets worse as you add more `if` options. If the credit rating is A, each of the additional `ifs` is still checked. With nested `ifs`, however, if the first `if` is true, none of the other `ifs` are checked.

Programmers have designed special charts that help demonstrate nested logic, such as the one shown in Figure 10.1. However, nothing seems to be as helpful as simply introducing a new statement into the language, such as the `switch` statement, whose very syntax lends itself well to a program's multiple-choice selection.

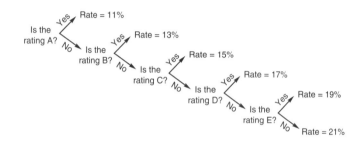

Figure 10.1.
A diagram that helps show embedded *if* logic.

STOP&TYPE Listing 10.1 uses an embedded `if-else` to perform multiple-choice selection. The user's favorite local TV channel is asked for, and an appropriate message prints.

Review   **What You Have Learned**

Embedded `if-else` statements let you select from among several alternatives, but embedded `ifs` are not very easy to maintain. As soon as you understand how embedded `if-else` statements work, you'll be ready to learn about the `switch` statement, which removes much of the multiple-choice selection burden from your programming shoulders.

▼ INPUT   LISTING 10.1. USING EMBEDDED if-else LOGIC TO SELECT AN APPROPRIATE MESSAGE.

```
1:// Filename: IFELSETV.CPP
2:// This program uses embedded if-else statements to print
3:// a message for the user. The printed message corresponds
4:// to the user's favorite television channel.
5:#include <iostream.h>
6:void main()
7:{
8:   int channel;
9:
```

continues

```
10:  cout << "In this town, there are five non-cable television ";
11:  cout << "channels." << endl;
12:  cout << "What is your favorite (2, 4, 6, 8, or 11)? ";
13:  cin >> channel;
14:  cout << endl << endl;    // Output two blank lines
15:
16:  // Use an embedded if to print appropriate messages
17:  if (channel == 2)
18:    { cout << "Channel 2 got top ratings last week!"; }
19:  else
20:    if (channel == 4)
21:     { cout << "Channel 4 shows the most news!"; }
22:      else
23:       if (channel == 6)
24:         { cout << "Channel 6 shows old movies!"; }
25:        else
26:         if (channel == 8)
27:           { cout << "Channel 8 covers many local events!"; }
28:          else
29:           if (channel == 11)
30:             { cout << "Channel 11 is public broadcasting!"; }
31:           else   // The logic gets here only if the
32:                  // user entered an incorrect channel
33:              { cout << "Channel " << channel
34:                     << " does not exist; it must be cable."; }
35:
36:  cout << endl << endl << "Happy watching!";
37:  return;
38:}
```

▼ OUTPUT

Note   Three different runs are shown to demonstrate the program's multiple-choice aspect.

```
In this town, there are five non-cable television channels.
What is your favorite (2, 4, 6, 8, or 11)? 6

Channel 6 shows old movies!

Happy watching!

In this town, there are five non-cable television channels.
What is your favorite (2, 4, 6, 8, or 11)? 2

Channel 2 got top ratings last week!

Happy watching!

In this town, there are five non-cable television channels.
What is your favorite (2, 4, 6, 8, or 11)? 3
```

```
Channel 3 does not exist; it must be cable.

Happy watching!
```

▼ ANALYSIS

If you understand `if`, just multiply that understanding by five and you'll understand this program! Seriously, embedded `if` statements do multiply the difficulty of following a program's logic.

One argument within the Visual C++ programming community concerns how programmers should indent embedded logic such as that in Listing 10.1. Some prefer to embed as shown here, while others want to put braces around each embedded `if` (which results in a series of several closing braces all grouped toward the end of the program). Still others want to align all the `if` and `else` bodies evenly so that the code doesn't get pushed too far to the right in the last few embedded statements.

If you prefer to embed `if-else` logic, and if you don't have a problem understanding such code (not everyone feels that nested `if`s are difficult), there is certainly nothing wrong with using it as done in Listing 10.1. However, after you learn about the `switch` statement in the next section, you'll probably prefer to use `switch` for much of your multiple-choice processing.

Note   Despite the advantages of `switch`, nothing beats `if-else` for straight-forward logic when only two choices must be made. Also, if the code is simple, use the conditional operator for efficiency. The `switch` statement can be overkill for simple choices. I'm not recommending that you cease to use `if-else` logic.

▶ **Making the *switch***

Concept   **What You Will Learn**

Use the `switch` statement to code multiple-choice logic. You will improve your program's clarity and make future maintenance much easier.

Unlike embedded `if-else` logic, the `switch` statement doesn't need a lot of fancy indentation that causes code to move closer to the right margin as the statement gets longer. Here is the format of `switch`. Even though the format looks a little intimidating, you'll see that `switch` is one of the easiest statements that Visual C++ offers.

```
switch (expression)
  {
    case (expression) :
      {   // Block of one or
          // more Visual C++ statements
      }
    case (expression) :
      {   // Block of one or
          // more Visual C++ statements
      }
    // If there are more case
    // statements, put them here
    case (expression) :
      {   // Block of one or
          // more Visual C++ statements
      }
    default :
      {   // Block of one or
          // more Visual C++ statements
      }
  }
```

switch might span more lines than shown in the format, depending on how many choices must be made. The expression following switch must evaluate to an integer or character-data type. Here is how switch works (using pseudocode again):

If the value of the switch expression matches that of the first case
  expression, execute the first block of code.
If the value of the switch expression matches that of the second case
  expression, execute the second block of code.
Continue looking for a match throughout the case expressions that
  compare to the switch's expression and execute the appropriate code.
If none of the case expressions matches the switch expression,
  execute the default block of code.

Did the pseudocode help? If not, looking at the following actual switch might:

```
cout << "What is the customer's credit rating (A, B, C, or D)? ";
cin >> rating;
switch (rating)    // The switch value must be an int or char
  {
    case ('A') :
      {
        loanRate = .11;
        break;
      }
    case ('B') :
      {
        loanRate = .13;
        break;
      }
```

```
case ('C') :
  {
    loanRate = .15;
    break;
  }
case ('D') :
  {
    loanRate = .17;
    break;
  }
default :
  {
    cout << "You didn't enter a valid rating." << endl;
    break;
  }
}   // Don't forget this required closing brace!
```

You should be able to read and understand this switch statement with little trouble. Ignoring the breaks for now, the user's credit rating determines exactly which block of code Visual C++ executes. If the rating is A, the first case block (the one that sets the loan rate to 11 percent) executes. If the rating is B, the second case block (the one that sets the loan rate to 13 percent) executes, and so on.

The default portion of switch tells Visual C++ what to do if none of the other case statements matches the switch expression's value. Therefore, if the user didn't enter an A, B, C, or D, the default block of code executes, which is nothing more than an error message for the user.

Warning   switch doesn't perform automatic uppercase and lowercase conversions. Therefore, if the user enters a lowercase a, b, c, or d, switch won't match any of the case expressions due to their uppercase forms.

Tip   Before entering a switch statement, your program should convert the switch expression to uppercase if you're using a character value for the switch expression.

The format and indentation that you see in this switch statement is fairly common. Be sure to remember the closing brace, because it's easy to forget. (Of course, the Visual C++ compiler won't let you forget it!)

STOP&TYPE   Listing 10.2 contains the television channel program that you saw in Listing 10.1. Instead of embedded if statements, switch makes the logic cleaner and easier to follow.

Note   The next section explains why so many breaks appear in `switch` statements.

Review   **What You Have Learned**

The switch statement gives you a maintainable statement that selects from one of many multiple-choice actions. A data value—either an integer or a character—decides which action executes.

▼ INPUT   LISTING 10.2. THE TELEVISION CHANNEL PROGRAM USING INSTEAD OF `if`S.

```
 1:// Filename: SWITCHTV.CPP
 2:// This program uses a switch statement to print a message
 3:// to the user. The printed message corresponds to the
 4:// user's favorite television channel.
 5:#include <iostream.h>
 6:
 7:void main()
 8:{
 9:  int channel;
10:
11:  cout << "In this town, there are five non-cable television ";
12:  cout << "channels." << endl;
13:  cout << "What is your favorite (2, 4, 6, 8, or 11)? ";
14:  cin >> channel;
15:  cout << endl << endl;    // Output two blank lines
16:
17:  // Use a switch to print appropriate messages
18:  switch (channel)
19:    {
20:      case (2) :
21:        {
22:          cout << "Channel 2 got top ratings last week!";
23:          break;
24:        }
25:      case (4) :
26:        {
27:          cout << "Channel 4 shows the most news!";
28:          break;
29:        }
30:      case (6) :
31:        {
32:          cout << "Channel 6 shows old movies!";
33:          break;
34:        }
35:      case (8) :
36:        {
37:          cout << "Channel 8 covers many local events!";
```

```
38:          break;
39:        }
40:      case (11):
41:        {
42:          cout << "Channel 11 is public broadcasting!";
43:          break;
44:        }
45:      default  :  // Logic gets here only if
46:                  // user entered an incorrect channel
47:        {
48:          cout << "Channel " << channel
49:               << " does not exist, it must be cable.";
50:        }
51:    }
52:
53:  cout << endl << "Happy watching!";
54:  return;
55:}
```

▼ OUTPUT

Note Notice that the output for this program is identical to that of Listing 10.1, despite the fact that a switch statement replaces the embedded if-elses.

```
In this town, there are five non-cable television channels.
What is your favorite (2, 4, 6, 8, or 11)? 6

Channel 6 shows old movies!

Happy watching!

In this town, there are five non-cable television channels.
What is your favorite (2, 4, 6, 8, or 11)? 2

Channel 2 got top ratings last week!

Happy watching!

In this town, there are five non-cable television channels.
What is your favorite (2, 4, 6, 8, or 11)? 3

Channel 3 does not exist, it must be cable.

Happy watching!
```

▼ ANALYSIS

The user's value is either 2, 4, 6, 8, or 11, and only one of the switch statement's blocks executes when one of those values matches a case expression's. If the user doesn't enter a correct value (one that matches the `case` statement's), the `default` section takes over and prints an appropriate message. `default` is a lot like a catch-all `if-else` statement. It handles any `switch` value not matched by a `case` statement.

Both the `switch` and the `case` expressions can contain variables and operators if you need to calculate a value, as long as the expression that you use results in an integer or character value.

Tip   A `default` section isn't mandatory. If previous input validation ensures that the user's value will match one of the `case` expressions, no `default` is needed.

▶ *break* Up That *switch*

Concept   **What You Will Learn**

The `switch` statement's `break`s ensure that each `case` block doesn't fall through and execute subsequent `case` blocks.

Although `switch` statements don't have to contain `break` statements, they almost always do. `break` ensures that each `case` doesn't fall through to the next `case` blocks. Here is a `switch` that contains no `break` statements:

```
switch (value)
  {
    case (1) : { cout << "You entered a 1" << endl; }
    case (2) : { cout << "You entered a 2" << endl; }
    case (3) : { cout << "You entered a 3" << endl; }
    case (4) : { cout << "You entered a 4" << endl; }
    default  : { cout << "I don't know what you entered!" << endl; }
  }
```

Tip   Notice the braces around each of the `case` blocks. Because each block has only a single statement, the braces aren't necessary. However, as with the `if`, the `while` loops, and the `for` loop, braces are always recommended.

Figure 10.2 shows the execution path if the user's value is 1. Notice that every `cout` executes!

```
                  switch (value)
                  { case (1) : { cout << "You entered a 1 \n"; }
                    case (2) : { cout << "You entered a 2 \n"; }
                    case (3) : { cout << "You entered a 3 \n"; }
                    case (4) : { cout << "You entered a 4 \n"; }
                    default  : { cout << "I don't know what you entered!\n"; }
                  }
```

Figure 10.2.
Without *break*, execution
falls through all *cout*s.

Here is the output when Visual C++ executes this `switch` without `break`s (assuming that value is equal to 1):

```
You entered a 1
You entered a 2
You entered a 3
You entered a 4
I don't know what you entered!
```

There's a big potential problem here! The `switch` statement will always fall through each `case` statement unless a `break` statement terminates each of the `case` blocks of code. If value had a 3, this would be the output:

```
You entered a 3
You entered a 4
I don't know what you entered!
```

The first two `case` statements don't execute, but as soon as Visual C++ finds a `case` to match the 3, Visual C++ executes all remaining `case` blocks of code.

Most of the time, your logic will require that you insert `break` statements to the end of each `case` block of code as done here:

```
switch (value)
{ case (1) :
    { cout << "You entered a 1"  << endl;
      break;
    }
  case (2) :
    { cout << "You entered a 2" << endl;
      break;
    }
  case (3) :
    { cout << "You entered a 3" << endl;
      break;
    }
   case (4) :
    { cout << "You entered a 4" << endl;
      break;
    }
```

```
        default  :
          { cout << "I don't know what you entered!" << endl;
            break;
          }
}
```

Figure 10.3 shows the action of this `switch` if `value` is equal to 1. The `case` blocks are now truly mutually exclusive; one and only one `case` block executes for each execution of the `switch`.

```
switch (value)
  { case (1) : { cout << "You entered a 1 \n";
                   break; }
    case (2) : { cout << "You entered a 2 \n";
                   break; }
    case (3) : { cout << "You entered a 3 \n";
                   break; }
    case (4) : { cout << "You entered a 4 \n";
                   break; }
    default  : { cout << "I don't know what you entered!\n";
                   break; }
  }
```

Figure 10.3.
With *break*, execution
terminates after one *cout*.

If the user enters a 1, here is the output:

```
You entered a 1
```

If the user enters a 3, here is the output:

```
You entered a 3
```

 Tip   Try to put the most often selected `case` at the top of the `switch` statement. The faster `case` matches the `switch` expression, the less searching Visual C++ has to do to find the right match, and the more efficient your code will be.

 Note   If you happen to put more than one `case` inside a `switch` with the same expression, Visual C++ matches only the first one.

The fall-through execution of the `case` code is actually to your advantage sometimes. For example, there could be a time when your program must calculate five values, or only four, or only three, or only two, or only one (such as when computing a country's, or a region's, or a state's, or a city's, or a person's sales values), depending on the data. You can arrange five `case` statements without `break`s to execute five calculations if the `switch` expression matches the first `case`, or four calculations if the `switch` expression matches the second `case`, and so on, creating a cascading flow of calculations.

Warning   One of the things that a `switch` can't do is choose from a range of values. For example, if you must execute the same code based on a 1, 2, or 3, and the same code for a 4, 5, or 6, you have to resort to the following coding technique:

```
switch (value)
   { case (1) :
     case (2) :
     case (3) : {    // The case code for 1, 2, or 3
                  break;
                }
     case (4) :
     case (5) :
     case (6) : {    // The case code for 4, 5, or 6
                  break;
                }
     default : {    // The code for other values
                  break;
                }
   }
```

You also can control range-checking by using a menu, as discussed in the Homework section at the end of this unit.

WHY IS THAT FINAL break THERE?

The Pascal programming language contains a CASE statement that works a lot like Visual C++'s `switch`. Pascal, however, guarantees that one and only one of the selected values will execute. If one of the options matches the CASE statement, Pascal executes only that code and terminates the statement without the need for `break` statements.

Visual C++ requires a little more work on your part if you want only a single `case` block of code to execute. You must insert `break` statements at the end of every `case` code if you don't want the execution to fall through the other `case` blocks. However, this extra effort gives you the ability to write a `switch` statement that terminates after a single `case` or one that cascades through the other `case` statements, which Pascal doesn't allow.

You might wonder why the `default` option needs a `break`. After all, when `default` finishes, won't Visual C++ move on to the next statement? There are no more `case` statements for the execution to fall through to. A `break` isn't required at the end of the `default` block of code, but try to get in the habit of including it. If you later rearrange the `case` blocks for efficiency, and one of the blocks that you rearrange is the `default` block, the `break` will already be there.

STOP&TYPE Listing 10.3 contains a program that prints the country's sales value, a region's sales value, a state's sales value, or the local sales value, depending on the user's request.

Review   **What You Have Learned**

The placement of break statements or the lack of break statements determines whether Visual C++'s case code falls through the other case blocks.

INPUT   LISTING 10.3. PRINTS FIVE, FOUR, THREE, TWO, OR ONE MESSAGES, DEPENDING ON THE USER'S REQUEST.

```
1:// Filename: NOBREAKS.CPP
2:// Not using break statements inside a switch lets
3:// you cascade through the subsequent case blocks
4:#include <iostream.h>
5:
6:void main()
7:{
8:  char request;
9:
10:  cout << "Sales Reporting System"  << endl << endl;
11:
12:  cout << "Do you want the Country, Region, State, or Local report";
13:  cout << " (C, R, S, or L)? ";
14:  cin >> request;
15:  cout << endl;
16:
17:  //
18:  // Convert to uppercase - letters are contiguous
19:  //
20:  if (request >= 'a' || request <= 'z')
21:    request += ('A' - 'a');
22:
23:  switch (request)
24:    {
25:      case ('C') :
26:        {
27:          cout << "Country's sales: $343,454.32" << endl;
28:        }
29:      case ('R') :
30:        {
31:          cout << "Region's sales: $64,682.01" << endl;
32:        }
33:      case ('S') :
34:        {
35:          cout << "State's sales: $12,309.82" << endl;
36:        }
37:      case ('L') :
38:        {
39:          cout << "Local's sales: $3,654.58" << endl;
```

```
40:          break;
41:        }
42:    default    :
43:        {
44:          cout << "You did not enter C, R, S, or L"  << endl;
45:          break;
46:        }
47:    }
48: return;
49:}
```

▼ OUTPUT

Note   Three different outputs are shown so that you can see how switch handles the different requests.

```
Sales Reporting System

Do you want the Country, Region, State, or Local report (C, R, S, or L)? c

The country's sales are $343,454.32
The region's sales are $64,682.01
The state's sales are $12,309.82
The local sales are $3,654.58


Sales Reporting System

Do you want the Country, Region, State, or Local report (C, R, S, or L)? L

The local sales are $3,654.58


Sales Reporting System

Do you want the Country, Region, State, or Local report (C, R, S, or L)? x

You did not enter C, R, S, or L
```

▼ ANALYSIS

This program contains four case blocks, as well as a default block that handles any unmatched expressions. All four sales figures are to be printed if the country's sales are requested, so no break appears in the first four case blocks to allow the execution to fall through.

The code in lines 20 and 21 converts the lowercase entry into uppercase. You might not know the numeric difference between 'a' and 'A', but you know that all the uppercase letters and the lowercase letters come together in the ASCII table. This code will work whatever the actual values of `'a'` and `'A'` are.

There is a `break` on line 40 so that a previous `case` execution doesn't fall through to the `default`'s code. Without that `break`, entering L (for local) would produce this output:

```
Sales Reporting System

Do you want the Country, Region, State, or Local report (C, R, S, or L)? L

The local sales are $3,654.58
You did not enter C, R, S, or L
```

Obviously, the `break` before the `default` block is needed to keep the error from appearing when the user enters a correct value.

▶ Using *switch* for Menus

Concept   **What You Will Learn**

Menus are common programming methods that give the user several options from which to choose.

Whenever you sit down in a new restaurant, what must you have before you order food? (From the title of this section, you already know what's coming!) You need a menu. You can't be expected to know in advance what food every restaurant will have (MacDonalds excepted!).

When your users sit down in front of your program, you can't always expect them to know what's possible either. You need to give them a choice of options that they can order. Such options usually are found on menus.

Obviously, the concept of a menu is nothing new to you, a top-notch Visual C++ programmer. You've been using the pull-down menus from Visual C++'s workbench throughout this book. When writing programs, you'll add menus to your programs so that your user can have access to a list of choices, just as you do in the workbench.

I'm not trying to fool you here! The menus that you write using this book won't be the fancy pull-down types that Visual C++ contains. Such menus are extremely difficult to code, and you have to learn to walk before you can run. The menus you write will do little more than display a list of choices such as these:

```
Here are your choices:
1. Print an employee report
2. Enter sales figures
```

3. Compute payroll
4. Exit the program
What do you want to do?

> ***Tip*** Despite the fact that this menu isn't of the fancy pull-down kind, its
> simplicity is its power. This kind of list menu is easy to code and easy for
> the user to use.

After you grab the user's input, your program must figure out what the user entered and execute the appropriate routine. Hey, that's a great job for the switch statement! One of the most common uses for switch is for menu processing. The multiple-choice selection that menus need matches the multiple-choice selection that the switch statement provides.

STOP&TYPE Listing 10.4 contains a menu that calculates different kinds of mathematical results based on the user's menu selection.

Review   **What You Have Learned**

The switch statement is perfect for writing menu selection code.

INPUT   LISTING 10.4. USING switch TO PERFORM THE USER'S CALCULATION.

```
1:// Filename: MATHMENU.CPP
2:// Uses a switch statement to perform
3:// menu actions for the user
4:#include <iostream.h>
5:
6:void main()
7:{
8:   const int PI = 3.14159;
9:   int menu;        // Will hold menu result
10:   int num;         // Will hold user's numeric value
11:   float result;    // Will hold computed answer
12:
13:   cout << "Math Calculations" << endl << endl;
14:   cout << "Please enter a number from 1 to 30: ";
15:   cin >> num;
16:   if ( (num < 1) && (num > 30));
17:      {
18:         return;  // Exit if bad input
19:      }
20:
21:   cout << "Here are your choices:" << endl << endl;
22:   cout << "\t1. Calculate the absolute value" << endl;
23:   cout << "\t2. Calculate the square" << endl;
24:   cout << "\t3. Calculate the cube" << endl;
```

continues

UNIT

10

Power with switch

```
25:  cout << "\t4. Calculate a circle's area" << endl;
26:  cout << "\t   using your radius" << endl;
27:  cout << endl << "What do you want to do? ";
28:  cin >> menu;
29:
30:  switch (menu)
31:    {
32:      case (1) :
33:        {
34:          result = ((num < 0)? -num : num);
35:          break;
36:        }
37:      case (2) :
38:        {
39:          result = num * num;
40:          break;
41:        }
42:      case (3) :
43:        {
44:          result = num * num * num;
45:          break;
46:        }
47:      case (4) :
48:        {
49:          result = PI * (num * num);
50:          break;
51:        }
52:      default  :
53:        {
54:          cout << "You did not enter 1, 2, 3, or 4" << endl;
55:          return;   // Terminate the whole program
56:                    // No need for a break
57:        }
58:    }
59:
60:  cout << endl << "Here is your computed value: "
61:       << result << endl;
62:  return;
63:}
```

▼ **OUTPUT**

Note   Two outputs appear.

```
Math Calculations

Please enter a number from 1 to 30: 10
Here are your choices:

1. Calculate the absolute value
2. Calculate the square
```

```
3. Calculate the cube
4. Calculate a circle's area
   using your radius

What do you want to do? 2

Here is your computed value: 100.00


Math Calculations

Please enter a number from 1 to 30: 6
Here are your choices:

1. Calculate the absolute value
2. Calculate the square
3. Calculate the cube
4. Calculate a circle's area
   using your radius

What do you want to do? 6
You did not enter 1, 2, 3, or 4
```

▼ ANALYSIS

One of four math calculations is performed, based on the user's request. The menu gives the user a nice display of every option available.

The program first asks for a number in lines 16 through 20. The `if` ensures that the user enters a value from 1 to 30. After the program accepts the user's number, the user sees the menu printed on lines 21 through 27. The user is to enter a value from 1 to 4. No fancy error checking is done. If the user enters a value that isn't in the range of 1 to 4, the program prints an error message (line 54) and exits via the `return` on line 55.

Note Without the `return` at the end of the `default` option, execution would fall through to print the message in line 60. Line 60's message should be printed only if the user entered a menu option from 1 to 4.

▶ Homework
General Knowledge

1. What is a disadvantage of nested `if-else` statements?

2. How can using a `switch` statement improve the readability of nested `if-else` statements?

3. Are braces required around every `case` block? Why or why not?

4. What kind of data type must the switch expression evaluate to?

5. What happens if none of the case expressions matches the switch expression?

6. Why would a programmer possibly want to reorder the case statements in a program?

7. What happens if you don't put break statements at the end of switch blocks?

8. What happens if more than one case block contains the same expression?

9. What do you insert in a case statement to capture an expression that doesn't match any of the other case expressions?

10. Which case block executes if you don't include a default block and none of the case expressions matches the value of the switch expression?

11. Why is it a good idea to put a break at the end of a default block of code?

12. True or false: The switch statement is one of the longest Visual C++ statements and therefore is the most complicated.

13. True or false: The default block is optional.

14. True or false: Forgetting to insert break statements at the end of switch blocks will introduce bugs into your program.

15. True or false: The switch statement requires the STDLIB.H header file.

16. True or false: switch statements improve the readability of nested for loops.

What's the Output?

17. What's the output of the following switch statement?

```
switch ('A') :
  { case ('A') : cout << "Apples" << endl;
    case ('B') : cout << "Bananas" << endl;
    case ('C') : cout << "Carrots" << endl;
    default    : cout << "Onions" << endl;
  }
```

Find the Bug

18. Although the following switch doesn't contain a syntax error, each line of code in each case is missing a couple of special characters that might come in handy later. What could you add to aid in the future maintenance of this switch?

```
switch (ans)
  { case (1) : cout << "The answer is 1" << endl;
    default : cout << "The switch statement is not finished." <<
endl);
  }
```

19. Rudy can't seem to get his `switch` statement to work. He's writing a program to control departmental duty reports, but too many departments print at once. Can you help Rudy by rewriting this `switch` so that each `case` block executes independently of the others?

```
switch (ans)
  { case (2) : { cout << "Your department isn't on duty today."; }
    case (5) : { cout << "Your department begins duty at 4:00"; }
    case (9) : { cout << "Your department works overtime Monday."; }
    default :  { cout << "Your department is in conference now."; }
  }
cout << "" << endl;
```

20. What's wrong with the following `switch` statement?

```
switch (choice)
  case (1) : { ans = 34 * sales;
               break; }
  case (2) : { ans = 56 * sales;
               break; }
  case (3) : { ans = 78 * sales;
               break; }
  default  : { ans = sales;
               break; }
```

Write Code That...

21. Ask the user for a number from 1 to 5. Using a `switch` statement, print the name of the number (for example, print two if the user enters 2). Include an error-checking loop to ensure that the user enters a number in the range of 1 to 5.

22. Wilma coded the following nested `if-else` statement, but she's having a hard time understanding it, even though it seems to be working correctly. Rewrite the statement as a `switch` to help Wilma's future program maintenance.

```
if (num == 1)
  { cout << "France" << endl; }
else if (num == 2)
  { cout << "Italy" << endl; }
  else if (num == 3)
    { cout << "England" << endl; }
    else { cout << "Greece" << endl; }
```

23. Although a `switch` statement can't deal directly with ranges of values, you can display a menu of ranges, with numbers 1 through the total number of menu options to the left of each range, and base a `switch` statement on the menu's ranges. Write a program that computes a sales bonus of $0 if the user sold fewer than 100 products, a sales bonus of $50 if the user sold between 101 and 200 products, and a sales bonus of $100 if the user sold more than 200 products.

Extra Credit

24. Write a program that calculates tolls for an interstate toll booth. Ask whether
the driver is in a car or a truck. Calculate a charge of $3.00 if the driver got on
the toll road within the last 75 miles, $3.50 if the driver got on the toll road
within the last 125 miles, and $4.00 if the driver got on the toll road more than
125 miles ago. If the vehicle is a truck, add an extra $1.00 for the added weight.
(Hint: Use one switch and one if statement.)

Upgraded Operators

STOP&TYPE In this lesson, you learned more about Visual C++'s operators and about its `switch` capabilities. You saw the following:

▶ Combining data types

▶ The `sizeof` operator

▶ Using the conditional operator

▶ Adding and subtracting one

▶ The difficulties involved with nested `if-else` statements

▶ Using `switch` to improve the readability of nested `if-else` statements

▶ Supplying menus for your users to help them select program options

Project 5 Listing. Using a `switch` statement to control a menu.

```
1:// Filename: PROJECT5.CPP

2:// Uses a switch statement to control a user's selection

3:#include <iostream.h>

4:

5:void main()

6:{

7:  int menu;

8:  float charge = 0.00;   // Holds total charge

9:

10:  cout << "** Computer Repair Center **" << endl << endl;

11:  cout << "What work was performed? Here are the choices: "
```

Description

1: A C++ comment that includes the program's filename.

2: A C++ comment that contains the program's description.

3: cout and cin need information in the IOSTREAM.H header file.

4: Extra blank lines make your program more readable.

5: All functions have names, and the first function in all C++ programs is main().

6: All functions begin with a left brace.

7: Defines an integer variable that will hold the user's chosen menu option.

8: Defines a floating-point variable that will hold a charge.

9: Extra blank lines make your program more readable.

10: Prints a title.

11: Prepares to print the menu.

continues

Project 5 Listing. continued

```cpp
12:        << endl << endl;

13:    cout << "\t1. Replaced the CPU and RAM" << endl;

14:    cout << "\t2. Replaced the RAM only" << endl;

15:    cout << "\t3. Repaired the monitor" << endl;

16:    cout << "\t4. Fixed stuck keys" << endl;

17:

18:    do

19:      {

20:        cout << endl << "What work was performed? ";

21:      cin >> menu;

22:      } while ((menu < 1) || (menu > 4));

23:

24:    // Store the charge based on the repair person's input

25:    switch (menu)

26:    {

27:      case 1 :  charge = 200.00F;    // Notice no break here

28:      case 2 :  charge += 150.00F;
```

Description

12: Continues the previous line, printing two new lines.

13: The first menu choice.

14: The second menu choice.

15: The third menu choice.

16: The fourth menu choice.

17: Blank lines help to make your program more readable.

18: The do-while loop always executes at least once, ensuring that the body with the user's question will be shown.

19: while loops use braces to contain the statements that are to be repeated.

20: Asks the user for the desired menu option.

21: Gets the user's input.

22: Keeps looping if the user doesn't enter a valid menu option.

22: Always check the user's input for validation.

23: Extra blank lines make your program more readable.

24: Place comments throughout your code.

27: Notice that there is no break here. If there is a CPU repair, there will always be a RAM replacement (see the menu), so execution will fall through to the second case as well.

25: Start of the switch statement that will select a case block based on the user's response to the menu.

26: The switch statement encloses its choices in braces.

27: The charge for a CPU repair is stored.

28: The charge for RAM replacement is stored.

28: Removing a break lets you cascade case code blocks.

continues

Project 5 Listing. continued

```
29:                break;

30:    case 3 :  charge = 75.00F;

31:                break;

32:    case 4 :  charge = 12.00F;

33:                break;

34:  }

35:

36:  // Print the results

37:  cout.precision(2);

38:  cout.setf(ios::showpoint);

39:  cout.setf(ios::fixed);

40:  cout << endl << "The total charge is $" << charge << endl;

41:}
```

Description

29: The break ensures that the execution won't fall through to the subsequent case blocks.

30: The charge for monitor repair is stored.

31: The break ensures that the execution won't fall through to the subsequent case blocks.

32: The charge for the keyboard repair is stored.

33: The break ensures that the execution won't fall through to the subsequent case blocks.

34: A final closing switch brace is always required.

35: Extra blank lines make your program more readable.

36: Place comments throughout your code.

37: Ensures that two decimal places print.

38: Makes sure the decimal point always appears.

39: Guards against scientific notation.

40: Prints the total charge.

41: A final brace ends all main() functions.

29: If execution fell through from the previous case, charge will hold $350. Otherwise, if the user selected only RAM replacement, the charge will be only $150.00.

▼ OUTPUT

```
** Computer Repair Center **
What work was performed? Here are the choices:
    1. Replaced the CPU and RAM
    2. Replaced the RAM only
    3. Repaired the monitor
    4. Fixed stuck keys
What work was performed? 5
What work was performed? 1
The total charge is $350.00
```

Lesson ▶

Looping Back and Forth

What *while* Is for

▶ What You'll Learn

▶ The format of while

▶ The other while: the do-while loop

▶ The for loop's structure

▶ Further control with countExpression

Computers do a lot of things that people find boring. They add and subtract. They print reams of information. They wait patiently while a user sits at the keyboard trying to find the Enter key. Computers do all these things without complaint as long as their programs contain no syntax errors (which, of course, none of your programs will!).

Not only do computers do all these things, but they do them very fast. Extremely fast. Their speed gives computers the added advantage of being able to perform multiple repetitions of the same tasks.

Definition—A *loop* is a program's repeated execution of the same set of instructions.

When your programs contain loops, they can repeat the same set of code a lot. The computer can repeat the code hundreds, even thousands, of times. Computers repeat so rapidly that the user usually notices no delay at all. Suppose you wrote a program that calculated payroll figures. Instead of running the same program over and over for each employee, the user would have to run the program only once. A loop within the program would keep calculating each employee's data until the entire payroll was finished.

Looping is a very important concept in programming. It is so important that Visual C++ provides three different forms of loops to repeat statements over and over: while and do...while loops, which do things over and over until some condition is true, and the for loop, which performs some actions a specific number of times.

▶ The Format of *while*

The while loop repeats as long as a relational test is true. As soon as the relational test becomes false, the while loop terminates and the rest of the program continues.

In programming, there will be times when you want to do the same task over and over again. For example, you might want to write a quiz program and ask the user the same question until he or she gives the right answer. You could write the same code over and over again, but often you want to do things hundreds or thousands of times—in which case your programs would get very long! Instead, you can use a loop. You decide what code you want to use repeatedly, and place it inside a loop. Inside the loop, you might ask a question and get new input over and over again or use other advanced techniques such as arrays to access different data each time around the loop. Each time around the loop, C++ can ask the question, "Should I do the loop again?" In the while loop, C++ asks the question before each time it starts executing the loop.

The while loop requires the while statement. while is a command, just as return, if, and else are commands.

Note   while isn't a library function. Therefore, it doesn't use any header files.

Definition—An *infinite loop* never stops executing.

When you want your program to execute the same series of statements over and over, one of the most important points to plan is when the loop should terminate. No matter how fast your computer is, if you write a program that contains a loop that loops without stopping, the endless infinite loop hangs up and the program never lets the user stop the program or return to Visual C++.

To keep loops from executing forever, you write a controlling relational test, just like the relational tests that appear inside if statements. The loop repeats as long as the relational test is true. Unlike an if statement, a while body keeps repeating as long as the while's relational test is true. The if statement's body executes only once if the if's relational test is true.

Warning   You must make sure that something inside the loop eventually changes the while's relational test. If the relation is true when the while first begins, and if nothing inside the body of the while ever changes the relational test, it executes forever. The loop will never stop, and you'll lose your title of "Master C++ Guru Programmer."

Tip   If you accidentally write a QuickWin program that contains an infinite loop, you can terminate the program by pressing Ctrl+Break or Ctrl+C. Visual C++ then stops the program and returns to the QuickWin window.

We're a few pages into this unit and you've yet to see a while loop. Enough introduction. Here's the format of the while loop:

```
while (relationalExpression)
  {
     // Block of one or more Visual C++ statements
  }
```

Just like if, while is a multiline statement. Also like if, parentheses must appear around the relational expression. The relational expression can contain one or more relational operators. If you use more than one relational operator inside the relational expression, use logical operators (&& and ¦¦) to combine the relational tests.

 Tip   Indent the body of the while loop so that when you maintain the program, you'll be able to spot where the loop's code begins and ends.

The body of the while loop doesn't require braces if it has only one statement. However, you should get in the habit of using the braces so that you won't forget them later if you add more statements to the while loop.

 Warning   Don't put a semicolon after the relational test's closing parenthesis. The while loop would then be an infinite loop, because Visual C++ would think that the body of the loop was a null statement (empty), and null statements can't change the loop's controlling relational test.

The relational test appears at the top of the while loop. The location of the test is important; if the while expression is false the first time through, the loop will not execute even once! The body of the while loop executes only if the relational expression is true, and it keeps executing as long as the relational expression is true. If and when the relational expression becomes false, the program continues at the statement following the while loop's closing brace.

Figure 11.1 illustrates the while loop's action. while is somewhat like a repeating if test. If the relational expression is true, the while body repeats its execution. If the relational expression is false, the while body stops executing and the program continues from there.

Figure 11.1.

The body of the while executes as long as the relational expression is true.

```
while (relTest)
  {
      // One or more
      // statements       Only if the test is
      // go here          true do the statements
  }                       in the body execute
// Rest of program
// continues
```

The following while loop prints Happy Birthday! on-screen 10 times. Notice that instead of using 10 separate couts, you need to specify only one inside a while loop that loops 10 times:

```
int count = 0;
while (count < 10)
  {
    cout << "Happy Birthday!" << endl;
    count++;    // VERY important!
  }
```

Why is it important to increment the `count` variable? If you don't increment `count`, the loop will be infinite! Remember that the body of the loop should always change something in the `while`'s relational test so that the relational test eventually becomes false and the loop can stop.

COUNTERS

The `count` variable in the preceding `while` loop is called a counter variable. Each time through the loop, the program increments `count`. Just as when you count 0, 1, 2, 3, and so on, `count` starts out holding a 0, and then 1, 2, 3, and so on, until Visual C++ increments `count` to the final value of 10. At this time, the relational test becomes false and the loop terminates.

STOP&TYPE Listing 11.1 contains a program that asks the user for an age. If the user enters an age less than 5 or more than 110, the program doesn't believe the user and asks again. Until now, if the user entered a bad value, the program stopped early. Now, you can keep asking the user until he or she enters a value within an expected range.

Review **What You Have Learned**

The `while` loop lets you repeat sections of your program as long as the relational test is true.

▼ **INPUT   LISTING 11.1. USING TO VERIFY USER INPUT.**

```
1:// Filename: USERAGE.CPP
2:// Uses a while loop to get an age from the user
3:#include <iostream.h>
4:void main()
5: {
6:   int age;
7:
8:   cout << "How old are you? ";
9:   cin >> age;
10:
11:   while ((age < 5) || (age > 110))
12:     {
13:       cout << "I'm not sure that I believe you are "
14:            << age << endl;
15:       cout << "Try again..." << endl << endl;
16:       cout << "How old are you? ";   // Get the age again
17:       cin >> age;
18:     }
```

continues

UNIT

11

What while Is for

```
19:    // The program continues if the user entered a reasonable age
20:    if (age < 16)
21:      {
22:        cout << "Your curfew is at 11:30 pm" << endl;
23:        cout << "Have fun!"  << endl;
24:      }
25:    else
26:      {
27:        cout << "You're old enough to drive, so be careful ";
28:        cout << "out there!" << endl;
29:      }
30:    return;
31: }
```

▼ OUTPUT

```
How old are you? -32
I'm not sure that I believe you are -32
Try again...

How old are you? 192
I'm not sure that I believe you are 192
Try again...

How old are you? 25
You're old enough to drive, so be careful out there!
```

▼ ANALYSIS

The user's entered age determines what the program does. First of all, if the user enters an age that isn't within the range between 5 and 110, the program prints an error message in lines 13 and 15. Actually, the program prints a warning, not an error, because as soon as the user enters a bad age, the program asks the user for another age and tests the age all over again via the loop in lines 11 through 18. The while will continue looping as long as the user's value isn't within the expected range.

The rest of the program primarily consists of an if-else in lines 19 through 27 that prints one message or another, depending on the user's age. Unlike the while, the if never repeats its body more than once. When the if body finishes, the program always continues on to the return, where it then returns to QuickWin and finishes.

 Note   This program contains two sets of duplicate lines: Lines 8 and 9 are repeated in lines 15 and 16. After mastering the second kind of while loop discussed in the next section (there are two), you'll see a way to eliminate the duplication of lines of code.

▶ The Other *while*: The *do-while* Loop

Concept

There is a second `while` loop, called the `do-while` loop, whose relational test appears at the bottom of the loop's body instead of at the top.

Visual C++ contains two `while` loops: the `while` loop that you read about in the preceding section and the `do-while` loop. Although these loops are similar, they differ in where they test their relation. Here is the format of `do-while`:

```
do
  {
    // Block of one or more Visual C++ statements
  }
while (relationalExpression);
```

As with the `while` loop, the braces around the body aren't required if it contains a single statement. However, you should use the braces in all cases for clarity and future maintenance. You must put parentheses around the relational expression. The final semicolon after the relational test is required to terminate the `do-while` statement.

You should use a `do-while` loop instead of a `while` loop when you want the body of the loop to execute at least once. The location of the `do-while`'s relational test causes execution to fall through and execute the body of the loop at least once. Only after the body executes once can the `do` loop check the relational test to see whether the loop should loop again or terminate. Only after the relational test is false will the rest of the program continue executing.

Definition—An *iteration* is one cycle through the body of a loop.

Note The `while` loop might never execute because Visual C++ checks the relational test before the body has a chance to execute. `do-while` doesn't test the relation until the loop executes one full iteration. Figure 11.2 shows how the `do` loop works as opposed to how `while` works (which you saw in Figure 11.1).

UNIT
11
What while Is for

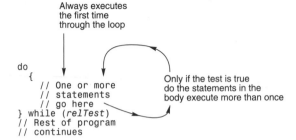

Figure 11.2.

The body of a do-while always executes at least once.

Here is a do-while that prints Happy Birthday 10 times:

```
int count = 0;
do
{ cout << "Happy Birthday!" << endl;
count++;
} while (count < 10);
```

STOP&**TYPE** Listing 11.1 asked the user for his or her age and printed an appropriate message. Listing 11.2 improves upon that program by using a do-while loop. The use of do-while as opposed to while means that you don't have to repeat the age prompt and the user's cin. However, an extra if is needed to capture any mistake the user makes.

Review ━━━━━━━━━━━━━━━━━━━━━━━━━━━━━━━━━━━ **What You Have Learned**

do-while ensures that the body of the loop executes at least once.

▼ **INPUT   LISTING 11.2. KEEP ASKING FOR A CORRECT AGE IF NEEDED WITH do.**

```
 1:// Filename: DOUSRAGE.CPP
 2:// Uses a do-while loop to get an age from the user
 3:#include <iostream.h>
 4:void main()
 5:{
 6:  int age;
 7:
 8:  // In the previous listing, two extra lines went here
 9:  do
10:    { cout << "How old are you? ";   // Get the age
11:      cin >> age;
12:      if ((age < 5) || (age > 110))
13:        { cout << "I'm not sure that I believe you are "
14:               << age << endl;
15:          cout << "Try again..." << endl << endl; }
16:    } while ((age < 5) || (age > 110));   // Quit after good input
17:
18:  // The program continues if the user entered a reasonable age
19:  if (age < 16)
```

```
20:    { cout << "Your curfew is at 11:30 pm" << endl;
21:      cout << "Have fun!" << endl;
22:    }
23: else
24:    {
25:      cout << "You're old enough to drive, so be careful ";
26:      cout << "out there!" << endl;
27:    }
28: return;
29:}
```

▼ **OUTPUT**

```
How old are you? 2
I'm not sure that I believe you are 2
Try again...

How old are you? 3224
I'm not sure that I believe you are 3224
Try again...

How old are you? 12
Your curfew is at 11:30 pm
Have fun!
```

▼ **ANALYSIS**

The use of do-while keeps the program from repeating these lines, as was done in Listing 11.1:

```
cout << "How old are you? ";   // Get the age again
cin >> age;
```

The use of do-while requires an extra if statement that Listing 11.1 didn't need. The if in line 12 ensures that the age warning message prints only if the user enters an age outside the range. Whether to use while without the extra if or do-while with the extra if is up to you.

▶ **The *for* Loop's Structure**

Concept

What You Will Learn

Learn the format of the for statement. A single for statement requires three values that control the loop.

The for statement makes for loops look rather difficult, but as you'll see, for loops aren't hard to understand. Visual C++'s syntax requirements for the for statement are a little strange looking, but Visual C++ has never been known for being a verbose language. Here is the format of the `for` loop:

```
for (startExpression; conditional; countExpression)
  {
  // Block of one or more Visual C++ statements
  }
```

When Visual C++ encounters a `for` statement, it follows these steps to perform a loop:

1. Perform the `startExpression`, which is usually just an assignment statement.
2. Test the conditional expression for a true or false result.
3. Perform the body of the loop if the conditional is true.
4. Perform the `countExpression`, which usually is an increment or decrement operation.
5. Go back to step 2.

When the conditional is tested and found to be false, Visual C++ stops looping and the program continues at the statement following the `for` loop. As with `while`, never put a semicolon right after the `for` statement's parentheses. However, semicolons are required inside the parentheses. Until now, you've never seen semicolons inside a statement. The `for` loop is the only statement that requires such semicolon placement.

If the body of the `for` statement contains a single statement, the braces aren't required. But, as with the `while` loops, braces are recommended even when the body contains only a single statement.

 Tip   You'll see that the semicolons inside the `for` statement aren't all that strange. Semicolons always terminate executable statements, and the `startExpression` and the `conditional` are individual statements inside `for`. The `for`'s two semicolons help separate the three statements inside the parentheses.

Definition—A *control variable* is a variable controlled and changed automatically by the `for` loop.

After reading through the action of `for` loops, you might feel as if they're just complicated `while` loops that are controlled by a conditional statement just as the `while` loops are. The `for` loop, however, is slightly different from either of the `while` loops, not only in its syntax but also in the way that it updates its important loop control variable for you.

 Tip   Can you see that indenting the body of the `for` loop, as you did with the `while` loops, makes the body of the loop stand out? You can tell at a glance where the loop body begins and ends.

Here is a sample `for` loop:

```
for (i = 1; i <= 10; i++)
  {
    cout << i << endl;
  }
```

When Visual C++ gets to this `for` loop, it writes the following output to the screen:

```
1
2
3
4
5
6
7
8
9
10
```

Visual C++ automatically updates the integer i each time the `for` loop executes. The body of this `for` loop executes exactly 10 times, hence the 10 lines in the output. Here are the parts of this `for` loop:

```
startExpression: i = 1

conditional: i <= 10

countExpression: i++
```

Next are the five actions of the `for` loop applied to this specific loop. Follow the actions listed here and you'll see how Visual C++ produced the numbers from 1 to 10:

1. Assigns 1 to the variable i. This two-line `for` loop assumes that you've already defined an integer variable named i. Visual C++ executes this `startExpression` only once before the loop begins.

2. Visual C++ tests the conditional, i <= 10, to see whether it's true or false. The first time Visual C++ enters the loop, i is 1 (due to the assignment just made in step 1) and the conditional is true, so Visual C++ executes the body of the loop.

3. The statement inside the loop body executes, the first time printing a 1 for i.

4. The `countExpression` executes, adding 1 to i, so that it stores a 2 in i.

5. Visual C++ goes back to step 2, testing the conditional again and executing the body of the loop nine more times until i contains 11. At that point, Visual C++ terminates the loop and the program continues.

Here is an equivalent `while` loop:

```
i = 1;
while (i <= 10)
  {
    cout << i << endl;
    i++;
  }
```

The while doesn't really require less typing than the equivalent for. The increment of i resides in the body of the while instead of in the loop's first statement as it does in the for. Also, the initial value of i must be set before Visual C++ ever begins the while loop, whereas the first line of the for initializes i to its first value.

The biggest difference between while and for is that you can tell at a glance, in a single statement, how Visual C++ controls for, whereas you must do more searching to find the controlling values of a while loop.

 Note   The for loop is not a good loop to use for input validation, but the while loops are good for this purpose, as you discovered in the previous unit. for is better when you know in advance exactly how many times you want a loop to execute. In the previous for loop, the body of the loop executed exactly 10 times, with the expressions inside the for statement controlling the 10 executions.

Figure 11.3 helps show the action of the for loop. The line traces the loop's execution path. Notice that the startExpression executes only once. Also, the loop's test is at the top, similar to a while loop's (but not a do-while loop, which tests at the bottom of the loop), meaning that there is a chance that the body of the for loop might never execute.

```
for (i=1;i<=10;i++)

    {
      cout <<i<<'\n';



    }
```

Figure 11.3.
The execution path of a
for loop.

If the conditional is false to begin with, as the following for statement's is, the body of the loop never executes:

```
for (i = 15; i <= 10; i++)     // The conditional is false from the start
   {
      cout << "This cout never executes!!";
   }
```

When this loop first begins, Visual C++ stores a 15 in i. The conditional test, i <= 10, is false, so Visual C++ terminates the loop and continues the program right after the loop without ever executing the body of the loop.

Tip   Visual C++ lets you define variables right before you use them for the first time. Therefore, if you need a control variable for only one for loop, you might consider defining that variable inside the for statement as done here:

```
for (int i=0; c<10; i++)    // Notice the int
```

STOP&TYPE Listing 11.3 contains a program that asks the user for five values, averages those values, and prints the average. A for loop ensures that the user is asked for the five values.

Review
What You Have Learned

The for loop initializes and increments control variables for you so that you can execute a loop a specific number of times.

▼ INPUT LISTING 11.3. USING A LOOP TO COMPUTE THE USER'S AVERAGE.

```
 1:// Filename: FORAVG.CPP
 2:// A for loop asks the user for five values.
 3:// As the user enters each value, a compound
 4:// assignment statement adds the values.
 5:// After all five values have been entered and
 6:// the loop ends, the program prints an average.
 7:#include <iostream.h>
 8:
 9:void main()
10: {
11:    float value, avg;
12:    float total = 0;
13:
14:    cout << endl << "** An Average Program **"
15:         << endl << endl;
16:
17:    // Loop five times
18:    for (int count = 0; count < 5; count++)
19:      {
20:        cout << "What is the next value? ";
21:        cin >> value;
22:        total += value;   // Add to the total variable
23:      }
24:
25:    // Now, compute and print the average
26:    avg = total / 5.0F;
27:    cout.precision(1);
28:    cout.setf(ios::fixed);
29:    cout.setf(ios::showpoint);
30:    cout << endl << "The average of your values is "
31:         << avg << endl;
32:    return;
33: }
```

UNIT

11

What while Is for

▼ OUTPUT

```
** An Average Program **

What is the next value? 34.5
What is the next value? 65.4
What is the next value? 78.9
What is the next value? 76.5
What is the next value? 43.2

The average of your values is 59.7
```

▼ ANALYSIS

The for loop on line 18 is similar to many that you'll see. This loop iterates exactly five times, as controlled by the loop's control variable, count. count begins at 0, and then continues incrementing each time through the loop until its value reaches 5. The conditional statement, count < 5, is then false and the loop terminates. Execution of the program then continues at line 24.

What if you wanted to average more than five values? You would have to change only two statements. You would have to change line 18's conditional statement to test for a value other than 5 and change the average calculation on line 26 because you could no longer divide by 5.

 Tip   To make the program even easier to change and update, change line 26 to this:

```
avg = total / count;
```

To change the number of average values now, you only need to change the loop's conditional test. When line 19's for loop finishes, count always holds the number of values that the user entered. To make the program even more maintainable, don't even conditionally test against a numeric literal on line 19. Instead, define a constant variable at the top of the program as done here:

```
const int NUMBER = 5;
```

Then make the for loop's conditional statement compare against the named constant:

```
for (count = 0; count < NUMBER; count++)
```

After you change the program as suggested here, you'll need to change only one line, the const, to make the program work with a different number of values.

▶ Further Control with *countExpression*

What You Will Learn

for loops don't have to increment. You can decrement the loop control variable as well as update the control variable with a value different from 1.

The third part of the for statement, the countExpression in parentheses, doesn't always have to increment the control variable. Inside the countExpression, you can decrement or update the control variable by any value your application requires. Consider the following for loop:

```
for (i = 10; i >= 1; i--)
  {
    cout << i << endl;
  }
cout << "Blast off!" << endl;
```

Notice that the control variable i begins at 10, not 0 or 1 as has been the case previously. The conditional statement stays true as long as i remains greater than or equal to 1. The countExpression decrements i. Here is the output from this loop and the subsequent cout:

```
10
9
8
7
6
5
4
3
2
1
Blast off!
```

You must be sure to initialize the control variables properly. The for loop is a compact way to initialize, test, and control a loop in a single statement.

One interesting thing to note is that the for loop's parentheses don't have to hold all three expressions. For example, instead of

```
for (num = 2; num <= 40; num += 2)
```

you can do this:

```
num = 2;
for ( ; num <= 40; )
```

```
{   // Body of loop goes here
  num += 2;    // Increment the control variable in the loop
}
```

Taking the expressions out of the for statement is sometimes warranted, especially when the user initializes the control variable's starting value with cin instead of your program initializing the value with an assignment statement. Nevertheless, for most uses of for loops, place all three expressions inside the for parentheses so that all control information is available at a glance in one statement.

► Homework
General Knowledge

1. What is a loop?

2. What's the difference between a loop and an infinite loop?

3. If your program enters an infinite loop, how can you stop the execution?

4. Why should you never put a semicolon at the end of the while loop's parentheses?

5. Why is it recommended that you put braces around the while and do-while loop bodies?

6. Which is better for looping a specific number of times: a while loop, a for loop, or a do-while loop?

7. How does a for loop differ from a while loop?

8. How does the format of a for loop help you spot the entire control of the loop in a single statement?

9. When are braces required around a for loop's body?

10. What happens when the conditional expression in a for loop becomes false?

11. True or false: The body of a do-while loop might never execute.

12. True or false: A for loop's body might never execute.

13. True or false: The semicolons inside the for loop are optional.

14. True or false: Visual C++ tests the for's condition before the first iteration of the loop.

What's the Output?

15. How many times do the letters abc print in the following code?

```
int c = 1;
while (c < 20)
```

```
    { cout << "abc" << endl;
      c++;
    }
```

16. How many times do the letters `abc` print in the following code?

```
int c = 0;
while (c <= 20)
    { cout << "abc" << endl;
      c++;
    }
```

17. What's the output of the following section of code?

```
for (c = 0; c <= 10; c += 3)
    { cout << c; }
```

18. What's the output of the following `for` loop? Will an error occur?

```
for (i = 5; i; i--)
    {
      cout << i << " "  << endl;
    }
```

Find the Bug

19. Can you find anything wrong with the following loop?

```
a = 10; b = 4;
while (a >= 10)
    { cout << "a is now " << a << endl;
      b += 2;
      cout << "b is now " << b << endl;
    }
```

20. Carl the Visual C++ coder wants to print a special warning message 10 times if his company's costs get too high. Carl coded the following, but the results aren't working exactly as he expected:

```
if (costs >= 25000.00)
    {  count = 0;
       while (count < 10)
         cout << "** Please lower costs immediately **"
              << endl;
         count++;
    }
```

Help Carl fix the problem.

Write Code That...

21. Write a program that defines a character array 80 bytes long. Ask the user for his or her first name (80 bytes is more than enough to hold anyone's response). Using an integer variable and a `while` loop, find the length of the user's name (the string's length). Hint: Add one to the integer variable each time through the loop and stop when you get to the terminator (`'\0'`). Note: The string length variable is a counter variable.

22. Use a `for` loop to print the letters of the alphabet in uppercase. To do this, use a character variable, initialize it (within the `for`) with `'A'`, and increment it using `++`. Although applying `++` to a character variable might seem wrong, remember that because Visual C++ maintains a close relationship between character variables and integer variables, you can interchange simple operations between them.

Extra Credit

23. Write a number-guessing game. Store an integer in a variable. Ask the user to guess the number between 1 and 100. If he guesses the variable's value, congratulate him. If he doesn't guess the value, give him a clue (higher or lower) and ask again. If the guess is 0, stop the program. (Hint: the checking will have to check two conditions, whether the guess was 0, or whether the guess was correct).

12

Controlling Loops and Branching

nesting

branch

break

continue

goto

▶ **What You'll Learn**

▶ Nested loops

▶ Terminating `for` early

▶ `break`

▶ `continue` as opposed to `break`

▶ (Not) using `goto`

This unit offers a variation on a theme. Because loops are themselves C++ statements, you'll find that loops can contain other loops. You'll see how to use the `break` statement to make an early exit from a `for` or `while` loop. With a new command, `continue`, you'll also learn about the opposite of `break`. The `continue` statement tells Visual C++ to continue with a loop a little earlier than it normally would iterate the loop.

In addition to the looping control that you've mastered, Visual C++ also includes another command named `goto`. Many veteran C++ programmers agree that `goto` isn't useful when it's overused, but you need to know how to code `goto` statements in case you run across them someday.

▶ **Nested Loops**

Concept   **What You Will Learn**

When you nest loops, one loop can control another, amplifying the power of loops.

Whenever you need to repeat a loop several times, put the loop inside another loop. Many newcomers to programming often find nested `for` loops to be a little tricky, but there is really nothing to them.

Perhaps an analogy to the real world would help introduce the concept of nested `for` loops. Your car's odometer is similar to five or six nested `for` loops, each going from 0 to 9. The far-right number iterates the fastest, visibly moving from 0 to 9 as you drive down the road. A `for` loop that tracked that right number would be nothing more than this:

```
for (tenth = 0; tenth <= 9; tenth++)
  { cout << tenth << endl; }
```

The far-right number (either a tenth-of-a-mile indicator or a tenth-of-a-kilometer indicator, depending on your country) isn't the only number that moves. All the others do so, but at a slower rate. For every 10 values that move in the tenth-of-a-mile indicator, one of the mile indicators moves. In other words, a nested loop that looks something like this controls the two far-right numbers:

```
for (miles = 0; miles <= 9; miles++)
  {
    for (tenth = 0; tenth <= 9; tenth++)
      { cout << miles << tenth; }
  }
```

What about the number that is third from the right? The tens indicator, which tells you how many tens of miles you've traveled, is yet another loop that iterates once for each of the miles iterations, like this:

```
for (tens = 0; tens <= 9; tens++)
  {
    for (miles = 0; miles <= 9; miles++)
      {
        for (tenth = 0; tenth <= 9; tenth++)
          { cout << tens << miles << tenths << endl; }
      }
  }
```

However many digits your odometer contains is the number of nested loops required to imitate the odometer.

Note When you nest `for` loops, the outside loop always loops slower than the inside loops, just as the far-right digits of your odometer change faster than the far-left ones. The outer loop changes only after the inner loop completely finishes.

Figure 12.1 shows how you can picture inside and outside loops. The nested loop at the bottom actually contains two separate `for` loops nested inside an outer loop. Both of the two nested loops completely finish their respective iterations before the outside loop iterates again. When the outside loop changes, the two inner loops start from the beginning to loop again.

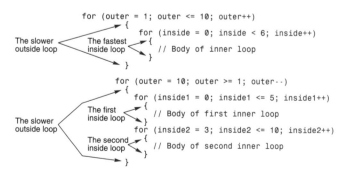

Figure 12.1.
Two kinds of nested loops.

STOP&TYPE The program in Listing 12.1 contains two nested loops.

Review   **What You Have Learned**

Embedding one loop in another produces a nested loop. Nested loops let you execute a loop more than once (a loop of loops).

▼ INPUT   LISTING 12.1. TWO NESTED LOOPS.

```
 1:// Filename: NESTFOR.CPP
 2:// Two nested loops
 3:#include <iostream.h>
 4:void main()
 5:{
 6:   int inner, outer;
 7:
 8:   // One loop nested in another
 9:   cout << "Showing the loop control variables:" << endl;
10:   cout << "Outer   Inner" << endl;
11:   for (outer = 0; outer < 2; outer++)
12:     {
13:       for (inner = 0; inner <= 3; inner++)
14:         {
15:           // The '\t' outputs a tab character
16:           cout << outer << '\t' << inner << endl;
17:         }
18:     }
19:
20:   cout << endl;   // Blank line between loop outputs
21:
22:   cout << "Here is a loop from 1 to 10, printed three times:" << endl;
23:   for (outer = 0; outer < 3; outer++)
24:     {
25:       for (inner = 1; inner <= 10; inner++)
26:         {
27:           cout << inner << ' ';
28:         }
29:       cout << endl;   // Executes once each outer iteration
30:     }
31:
32:   return;
33:}
```

▼ OUTPUT

```
Showing the loop control variables:
Outer   Inner
0       0
0       1
```

```
0      2
0      3
1      0
1      1
1      2
1      3
```

```
Here is a loop from 1 to 10, printed three times:
1 2 3 4 5 6 7 8 9 10
1 2 3 4 5 6 7 8 9 10
1 2 3 4 5 6 7 8 9 10
```

▼ ANALYSIS

By seeing printed loop control variable values in line 16, you can see how the outer loop variable changes (from 0 to 1) more slowly than the inner loop variable changes (from 0 to 3). The reason that the inner loop changes more rapidly is that the inner loop always completes all its iterations before the outer loop has a chance to iterate again.

The second half of the output shows the values from 1 to 10 being printed. A simple for loop in lines 25 through 28 controls the numbers. However, to print that set of 10 numbers three times, an additional outer loop that iterates three times appears, beginning on line 23.

Note carefully the indentation. This makes it easy to follow where each loop begins and ends. For example, it becomes clear that the end of line marker in line 29 belongs to the outer for loop and only gets executed once for each list of 10 numbers.

 Tip A clock for football makes a useful analogy for nested loops. The quarter clock moves from 15 minutes down to 0. That countdown happens once each quarter. The quarter count from 1 to 4 increments much more slowly than the minute count within each quarter.

 # Take a *break*?

Concept   **What You Will Learn**

The break statement lets you terminate loops before their natural conclusion.

The break command exits the current loop in progress. You use break only inside a loop such as a while, do-while, or for loop. The break exits the execution of the loop only, not the entire program. return exits the entire program (when used in main()), regardless of the loop. Therefore, you can now exit a loop in two ways:

▶ Through the normal termination of the loop when the relational test finally becomes false

▶ Through the termination of the loop through the use of the `break` statement

No matter how your program's loop finishes, the rest of the program will continue as usual.

Note In DOS programs, there is another function you can call, `exit()`, which immediately stops the program wherever it is. (You need to include STDLIB.H to use `exit()`. `return` and `break` are C++ commands that do not need headers.) Figure 12.2 shows the actions of `return`, `exit()`, and `break`.

```
// An outline of a program
main()
{
   //
   if (i == 10)
      { exit(1); }  ◄─────── Exits the program

   //
   while (a < b)
   { if (i >= 35)
         break;  ◄─────────── Exits the current loop
   }

   //
   if (i <= 120)
      { return 0; }  ◄─┐
                       │
   //                  ├──►  Exits the function
   return 0;  ◄────────┘
}
```

Figure 12.2.
The actions of `return`, `exit()`, and `break`.

Warning `break` terminates only loops and `switch` statements, not `if` statements.

You'll almost always enclose `break` code in `if` blocks. You simply don't write code that always executes `break`. A `break` inside a `while` or `for` loop invalidates the whole use of the loop unless the `break` appears in an `if`. The `if`'s relational test lets the loop continue looping until the conditions are right for breaking out of the loop early.

STOP&TYPE Listing 12.2 contains both a `break` and a `return`. The execution of either depends on the user's response.

Review   **What You Have Learned**

`break` terminates the current loop and `return` terminates the current function.

```
 1:// Filename: BREXIT.CPP
 2:// Demonstrates both break and return
 3:#include <iostream.h>
 4:
 5:void main()
 6:{
 7:  int count=0;
 8:  char ans;
 9:
10:  // The following loop prints "Hi" five times only
11:  // as long as the user keeps requesting the word.
12:  // Whether the user terminates the loop early or
13:  // not, the program continues executing.
14:  while (count < 5)
15:    {
16:      cout << "Hi" << endl;
17:      cout << "Do you want to see it again (Y/N)? ";
18:      cin >> ans;
19:      if ( ans == 'N' || ans == 'n')
20:        {
21:          break;
22:        }
23:      count++;
24:    }
25:
26:  cout << endl;
27:
28:  // The following loop prints "Bye" five times only
29:  // as long as the user keeps requesting the word.
30:  // The difference here from the previous section
31:  // is that the entire program, not just the loop,
32:  // terminates if the user requests termination.
33:
34:  count = 0;
35:  while (count < 5)
36:    {
37:      cout << "Bye" << endl;
38:      cout << "Do you want to see it again (Y/N)? ";
39:      cin >> ans;
40:      if (ans == 'N' || ans == 'n')
41:        {
42:          return; // Exit current function
43:        }
44:      count++;
45:    }
46:
47:  // The following cout executes ONLY if the user let
48:  // the previous loop execute to its natural termination
```

UNIT

12

Controlling Loops and Branching

continues

```
49:  cout << "That's all, folks!" << endl;
50:
51:  return;   // Return to QuickWin
52:}
```

▼ OUTPUT

```
Hi
Do you want to see it again (Y/N)? y
Hi
Do you want to see it again (Y/N)? Y
Hi
Do you want to see it again (Y/N)? y
Hi
Do you want to see it again (Y/N)? y
Hi
Do you want to see it again (Y/N)? y
Bye
Do you want to see it again (Y/N)? y
Bye
Do you want to see it again (Y/N)? y
Bye
Do you want to see it again (Y/N)? N
```

▼ ANALYSIS

The top of the output shows the user letting the while loop continue until its natural conclusion (after five iterations). The test in lines 19 and 40 allows users to answer in upper or lowercase, although if they type anything but an n, the program will continue. If the user enters n or N in response to the question, the break executes, terminating the while loop on line 24. (The if being placed after the output keeps the break from executing the first time through the loop.)

The second part of the program contains a similar set of lines that print Bye until the user enters n or N (line 40), or until the loop finishes execution after five iterations. If the user terminates the loop early, the return in line 42 makes sure that the program terminates completely and the cout in line 49 never gets a chance to execute. If the user doesn't terminate the loop early in response to the question in line 40, line 49's cout executes because the return never executes.

> *Note*   The break statement also forces an early exit from a for loop.

In Unit 11, you saw how the for statement controls loops a specific number of times via the loop's control variable. The for statement does a lot for you. It initializes the control variable, tests the condition, and updates the control variable each time through the loop. You often use the for loop when you want a loop to execute a specific number of times. Depending on the data or the user's input, however, your program might have to terminate the for loop a little early. Using break inside an if statement gives you that early termination in the same way as in the while statement.

Although the following for loop appears to execute 10 times, the first iteration doesn't even complete due to the break:

```
for (i = 0; i < 10; i++)
  {
    break;   // Tell Visual C++ to ignore the remaining iterations
    cout << i << endl;
  }
```

break terminates for loops in the same manner that it terminates while loops. When you write nested loops, a break statement terminates only the loop it resides in, not any surrounding outer loops. In other words, break forces Visual C++ to break out of the current loop, reentering the body of the next-outermost loop:

```
for (out = 0; out < 10; out++)
  { for (in = 0; in < 5; in++)
    { if ((in * out) % 2)
        { break; }   // Terminate inner loop if product is odd
      cout << "Looping" << endl;
    }
  }
```

When the product of the inner loop control variable (in) and the outer loop control variable (out) is an even number, the break statement doesn't force Visual C++ to terminate both loops because break terminates only the current loop. Because the break resides in the innermost loop, the innermost loop is the one that terminates as a result of the break. Figure 12.3 shows how the break works.

Figure 12.3.
Breaking out of the current loop.

```
for (out = 0; out < 10; out++)
  { for (in = 0; in < 5; in++)
    { if ((in * out) % 2)
        { break; }                    Terminate the inner
      cout <<'\x07';   // Ring the bell    loop and perform
                                         another outer loop
    }                                    iteration
  }
```

 STOP&TYPE Listing 12.3 contains a simple program that asks the user for his or her dog's name. The program then prints the name 10 times. The user can terminate the loop early by triggering the break.

Review

What You Have Learned

break causes the current loop to quit early.

UNIT

12

Controlling Loops and Branching

▼ **INPUT   LISTING 12.3. USING** break **IF THE USER WANTS TO QUIT THE LOOP EARLY.**

```
1:// Filename: FORBREAK.CPP
2:// Prints a dog's name 10 times
3:// (or less if the user dictates)
4:#include <iostream.h>
5:void main()
6:{
7:  char ans;          // Will hold a Y or N answer
8:  int count;         // The loop control variable
9:  char dName[25];    // Will hold the dog's name
10:
11:  cout << "What is your dog's name? ";
12:  cin >> dName;
13:
14:  cout << "I'll now print the name ten times (maybe)..." << endl;
15:
16:  for (count = 0; count < 10; count++)
17:    { cout << dName << endl;
18:      cout << "Do you want to see the name again (Y/N)? ";
19:      cin >> ans;
20:      if ((ans == 'N') || (ans == 'n'))
21:        {
22:          break;  // Terminate early
23:        }
24:    }  // Iterate again if not broken out of the loop
25:
26:  cout << "That's a nice dog!";
27:  return;
28:}
```

▼ **OUTPUT**

```
What is your dog's name? Luke
I'll now print the name ten times (maybe)...
Luke
Do you want to see the name again (Y/N)? Y
Luke
Do you want to see the name again (Y/N)? Y
Luke
Do you want to see the name again (Y/N)? Y
Luke
Do you want to see the name again (Y/N)? N
That's a nice dog!
```

▼ **ANALYSIS**

This program is fairly simple. It asks the user for his or her dog's name in lines 14 and 15. Due to cin's limitations, make sure that you enter only a single name and not a name such as Bow Wow.

Tip You can get more than one word at a time using the `cin.getline()` function call. You'll see examples of this starting in Lesson 7.

As soon as the user enters the dog's name, the program loops 10 times, with the loop control variable `count` moving from 0 to 9 before the `for` loop terminates. Line 16 controls the loop. Inside the loop, however, a question on line 18 asks the user if he or she wants to see the name again. If the user tires of seeing the dog's name before the 10 iterations print, the `break` on line 22 terminates the loop early and the program ends.

▶ *continue* as Opposed to *break*

Concept ▐ **What You Will Learn**

The `continue` statement tells Visual C++ to iterate once again, even if the body of the loop hasn't completed.

Visual C++ contains a `continue` statement, which performs a job that is virtually the opposite of that of the `break` statement. Whereas `break` terminates a loop early, `continue` causes an immediate and new iteration of the current loop. The `continue` always checks the `for` or `while` condition so that the loop will end properly.

Here's a simple example. In the following code fragment, the loop iterates only once due to the `break` statement, and the second `cout` never executes:

```
for (i = 0; i < 5; i++)    // Seems to loop five times
  {
    cout << "Adam " << endl;
    break;
    cout << "Eve " << endl;    // Never executes
}
```

The next code fragment contains the same code, except that a `continue` statement replaces the `break`. Of the two `cout`s, only the first one prints. Unlike the preceding code fragment, however, the `continue` keeps the loop iterating through all of its cycles, unlike `break`, which tells Visual C++ to forget the rest of the iterations:

```
for (i = 0; i < 5; i++)    // Does loop five times
  {
    cout << "Adam " << endl;
    continue;
    cout << "Eve " << endl;    // Never executes
  }
```

UNIT

12

Controlling Loops and Branching

This second code fragment prints Adam five times, but Eve never prints. The continue tells Visual C++ to iterate the loop once again. Of course, on the loop's final iteration (when i is 4), the continue causes the loop to iterate once again, but the loop doesn't iterate because the control variable is used up or past its final value. Figure 12.4 shows the difference between break and continue using these code fragments.

```
for (i = 0; i < 5; i++)  // Seems to loop five times
    { cout <<"Adam \n";
      break; ─────────────
      cout <<"Eve \n";    // Never executes      Terminate the loop
    }
```

```
for (i = 0; i < 5; i++)  // Does loop five times   Another iteration
    { cout <<"Adam \n";
      continue; ─────────
      cout <<"Eve \n" ;   // Never executes
    }
```

Figure 12.4.
continue iterates the loop again, unlike break.

Note   You also can use continue on while loops, just as you can with break.

There might be times when the body of your loop processes data (through calculations and I/O) and—depending on the values of the data—you don't want to process each data value completely. An early continue statement can make sure that the second part of the loop's body doesn't always execute for every data value.

Warning   If you place a break or continue outside an if body, Visual C++ displays a warning message telling you that there is unused code in your program if any code follows the break or continue. Therefore, programs you compile with loops, such as the ones contained in the previous code fragments, result in compiler warnings because Visual C++ knows that the second cout never executes. If, however, you place the break or continue statement inside an if's body, Visual C++ doesn't display the warnings because the break and continue will change the loop's execution only when the if's conditional is true.

Note   As with break, if you place a continue inside a nested loop, the continue executes another iteration of the current innermost loop, not the outer loop.

STOP&**TYPE** Listing 12.4 contains a program that asks the user for five values that repre-sent each day's sales. A `for` loop ensures that only five values are asked for. As the user enters the five values, the body of the `for` loop totals the sales for the week. Not all weeks will have five days' worth of sales, however. If the week had a holiday, the user should enter -99 for that day's sales, which triggers the `continue` statement.

Review **What You Have Learned**

`continue` forces an early iteration of the loop.

▼ **INPUT   LISTING 12.4. `continue` LETS THE PROGRAM CONTROL THE EXECUTION OF THE SECOND PART OF A LOOP.**

```
 1:// Filename: CONTINUE.CPP
 2:// Uses continue when data is missing
 3:#include <iostream.h>
 4:
 5:
 6:void main()
 7:{
 8:  int count;          // Loop control variable
 9:  float dSales;       // Will hold each day's sales
10:  float wSales = 0;   // Weekly total
11:
12:  // Set up the loop for a possible five iterations
13:  for (count = 0; count < 5; count++)
14:    {
15:      cout << "Enter the sales for day #" << (count + 1)
16:           << " (-99 for none): ";
17:      cin >> dSales;
18:      if (dSales < 0.0)
19:        { continue; }
20:
21:      // The following statement executes ONLY if a
22:      // valid daily sales total was just entered
23:      wSales += dSales;
24:    }
25:
26:  // Print the week's total
27:  cout.precision(2);
28:  cout.setf(ios::showpoint);
29:  cout.setf(ios::fixed);
30:  cout << endl << "The weekly total is $"
31:       << wSales << endl;
32:  return;
33:}
```

UNIT

12

Controlling Loops and Branching

▼ **OUTPUT**

```
Enter the sales for day #1 (-99 for none): 546.77
Enter the sales for day #2 (-99 for none): -99
Enter the sales for day #3 (-99 for none): 434.56
Enter the sales for day #4 (-99 for none): 886.31
Enter the sales for day #5 (-99 for none): 905.42

The weekly total is $2773.06
```

▼ **ANALYSIS**

This program's continue statement lets the for loop process very intelligently. The for loop in lines 13 through 24 normally executes five times due to the loop control. Each iteration represents a day of the week. The user is to enter each day's sales value when prompted by the cout in lines 15 and 16.

Line 15 adds 1 to count when printing the prompt for each day's sales because line 15's for loop begins at 0, not 1. However, if there is no sales figure for the user to enter (as would be the case for holidays), the user enters -99 and the loop iterates again, getting another value.

As soon as the user enters all the values for the week, the program prints the total weekly sales value on lines 27 through 31 with extra code that ensures that two decimal places will always print.

▶ **Moving Around with** *goto*

	What You Will Learn

goto lets your program execute in any order you desire.

Many Visual C++ programmers write all kinds of Visual C++ programs and never use the goto statement. Old programming languages, especially FORTRAN and the pre-QBasic BASIC languages, don't have enough rich control commands such as while and do-while to eliminate goto entirely.

***N**ote*   In today's world of modern programming languages, goto is rarely used, except when a programmer writes programs in low-level assembly language where goto-like statements are mandatory for many operations.

Definition—A *branch* occurs when one section of a program triggers the execution of a different section.

Visual C++ includes a goto just in case you need one. Before studying goto, keep in mind that you can write any program without goto. Use goto only when its meaning is obvious. goto branches the current program's execution to a different part of the program. In other words, instead of executing a program sequentially, line by line, goto tells Visual C++ what line of your program to execute next.

goto AND MAINTAINABILITY

If you put too many goto statements in your programs, you will soon find that your programs are virtually impossible to follow. Until you learn about goto, all your programs execute in one of two ways:

▶ Sequentially, line-by-line

▶ In a loop, with one or more statements repeating until a condition becomes false

Both of these execution orders are easy to follow, especially if you indent the bodies of your loops. It's very easy to spot where a loop begins and ends. If your program doesn't contain a loop, but instead executes sequentially from top to bottom, it's even easier to follow.

Once you insert goto statements in a program, the program's execution is at the mercy of the goto statements. The execution might jump from one part of the program to another and do so several times. The "need" to use a goto is usually a symptom of bad code.

Here is the format of the goto statement:

```
goto statementLabel;
```

statementLabel follows the same naming rules that variables follow (see Lesson 3 for a review of variable-naming conventions). Here is a sample goto:

```
goto getInput;
```

When Visual C++ encounters this goto, it looks from the top of the current function to the bottom for a statement label named getInput. If Visual C++ doesn't find a statement label named getInput, you get an error message.

A statement label always appears to the left of an executable Visual C++ statement. For example, all of the following statements have statement labels in front of them:

```
getInput: cin >> amount;
here: for (i = 0; i < 10; i++)
```

Notice that a colon (:) always separates a statement from its label.

UNIT

12

Controlling Loops and Branching

Warning   Never put a colon after the label's name in the goto statement. Use a
colon only after the label name when the label appears before code, as
shown in the preceding two statements.

Without the colon, Visual C++ would be confused by a label that is directly before a legal Visual C++ statement. The colon tells Visual C++, "Here is a label, and it appears before a statement." Never put more than one label with the same name in the same function.

When Visual C++ encounters a goto statement, it doesn't continue executing the program on the line following the goto. Instead, Visual C++ transfers control (branches) to the statement label and then continues from there. Unlike loops that always repeat again at the top of the loop, a goto might never come back to its point of origin.

Note   continue, break, and return provide safe methods of implementing a
goto in a program. When you use the correct commands, together with
sensible use of compound statements (blocks), there is really no need to
ever use a goto.

Note   There is no Stop and Type for this section due to the author's dislike of
the goto statement.

▶ Homework
General Knowledge

1. How can you terminate a for loop early?
2. How can your program force an early execution of the loop's next cycle?
3. What's the difference between break and continue?
4. Will break and continue work for while, do-while, and for loops?
5. Which kind of loop—while, do-while, or for—is usually the one that uses continue?
6. What's the difference between return and break?
7. Why should a break fall within an if block instead of residing as regular lines of a Visual C++ program?
8. Why does continue rarely appear without an if preceding it?
9. What does goto do?
10. Why is goto considered a bad programming statement?

11. Which variable controls the inner loop and which controls the outer loop in the following code?

```
for (ctr1 = 10; ctr1 > 5; ctr1-)
  { for (ctr2 = 1; ctr2 < 4; ctr2++)
      { cout << ctr1 << "  " << ctr2; }
  }
```

12. Does the outer loop of two nested loops iterate faster or slower than the inner loop? Why?

13. True or false: There can be more than one label with the same name, but only one goto to that label.

14. True or false: You can't use continue in nested loops.

15. True or false: You can't use break in nested loops.

16. True or false: The break statement requires a header file.

17. True or false: Visual C++ displays a warning message when you compile a program that has a break or continue.

18. True or false: When you nest loops, continue terminates the execution of the inner loop only.

What's the Output?

19. How many times does x print?

```
for (count = 0; count < 5; count++)
  {
    cout << 'X';
    break;
  }
```

20. How many times does x print?

```
for (count = 0; count < 5; count++)
  { cout << 'X';
    continue;
  }
```

21. Here's some spaghetti code! What's the output?

```
#include <iostream.h>
void main()
{
  goto a;
e:
  goto f;
c:
  cout << "a" << endl;
  goto d;
b:
  cout << "d" << endl;
  goto c;
```

```
d:
  cout << "c" << endl;
  goto b;
a:
  cout << "b" << endl;
  goto e;
f:
  return;
}
```

22. How many times will an x appear in the following nested for loop?

```
for (outer = 0; outer < 5; outer++)
  { for (inner = 0; inner < 3; inner++)
      { cout << 'X'; }
  }
```

Find the Bug

23. Mary Jo Beth can't get her program working. It seems to be hung up on this statement:

```
goto calcPayroll:
```

Help Mary fix the problem.

24. The following three lines appear together in a program. Although there is nothing technically wrong with the statements, something is unnecessary. What is unnecessary and why?

```
  cin >> rate;
  goto here;
here: pay = rate * hours;
```

25. When Pete's program gets to the following statement, it seems to hang up. Pete has studied the code for several hours without figuring out the problem. Tell him what he's doing wrong (and why he should consider a different career).

```
makeLoop: goto makeLoop;    // Transfer control
```

26. Foster Forsythe is nesting for loops, but they don't seem to be working properly. Will you please help him? Here is the part of the program that is giving him trouble:

```
for (ctr1 = 1; ctr1 <= 10; ctr1++);
  { for (ctr2 = 1; ctr2 <= 5; ctr2++)
    { value = ctr1 * ctr2;
      cout << value << endl;
    }
  }
```

27. Rewrite the following code using a do-while statement:

```
AskAgain:
  cout << "What is your first name? ";
  cin >> fName;
  if ((fName[0] < 'A') || (fName[0] > 'Z'))
    { goto AskAgain; }    // Make sure user enters a word
                          // and not special characters
```

Write Code That...

28. Write a program that asks the user for four weekly sales values. Add to a sales total as the user enters a new value and print the total sales after the user enters all four values. Just in case the store closes for repairs one week, see whether the user enters a negative value for a sales figure. If so, terminate the sales entry early and average the number of weeks the user actually entered.

29. Rewrite Listing 12.4 (CONTINUE.CPP) so that the loop terminates completely when the user enters -1 for a daily sales figure. The loop will now have both a break and a continue, and the weekly total will update only if neither the break nor the continue executes. Don't check for an exact match for -1 or -99 because the user enters the daily values as floating-point numbers and you can't accurately test for floating-point equality.

Extra Credit

30. Write a program with two nested loops that produces the following output:
```
ABCD
ABC
AB
A
```

31. Write a program that asks the user for test scores. Enter all test values as integers to keep things simple. The program is to continue until the user enters -99 in order to obtain the average or until she enters five values (there were only five tests this term). If the user enters -99, it means that she took fewer than five tests and is ready for the average early. (Hint: break might help with the early loop termination.) As the user enters each test average, add the average to a total variable and increment a counter variable (the loop's counter variable will work for the test count). As soon as the user enters five values or -99 (indicating that there are no more test scores), compute a floating-point average and print the result. Be sure that you congratulate the user for an average of more than 90 percent!

32. Write a program that asks the user for temperature readings for the last 10 days. Compute the average temperature. If the user enters a temperature below freezing, make sure that a continue causes the program to ignore the reading (average in only temperatures above freezing). Keep track of how many above-freezing temperatures the user enters (via a counter variable) and compute the average based on the number of valid values entered.

Looping Back and Forth

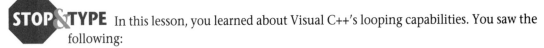 In this lesson, you learned about Visual C++'s looping capabilities. You saw the following:

▶ Loops repeat sections of code.

▶ The while loop tests a condition at the top of the loop and loops as long as the condition is true.

▶ Loops and the if statement differ because the body of an if executes one time at most.

Project 6 Listing. Using a for **loop to compute interest controlled by the user's input.**

```
1:// Filename: PROJECT6.CPP1: A C++ comment that includes the program's filename.

2:// Computes interest over a number of periods

3:#include <iostream.h>

4:#include <iomanip.h>

5:

6:void main()

7:{

8:  int periods;       // Number of periods in the loan

9:  int count;         // Loop control variable

10:  float intRate;     // Interest rate per period

11:  float principal;   // Loan amount

12:
```

▶ The do-while loop tests its condition at the bottom of the loop, ensuring that the loop always executes at least once.

▶ The break statement terminates the current loop.

▶ The for loop gives you more control when you know in advance the number of iterations required by the loop.

▶ When you nest loops, the inner loop iterates faster than the outer loop.

Description

1: A C++ comment that includes the program's filename.

2: A C++ comment that contains the program's description.

3: cout and cin need information in the IOSTREAM.H header file.

4: You need to include iomanip.h.

5: Place blank lines throughout a program for readability.

6: All functions have names, and the first function in all C++ programs is main().

7: All functions begin with a left brace.

8: Defines an integer variable that will hold the number of periods in the loan.

9: Defines an integer variable that will control the for loop.

10: Defines a floating-point variable that will hold the interest rate.

11: Defines a floating-point variable that will hold the loan principal (the amount borrowed).

12: Extra blank lines make your program more readable.

1: You saw another version of this program in Unit 7, but that program didn't have the looping capability that this program does. As a result, Unit 7's program was longer and less flexible!

9: All for loops require a loop control variable.

continues

Project 6 Listing. continued

```
13:  cout << "Welcome to loan central!" << endl;    // Title

14:  cout << "------------------------" << endl << endl;

15:

16:  cout << "How much was the loan for? ";

17:  cin >> principal;

18:

19:  cout << endl << "What is the interest rate (i.e., .03 ";

20:  cout << "for 3%) per period? ";

21:  cin >> intRate;

22:

23:  cout << endl << "How many periods are in the loan? ";

24:  cin >> periods;

25:

26:  for (count = 0; count < periods; count++)

27:    { principal *= (1 + intRate); }    // Compounds the interest

28:

29:  cout.precision(2);

30:  cout.setf(ios::showpoint);
```

Description

13: Prints a title.

14: Underlines the title on-screen with hyphens.

15: Extra blank lines make your program more readable.

16: Prompts the user for the amount of the loan (the principal).

17: Gets the principal from the user.

18: Extra blank lines make your program more readable.

19: Prompts for the interest rate. The user is reminded to enter the interest as a decimal.

20: The rest of line 19's cout.

21: Gets the interest rate.

22: Extra blank lines make your program more readable.

23: Prompts for the number of periods in the loan (called the loan term).

24: Gets the term from the user.

25: Extra blank lines make your program more readable.

26: The for loop ensures that the interest calculation computes for the full term entered by the user in line 25.

26: The for loop compounds the loan in one step.

27: The body of the for loop is only a single statement. The principal increases by the amount of each period's interest rate.

28: Extra blank lines make your program more readable.

29: Ensures that two decimal places print.

30: Prints the decimal point.

continues

Project 6 Listing. continued

```
31:   cout.setf(ios::fixed);

32:   cout << endl << "$" << principal << " total amount owed after "

33:        << periods << " periods." << endl;

34:   return;

35:}
```

Description

31: Guards against scientific notation.

32: Prints the computed loan principal including all accrued interest.

33: Continues the loan balance's printing.

34: Returns to QuickWin control window.

35: main()'s closing brace to terminate the program.

▼ OUTPUT

```
Welcome to loan central!
.......................
How much was the loan for? 2500.00
What is the interest rate (i.e., .03 for 3%) per
period? .11
How many periods are in the loan? 5
$4212.65 total amount owed after 5 periods.
```

Lesson ▶

7

Break It Up with Functions

13

Building Your Own Functions

passing by address

passing by value

prototypes

recursion

structured program

▶ What You'll Learn

- ▶ Separating code
- ▶ Local and global variables
- ▶ Sharing variables among functions

So far, every program you've written has contained one and only one function that you wrote—main(). Visual C++ programs can contain many more functions that you write. The longer your program is, the better it is to break it into several small functions. By following a building-block approach, you separate routines into their own areas and make debugging easier because you can focus on specific problems without letting the rest of the code get in your way.

Writing a function in addition to main() does require a little fancy programming footwork, but writing multiple functions isn't difficult at all.

▶ Separating Code

Concept   **What You Will Learn**

A program with many small functions is a lot easier to maintain than one long program. When writing separate functions, you have to manage the communication between those functions so that they can "talk" to each other.

Why does a book contain separate chapters? For one thing, one long, continuous book would seem to drag on and on. Chapters give the reader breaks, even if the reader starts another chapter right after finishing one. Chapters give the reader a sense of accomplishment.

More important, separate chapters—especially in a technical book such as this one—allow the reader to zero in on specific topics. Suppose that you picked up this book already knowing how to program in Visual C++, but you'd never taken the time to master the switch statement. You wouldn't need to read the entire book. Instead, you could turn directly to Unit 10 and get exactly the information you needed without the rest of the text getting in the way.

Definition—A *structured program* is a modular program that contains one function for each task the program does.

Structured programming becomes a habit when you begin to use it. People are used to breaking large tasks into smaller, more manageable ones. Programs often need to be broken down.

Suppose that you are writing a program that computes and prints payroll figures for employees. As the payroll clerk enters each person's payroll figures, the program should perform input validation, compute payroll results, compute tax amounts, and print the results.

Here is a skeleton version of what such a program might look like:

```
void main()
{
  // This is only an outline of a program
  //
  // Visual C++ code to validate employee data
  //
  // Visual C++ code to calculate payroll amounts
  //
  // Visual C++ code to compute taxes
  //
  // Visual C++ code to print the results
}
```

Note   This program would more likely contain a large loop that continued running until all employee data was entered, validated, and printed, but we're keeping things simple for now.

There's nothing wrong with building a program such as this. For a real-world payroll system, however, this program would be extremely long. If the employee payroll figures were computed incorrectly, you would have to find exactly where in main() the problem occurred. Tracking such a bug would require you to make sure that the input validation code, the calculation code, and the printing code all worked properly.

If, however, you structured the program into separate functions, putting only one task in each function, you could more easily test each routine separately. Changing one routine wouldn't be likely to introduce as many bugs in other areas, as would be the case with one long program.

Tip   Each separate function might be several lines long. The important thing to keep in mind when writing separate functions is that each function should do, at most, one task. As a rule of thumb, each function shouldn't be longer than a single screen's length. If it is any longer, the function probably does too much work and you should break it into more functions.

When you write a function, you must start it with a name, parentheses, and surrounding braces, just like with main(). For example, here is the familiar outline of main():

```
void main()
{
```

```
  // First, define any variables
  // The body of main() goes here
}
```

When writing additional functions, keep this format in mind. Here is the outline of a function called CalcWages():

```
void CalcWages()
{
  // First, define any variables
  // The body of CalcWages() goes here
}
```

You never explicitly call the main() function. The runtime system always begins at the main() function. However, if you want to execute (or call, in Visual C++ terminology) another function in your program, you call that function by name. In fact, you have already seen this when using the string copy (strcpy) and string length (strlen) functions in Unit 6. For example, if you want main() to call the CalcWages() function, main() could do so with this statement:

```
CalcWages();    // Call the CalcWages() function
```

After CalcWages() finished, main() would regain control and continue on its way. Of course, any function can call any other function. After main() calls a function, that called function might in turn call yet another function.

 Tip

In really good programs (the ones that you write), main() should be little more than a controlling function for the other functions. In other words, main() should contain very few Visual C++ statements other than function calls to other functions. In a way, main() acts like a table of contents for your program, controlling the execution of the rest of the code. If you need to change the program later, main() gives you the "big picture" that shows you how the rest of the program operates.

One additional advantage of separate functions is that you can call a routine more than once from different places in the program. For example, if you wanted to print your company's name and address at the top of every screen and report produced by a program, you could write a single function named PrintCompanyInfo() and call it from anywhere in the program in which the company information needed to appear.

Note   As you saw with main(), the function call should be described with a *return type*. When a return type is void, it means that no data is returned. This will be covered later in the next unit, for now just accept that function definitions start with void.

STOP&TYPE Listing 13.1 contains a version of the payroll program described earlier. Instead of having one long main() function, this program is broken into several separate functions, each of which accomplishes a single task.

Review **What You Have Learned**

Break your programs into several small functions to aid in debugging and to decrease the number of bugs.

Warning Listing 13.1 isn't a working program, only the outline of one.

▼ **INPUT   LISTING 13.1. AN OUTLINE OF A STRUCTURED PAYROLL PROGRAM.**

```
 1: void main()
 2: {
 3:   // This is only an outline of a program
 4:   //
 5:   GetInput();    // Get and validate the input data
 6:   CalcWages();   // Calculate the payroll results
 7:   CalcTaxes();   // Calculate the payroll taxes
 8:   PrintResults();  // Print the results
 9:   return;        // Return to the IDE
10: }
11:
12: //********************************************
13: void GetInput()
14: {
15:   // Visual C++ code to validate employee data
16:   return;   // Return to main()
17: }
18:
19: //********************************************
20: void CalcWages()
21: {
22:   // Visual C++ code to calculate payroll amounts
23:   return;   // Return to main()
24: }
25:
26: //********************************************
27: void CalcTaxes()
28: {
29:   // Visual C++ code to compute taxes
30:   return;   // Return to main()
31: }
```

continues

```
32:
33: //************************************************
34: void PrintResults()
35: {
36:   // Visual C++ code to print the results
37:   return;   // Return to main()
38: }
```

 Note   There is no output for Listing 13.1 because the program is incomplete as shown.

▼ ANALYSIS

Look at main() (lines 1 through 10). It controls the flow of the rest of the program. You can glance at main() and tell what the rest of the code does without wading through the rest of the code! Of course, using meaningful function names and ample comments helps make main() a true "control panel" that describes the rest of the code.

After the program is broken into separate functions, the code is certainly longer than the all-in-one function version you saw earlier. However, brevity isn't the key to structured programs—readability is.

In this listing, main() is the only function shown that calls another function. However, that doesn't have to be the case. Any of the subsequent functions could call any other function. The separating asterisk comments aren't required, but they do help you find where each function begins and ends.

Definition—*Recursion* occurs when one function calls itself or when two functions call each other.

 Warning   As with infinite loops, you can get into trouble if a function calls itself, or if function A calls function B and function B then calls function A. Recursive techniques can be helpful in advanced programming, but for now you'll want to stay away from them. (You'll be *cursing* your *recursive* programs!) If you write recursive functions without knowing exactly how to eliminate infinite recursion calls, you'll get a runtime error called *stack overflow*. Believe me, you don't want to overflow your stack!

▶ **Local and Global Variables**

Concept

Variables have either local or global scope. Their scope determines whether or not another function can use them.

Definition—A *local variable* can be used only within the block in which you define it.

All variables that you've defined in this book have been local variables. In other words, if you were to define a variable after `main()`'s opening brace, another function couldn't use that variable for anything. Only `main()` could use it. Perhaps you can see a problem: If separate functions are better than one long function, how can those functions work with the same data? If the user enters payroll values in one function, how can another function calculate with those values?

Definition—A *block* is code between braces.

The concept of a block becomes important when discussing local variables. Variables aren't local to functions, but variables are local to blocks. For example, all the variables you've defined so far have been local to `main()` simply because you defined them at the top of `main()`'s primary block. A function always contains at least one pair of braces; therefore, a function always contains at least one block.

You can define variables at the top of any block, not just at the top of a function. When the block ends, all variables defined at the top of that block go away forever! When a block ends, all variables defined at the top of that block disappear and can never be used again unless you define them again elsewhere and reinitialize the variable with a new value.

Consider the following `main()` function:

```
void main()
{
  int i = 9;       // Local to main()'s large block
  cout << "i is " << i << endl;
    {                 // Begin a new block
      int j = 17;   // Local to this block only
      cout << "j is " << j << endl;
    }               // j goes away!
  cout << "i and j are " << i
      << " and " << j << endl;   // Error!!!
  return;
}                // i goes away here!
```

`i` is local to the entire `main()` function because it's defined right after `main()`'s opening brace. `i` doesn't go away until its block ends at the end of `main()`. Therefore, from `main()`'s opening brace to its matching closing brace, `i` is active and is said to be visible.

j is a different story. Notice that the code doesn't define j until a new block begins. j is defined at the top of main()'s inner block; therefore, j is available (visible) only within that block. At the location of the inner block's closing brace, j disappears, causing an error on the subsequent cout that occurs right before return.

You might not be opening new blocks in the middle of a function and defining new variables inside them as done here, but it's vital that you understand the following:

▶ All local variables are available from their point of definition down in whatever block they appear in.

▶ When a block ends, all the variables defined in that block go away completely.

▶ An outer block's variables are always visible to a nested block, unless they are hidden by an identically named variable declared in the nested block.

Definition—A *global variable* is visible throughout the rest of the program.

The opposite of a local variable is a global variable. At first, it seems as if global variables are the answer for multifunction programs, because they let more than one function see the same variable. However, global variables lend themselves to sloppy programming practices, so you should avoid defining too many of them.

You must define a global variable before a function begins. That is, you must define the variable before a function name or between two functions (after one function's closing brace and before another's beginning line). If you define global variables, it is good practice to define all of them before main() even though Visual C++ lets you define them later between other functions. Putting all your global variable definitions in one location helps you find them later.

All global variables are visible from their point of definition down in the source code. That is, after you define a global variable, any statement in any function that follows that global variable will be able to use it. The global variable won't go away until the program ends.

Warning   You can't use a global variable before its definition.

The problem with global variables is that they're too visible. All functions that follow their definition can access the global variables whether they need to or not. Local variables keep data on a need-to-know basis. Only functions that define local variables can use them, but any function can use visible global variables. One problem with global variables is that you can too easily change a global variable in one function and then inadvertently reinitialize that variable in another function. Also, global variables are sometimes difficult to find. If you define global variables at the top of a 20-page program, and you're working in the middle of that program, you'll have to flip back and forth from the beginning to the middle to see how those variables were defined. When you use local variables, their definitions always appear close to their usage.

All this discussion of local and global variables presents the following problem: With rare exceptions, you should use only local variables, but doing so keeps other functions that need access to those variables from using them. Luckily, you can teach Visual C++ to share data between only those functions that need access to certain variables. You'll learn how Visual C++ shares data between specific functions in the next section.

It is time to correct something that was said earlier in the book. With local scope, it is quite acceptable to use the same name in the program several times, as long as the scope is different. This doesn't mean that using the same name all the time is efficient or necessarily a good idea. Instead, it is a rule, which means that you can write a function without worrying about names used elsewhere in the program. For example, when writing loops, tradition has it that the loop counter is called i. It would be very inconvenient if every for loop you write had to invent a new counter name. However, if you call a function that also uses a for loop using i, the program needs to know that the i you refer to is the local i and not the calling function's i.

A further complication is that C++ does not stop you reusing a name in a new block that has already been declared. The rule is that where there is a duplicate name, C++ will use the nearest declaration. Look at the following example:

```
#include <iostream.h>
void main()
  {
    int counter = 0;
      { // a new block
        int counter = 5;
        counter++;
      }
    cout << counter;
    return;
  }
```

In this snippet of code, the increment (++) is applied to the new block counter. This variable then disappears and cannot be seen by the main counter. So the result of the code snippet is to print:

0

Note   When a name is reused, the type can be different.

STOP&TYPE Listing 13.2 contains a program with both local and global variables.

Review

Local variables are safe, but they're visible only within the block in which you define them. Global variables often are messy and lead to program bugs, but they allow for mass sharing of data.

▼ INPUT   LISTING 13.2. A SIMPLE PROGRAM WITH THREE GLOBAL AND THREE LOCAL VARIABLES.

```
1:// Filename: LOCGLO.CPP
2:// Defines six variables, two local and two global
3:// and one both local and global
4: #include <iostream.h>
5:
6: // Define two global variables
7: int global1 = 10;   // Global variables can be any data
8: int global2 = 20;   // type, just as local variables can be
9: int both1   = 30;   // a global variable
10:
11: void main()
12: {
13:   int local1 = 14;
14:
15:   // The next line shows that globals are available
16:   cout << "At the top of main(), " << endl;
17:   cout << "The globals are " << global1 << ", " << global2
18:       << " and " << both1 << endl;
19:   cout << "The local variable local1 is " << local1 << endl;
20:
21:   // Create a new block
22:   {
23:     int local2 = 21;   // Local to this block only
24:     int both1 = 90;    // Local to this block only
25:                        // It hides global both1
26:     cout << endl <<"In main()'s inner block, the globals are";
27:                        // Globals are still available
28:     cout << " " << global1 << " and " << global2 << endl;
29:
30:     cout << "Printing both1 sees the local variable "
31:         << both1 << endl;
32:
33:     cout << "The local variable local1 is "
34:         << local1 << endl;
35:     cout << "The local variable local2 is "
36:         << local2 << endl;
37:
38:     both1++;
39:     cout << "The increment only sees local both1 - now "
40:         << both1 << endl;
41:
42:     cout << "(local2 and local both1 about to disappear...)"
```

```
43:          << endl;
44:    }   // This terminates all valid use of local2
45:        // and the local version of both1
46:
47:    cout << "Toward the end of main(), the globals are";
48:    cout << " " << global1 << ", " << global2
49:          << " and " << both1 << endl;
50:
51:    cout << "See how global both1 was not affected by the ++"
52:          << endl;
53:
54:    cout << "The local variable local1 is " << local1 << endl;
55:    cout << "The local local2 and local both1 "
56:          << "are no longer valid.";
57:
58:    return;
59: }   // All variables go away at end of execution
```

▼ OUTPUT

```
At the top of main(),
The globals are 10, 20 and 30
The local variable local1 is 14

In main()'s inner block, the globals are 10 and 20
Printing both1 sees the local variable 90
The local variable local1 is 14
The local variable local2 is 21
The increment only sees local both1 - now 91
(local2 and local both1 about to disappear...)
Toward the end of main(), the globals are 10, 20 and 30
See how global both1 was not affected by the ++
The local variable local1 is 14
The local local2 and local both1 are no longer valid.
```

▼ ANALYSIS

Figure 13.1 helps to show where each of the variables in Listing 13.1 is defined and where each loses its visibility. It's important to note that if the program contained additional functions below main(), the global variables global1 and global2 would be fully visible to those functions.

After main()'s inner block finishes in line 44, local2 goes away completely. The program defines local2 at the top of the inner block, right after the opening brace in line 23, and local2 goes away when the block ends (where the matching closing brace appears in line 44). local1 exists for the whole of main. global1 and global2 exist for a slightly longer time, from just before main starts to just after main ends.

both1 is first declared as a global variable in line 9. In the outer main block, only the global both1 exists, and this is printed out in line 18. The second declaration of both1 in line

24 does not destroy the original declaration of line 9. This is shown by the increment in line 38, which sees the local both1. The program prints the changed value in line 40. The local both1 disappears at the end of the inner block in line 44, and you can see in line 49 that the original both1 is affected by neither the local declaration in line 24 nor the increment in line 38.

```
                                  // Define 2 glogbal variables
                                  int g1 = 10; // Global variables can be any data
                                  int g2 = 20; // type just as local variables can be
        Two                                   First local created
        globals                   { void main()
        created                     int 11 = 14;
                                    clrscr();


                                  // the next line shows that globals are available
                                  cout << "At the top of main(), \n";
                                  cout << "The globals are " <<g1 << " and " << g2 << '\n';
                                  cout << "The local variable 11 is "<<11<<'\n';

        Second                    // Create a new block
        local                     {
        created                     int 12 = 21; // Local to this block only
                                    cout << "\nIn main()'s inner block, the globals are";The
                                    cout<<" "<<g1<<" and "<<g2 <<'\n'; // Still available
                                    cout << "The local variable 11 is " << 11 << '\n';     inner
                                    cout << "The local variable 12 is " << 12 << '\n';     block
                                    cout << "(11 is about to disappear...)\n\n";
        Second                    } // This terminates all valid use of 12
        local
        goes away                 cout << "Towards the end of main, the globals are";
                                  cout<< ' '<<g1<<" and "<<g2<<'\n';//Still available
                                  cout << "The local variable 11 is " << 11 << '\n';
                                  cout << "The local 12 is no longer valid.\n";

        No more                   return;
        variables   } // All variables go away now
```

Figure 13.1.
Pointing out the local and global variables.

Scope is a feature of C++ that is designed to make programs more maintainable. The use of local variables reduces problems often called *side-effects*. The problem of debugging programs is that you can easily examine code—even as it executes using the Visual C++ debugger—and understand how the code you are watching is affected by changes in variable values. It is much harder to understand how code in a different part of the program is affected. A global variable enables you to accidentally affect how an unrelated function works. This problem is so important that C++ introduces a completely new way of organizing the visibility of variables called *classes*, which we will cover in Lesson 11.

▶ Sharing Variables Among Functions

Concept   **What You Will Learn**

To share local variables between two functions, you must pass the variables—not unlike a quarterback does with a football—from the calling function (the quarterback) to the receiving function (the receiver).

This section shows you how to pass data from one function to another. The passing described here is one-way. In the next section, you'll learn how to return a value from one function to another function. This section also finally tells you why you have to put parentheses after function names!

When a function needs to work with values, the calling function passes the values inside the parentheses. The receiving function's code will have a similar group of parentheses with variables inside to capture that passed data. Remember that the values you pass are called arguments and the receiving variables are called the parameters of the function. (Don't be too worried by this fine distinction; most people use the terms interchangeably.)

Parameters are the vehicles in which you pass data from one function to the next. Ordinarily, one function can't access another's local data. However, if a function passes one or more of its local data values as arguments, another function can receive that data and work with it as if it had access all along.

If you want `main()` to pass two integer values, `v1` and `v2`, to a function called `GetThem()`, `main()` could pass the values like this:

```
GetThem(v1, v2);   // Call the GetThem() function and pass two values
```

The first two lines of `GetThem()` would look something like this:

```
void  GetThem(int v1, int v2)
{
```

Definition—A function *definition* is the function's first line, which names the function and describes the parameters.

When a function receives one or more parameters, you can't leave the function's definition line with empty parentheses. The parentheses must describe to the function exactly what data is coming, as well as the data types. Figure 13.2 helps describe the process and terminology of passing data from `main()` to `GetThem()`.

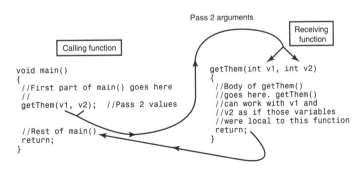

Figure 13.2.

Passing data requires a little setup in the function's definition line.

There are three ways to pass data from one function to another:

▶ By value

▶ By address

▶ By reference

The method you use depends on your data and application. As you might imagine, the way you pass variables depends on what you need to do with them. C++ enables you to control whether the receiving routine can change the value of the variable as seen by the called function.

Passing by Value

Passing by value is sometimes called *passing by copy*. When you pass an argument from one function to another, the argument's value is passed to the receiving function, but the variable itself isn't passed.

It's vital for you to understand that passing by value means that the receiving function can't change the passing function's variable in any way. Only the value of the passing function's variable—not the variable itself—is passed. When the value gets to the receiving function, the receiving function accepts that value into its own local variable parameter and works with its own variable that contains the passed value. However, nothing the receiving function does will change anything in the passing function. The receiving function can use the local variable as if it had been declared as a local variable.

STOP&TYPE Study the program in Listing 13.3. main() is the passing function and getIt() is the receiving function. The argument i is passed from main() to getIt(). No special syntax is needed. By default, Visual C++ passes the data by value.

Review   **What You Have Learned**

Passing by value is safer than passing by address. When you pass by value, the "owner" of the original variable—the passing function—passes the variable's value but retains all rights to that variable. The receiving function simply uses the value in its own variable without changing the passing function's version of the variable.

▼ **INPUT   LISTING 13.3. PASSING FROM main() TO getIt() BY VALUE.**

```
1:// Filename: VALUPASS.CPP
2:// Passes an argument from main()
3:// to another function by value
4:#include <iostream.h>
5:
```

```
 6:void GetIt(int i);    // The function's prototype
 7:
 8:void main()
 9:{
10:   int i;
11:
12:   cout << "I'm now in main()... " << endl;
13:   cout << "Please enter a value for i: ";
14:   cin >> i;
15:
16:   getIt(i);    // No data types, just the variable
17:
18:   cout << endl << endl;
19:   cout << "Back in main(), the value is still "
20:        << i << endl;
21:   return;    // Return to the QuickWin
22:}
23://************************************************************
24:void getIt(int i)
25:{
26:   // getIt() now has a local variable called i also
27:   cout << endl << endl
28:        <<"Just got to getIt() and i is " << i << endl;
29:
30:   i *= 5;
31:
32:   cout << "After multiplying by 5, i is now " << i << endl;
33:   return;    // Return to main()
34:}
```

▼ OUTPUT

```
I'm now in main()...
Please enter a value for i: 3

Just got to getIt() and i is 3
After multiplying by 5, i is now 15

Back in main(), the value is still 3
```

▼ ANALYSIS

By studying the output, you can see that getIt() can change i only inside getIt(). After getIt() returns control to main(), you see that main()'s i was left intact with its original value. main()'s i and getIt()'s i are two completely different variables. One is main()'s local variable and the other is getIt()'s local variable.

One interesting thing to note is that getIt() didn't even have to call the variable i. If getIt()'s definition line read

```
void getIt(int myVal)
```

getIt() would print and multiply myVal by 5, and the results would be identical to the preceding output. Only the value of main()'s i was passed, not the variable itself.

main() didn't have to list i's data type in the parentheses on line 16 because main() already knows i's data type. Only the receiving function, which knows nothing about the argument before the pass, must be told the data type of the value being sent.

 Warning   Never put a semicolon at the end of a function's definition line. For example, line 24 would never have a semicolon at the end of it. At the point where you call a function, however, you must put a semicolon, as done in line 16.

Figure 13.3 shows how main() sends the value of the variable, and not the variable itself, to getIt(). This figure assumes that the user entered a 3, as shown in the previous output.

```
// Filename: VALUPASS.CPP
// Passes an argument from main()
// to another function by value
#include <iostream.h>
#include <conio.h>
getIt(int i);   // the function's prototype

void main()
{
  int i;
  clrscr();

  cout << "I'm now in main()... \n";
  cout << "Please enter a value for i: ";
  cin >> i;

  getIt(i);  // No data types, just the variable

  cout << "\n\nBack in main(), the value is still "<<i<<'\n';
  cout << "Press a key to return to the IDE...";
  getch();
  return;  // Return to the IDE
}
//*********************************************************
getIt(int i)
{
  // getIt () now has a local variable called i also
  cout << "\n\nJust got to getIt() and i is " << i << '\n';
  i *=5;
  cout << "After multiplying by 5, i is now " << i << '\n';
  return 0;  // Return to main()
}
```

Figure 13.3.

main() passes the value of 3, not i.

If more than one value was passed from main() to getIt(), all the values would be sent, but the receiving function couldn't change main()'s copy of the variables. When you pass more than one variable, separate the variables with commas. When a function receives more than one parameter, separate the receiving data types and parameters with commas. For example, if main() passed an integer named i, a character named c, and a floating-point value named x to getIt(), the line in main() might look like this:

```
getIt(i, c, x);   // Pass three values
```

The definition of getIt() would look like this:

```
void getIt(int i, char c, float x)    // Definition line
```

As mentioned earlier, getIt() could have renamed the argument values and used the new names as its parameters, but getIt() could never change main()'s copy of any of the variables. A parameter is a declaration of local scope. It will hide a like-named global variable, and a local variable in main does not exist in other functions. (Recall that a local variable does not exist after the closing brace of the function.) A function that is called is not within the scope of a calling function.

Detour for a Moment with Prototypes

We're not done with Listing 13.3. Aren't you curious about the duplication of getIt()'s definition line in line 6? Line 6 is called a prototype. All functions that you write using Visual C++ must include a prototype.

Definition—A *prototype* models a function's definition.

As you know, you must declare all variables before you can use them. Also, you must declare all functions before you call them. main() is the exception because it's already known by the runtime system that runs your program. (main() is known as a self-prototyping function.)

Declaring (prototyping) a function almost seems like overkill because it's so easy. To prototype a function, you must copy the function's definition line (the function's first line with parameters and everything else) to the top of your program. The best place to prototype your program's functions is right after your #include directives. As long as you prototype anywhere before main(), you'll be okay, but most people prototype right after the #includes.

A prototype tells Visual C++ what to expect. For instance, if you tell Visual C++ via a prototype that a particular function should receive a float followed by a double, but in the program you inadvertently pass the function a char followed by a double, Visual C++ can catch the error during compilation. Without the prototype, Visual C++ would have to promote the value any way it could, and a char doesn't promote very well to a double. Your program results would be incorrect, and it would be difficult to track down the error and figure out exactly where your data got messed up.

Note   In C++, the protoype is correctly termed a *declaration*. When you give the full body of the function, this is called the *definition* of the function. You must always declare a function before using it in your code, but you can define it any time you like. Also, a definition counts as a declaration too.

Many Visual C++ programmers prototype their functions right before compiling. With Visual C++, that's easy to do. Follow these steps to copy and paste function definitions into prototypes:

1. Highlight the function's definition (the first line in the function) by clicking and dragging the mouse or by holding down the Shift key and pressing the arrow keys until the line you want is highlighted.

2. Select Edit Copy (Ctrl+C or Ctrl+Ins) to copy the highlighted line to the Windows clipboard.

3. Move the cursor to the top of the program and insert a new line where you want the prototype to go.

4. Select Edit Paste (Ctrl+V or Shift+Ins) to copy the clipboard's line to the prototype area.

5. Add a semicolon to the end of the prototype. All prototypes require semicolons so that Visual C++ can distinguish a prototype from a function's definition line.

AH, IT MAKES SENSE NOW!

You've been dutifully including the appropriate header files, such as IOSTREAM.H and STRING.H, as needed. Until now, you've never fully understood why they're needed. Each time you learned a function that required a different header file, you began using that header. Now you know enough to understand why those header files are so important.

As mentioned a moment ago, you must prototype all functions before you can use them. The only exception is `main()`. That means that you must prototype functions that you didn't even write, such as `strcpy`.

What does the prototype for `strcpy()` look like? You don't know, yet you've already been prototyping `strcpy()` and all the other library functions. When Visual C++ supplies a library function, it prototypes that function for you in one of the header files. Therefore, when you include a header file, you're including a ton of prototypes for all functions you might use that are related to that header file. By including STRING.H, for instance, you started prototyping `strcpy()` from the very beginning. (The adventurous among you might want to open up the include file in `C:\msvc\include\string.h` to see what you can find. Aside from some technical stuff, which we won't worry about, you should be able to find a prototype for the string functions that you can recognize.)

If, in the beginning, I had gone into a lot of detail about the need to define all functions with a prototype before you call them, you might have given up too early. Now that you understand prototypes, the header files should make a lot more sense.

A prototype doesn't need to have the actual parameter names listed inside its parentheses, only the data types. The following are considered to be identical prototypes for a function named CalcIt():

```
void CalcIt(float i, double d, char c);

void CalcIt(float, double, char);
```

A prototype helps Visual C++ with data types, not variable names, so names aren't needed in the prototype itself. Parameter names are needed, however, in the function's definition line. Most programmers use the cut-and-paste method described earlier to create their prototypes; therefore, most programmers' prototypes do contain parameter names.

Tip   Although you don't need the parameter name, it is very useful to put the name in to help describe what the parameter does.

Another Detour to Address

Definition—*Passing by address* means that the variable itself (its location in memory) is passed and received.

The second way of passing data to a function is passing by address. First, what is an address? An address is the location in memory of a variable. When you name a variable, C++ sets aside a piece of memory and C++ also makes a note internally of where that variable has been put. Unlike some languages, C++ let's the programmer find this address value. To ask for the address of a variable, you can use this syntax:

```
addressOfVariable = &someVariable;
```

in which the & means *address of*.

However, you cannot hold an address in just any data type. C++ holds addresses as *pointers* and each data type has its own pointer type. So, when a pointer is declared, C++ needs to know the data type and that the variable is to hold a pointer, using the pointer operator (*). Yes, it does look like the multiplication symbol. C++ has to use the context to work out what was meant. Here is an example:

```
int i = 5; // integer
int *iptr; // pointer to integer
iptr = &i; // iptr now holds the address of i
```

The final trick is to know how to get the variable back from a pointer. The answer is that you use the dereference operator. The bad news is that it looks remarkably the same as multiply and the pointer declaration symbol, *. Here is a further example to show you how it works:

```
int i = 5; // integer
int j = 10;
```

```
int *iptr;    // pointer to integer
iptr = &i;    // iptr now holds the address of i
j = *iptr;    // j now holds 5, the contents of
              // the place iptr points to
*iptr = 77;   // the place where iptr points to, i,
              // now holds 77
```

Note   We will cover pointers in further detail in Lesson 8.

Having had another minor detour, let's get back to discussing what this has to do with function calls. Note the last statement in the previous code snippet. It enables you to update a variable by using its address. This gives a way of beating C++'s safety belt of copying the value, which stops you from updating the real value of the variable. If you take the address of a value that you want to update in a program and then pass that as a parameter, even if C++ copies that address, you can still access the same memory location that you passed. So, when Visual C++ passes a variable by address, in effect it passes the variable itself, which means that the receiving function can change the calling function's variable. When the calling function regains control, any variable just passed by address might be changed if the called function changed the argument.

Aside from character arrays, you haven't looked at arrays in much detail, but there is a significant difference in an array variable and a normal variable: An array variable is really a pointer in disguise. So when you pass an array as a parameter, you are really passing its address. This means that when you pass an array, you are effectively passing the contents of the array by address. Therefore, when you pass an array, the contents of the array can also be changed.

STOP&TYPE   Passing by value is safer than passing by address because the called function can't change the calling function's variables. However, there are times when you want the called function to change the calling function's variables. For example, Listing 13.4 contains a program that asks the user for his or her name in `main()`. The user's name is then passed to `ChangeIt()`, where the first and last characters in the name are changed to #. When `main()` regains control, it prints the name array, showing that the called function did indeed change `main()`'s version of the array.

▼ INPUT   LISTING 13.4. PASSING AN ARRAY IS PASSING BY ADDRESS.

```
 1:// Filename: PASSADDR.CPP
 2:// Passing an array means that the called function
 3:// can change the same variable as in the calling function
 4:#include <iostream.h>
 5:#include <string.h>
 6:
 7:void ChangeIt(char userName[30]);    // Prototype
 8:
 9:void main()
10:{
```

```
11:   char userName[30];
12:
13:   cout << "What is your name? ";
14:   cin.getline(userName, 30);
15:
16:   // Send the name to changeIt() by address
17:   ChangeIt(userName);
18:
19:   cout << "After a return to main(), here is your name: ";
20:   cout << userName;
21:   return;
22:}
23://**********************************************************
24:void ChangeIt(char userName[30])
25:{
26:   int endPlace;
27:   userName[0] = '#';   // Change first letter in name
28:   endPlace = strlen(userName) - 1;   // Find location of
29:                                      // final letter in name
30:   userName[endPlace] = '#';
31:
32:   return;   // Return to main() - optional
33:}
```

▼ OUTPUT

```
What is your name? Graham Ward
After a return to main(), here is your name: #raham War#
```

▼ ANALYSIS

The user fills the array named userName with a string value at line 14. On line 17, main()
then passes the array named userName to the function named ChangeIt(). ChangeIt()
changes the first and last letter of the name to pound signs.

The ChangeIt() function changes main()'s array because all arrays are passed by address.
Therefore, when ChangeIt() overwrites two letters with pound signs, main() knows about
the change. When ChangeIt() returns to main(), the array is still changed. main() displays
the array in line 20. As you can see from the output, the array that main() displays is
indeed the array that ChangeIt() changed. You can't pass an array by value. Therefore,
you must be on guard when passing arrays. Always be aware that the called function
could change the array. If the called function does change the array, the calling function's
array will reflect those changes.

 Tip It turns out that when you pass an array to a function, you don't have to
put the subscript in the receiving function's parameter brackets. The 30 in
line 24 is optional, although Visual C++ can use it to make sure that the
arrays are the same size.

Passing a nonarray variable by address requires some of that really strange syntax that you saw briefly earlier. Perhaps it's best that the designers of Visual C++ included the extra syntax, because that might make you pass by address only when you need to. It's important when writing long, structured programs (especially if you're on a team of programmers writing a large system) to make sure that only functions that need to change variables get a chance to do so.

To pass a nonarray variable by address, precede the parameter in the calling function with an ampersand (&), the *address of* operator. The ampersand tells Visual C++ that you want that specific nonarray variable passed by address. Visual C++ therefore passes the variable by address and lets the called function change the variable in both places.

Tip   Instead of passing nonarrays by address, pass them by reference as described in the next section. Passing by reference does not require the messy syntax that is required when passing nonarrays by address, but passing by reference achieves the same effect. Learn both methods, however, so that you can recognize other people's code when they pass nonarray variables by address.

STOP&TYPE In addition to including an ampersand in the calling function, you must also precede the variable with an asterisk (*) in the receiving function wherever the variable appears. It looks quite awkward, as you can see in Listing 13.5.

▼ INPUT   LISTING 13.5. PASSING AN INTEGER BY ADDRESS AND A CHARACTER BY VALUE.

```
 1:// Filename: OVERRIDE.CPP
 2:// Overrides the default method of passing
 3:// a nonarray variable. This program passes
 4:// a nonarray variable by address and,
 5:// therefore, requires some extra notation.
 6:#include <iostream.h>
 7:
 8:void ChangeIt(int *i, char c);
 9:
10:void main()
11:{
12:  int i;
13:  char c;
14:
15:  // Assign two values in main()
16:  i = 10;
17:  c = 'X';
18:
19:  cout << "Before leaving main(), i and c are "
20:       << i << " and " << c << endl;
```

```
21:
22:   ChangeIt( &i, c);   // Pass the integer by address
23:
24:   cout << "Back in main(), i and c are "
25:        << i << " and " << c << endl;
26:   return;
27:}
28://*********************************************************
29:void ChangeIt(int *i, char c)
30:{
31:   *i = 26;
32:   c = 'p';   // main()'s version of c won't change
33:              // but we can still use c locally
34:
35:   return;   // Return to main()
36:}
```

▼ OUTPUT

```
Before leaving main(), i and c are 10 and X
Back in main(), i and c are 26 and X
```

▼ ANALYSIS

If ChangeIt() were longer and had referred to i several times throughout the function, i would have needed an asterisk (*i) every place it appeared. Again, overriding the passing of nonarray data requires some strange syntax, but when a function has to change another function's data, passing by address is a good way to accomplish that change.

Passing by Reference

C++ provides a third way to pass data between functions that C++'s predecessor, C, does not support. When you pass data by reference, if the called function changes the data, C++ applies those same changes to the calling function's data.

The end result of passing by reference is identical to that of passing by address with one exception: You don't need to mess with all the strange overriding syntax when passing nonarrays by reference. As you learned at the end of the previous section, if you pass nonarrays by address you must precede the passed arguments with ampersands and also precede all parameters in the called function with asterisks. When passing variables by reference, you only have to precede the receiving parameters with ampersands.

 Warning Be careful when passing by reference! Remember that any changes applied to the receiving parameters will also apply to the sending function's arguments.

STOP&TYPE Listing 13.6 shows a program that passes several parameters by reference. The called functions change the calling function's arguments.

▼ INPUT   LISTING 13.6. PASSING ARGUMENTS BY REFERENCE.

```
 1:// Filename: POOL.CPP
 2:// Calculates the cubic feet in a swimming pool
 3:#include <iostream.h>
 4:
 5:void GetValues(int &length, int &width, int &depth);
 6:void CalcCubic(int length, int width, int depth, int &cubic);
 7:void PrintCubic(int cubic);
 8:
 9:void main()
10:{
11:    int length, width, depth, cubic;
12:
13:    GetValues(length, width, depth);
14:    CalcCubic(length, width, depth, cubic);
15:    PrintCubic(cubic);
16:    return;
17:}
18://********************************************************
19:void GetValues(int &length, int &width, int &depth)
20:{
21:    cout << "What is the pool's length? ";
22:    cin >> length;
23:    cout << "What is the pool's width? ";
24:    cin >> width;
25:    cout << "What is the pool's average depth? ";
26:    cin >> depth;
27:    return;
28:}
29://********************************************************
30:void CalcCubic(int length, int width, int depth, int &cubic)
31:{
32:    cubic = length * width * depth;
33:    return;
34:}
35://********************************************************
36:void PrintCubic(int cubic)
37:{
38:    cout << endl
39:         << "The pool has " << cubic << " cubic feet";
40:    return;
41:}
```

▼ OUTPUT

```
What is the pool's length? 12
What is the pool's width? 33
```

```
What is the pool's average depth? 4

The pool has 1584 cubic feet
```

▼ ANALYSIS

`main()` is nothing more than a function-calling control function. However, on line 11, `main()` defines three variables to be used in subsequent calculations. `main()` calls `GetValues()` on line 13. The job of `GetValues()` is to collect user values for `main()`'s three variables. `main()` passes the three arguments by reference due to the ampersands in front of each parameter in the function declaration on line 5 and the function defintion starting in line 19, which must match.

Once it is passed by reference, when `GetValues()` changes a parameter through the user's keyboard entry, the values change in `main()` as well. In `CalcCubic`, the only value that needs to be updated is the result of the calculation, `cubic`. For safety, the only value that the function is allowed to change is `cubic`; all the other arguments are passed by value in line 30. Therefore, if the programmer made a mistake in the calculation and accidentally put the result into `length`, `CalcCubic` would be the only function that had the wrong value in `length` after the mistake.

Finally, when printing the result in line 36 (`PrintCubic`), the function does not change the value, so there is no need to allow `cubic` to be updated.

Review

What You Have Learned

In this section, you learned that there are three ways to pass variables from one function to another. When you pass by value, the called function can't change the calling function's variables. When you pass by address, the called function can change the calling function's variables. Passing by reference performs the same job as passing by address, but you can pass nonarrays by reference without the messy syntax required when you use address passing.

► Homework
General Knowledge

1. Which is better, a program with one long `main()` function or a program with lots of smaller functions?

2. What's one advantage of structured programs?

3. Why are modular programs with lots of functions easier to maintain than programs with only one or a few long functions?

4. What is recursion?

5. Variables can be defined in two places in a program. List the two places.

6. What's the difference between local and global variables?

7. What's a block?

8. Which variable is safer, a local or a global variable?

9. When does a local variable go away?

10. When does a global variable go away?

11. What are the three ways you can pass variables?

12. Which is safer, passing by address or by value?

13. What's another name for passing by value?

14. How can you pass a nonarray variable by value?

15. How can you pass a nonarray variable by address?

16. How do you pass a variable by reference?

17. What's a prototype?

18. How can prototypes help eliminate bugs?

19. How can you prototype library functions such as `strlen()`?

20. Why don't you need to prototype `main()`?

21. Suppose `main()` passes a variable by value. If the called function changes the parameter, will `main()`'s value also change?

22. Suppose `main()` passes a variable by address. If the called function changes the parameter, will `main()`'s value also change?

23. Suppose `main()` passes a variable by reference. If the called function changes the parameter, will `main()`'s value also change?

24. True or false: Once you define a local variable, all functions in the program can use the variable.

25. True or false: You can't use a global variable before its definition.

26. True or false: The following is a prototype.

```
void aFunction(void)
```

27. True or false: The following is a prototype.

```
void aFunction(void);
```

28. True or false: You can pass an array by value.

What's the Output?

29. What's the output of the following program?

```cpp
// Filename: U16OUT1.CPP
#include <iostream.h>
void DoubleIt(int i);

void main()
{
  int i = 19;

  DoubleIt(i);
  cout << "i is now " << i << endl;
  return;
}
//***************************************************
void DoubleIt(int i)
{
  i *= 2;
  return;
}
```

30. What's the output of the following program?

```cpp
// Filename: U16OUT2.CPP
#include <iostream.h>
void DoubleIt(int *i);

void main()
{
  int i = 19;

  DoubleIt(&i);
  cout << "i is now " << i << endl;
  return;
}
//***************************************************
void DoubleIt(int *i)
{
  *i *= 2;
  return;
}
```

Find the Bug

31. What's wrong with the following function?

```cpp
void SqThem(i, j)
{
  i = i * i;
  j = j * j;
  cout << "i squared is " << i << endl;
  cout << "j squared is " << j << endl;
```

```
    return;
}
```

Write Code That...

32. Write a program that prints, in main(), the double-precision area of a circle, given that a user's double-precision radius is passed to the function. The formula for calculating a circle's area is

```
area = 3.14159 * (radius * radius)
```

33. Rewrite the following function to receive and process its parameters by address instead of by value:

```
void DoubleThem(float x, float y)
{
  x *= 2.0;
  y *= 2.0;
  cout << "The first parameter is now " << x << endl;
  cout << "The second parameter is now " << y << endl;
  return;
}
```

34. Rewrite the following function to receive and process its parameters by reference instead of by value:

```
void DoubleThem(float x, float y)
{
  x *= 2.0;
  y *= 2.0;
  cout << "The first parameter is now " << x << endl;
  cout << "The second parameter is now " << y << endl;
  return;
}
```

35. Write a program whose main() function calls a function that asks the user for a number from 1 to 80. (Keep looping if the user enters a value outside that range.) Return to main() and pass that number to a function named asterisk(), which will print that number of asterisks in a line across the screen.

Extra Credit

36. Write a program that, in main(), asks the user for the number of vacation days he or she has left at work this year. As soon as the user enters the number of days, pass that value to a second function. In the called function, print the number of hours of vacation that the user still has (24 times the number of days). Print the message Enjoy! if the user has more than five days of vacation time. Return to main() and terminate the program as usual.

37. Write a function that receives two integers by address. Switch the values of the two integers in the function. Due to the passing by address, when the called function returns control to the calling function, the values will still be swapped in the calling function.

14

More on Functions

▶ What You'll Learn

▶ Returning values

▶ Same function, different types

▶ Typesafe parameters

▶ Argument matching: sorting out which function to use

▶ Default parameters

In the previous unit, you learned how to pass data between functions. Passing data around is an important requirement in Visual C++ programming. As you continue, you will see another method by which you can return a value to the calling function. Then you will explore the restrictions of type safety, and look at the way C++ provides special features to enable you to work safely and easily with different types.

Often you will want to make functions multipurpose. C++ recognizes this by giving you default parameters, which are a great way to avoid unwieldy parameter lists.

▶ Returning Values via *return*

Concept   **What You Will Learn**

The `return` statement gives your functions the capability to return a single value from a called function.

You've already seen the passing of data *to* a function. Using the `return` statement, you can see how to return a value *back* to the calling function. Every program in this book has used the `return` statement at the end of `main()`. The `return` command can also take a value:

```
return 1;
```

Sometimes, Visual C++ programmers put the `return` value in parentheses:

```
return (0);
```

You can return, at most, one value from a function! As Figure 14.1 shows, you can pass several parameters to a function, but you can return only one.

Although Figure 14.1 contains an outline of two functions, you can see that the calling function's function call looks unlike any you've seen so far. Instead of calling `AFunction()` on a line by itself,

```
AFunction(a, b, c);
```

main() assigns AFunction to a variable like this:

```
value = AFunction(a, b, c);
```

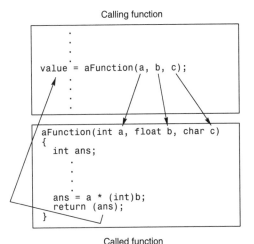

Calling function

```
value = aFunction(a, b, c);
```

```
aFunction(int a, float b, char c)
{
    int ans;
    .
    .
    .
    ans = a * (int)b;
    return (ans);
}
```

Called function

Figure 14.1.
At most, you can return
only a single value.

The assignment is needed to hold AFunction()'s return value. In other words, when a function returns a value, you should have some way to capture that return value.

> **Note**   If a function returns a value, the calling function doesn't have to capture the value. However, although the calling function can ignore the return value, a return value must always be provided.

Before you look at a program that uses a return value, there's one more thing you should know. If a function returns a value, you must tell Visual C++ what kind of value that function is returning. Put the return value data type before the function name. If a function isn't going to return a value, you must put void before the function name.

Therefore, you know from the following function definition, without looking at its return statement, exactly what kind of data the function returns:

```
double FunctionA(int i, float j)
```

This function returns a double value. The return data type appears on the same line as the function definition so that you can specify the return data type in the prototype as well. Here is the prototype for the preceding function:

```
double FunctionA(int i, float j);
```

If you don't specify a `return` value, Visual C++ assumes that you're returning an integer. Therefore, the following function prototypes are identical:

```
int Compute(int age, float factor);

Compute(int age, float factor);   // Assumed to return an int
```

However, C++ syntax is confusing enough without leaving such things to memory. (You would probably guess that the default was `void` and be puzzled as to why the compiler threw an error on a `return` statement without a value.) Therefore, C++ programmers always specify the return type, even if it is `int`.

Because you can write a program that can return a value using a reference or address of parameter, you might wonder why you would bother with a `return` value. The answer is that it is very handy to be able to call functions in the middle of a calculation, or even in a parameter list. For example, imagine that the POOL.CPP program in the previous unit (Listing 13.6) had a `CalcArea` function. In that case, `CalcCubic` could be written like this:

```
// CalcArea function
int CalcArea(int length, int width)
   {
     return (length * width);
   }
// new CalcCubic
void CalcCubic(int length, int width, int depth, int &cubic)
   {
      cubic = CalcArea(length,width) * depth;
      return;
   }
```

Note that the `return` value can be an expression and that the function can be used exactly like a variable (though you cannot assign into a function `return` value). You can use the `return` value of a function as an argument to another function:

```
int CalcArea(int length, int width)
   {
     return (length * width);
   }
// another CalcCubic
int CalcCubic(int area, int depth)
   {
      return area * depth;
   }
void main()
   {
      cout << "Cubic is " << CalcCubic(CalcArea(5,4),5);
   }
```

You have to carefully count the parentheses to follow this. Visual C++ will first work out all the functions in the argument list before continuing with the function call.

You can have more than one `return` statement in a function. This can pass different values back as long as the types match the return type.

STOP&TYPE Listing 14.1 contains a program that uses three functions (including `main()`). The first function that `main()` calls asks for the user's name, and the second calculates the number of years left until the user's retirement.

Review ▬▬▬▬▬▬▬▬▬▬▬▬▬▬▬▬▬▬▬▬ **What You Have Learned**

The passing and returning of data provide Visual C++'s vehicle for sharing data. You can pass data by value or by address. The method you use depends on whether you want the receiving function to be able to change the calling function's variables.

▼ **INPUT   LISTING 14.1. PASSING AND RETURNING VALUES.**

```
1:// Filename: PASSRET.CPP
2:// Program that passes by value and by address.
3:// This program also demonstrates prototypes and
4:// how to return a value from one function to
5:// the calling function.
6:#include <iostream.h>
7:
8:void GetUserName(char userName[50]);
9:int ComputeRetire(int age);
10:
11:void main()
12:{
13:   char userName[50];
14:   int age = 0;
15:   int yearsToRetire = 0;
16:
17:   GetUserName(userName);    // Fill the array in the function
18:
19:   cout << "How old are you, " << userName << " ?";
20:   cin >> age;
21:   yearsToRetire = ComputeRetire(age);// Pass and return values
22:
23:   cout << "You have " << yearsToRetire
24:        << " years until retirement at 65" << endl;
25:
26:   return;
27:}
28://*************************************************************
29:void GetUserName(char userName[50])    // 50 is optional here
30:{
31:   cout << "What is your name? ";
```

continues

```
32:   cin.getline(userName,50);
33:   return;   // No need to return anything
34:}
35://*********************************************************
36:int ComputeRetire(int age)
37:{
38:   return (65 - age);   // Return the number of years until 65
39:}
```

▼ **OUTPUT**

```
What is your name? Andy Smith
How old are you, Andy Smith? 40
You have 25 years until retirement at 65
```

▼ **ANALYSIS**

Lines 8 and 9 contain prototypes for the two functions that follow main(). Always put main() first in your programs. Not only is main() executed first, but other Visual C++ programmers who might maintain your programs expect main() to appear first.

In line 17, main() calls the next function in the program, GetUserName(). main() passes the character array to this function so that the function can fill the array. Visual C++ receives all arrays by address, so when the user enters a value into the array within the GetUserName() function, main()'s array also gets filled at the same time. When you pass an array, a copy of the array values doesn't get sent. Instead, Visual C++ passes the actual array.

The cout in line 19 shows that the user's name resides in main()'s array when GetUserName() returns control to main(). After the user enters his or her age, main() passes the age in line 21 to the ComputeRetire() function. The body of ComputeRetire() consists of a single statement—the return statement on line 38—that computes the number of years until the user reaches 65. As you can see from line 38, you can return an expression from a function instead of a single variable if you choose.

There is no reason for main() to pass age by address to ComputeRetire(), because ComputeRetire() doesn't need to change main()'s age value. It only uses age to compute the retirement years. You won't find any global variables in Listing 14.1 because they're not needed. There is rarely ever a need for them.

▶ *const* **Parameters**

What You Will Learn

const parameters enable you to stop the function-changing values of arguments even if passed by reference or by address.

Definition—const means the value cannot be changed.

In the last unit, you saw that arrays were passed by address; therefore, the called function was allowed to change the value of the passed array. There are two places where this could mean trouble:

▶ Passing a const value or a literal

▶ Passing a variable that the programmer does not want changed

If the program was allowed to pass a const value to a function, the "unchangeability" of a const would be broken. Worse, a literal only exists as a piece of text in your program. How could the compiler change it?

```
void PrintIntRef(int & i);
void main()
   {
      PrintIntRef(1);    // error C++ cannot change 1
```

C++ has a simple rule: You can't pass constant values to a nonconstant parameter. A pass by value parameter is a constant parameter, so that is not a problem. However, a pass by address or pass by reference parameter means that the calling value can be changed. By declaring the parameter const, you can tell C++ that although you pass by address or reference, you promise that the called function will not change the argument's value. In fact, Visual C++ then won't let you write code that changes the value in the called function because it treats the parameter as a const that is initialized with the argument value. When you declare a const parameter, Visual C++ can automatically treat a non-const value as a const value. You declare a const parameter as follows:

```
void PrintIntRef(const int& printValue);
```

This means that it will not change printValue even though it is passed the real printValue, not a copy. Similarly,

```
void PrintString(const char str[]);
```

tells the programmer that the string will not change when the array is passed.

The real benefit of this to a programmer is that you can use routines that someone else has written and know which parameters might be changed by the routine and which might not. You saw in the last unit that a pass by value parameter did the same job. When passing large amounts of data, it is more efficient to pass by reference. Of course, you don't have the choice with an array; they are always passed by address.

UNIT

14

More on Functions

Listing 14.2 shows how you can use const to tell the rest of the program that you are being careful not to change array data.

▼ INPUT   LISTING 14.2. USING const TO STOP FUNCTIONS FROM CHANGING DATA.

```
1:// Filename: INITIALS.CPP
2:// Shows a routine that given a name
3:// finds the initials
4://
5:
6:#include <string.h>  // header for strlen function
7:#include <iostream.h>
8:
9:// GetInitials prototype: returns 1 if successful,
10://                        0 if fails
11:int GetInitials(char initials[],const char name[]);
12:
13:void main()
14:  {
15:     char initials[15] = ""; // Allow for silly strings
16:     char name[30] = "";
17:     while (1)               // Do forever
18:        {
19:            cout << "Type name, (0 to quit): ";
20:            cin.getline(name,30);
21:            if (name[0] == '0')// Stop when the user asks
22:              break;
23:
24:            //
25:            // Extract the initials, and report if error
26:            //
27:            if (GetInitials(initials,name))
28:               {
29:                  cout << "The initials for '" << name
30:                       << "' are: '" << initials << "'" << endl;
31:               }
32:            else
33:               {
34:                  cout << "Something wrong with '"
35:                       << name << "'" << endl;
36:               }
37:        }
38:  }
39://*************************************************************
40:int GetInitials(char initials[],const char name[])
41:  {
42:    int count = 0;
43:    int initialCount = 0;
44:
45:    int length = strlen(name);
46:    if (length == 0) // error if no string
47:      return 0;
48:
```

```
49:     while (count < length)
50:       {
51:         while (count < length
52:               && name[count] == ' ')
53:           count++;
54:         if (count < length)
55:           {
56:             initials[initialCount] = name[count];
57:             initialCount++;
58:             count++;
59:           }
60:         while (count < length
61:               && name[count] != ' ')
62:           count++;
63:       }
64:     initials[initialCount] = '\0';// Ensure terminated string
65:     return (initialCount > 0);    // Success if found
66:                                   // one or more initials
67:   }
```

▼ OUTPUT

```
Type name, (0 to quit): Gary Smith
The initials for 'Gary Smith' are: 'GS'
Type name, (0 to quit): Stefan Winman
The initials for 'Stefan Winman' are: 'SW'
Type name, (0 to quit): Kenneth Lee Michael Noble
The initials for 'Kenneth Lee Michael Noble' are: 'KLMN'
Type name, (0 to quit):
Something wrong with '       '
Type name, (0 to quit): 0
```

▼ ANALYSIS

The GetInitials prototype in line 11 tells the programmer a lot about the function without needing much explanation. GetInitials tells what the function does, the non-const character array called initials is a big clue that the result is returned into the first parameter, and the second parameter is a clue that the name to be examined should be passed in the second parameter. It is not clear what the returned int is for, so this is documented by way of a comment in lines 9 and 10.

The program simply loops, asking for input and processing the result. In line 17, there is an odd statement, while(1). This means the loop will never end. Fortunately, the programmer has done this deliberately and has remembered to put a test in line 21 to stop the loop if the user enters a 0.

The call in line 27 is a typical C++ statement when a function returns success or failure. Remember that the if statement tests the expression to see whether it is zero or nonzero. The GetInitials function has been written to return a value that says whether the function worked, and the if statement can easily test this value. It does not have to be stored somewhere first. Would the following have been more clear?

```
if (GetInitials(initials,name) != 0)
```

Using the result, the program can put out an error message or the answer as appropriate.

The function definition in line 40 tells the programmer that he can pass any length of string to the program because the special [] notation has been used for the array. Lines 45 to 47 check that there is something worth processing, returning a failed value if the string length is zero.

In lines 49, 51, and 54, the program checks the length of the string before allowing the value of the character to be examined. This makes sure that the program does not fall off the end of the string. Remember that string lengths are a bit confusing. The last real character of the string is at the `string length - 1` position because the character arrays start at zero.

The `while` loop in line 49 ensures that each word is processed. For each word in the string, the loop in lines 51 to 53 skips any blanks (notice there are no brackets around line 53). In line 54, the program knows that there is either a nonblank character or that the string is ended. If there is a valid character, this is stored away and the program moves on. In line 57, a count is maintained of how many initials have been found. In lines 60 to 62, the program skips forward through the word until it finds a space or the end of string terminator. At this point, the main `while` loop decides whether to terminate on the end of string or to carry on with the next word.

In line 64, you must make sure that the `initials` result is a valid string by placing a terminator on the end. In line 65, there is a simple test on the `initialCount`. If there were no initials—for example, in a blank string—the test would be false and the test would evaluate to a `0`. Otherwise, the test would be true and `1` would be returned.

▶ **Typesafe Parameters**

	What You Will Learn

Visual C++ typing means that you have to be careful about the arguments you pass to parameters.

Definition—*Typesafe* means that C++ stops mistakes caused by mixing up different types.

To understand how Visual C++ works with parameters, you need to do some revision on C++'s typing mechanism. Remember that C++'s main aim of typing is that you cannot accidentally assign a variable of one type into another. To be friendly, C++ does know that some type conversions are safe and performs them automatically, and also provides the casting mechanism to enable the programmer to force the language to change types. When passing by value, C++ has an easy job. All it needs to do is create a temporary value of the right type if the argument and parameter are different types. If C++ knows how to convert one type to another (such as an int to a float), it can do so. When passing by reference, things get more complicated. In the last unit, you saw that when passing a reference, the parameter used is actually the argument passed, not a copy. This means that C++ has a problem when a reference parameter is of a different type than that of an argument passed to it. Consider this example:

```
#include <iostream.h>

void PrintInt(int i);
void PrintIntRef(int & i);

void main()
  {
    float value = 19.99
    PrintInt(value);     // ok, but will lose decimals
    PrintIntRef(value); // Error!
  }
```

C++ does not need to see the body of PrintIntRef to know it has trouble. It must use an int in PrintIntRef when it is being handed a float. Even the explicit cast

```
PrintIntRef((int)value);
```

will not do the trick. C++ must have an int. One solution is to make a temporary value. Another solution is to consider why you are trying to print a float with an int printing function, which is a nasty mistake. Or another solution is to write a PrintFloatRef function.

▶ Same Function, Different Types

Concept

What You Will Learn

Visual C++ enables you to have more than one function with the same name using *function overloading*.

C++ needs different functions to deal with different types. This is not a big deal because different types might need different code, but it is difficult trying to invent names to deal with the different combinations of types. Imagine that you have a print function that codes the cout statements for a different number of decimal places for float and

UNIT

14

More on Functions

doubles. (Remember that a `double` is like a `float`, except it can hold more digits of precision.) You would have to code the following:

```
void PrintFloat(float outputNumber,int decimalPlaces)
  {
   cout.precision(decimalPlaces);
   cout.setf(ios::showpoint);
   cout.setf(ios::fixed);
   cout << outputNumber;
  }
```

And, similarly, the following:

```
void PrintDouble(double outputNumber,int decimalPlaces)
// same code as before
```

Inventing names for these examples is easy. But what if several parameters need handling in this different way? C++ has a handy mechanism called function overloading. This enables you to use the same name for more than one function. Visual C++ tells them apart by looking at the *function signature*. The function signature is the name of the function and the type of each parameter. It does not include the return type, so you cannot have a function that returns a different type with the same parameter list. For example,

```
void Print(int value);
void Print(float value);
```

are allowed to be declared in the same program. When you call these functions, Visual C++ looks at the type of the argument to decide which function to call. So, given the previous functions, the code snippet that follows needs to sort out which version to call.

```
void main()
  {
    int i = 5;
    float f = 1.25;
    Print(i);      // calls Print(int)
    Print(f);      // calls Print(float)
    Print((int)f); // calls Print(int)
```

The calls get sorted out by looking at the type of the arguments.

You do not even need the same number of parameters in the different function declarations. Remember the pool calculation? You could develop a `CalcCubic` that takes three dimensions, or you could use an area and another single dimension like this:

```
int CalcCubic(int length, int width, int depth);
int CalcCubic(int area, int depth);
void main()
  {
    int area = 50;
    int aveDepth = 5;
    int cube = CalcCubic(area,aveDepth);
    // Second version called as only two int arguments
```

The great thing about overloading is that you can have lots of functions that do the same thing to different parameters. However, you must be careful to not use the same name for different functions that do different things. Normally, if you choose a vague name, it will not be clear what the function does, and the programmer calling the function might be surprised when the expected function does not happen:

```
// Calculate the area of a circle
int Circle(int radius);
// Calculate the area of a rectangle
int Rectangle(int length, int width);
// Print a rectangle
int Rectangle(int left, int top, int right, int bottom);
```

The programmer writing a geometry calculation might use the circle area function and be surprised that the second Rectangle function does not calculate the area of a rectangle as well.

▶ Default Parameters

Concept

Use default parameters to simplify parameter lists and combine similar functions.

Definition—A *default parameter* specifies what value should be used if an argument is missing.

Default parameters are to C++ functions what automatic gear selection is to a car. You can let C++ decide what value a parameter can have, or you can fiddle around with the call and give it a specific value, just as you can leave an automatic gearbox in drive or choose a specific gear with the gear shift.

Why would you want to do this? Often, you want to write functions that are similar except for some optional features. These optional features might need extra data (that means new parameters for a function) so that the new features can work. There is no problem adding extra parameters, but they are a nuisance to provide if you do not want them. Here is how you declare a default parameter:

```
int CalcCubic(int length, int width, int depth = 5);
```

This means that depth, when not explicitly stated, will be 5. The default value should only be specified once, and specification should be in the function prototype so that the calling functions know about the default. The following calls produce the same result:

```
cube = CalcCubic(10,6,5);
cube = CalcCubic(10,6);
```

There is a simple rule for default parameters: After a parameter is defaulted, all of the following parameters in the function call must be defaulted. This means that you are not allowed to declare

```
int Cubic(int length, int width = 5, int depth); // Wrong!
```

because you would still have to supply a value for `depth` when trying to default `width`. When putting several defaults into a parameter list, the order of parameters is decided by how frequently you expect to omit the parameter.

For example, you might develop your specialized floating point printing routine so that it automatically prints out two decimal places unless there is a special requirement:

```
void Print(float value, int noOfDPs = 2);
main()
  {
    float length = 12.25F;
    float width = 5.50F;
    float depth = 4.75F;
    Print(length);
    Print(width);
    Print(depth);
    float cube = CalcCube(length,width,depth);
    Print(cube,6); // six places for full accuracy
```

You can also use a default parameter to control function logic. If a function needs to do nothing most of the time, the default parameter can be used with a value that says "do nothing." Then when the programmer needs the special situation, the parameter can be set as in the following example:

```
float CalculateTax(float pay, int promptForRate = 0)
  {
    if (promptForRate)
      {
        cout << "What is tax rate?";
        cin >> taxRate;
      }
    else
      {
        taxRate = 0.25;
      }
    // Calculate tax
  }
```

This routine might have been designed to be used as a routine to calculate tax in a standard way, or if the programmer chooses, the routine can be used to ask for a tax rate if a nonzero value has been set.

 Tip   There is a useful trick for pass by address parameters that you can use. If you want an optional pass by address parameter, you can set a default value of 0. In your called routine, you can test the parameter itself (not the dereferenced value) to see whether it has been set. Here's an example:

```cpp
void Default(int * i = 0, const char str[] = 0);
void main()
  {
    Default();
    Default(23,"Hello World!");
  }
void Default(int * i,const char str[])
  {
    if (i == 0) // test address of i not *i
      {
        // No i parameter
        // (and cannot be a str either - why?)
      }
    if (!str) // another way of testing for zero
      {
        // no str parameter
      }
  }
```

Argument Matching: Sorting Out Which Function to Use

Concept   **What You Will Learn**

C++ has a sequence for parameter matching to decide which overloaded function to call.

Definition—An *overloaded function* is more than one function with the same name but different parameter lists.

Definition—*Argument matching* is the process C++ uses to determine which version of an overloaded function to call.

You can't declare two functions with the same parameter list, but what happens in the following case?

```cpp
void Print(float value, int dps = 2); // specify precision
void Print(float value);              // standard cout print
```

The compiler will accept these declarations as different. When you call the first example with Print(value,5), the compiler can see which version you wanted by the two parameters. But if the program calls Print(value), there would be a problem. The call would be *ambiguous;* Visual C++ would not know whether you meant to call the first Print with a default of 5 or the second version with no parameter. Visual C++ makes the decision easy for itself, in that case. It will not use either version, and it tells you at compile time that it can't tell the calls apart. In this example, either the two functions do the same thing and the second version is redundant, or the one version should be renamed.

Now consider a trickier example. C++ automatically converts types if it cannot find a match. It searches for the next best function to call, if any. So, if you have

```
void Print(int);
void main()
  {
    Print(3.3F);  // Pass a float
```

and you pass Print(int) a float, C++ automatically converts the value to a float.

Add a Print(char):

```
void Print(int);
void Print(char);
void main()
  {
    Print(3.3F);  // Pass a float
```

C++ first checks to see whether there is a function that is an exact match. If there is not, it checks for all possible functions to which it can convert the number. Perhaps surprisingly, C++ can change a float to a char as well as to an int. (Remember that a char is almost like an int.) When it tries to match your call to Print with a float, C++ can't guess which version you really meant:

```
void Print(int){}
void Print(char){}

int main()
  {
    float f = 4.5;
    Print(1);       // OK, 1 is type int
    Print('C');    // OK, 'C' is a char
    Print(f);       // Ambigous, can convert to either
    Print("Hello World!"); // Error! no match at all for char[]
    Print((int)f);// OK, cast tells C++ which version to use
  }
```

C++ has a lot of work to do to sort out how to match parameter lists with defaults and type conversions. What C++ does is work through a sequence:

1. Look for an exact match, including default parameters. If only one function is found, use it. If more than one function is found, report ambiguous function error.

2. Look for all matches through C++ automatic type conversion (called promotion). If only one function is found, use it. If more than one function is found, report ambiguous function error.

3. Look for user-specified conversions. (In C++, you'll see that you can invent our own types called classes.) Perform matching again.

Don't worry about this last step; it's only included here for completeness. The important message is that you can sort out an ambiguous function call by using a cast to force a parameter to be an exact match, but only if the function signature itself is not ambiguous.

The process becomes even more complicated with multiple parameters, but basically if it does not find an exact match, it looks at all the nearest matches and chooses the function where the most parameters match exactly. The exact rules are very complicated, but C++ programmers should avoid writing overloaded functions with only slightly different parameter lists, so normally the match is quite easy to find.

Here is something for you to think about. In C++, the operators such as +, -, and << can be thought of as functions. Can you see that cout overloads the << operator function to work with different types?

STOP&TYPE In Listing 14.3, you see an example of using overloaded functions and defaults.

▼ **INPUT LISTING 14.3. OVERLOAD.CPP SHOWS HOW ONE FUNCTION NAME CAN BE SHARED BY SEVERAL FUNCTIONS.**

```
1:// File : OVERLOAD.CPP
2:// Demonstration of overloading and defaults.
3:// in a program that prints loan repayments
4:#include <iostream.h>
5:
6:
7:const int TRUE = 1;
8:const int FALSE = 0;
9:
10:void Print(int i, int newline = FALSE);
11:void Print(float f, int newline = FALSE, int width = 5);
12:void Print(char str[],int newline = FALSE);
13:
14:void main()
15:  {
16:    float amount = 0;
17:    float rate = 0;
18:    float repayment = 0;
19:
20:    Print("Enter amount to repay: ");
21:    cin >> amount;
22:    Print("Enter interest rate per annum: ");
23:    cin >> rate;
24:
25:    Print("Amount of loan: ");
```

continues

```
26:      Print(amount,TRUE);
27:      Print("Interest rate: ");
28:      Print(rate, TRUE);
29:      Print("Repayment table", TRUE);
30:      Print("--------------", TRUE);
31:      Print("Months\tRepayment\tMonthly Amt",TRUE);
32:
33:      // Print a table for 3 to 48 months in 3 monthly intervals
34:      for (int months = 3; months <= 48; months+=3)
35:        {
36:          // Interest will be rate * months / 12
37:          if (rate >= 0)
38:            {
39:              repayment = amount
40:                          + amount * rate * months / 12 / 100;
41:              Print(months);
42:              Print("\t");
43:              Print(repayment,FALSE,8);
44:              Print("\t");
45:          // C++ will also recognize the type of an expression
46:              Print(repayment / months,TRUE,8);
47:            }
48:
49:        }
50:      return;
51:
52:  }
53://***********************************************************
54:void Print(int i, int newline)
55:  {
56:    cout << i;
57:    if (newline)
58:      cout << endl;
59:  }
60://***********************************************************
61:void Print(float f, int newline,int width)
62:  {
63:    cout.precision(2);
64:    cout.setf(ios::showpoint);
65:    cout.setf(ios::fixed);
66:    cout.width(width);
67:    cout << f;
68:    if (newline)
69:      cout << endl;
70:  }
71://***********************************************************
72:void Print(char str[], int newline)
73:  {
74:    cout << str;
75:    if (newline)
76:      cout << endl;
77:  }
```

▼ OUTPUT

```
Enter amount to repay: 6000
Enter interest rate per annum: 6.5
Amount of loan: 6000.00
Interest rate:  6.50
Repayment table
---------------
Months  Repayment       Monthly Amt
3        6097.50         2032.50
6        6195.00         1032.50
9        6292.50          699.17
12       6390.00          532.50
15       6487.50          432.50
18       6585.00          365.83
21       6682.50          318.21
24       6780.00          282.50
27       6877.50          254.72
30       6975.00          232.50
33       7072.50          214.32
36       7170.00          199.17
39       7267.50          186.35
42       7365.00          175.36
45       7462.50          165.83
48       7560.00          157.50
```

UNIT 14
More on Functions

▼ ANALYSIS

In lines 10 to 12, the prototypes for the overloaded Print functions are declared. These also use an extra parameter to enable the programmer to easily code when newlines are to be inserted in the output.

The main body of the code, starting at line 14, asks the user some questions and reports the answers in a neat form to confirm that the program has understood the input. In lines 25 to 31, the char[] and float versions of Print are called, with some skipping lines and some not.

The main for loop that starts in line 34 drives a listing of repayments over three monthly intervals up to 48 months. In line 41, it calls the int version of Print.

Perhaps the more difficult one to recognize is which version is called in line 46. The rules of the expression are that the type of an expression is expanded to the biggest type of the values in the expression. So, just as repayment is a float, the result of the expression is a float, even though months is an int.

Even if the expression had been an int, the same function would have been called. Why? The rules on parameter matching say that there is no exact match for a Print function with three parameters, but no other version of Print has three parameters. Automatically converting an int to a float allows Visual C++ to come up with a good match of the arguments given to it. Visual C++ would not try to match to the Print(int,int) version because of the extra parameter.

▶ More On Structured Programming

This lesson began with a discussion on structured programming, and it is going to end with one! Now you can see how you can break up a large program into lots of small ones. You have a technique for breaking a big problem into many small problems, and you can solve many small problems quicker than one big problem.

When you write a program, you can quickly draft an outline of what it should do by writing a main() that simply consists of function calls. Function by function, you can then decide the detail of how each function performs its task (perhaps even breaking down the called functions into several functions themselves). Often you can decide at the high level what parameters the functions will need. This top-down programming technique enables you to concentrate on a sensible structure to your code. If you just start at the beginning and work to the end, you are more likely to end up with a heap of spaghetti code, because you will not have considered properly how a big function can be broken down.

For really complicated programs, you can write dummy functions that do nothing except assign sensible return values and perhaps a comment as to what they are supposed to do. This means that you do not always have to write all the code before you can start testing your program. This technique is called *stepwise-refinement*, making your program more detailed step by step.

 Note   This lesson began by separating a payroll program into different functions. This lesson's project contains the full code and a description of the program.

▶ Homework
General Knowledge

1. How many values can a function return at any one time?
2. Why don't you need to return global variables?
3. What is the default return type of a function if one isn't specified?
4. Do you think that return works like passing by value or passing by reference? Explain why.
5. Are const parameters useful for pass by value parameters?
6. Are const parameters useful for pass by address parameters?
7. Are const parameters useful for pass by reference parameters?

8. In what order should the following be placed in a Visual C++ program?

```
main()
functions
function prototypes
includes
```

9. When is it sensible to use const and strings?

10. What is an overloaded function?

11. When should you use a default parameter?

12. What is an ambiguous function definition?

13. True or false: A return value that is an expression must be placed in parentheses.

14. True or false: A function that returns a value can be passed only a single parameter.

15. True or false: A function that calls another function with a return value must receive the return value into a variable.

16. True or false: A const parameter tells C++ to convert a literal parameter into a changeable parameter.

17. True or false: C++ uses automatic type conversion to match calling functions to called functions.

18. True or false: C++ will always match calling to called functions when the function name is the same.

19. True or false: Defaulting parameters can be in any order compared with nondefaulting parameters.

20. True or false: Default parameters are ignored by C++ when argument matching.

What's the Output?

The following two questions contain complete programs. Look at the programs and decide what the output should be. You should note which version of the overloaded functions is called and why.

21.
```
#include <iostream.h>
#include <string.h>
void Replace(char str[])
  {
    strcpy(str,"Hello World!");
  }
void Replace(int i)
  {
    i = 99;
  }
void main()
```

UNIT

14

More on Functions

```
    {
      int j = 50;
      char hi[30] = "Hi there!";
      Replace(j);
      Replace(hi);
      cout << hi << endl << j;
    }
```

22. `#include <iostream.h>`

```
    void Print(int i);
    void Print(float f, int skip = 0);
    void main()
      {
        float f = 3.3;
        Print(f);
      }
    void Print(int i)
      {
          cout << "Integer" << endl;
      }
    void Print(float f, int skip)
      {
        cout << "Float";
        if (skip != 0)
          cout << endl;
      }
```

Find the Bug

23. Why won't this code compile?

```
    #include <iostream.h>

    void Print(int i);
    void Print(float f, int skip = 0);
    void main()
      {
        Print(3.3);
      }
    void Print(int i)
      {
          cout << "Integer" << endl;
      }
    void Print(float f, int skip)
      {
        cout << "Float";
        if (skip != 0)
          cout << endl;
      }
```

24. Suzi has amended Pippa's program to print a more suitable message (in her opinion). Why doesn't it work, and will Suzi see an error in her compile or when the program runs?

```
#include <iostream.h>
#include <string.h>
int NameLength(const char name[]);
void main()
  {
    char testName[30] = "Philippa Spencer";
    int length = NameLength(testName);
    cout << testName << " " << length;
  }
int NameLength(const char name[])
  {
    // Suzi's change
    strcpy(name,"Philippa is silly");
    // End of Suzi's change
    int count = -1;
    while (name[++count]);
    return count;
  }
```

25. Was Pippa's code correct before Suzi changed it?

Write Code That...

26. Write overloaded function prototypes for two functions: one that converts inches with decimal places to millimeters with no decimal places, and another that converts back again.

27. Write a prototype equivalent to the following that explicitly includes the return data type:

```
event(int a);
```

28. Write a program that prints the square of a number that the user gives you without using an assignment statement.

Extra Credit

29. Write a program that asks for people's names and their scores at Minesweeper. After each entry, put out a message to say Sorry, not good enough or Best so far!. After each input, ask the user whether there is another score; at the end, put out a message declaring the winner. Use a single function to put out the messages. Only the winning message will show the player's name.

30. Write a program with a function called Swap that allows two strings, two ints, or two floats to be changed over. The program must be able to swap an int and a float. Use the main program to prove that all combinations work.

UNIT
14
More on Functions

Break It Up
with Functions

STOP&TYPE In this lesson, you learned about functions. You saw the following:

▶ Writing your own functions.

▶ How to determine the difference between local and global variables.

▶ How to pass data to a function.

Project 7 Listing. A multifunction program that passes data between functions.

```
1:// Filename: PROJECT7.CPP

2:// A multifunction program that computes payroll amounts

3:#include <iostream.h>

4:#include <iomanip.h>

5:

6:void GetPayrollInput(char name[], float &rate, int &hours);

7:float CalcWages(float rate, int hours);

8:float CalcTaxes(float pay, float taxRate = 0.34);

9:void PrintResults(const char name[],float pay, float taxes);

10://

11:// Overloaded input functions to get individual values

12://
```

▶ How to return data from a function.

▶ How to use the same function name with different parameters.

▶ How to default values.

Description

1: A C++ comment that includes the program's filename.

2: A C++ comment that contains the program's description.

3: The cout and cin commands need information in the IOSTREAM.H header file.

4: You need to include iomanip.h.

5: Blank lines improve your program's readability.

6: Prototype of payroll input function.

6: Prototype all functions.

7: Prototype of wages calculation function.

8: Prototype of taxes calculation function with default parameter for tax rate.

8: The tax rate is defaulted if rate is not present.

9: Prototype of printing function.

10: Comments improve readability.

11: Comments improve readability.

12: Comments improve readability.

continues

Project 7 Listing. continued

```
13:void GetInput(const char prompt[],char string[]);

14:void GetInput(const char prompt[],float& number);

15:void GetInput(const char prompt[],int& number);

16:void main()

17:{

18:  int hours;

19:  float rate, pay, taxes;

20:  char employee[30];

21:  GetPayrollInput(employee, rate, hours);// Get the input data

22:  pay = CalcWages(rate, hours);// Calculate payroll results

23:  taxes = CalcTaxes(pay);       // Calculate payroll taxes

24:  PrintResults(employee, pay, taxes);    // Print the results

25:  return;    // Return to QuickWin

26:}

27://***********************************************************

28:void GetPayrollInput(char name[], float &rate, int &hours)

29:{
```

Description

13: Prototype of overloaded input function, string version (employee name).

13: C++ distinguishes different overloaded functions by parameter data types.

14: Prototype of overloaded input function, `float` version (hourly rate).

15: Prototype of overloaded input function, `int` version (hours).

16: `main()` begins.

16: Keep `main()` as simple as possible.

17: All functions begin with an opening brace.

18: An integer variable that will hold the number of hours worked.

19: `float` variables to hold various payroll values.

20: A `char` array to hold the employee name.

21: Passes `rate` and `hours` by reference so that `GetPayrollInput()` can change them and keep those changed values in `main()`.

21: The function receives the variables by reference.

22: `CalcWages()` uses the `rate` and `hours` figures to calculate and return the gross pay. `main()` captures the return value in `pay`.

23: `CalcTaxes()` uses the gross pay to calculate and return the taxes. `main()` captures the return value in `taxes`.

23: The tax rate parameter is not specified; therefore, the default is used.

24: The employee, gross pay, and taxes are sent to `PrintResults()` to be displayed on-screen.

25: Always return from `main()` to QuickWin.

26: A final brace ends all `main()` functions.

27: A line of asterisks helps to separate functions.

28: The definition (first line) of `GetPayrollInput()`. Receives three parameters: name by address, rate, and hours by reference.

29: All functions begin with an opening brace.

continues

Project 7 Listing. continued

```
30:  // Code to get employee data

31:  GetInput("Employee name? ",name);

32:  GetInput("How many hours did this employee work? ",hours);

33:  GetInput("What is the pay rate per hour? ",rate);

34:  return;   // Return to main()

35:}

36://************************************************************

37:void GetInput(const char prompt[], char string[])

38:  {

39:    cout << prompt;

40:    cin.getline(string,30);

41:    return;

42:  }

43://************************************************************

44:void GetInput(const char prompt[], float& number)

45:  {

46:    cout << prompt;
```

Description

30: Comment to explain the function.

31: Call another function to get the employee name.

31: Break down a complicated function into several easier steps by using function calls.

32: Call another function to get hours worked.

33: Call another function to get rate per hour.

34: Return to `main()` having passed data back via reference parameters.

35: A final brace ends a function definition.

36: A line of asterisks helps to separate functions.

37: The definition of `GetInput()`, which retrieves a string.

37: The passing of the prompt means that the function could be reused to get other values in the program.

38: All functions begin with an opening brace.

39: Use `cout` to output a prompt for user input.

40: `cin.getline` retrieves a whole line of text up to a maximum number of characters.

41: `return` to the calling function, `GetPayrollInput`.

42: A final brace ends a function definition.

43: A line of asterisks helps to separate functions.

44: The definition of `GetInput()` for a `float`. Receives a `const char` array so that the calling program can send literal for prompt.

44: By breaking down the function, each step is small and easy to understand.

45: All functions begin with an opening brace.

46: Use `cout` to output a prompt for user input.

continues

Project 7 Listing. continued

```
47:    cin >> number;

48:    return;

49: }
```

```
50://**********************************************************

51:void GetInput(const char prompt[], int& number)

52: {

53:    cout << prompt;

54:    cin >> number;

55:    return;

56: }
```

```
57://**********************************************************

58:float CalcWages(float rate, int hours)

59:{ // Code to calculate payroll amounts

60:    return (rate * (float)hours);    // Return to main()

61:}
```

```
62://**********************************************************

63:float CalcTaxes(float pay, float taxRate)
```

Description

47: `cin >>` retrieves a `float`.

48: `return` to the calling function, `GetPayrollInput`.

49: A final brace ends a function definition.

50: A line of asterisks helps to separate functions.

51: The definition of `GetInput()` for a `float`. Receives a `const char` array so that the calling program can send literal for prompt.

52: All functions begin with an opening brace.

53: Use `cout` to output a prompt for user input.

54: `cin >>` retrieves a `float`.

55: `return` to the calling function, `GetPayrollInput`.

56: A final brace ends a function definition.

57: A line of asterisks helps to separate functions.

58: Defines the function that calculates gross pay. This function receives a floating-point and an integer parameter passed by value.

58: You can return at most one value.

59: Scatter comments throughout your code.

60: Returns the wages (the number of hours multiplied by the rate per hour).

61: A final brace ends all functions.

62: A line of asterisks helps to separate functions.

63: Defines the function that calculates taxes. Requires a `float` and the tax rate both passed by value, which can be defaulted (line 6).

continues

Project 7 Listing. continued

```
64:{ // Code to compute taxes

65:  return (pay * taxRate);   // Return to main()

66:}

67://*************************************************************

68:void PrintResults(const char name[], float pay, float taxes)

69:{   // Code to print the results

70:  cout.precision(2);

71:  cout.setf(ios::showpoint);

72:  cout.setf(ios::fixed);

73:  cout << endl << name << " earned a total of $"

74:       << pay << endl;

75:  cout << "Before $" << taxes << " in taxes." << endl;

76:  return;   // Return to main()

77:}
```

Description

| 64: | Scatter comments throughout your code. |

| 65: | Returns the taxes to `main()`, which are simply the gross pay multiplied by the tax rate. |

| 66: | A final brace ends all functions. |

| 67: | A line of asterisks helps to separate functions. |

| 68: | Defines the function that prints the results, and requires a `char` array passed by address and two parameters passed by value. |

| 69: | Scatter comments throughout your code. |

| 70: | Ensure that two decimal places print. |

| 71: | Always show the decimal point. |

| 72: | Guard against scientific notation. |

| 73: | Prints the employee's gross pay. |

| 74: | The long cout is concluded. |

| 75: | Prints the employee's tax requirement. |

| 76: | Returns to `main()`. |

| 77: | A final brace ends all functions. |

▼ **OUTPUT**

```
Employee name? Keith Gutteridge
How many hours did this employee work? 40
What is the pay rate per hour? 25.50

Keith Gutteridge earned a total of $1020.00
Before $346.80 in taxes.
```

Lesson ▶

Lots of Data

15

Arrays Multiply Storage

element

key value

sequential search

parallel arrays

numeric arrays

▶ What You'll Learn

▶ Array basics

▶ Searching through arrays

There is little need to explain arrays in great detail here because you already know all about them! You've been working with character arrays since Lesson 3. This unit simply explains more about how Visual C++ stores arrays and introduces arrays of data types that are different from the char data types you've been working with.

In addition to character arrays, you can create arrays of any data type. You can define an integer array, a floating-point array, and a double floating-point array. Any time you need lists of values, it's a lot easier to define the list as an array instead of as differently named variables. You can step through all the elements of an array with a for loop, and you'll often need to process and print elements throughout an array.

▶ Array Basics

Concept

What You Will Learn

Review the terminology of arrays and explain how arrays reside in the computer's memory.

Figure 15.1 shows a character array named cArray with five values. Each individual value in the array is an *element*. The subscripts range from 0 to 4 for a five-character array. No matter what kind of array you define, each value in the array is called an element, and the number that references each element is also a subscript.

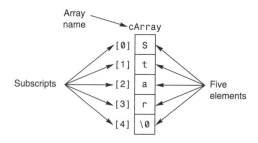

Figure 15.1.
A five-element character array holding a string.

As you know, character arrays hold strings. In Visual C++, arrays can be taught much earlier than in other programming languages (or at least character arrays can be). When a character array holds a string value, treating the array as a single but aggregate string value with the individual elements holding individual characters makes a lot of sense. (Other programming languages store strings in string variables.)

You might not see the need for numeric arrays at this time. After all, if you defined an array of 25 integers, you would never refer to the entire integer array as a single entity. The concept of doing something with a single group of 25 numbers doesn't make as much sense as treating a character array holding a string as a single group.

In reality, you work with lists of numbers all the time. When your program must process several numeric values, array storage is perfect for holding and stepping through those values. Although you don't refer to the array aggregately in the same way that you do a character array holding a string, numeric arrays are extremely important in computing.

To help with your understanding of numeric arrays, let's review the basics of character arrays. The array in Figure 15.1 might be initialized like this:

```
char cArray[5] = "Star";
```

Visual C++'s syntax for initializing strings in character arrays, as shown here, doesn't apply to numeric arrays. There's no need to worry about a null zero at the end of numeric arrays because only strings need null zero values at their termination. If you define and initialize a numeric array at the same time, you must initialize the array's individual elements one at a time. Use braces to initialize individual elements in the array.

Here's how you would initialize cArray one element at a time:

```
char cArray[5] = {'S', 't', 'a', 'r', '\0'};
```

This definition is identical to the previous one, except that it's a little more tedious for you to type. Nevertheless, this character-by-character initialization will prepare you for the syntax required for all numeric array initialization. Visual C++ automatically adds the terminator zero to the end of the string when you assign an initial string value.

When you define and initialize an array at the same time, you don't need the initial subscript. The following definition is identical to the preceding one:

```
char cArray[] = {'S', 't', 'a', 'r', '\0'};   // Visual C++ counts the
                                              // elements for you
```

When you (or Visual C++) reserve five array elements, don't try to store six or more elements in the array! If you do, you will overwrite memory that might be holding other kinds of variables. If you need to define a large array, you can always define the array with extra elements. The following array definition holds the four-character string Star with a terminator, but it also has extra reserved room in case you need to store a longer string in the array later:

```
char cArray[35] = {'S', 't', 'a', 'r', '\0'};
```

Character arrays might hold individual characters and not strings. If that's the case, don't worry about the terminator. It exists only to terminate strings.

UNIT

15

Arrays Multiply Storage

Note   String functions such as `strlen()` and `strcpy()` rely on the terminator. If you define an array to hold a list of individual characters, such as a class's letter grades, you'll never treat the array as if it holds a string; therefore, you don't have to make sure the terminator is at the end of the array.

Warning   Unlike most programming languages, Visual C++ doesn't complain if you store a value in an undefined array element. For example, the statement

```
cArray[3200] = 'X';    // Oops!
```

puts an X approximately 3,200 memory locations after the start of the 35-character array named `cArray`. Who knows what the X will overwrite? Whatever happens, you'll realize something has gone awry when your computer freezes or reboots because the X overwrote an important area of memory or changed a critical internal program value!

Moving to numeric arrays is now easy. If you want to define a five-element integer array named `nums`, you can do so like this:

```
int nums[5];    // Define an integer array
```

You also can initialize the array at the same time you define it:

```
int nums[5] = {2, 4, 6, 8, 10};    // Define and initialize the array
```

Figure 15.2 shows how the integer array looks in memory. Notice that an integer array and a character array are the same except for these two things:

▶ Numeric arrays contain numeric values and not character values.

▶ Numeric arrays don't use a terminating zero.

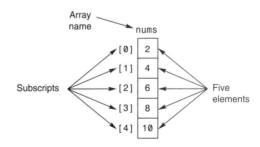

Figure 15.2.
A five-element integer array holding five integers.

As with character arrays, you don't need to specify the initial subscript if you define the array with its maximum number of values up front. This array definition matches the preceding one:

```
int nums[] = {2, 4, 6, 8, 10};    // Defines and initializes the array
```

Warning   If you define an array without assigning initial values at the time of definition, be sure to use an initial subscript. The following array definition is incorrect. Visual C++ reserves no storage for the array!

```
int array[];   // There must be a subscript
               // or initial values
```

Here is another integer array definition:

```
int values[] = {10, 9, 8, 7, 6, 5, 4, 3, 2, 1, 0};
```

Despite the fact that a 0 is in values's last element, that 0 is considered an integer zero, because there is no string in the array. In other words, it is considered a valid part of the array data.

If you don't initialize an array when you define it, you must fill the array one value at a time. For example, this is not possible in the body of the program:

```
values[] = {10, 9, 8, 7, 6, 5, 4, 3, 2, 1, 0};
```

And neither is this:

```
values = {10, 9, 8, 7, 6, 5, 4, 3, 2, 1, 0};
```

In the body of the program, you must assign each value to each array element one at a time. Later in this unit, you will learn some techniques that most programs use to initialize arrays.

The following two array definitions reserve two numeric arrays. The first array is a double array and the second is a long int array:

```
double factors[25];      // Defines an array of 25 doubles

long int weights[100];   // Defines an array of 100 long integers
```

At the time you define these arrays, you could initialize them with a few values, like this:

```
double factors[25] = {4244.56, 78409.21, 2930.55433, 569401.34};

long int weights[100] = {43567, 70935, 32945, 102, 49059};
```

If you define an array of a specific size but initialize fewer elements as shown here, Visual C++ zeros out every remaining element in the array. In other words, the first five elements of weights contain the values inside the braces (from 43567 to 49059), and the remaining elements hold zero.

If you don't initialize any elements, don't rely on Visual C++ to initialize them for you! Visual C++ doesn't automatically initialize vals to zeros given this definition:

```
int vals[100];   // Defines but doesn't initialize vals
```

UNIT **15**

Arrays Multiply Storage

Tip If you want to initialize an array to all zeros, initialize it with a single zero:

```
int vals[100] = {0};    // The entire array now holds 0
```

ARRAY SPACE

Each element in an array requires a different subscript. All arrays, no matter what data type they are, start at subscript 0. The next array element is subscript 1, and so on.

Each element in an array of double values will consume more memory than each element in an array of character values. A five-element character array will consume much less space than a five-element double floating-point array. You reference both, however, with the subscripts 0 through 4.

If you want to know how much memory an array consumes, use the `sizeof` operator on the array name. The following statement stores the total amount of memory taken by the array named `factor` to `mem`:

```
mem = sizeof(factor);
```

If `factor` were a character array, `mem` would hold a much smaller number than if `factor` were a floating-point array because each element in the character array would take much less memory. `sizeof` returns the total amount of memory an array is defined as. `sizeof` has nothing to do with how many values you've actually initialized with data.

Many times, you can't initialize an array when you first define it. The user's input or data from a disk file or calculations might fill the array with values in the body of the program. The assignment operator stores values in arrays. Given the array definition

```
float ara[10];    // Define an array of 10 floating-point values
```

you can later store a number in the first element with an assignment like this:

```
ara[0] = 293.05;
```

You can also get an element with `cin` to let the user assign a value to the element:

```
cout << "What is the next value? ";
cin >> ara[4];
```

The following `for` loop stores the values 0 through 450 in an integer array that's assumed to be defined to hold at least 451 elements (one for element 0):

```
for (s = 0; s <= 450; s++)
{ iArray[s] = s; }
```

STOP&TYPE Listing 15.1 contains a simple program that defines an array of seven floating-point values. The user initializes each value with a daily temperature in Fahrenheit. The program then applies a calculation to each element to convert those Fahrenheit values to Celsius. When all values have been converted, the program prints the Celsius readings.

Review

What You Have Learned

You can define an array of any data type and step through each element.

▼ INPUT LISTING 15.1. CONVERTING A WEEK'S WORTH OF TEMPERATURE READINGS.

```
1:// Filename: ARRTEMP.CPP
2:// Fills an array with seven temperature readings, converts
3:// those readings to Celsius, and prints the results
4:#include <iostream.h>
5:
6:
7:void FillTemps(float temps[7]);
8:void CalcCelsius(float temps[7]);
9:void PrintCelsius(float temps[7]);
10:
11:void main()
12:{
13:
14:   float temps[7];   // The user will initialize the array
15:
16:   FillTemps(temps);     // Get the seven values from the user
17:   CalcCelsius(temps);   // Convert the values to Celsius
18:   PrintCelsius(temps);  // Print the Celsius readings
19:
20:   return;
21:}
22://*********************************************************
23:void FillTemps(float temps[7])
24:{
25:   int ctr;
26:   cout << "** Temperature Conversion **" << endl;
27:   cout << "---------------------------" << endl << endl;
28:   for (ctr = 0; ctr < 7; ctr++)
29:     {
30:       cout << "What is the Fahrenheit reading for day #"
31:            << (ctr+1) << "? ";
32:       cin >> temps[ctr];
33:     }
34:   return;
35:}
36://*********************************************************
37:void CalcCelsius(float temps[7])
```

continues

```
38:{
39:   // Change each temperature to Celsius
40:   int ctr;
41:   for (ctr = 0; ctr < 7; ctr++)
42:     {
43:        // The Fs after the numbers are floats not Fahrenheits
44:        temps[ctr] = (temps[ctr] - 32.0F) * (5.0F / 9.0F);
45:     }
46:   return;
47:}
48://**********************************************************
49:void PrintCelsius(float temps[7])
50:{
51:   // Print the Celsius readings
52:   int ctr;
53:   cout.precision(1);
54:   cout.setf(ios::showpoint);
55:   cout.setf(ios::fixed);
56:   cout << endl << "Here are the equivalent Celsius readings:"
57:        << endl << endl;
58:   for (ctr = 0; ctr < 7; ctr++)
59:     {
60:        cout << "Day #" << (ctr + 1) << ": "
61:             << temps[ctr] << endl;
62:     }
63:   cout << endl << "Stay warm!" << endl;
64:   return;
65:}
```

▼ **OUTPUT**

```
** Temperature Conversion **
_ _ _ _ _ _ _ _ _ _ _ _ _ _

What is the Fahrenheit reading for day #1? 65.7
What is the Fahrenheit reading for day #2? 45.4
What is the Fahrenheit reading for day #3? 32.1
What is the Fahrenheit reading for day #4? 28.3
What is the Fahrenheit reading for day #5? 24.5
What is the Fahrenheit reading for day #6? 67.8
What is the Fahrenheit reading for day #7? 76.2

Here are the equivalent Celsius readings:

Day #1: 18.7
Day #2: 7.4
Day #3: 0.1
Day #4: -2.1
Day #5: -4.2
Day #6: 19.9
Day #7: 24.6

Stay warm!
```

▼ ANALYSIS

One of the first things to note about this program is that all the temperature readings are asked for in advance, all at once, before any calculation is performed. You could never program this way without arrays. Arrays give you the ability to capture all your data in a loop and then process that data all at once. Without arrays, you would have to use separate variable names for each temperature and ask for the seven readings using seven different sets of the same I/O code.

main() is a controlling function that dictates what the rest of the program is to do. If you hadn't read the description of the program beforehand, you could still figure out the entire program's job by studying main(). One of the many advantages of structuring your program into smaller modules is the readability of the main() function.

The FillTemps() function in lines 23 through 35 gathers all the temperature readings in one for loop. As you begin to write longer and more powerful programs (this is one of the longest programs in this book so far), you'll see that gathering data up front, before processing, often helps eliminate messy get-a-value, calculate-a-value code. By storing data in an array first, you can better structure your programs. When you begin to write really big programs (several pages long), everything you can do to help streamline the code will save you time during both program development and debugging.

Tip Do you think that this long program is difficult to understand? On the contrary; you probably think it's rather simple. However, this program is one of the most complex in this book so far! You're now at the point where more advanced Visual C++ code seems easy. The structuring of programs into smaller functions helps you see "the big picture" better than before.

This program always passes the array by address. Therefore, the functions can all change the array. When they do, main()'s version also is changed because the functions operate on the same array as main(), not on a copy as would be the case with data passed by value.

Note You might think that a global array of temperatures would be better than passing the same local array through all the functions. It's true that a global variable makes sense if every function in the program—or at least most of the functions—needs access to the variable. However, my desire to shy away from global variables as much as possible dictated the use of one local array instead. The extra practice at passing data between functions is good for you.

UNIT

15

Arrays Multiply Storage

► **Searching Through Arrays**

Concept

One of the most important features of array processing is searching through an array for specific values. You can tell your computer to find a customer balance, receivable amount, or payroll figure, and it responds in a snap—even if the program has to search through hundreds of values.

Definition—A *key* is a value you're looking for in an array or a file.

Searching an array for a particular value is simple. Array searching requires no new commands, just an application of the commands you already know. Once an array is filled, finding a value requires starting at the beginning of the array and comparing the next array element with a key value.

Note   All kinds of searching techniques for computers have been developed. The technique discussed in this unit—the sequential search technique—is the most popular and one of the easiest, but it's also one of the slowest. Unless your programs often search through huge arrays of data, however, the sequential search gives you more than enough power to find a match in a short time.

For example, suppose you need to see whether a customer properly filled out his or her customer number on a mailing that you recently sent. You can scan the customer ID list, an array of values, looking for the customer's ID (the key).

When you search an array for a key value, one of three things will happen:

► You'll find a match.

► You won't find a match.

► You'll find more than one match.

Your data will dictate whether you'll allow duplicate keys. In other words, you don't want two customers with the same customer ID number. Therefore, every time you add a customer to your files, through array processing you'll want to make sure that the customer isn't already on the list. Other times, you'll want to allow two or more equal values in an array. A list of student test scores might produce two or more students who happened to make the same grade on a test.

Searching an array makes the assumption that the array already has data. There are three primary ways that you fill arrays with values:

- ▶ Assignment statements
- ▶ Data entry from the user
- ▶ Disk file input

This book has spent a lot of time assigning values with the assignment operator, but most real-world data comes from the user or the disk. You can't know when you write a program exactly what values that program will eventually process, so you can rarely assign data in assignment statements. You can't predict how much a customer will buy, so you have to wait for the clerk at the computer to enter the amount.

The rest of the programs in this unit assign array values directly or through user input because you have yet to learn about file I/O. Lesson 11 explains how to use disk files for storage. When you start a program that manages disk file data, probably one of the first things the program will do is read the disk values into an array. Therefore, a prerequisite for learning about disk files is learning how to work with arrays.

Tip In Lesson 12, you'll learn about random file access, which is a fancy term that basically means treating a disk file as if it were one large array. Instead of taking up valuable memory, you can keep the data on the disk and apply this lesson's array techniques to the file itself. As you can see, array processing is vital for your future programming.

Here is a simple loop that searches an array with MAX values, looking for the user's match:

```
cout << "What is your customer code? ";
cin >> userKey;
match = 0;    // No match is made yet
for (c = 0; c < MAX; c++)
{ if (customers[c] == userKey)
{ match = 1;
break; }    // 1 is true
}
if (match)
{ cout << "You are already in the list"; }
else
{ cout << "You are not in the list"; }
```

In this code fragment, userKey is the key value that you're looking for. Searching almost always involves a variable that holds a true or false result. Either the search key was found in the array (true) or it was not found (false). In this code, the match variable begins as false before the search begins. If there is a match of the customer's number to an array element, match is set to 1 (true) and the break terminates the for loop because there is no reason to look through the remaining elements.

Note If you were applying this sequential search against an array that holds duplicate keys, you wouldn't break out of the loop but would continue searching. Such searches often add all of the matches found (using a counter variable). A weather center might look through an array of last year's temperature readings for all values below freezing, counting the number of values that meet that criteria. Because two or more days could be below freezing, you wouldn't stop the search after finding just one.

ARE YOU "JUST A NUMBER"?

Do you get tired of feeling as if utilities and credit card companies think of you as just a number instead of a real person? Blame the computer!

Many names, such as McNeal and St. John, have far too many variations to be used as a key when searching with a program. McNeal might be entered as `McNeal`, `Mc Neal`, `Mcneal`, or `Mc.Neal`, depending on the person doing the data entry. An integer or character string is a much more accurate way of assigning specific values to people. The customer code of 734AB has little ambiguity other than the possibility of the user entering lowercase letters, which your program can convert itself or by calling a Visual C++ library routine (see Lesson 12).

When businesses computerize their records, they must assign their customers, vendors, and products unique IDs (key-searching values) to speed up the searching. Ideally, these computerized filing systems ultimately save you lots of money over file-cabinet organization. Can you imagine how long it would take a credit card company to go through miles of filing cabinets looking for your balance when you wanted to charge something? Computers speed up important business processing, and that saves you—the customer and consumer—lots of dough.

Before looking at code that searches an array, you've got one more concept to understand. Look at Figure 15.3, a spreadsheet-like representation of a customer file. The first column is a list of customer IDs, the second column contains customer balance amounts, and the third column is the customers' last purchase amount.

Definition—*Parallel arrays* are several arrays with the same number of elements that work in tandem to produce data.

Customer ID	Balance	Last purchase amount
4543	5,567.65	656.78
2934	345.43	19.83
1902	1,001.34	1,001.34
4967	3,249.55	573.68
8092	657.84	657.84
4234	2,384.56	1,290.45

Figure 15.3.
A three-array representation of customer data.

Rarely will you have to search a single array to look for a value. More likely, you'll have to search several parallel arrays. Figure 15.3 contains three parallel arrays. The first array is the customer ID, the second array is the balance, and the third array is the last purchase amount. Each array would be parallel, meaning that the first element ID in the first array would have the balance shown in the first element of the second array. That same customer's last purchase amount is listed in the first element of the third array. For example, customer number 4967 has a balance of $3,249.55 and last made a purchase of $573.68.

Here's how parallel arrays work: The data from the arrays would probably come from a disk file, as discussed earlier. After the arrays are filled with their values, a customer comes into your store to buy something. The first thing you do is have a program look through the customer ID array. When the customer's ID is found, use that element number to look in the balance array to see whether the customer's balance is too high to buy something. If so, the customer must pay some of the balance. You could use this same procedure to see whether the customer's last purchase was large, in which case you might want to give a special discount today.

The arrays that you've learned about in this book are called *single-dimensional* arrays. Visual C++ supports multidimensional arrays, which hold data in a tabular format, but multidimensional arrays aren't as commonly used in Visual C++ as they are in other programming languages. You can rarely replace parallel arrays with multidimensional arrays, even though multidimensional arrays have a tabular format similar to that of Figure 15.3. Multidimensional array elements must all be the same data type, which limits their use as a replacement for parallel arrays.

Also, Visual C++ doesn't really have built-in support for multidimensional arrays as other languages do. To create a multidimensional array, you must create an array of arrays, which can greatly increase program complexity without adding a lot of benefit.

If you're lost, that's fine because this book doesn't discuss multidimensional arrays any further. Again, their use is limited, and taking the time to discuss them in detail here would take away space from more important material. Later, you will see another way of holding different types of values in a single-dimensional array.

STOP&TYPE Listing 15.2 contains an inventory program. Initialization statements fill the parallel arrays with product ID numbers, product amounts, product prices, and product reorder levels. The user enters a product ID, and the program then displays the product's inventory figures.

Review   **What You Have Learned**

> Searching parallel arrays requires that you look for a match on a key value. If a match is found, the matching elements in the other arrays provide additional data.

▼ INPUT   LISTING 15.2. DISPLAYING INVENTORY INFORMATION.

```
 1:// Filename: INVSRCH.CPP
 2:// Demonstrates the sequential parallel array searching
 3:// technique. An inventory ID number is asked for. If
 4:// the ID is found in the arrays, that product's
 5:// inventory data is displayed for the user.
 6:#include <iostream.h>
 7:#include <iomanip.h>
 8:
 9:int GetKey();
10:int SearchInv(int keyVal, int prodID[]);
11:void PrintData(int foundSub, int prodID[], int numItems[],
12:               float price[], int reorder[]);
13:
14:const int INV = 10; // Products in this sample array
15:
16:void main()
17:{
18:
19:  // First, initialize a few sample elements
20:  // Product IDs
21:  int prodID[INV] = {32, 45, 76, 10, 94,
22:                     52, 27, 29, 87, 60};
23:  // Number of each product currently in the inventory
24:  int numItems[INV] = {6, 2, 1, 0, 8,
25:                       2, 4, 7, 9, 3};
26:  // Price of each product
27:  float price[INV] = {5.43, 6.78, 8.64, 3.32, 1.92,
28:                      7.03, 9.87, 7.65, 4.63, 2.38};
29:  // Reorder levels
30:  int reorder[INV] = {5, 4, 1, 3, 5,
31:                      6, 2, 1, 1, 4};
```

```
32:    int keyVal, foundSub;
33:
34:    // The program's primary logic begins here
35:    keyVal = GetKey();    // Ask the user for an ID
36:    foundSub = SearchInv(keyVal, prodID);    // Search the inventory
37:    if (foundSub == -99)
38:      {
39:        cout << "That product is not in the inventory.";
40:        return;
41:      }
42:    // Here only if the item was found
43:    PrintData(foundSub, prodID, numItems, price, reorder);
44:    return;
45:}
46://***********************************************************
47:int GetKey()
48:{
49:    // Ask the user for an ID
50:    int keyVal;
51:    cout << "** Inventory Search Program **" << endl;
52:    cout << endl << endl << "Enter a product ID: ";
53:    cin >> keyVal;
54:    return (keyVal);
55:}
56://***********************************************************
57:int SearchInv(int keyVal, int prodID[])
58:{
59:    // Search the ID array and return the subscript of
60:    // the found product, or return -99 if not found
61:    int foundSub = -99;
62:    int c;
63:    for (c = 0; c < INV; c++)
64:      {
65:        if (keyVal == prodID[c])
66:          {
67:            foundSub = c;
68:            break;
69:          }
70:      }
71:    // The -99 will still be in foundSub
72:    // if the search failed
73:    return (foundSub);
74:}
75://***********************************************************
76:void PrintData(int foundSub, int prodID[], int numItems[],
77:       float price[], int reorder[])
78:{
79:    // Print the data from the matching parallel arrays
80:    cout << setprecision(2);
81:    cout.setf(ios::showpoint);
82:    cout.setf(ios::fixed);
83:    cout << endl << "Product ID: " << prodID[foundSub]
84:        << "\tNumber in stock: "
85:        << numItems[foundSub] << endl;
```

continues

```
86:    cout << "Price: $" << price[foundSub] << "\tReorder: "
87:         << reorder[foundSub] << endl;
88:    return;
89:}
```

▼ OUTPUT

Note   Two runs of output are shown.

```
** Inventory Search Program **

Enter a product ID: 13
That product is not in the inventory.

** Inventory Search Program **

Enter a product ID: 94

Product ID: 94   Number in stock: 8
Price: $1.92     Reorder: 5
```

▼ ANALYSIS

main(), from lines 16 through 31, consists primarily of array initialization. As mentioned earlier in this unit, your real-world programs will probably initialize arrays from disk files or user input. Inventory programs are almost always designed to initialize from a disk file because the user shouldn't be expected to enter the inventory data each time he or she runs the program.

After the arrays are initialized, main() controls the rest of the program. The user enters a product ID in the GetKey() function. SearchInv() searches the product ID array, looking for a match. If the product ID isn't found, SearchInv() stores -99 for the subscript, which indicates that the ID isn't in the list and causes an error to appear in main(). If a match is found, the subscript for that product's parallel arrays is returned to main(), where it's passed on to the PrintData() function, along with the four parallel arrays.

PrintData() then uses the subscript of the found product to print the inventory information from the arrays. When main() regains control, the program quits and returns to the Visual C++ QuickWin window.

The logic in this program is fairly complicated, yet you should have little trouble understanding what's going on. No new commands or library functions are needed. Arrays make stepping through and searching a list of values simple. When you add file I/O to a program such as this, reading that file's data directly into the arrays, you have a full-featured inventory searching program.

When you complete the questions at the end of this unit, try your hand at the last two Extra Credit exercises. They require that you write a program similar to this inventory program and add some updating and reporting functions. You'll develop a full-featured inventory-balance control system based on what you already know.

Note   Fewer than seven lessons ago, you were figuring out the difference between an integer and a floating-point value. Now you're writing high-level business programs!

▶ Homework
General Knowledge

1. Besides `char`, what other data types can you store in arrays?

2. Do numeric arrays end with null zeros? Why or why not?

3. What is the starting subscript value for integer arrays?

4. How many array elements does the following array definition reserve?

```
double values[16];
```

5. How many array elements does the following array definition reserve?

```
int ages[] = {23, 54, 32, 39, 40, 69, 74, 57, 12};
```

6. Why will the following array definition fail to reserve storage?

```
float weights[];
```

7. How can you find out how much memory the following array consumes?

```
long double scientific[25];
```

8. What's the easiest way to initialize a 100-element integer array with zeros?

9. Why do arrays usually make programs more readable instead of less so?

10. What is a key?

11. If you allow for no duplicate values in an array, what are the two possible results of an array search?

12. If you allow for duplicate values in an array, what are the three possible results of an array search?

13. What are the three ways that programs initialize arrays?

14. Why do computerized systems often rely on integer-based or character-based keys instead of people's names?

15. Why would you use parallel arrays?

16. If you pass a floating-point array to a function and the function changes it, does the array change in the calling function also?

17. True or false: The following array named `values` terminates with a terminator:

```
int values[] = {5, 2, 1, 9, 8, 0};
```

18. True or false: An error message displays when you attempt to store a value in an array subscript higher than the number of elements you've defined.

19. True or false: Both of the following arrays consume the same amount of memory:

```
int vals[8];
double vals[8];
```

20. True or false: Both of the following arrays contain nine elements:

```
int vals[8];
double vals[8];
```

21. True or false: All elements in an array must be the same data type.

22. True or false: Visual C++ initializes all arrays with zeros if you don't store values in arrays when you define them.

What's the Output?

23. Given this array definition and initialization

```
int ara[] = {1, 2, 3, 4, 5, 6, 7, 8, 9};
```

what does the following code produce?

```
for (c = 8; c >= 0; c—)
  { cout << ara[c] << endl; }
```

Find the Bug

24. Mike has written an array-searching routine that doesn't work consistently. Perhaps you can help him spot the problem.

```
cin >> keyVal;
for (i = 0; i < NUM; i++)
  { if (ara[i] == keyVal)
      { found = 1; }   // Found a match
    else
      { found = 0; }   // Not at this element
  }
```

Write Code That...

25. This one's easy! Rewrite the temperature conversion program in Listing 15.1, changing all the hardcoded literal 7s to one named constant named DAYS. After you replace 7 with the named constant, change the constant to 21 and rerun the program. The program now asks for three week's worth of data. It's important to realize what you just accomplished; with arrays, the total number of items you have to process is a trivial concern. Once you write a program that contains array processing, all you have to do is modify the array size and `for` loop limits with the defined constant, and none of the rest of the program has to change. Without arrays, you would have to add more variables and more sections of repeated code.

26. Rewrite the INVSRCH.CPP inventory-searching program in Listing 15.2 to allow for more than one search with each run. Put a `do-while` loop in the `main()` function so that the user can look up more than one product. If the user enters an incorrect product ID, print an error message but don't terminate the program. Only when the user enters `-99` for the product ID (and let the user know that a `-99` will terminate the program) should the loop, and therefore the program, terminate.

Extra Credit

27. Write an inventory balance program using the parallel array data shown in Figure 15.3. You can use a lot of the code from the inventory program in Listing 15.2 as a basis for this program. Ask the user (in a loop) for a product number. Print the inventory's balance and the reorder level, and print a reorder request if the stock balance is below the reorder level (which indicates that the balance is too low and you are going to run out of stock).

28. Add the following menu to the program you wrote in question 27:

```
Here are your choices:
  1. Display a product balance information
  2. Update a product's stock with a receipt (+) or issue (-)
  3. Print a list of all products which need reordering
  4. Exit the program
What do you want to do?
```

If the user selects the second option, ask him or her for the ID of the product. If the ID exists, ask for receipt or issue amount. Let the user enter a negative number for an issue and then use the number to update the inventory array. If the user requests the third option, step through the array and check each item. For each item, test the number of items (stock) in the array for items below the reorder level (in other words, step through two arrays at once). Print the reorder list on-screen, outputting reorders as you find them.

UNIT

15

Arrays Multiply Storage

Pointers
Simplified

▶ **What You'll Learn**

▶ Inside memory

▶ Pointer variables

▶ The marriage of arrays and pointers

▶ Pointers to characters

▶ Arrays of pointers

Definition—*Pointer variables* point to other variables.

This unit takes you into the world of advanced Visual C++ programming by teaching you about pointer variables. Be warned: At first, pointer variables seem to add more work without offering any advantages. Be patient! Before this unit ends, you'll see how pointers let you write programs that manipulate string data in arrays. Until you learn about pointers, you can't keep track of string data using an array.

Note   Pointer variables are often just called pointers.

Although pointers are considered advanced, the true power of Visual C++ doesn't appear until you master pointers. Many programming languages, such as COBOL, FORTRAN, and QBasic, don't support pointers. Those languages can't provide for the advanced data management that you'll read about in Lesson 9.

Enough convincing! Let's get to the point.

▶ **Inside Memory**

Concept   **What You Will Learn**

To understand pointers, you must understand computer memory.

Definition—*RAM* stands for *random access memory.*

The memory inside your PC, often called RAM, holds your program, data, and operating system. There are really two types of memory if you count the disk drive. The disk, however, is long-term memory. Your PC can't process any program or data on the disk until you or another program reads the disk contents into RAM.

Note   To keep things simple, RAM will be called memory throughout the rest of this book. ROM, a special kind of read-only memory, isn't discussed here.

Your computer can process only data stored in memory. Therefore, your computer's memory is vital and closely tied to your computer's processor. Until now, you didn't need to know much about memory to run Visual C++ programs. However, a thorough understanding of pointers isn't possible until you really understand the makeup of your computer's memory storage.

Figure 16.1 shows an overview of memory as viewed by Visual C++. When you run Windows or OS/2, you'll have to give up even more memory for your operating environment, but usually there's still enough memory left to write virtually any program you need.

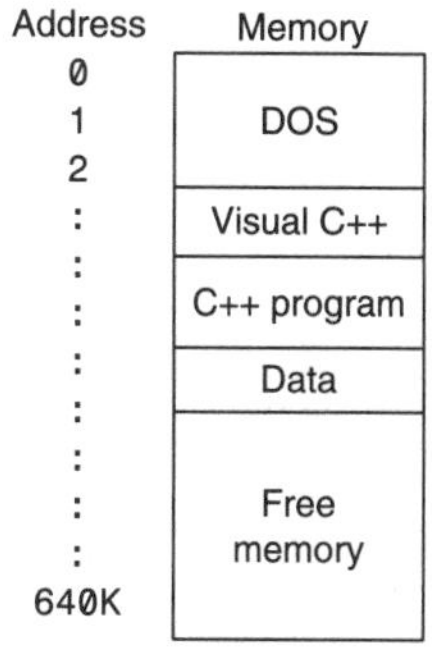

```
Address        Memory
   0        ┌──────────────┐
   1        │     DOS      │
   2        ├──────────────┤
   :        │  Visual C++  │
   :        ├──────────────┤
   :        │ C++ program  │
   :        ├──────────────┤
   :        │     Data     │
   :        ├──────────────┤
   :        │              │
   :        │     Free     │
   :        │   memory     │
 640K       └──────────────┘
```

Figure 16.1.
Your PC's memory layout.

The Address column in Figure 16.1 is very important for this unit. Each memory location in your PC has a different address, just as your house has an address different from the rest of the world. The PC's addresses are sequential numbers that begin at 0 and increment at each memory location through the highest memory location.

When you define a variable, Visual C++ finds the next empty address in the data area and sticks the variable at that location. Visual C++ keeps track, through an internal table, of where each variable resides. As you already know, Visual C++'s data types consume different amounts of memory, so variables are rarely stored in back-to-back addresses. Integers take two bytes, long integers take four, and so on.

After the variable definitions

```
main()
{
  int i = 19;
  char c = 'X';
  float f = 3.453;
```

Visual C++ would store the data in memory to look something like the memory in Figure 16.2. Of course, the variables probably wouldn't be placed exactly at the addresses in the figure, but the important thing to note is that each variable starts at a given address and different data types take different amounts of memory.

UNIT

16

Pointers Simplified

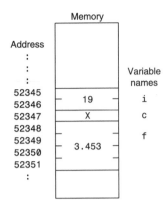

Figure 16.2.
Three defined variables in memory.

Aren't variable names great? Without variable names, you would have to remember the address of every data value your program worked with.

Review   **What You Have Learned**

Each memory location in your computer contains a specific address. When you define variables, Visual C++ finds unused memory locations and stores the variables there. When you refer to a variable by name, Visual C++ finds that variable's address and works with the value stored there.

Note   There is no Stop and Type section here due to this section's conceptual nature.

▶ **Pointer Variables**

Concept   **What You Will Learn**

As with all other kinds of variables, you must define and initialize pointer variables before you can use them.

A pointer variable is just that—a variable. You already know that you must define all variables before you can use them, and pointers are no exception. When you define variables, the following things happen:

▶ You tell Visual C++ to find an empty place in memory.

▶ You tell Visual C++ what to call the variable.

▶ You might put something in the variable.

You don't always put a value in every variable at the time you define the variable, but you can, as you already know.

Nothing's new here so far. It's important to realize that when you request a pointer variable, you do exactly the same thing as when you request a nonpointer variable. If you were defining an integer variable, you'd do this:

```
int i;   // No initial value
```

When you define pointer variables, you must tell Visual C++ that the variable is a pointer. Visual C++ knows that this variable named i is a simple integer variable.

To define a pointer variable, you must include one extra symbol. Here's how you would define a pointer variable named iPtr:

```
int * iPtr;   // No initial value
```

The * is not the multiplication operator. It's called a dereferencing operator when used in this context. Without the *, Visual C++ wouldn't know that iPtr is supposed to be a pointer variable. Without the *, Visual C++ would think that iPtr was another integer variable; therefore, you couldn't perform pointer access with iPtr.

 Tip The spacing around the * isn't important. All of the following variable definitions are equivalent:

```
int * iPtr;
int *iPtr;
int* iPtr;
```

The * must be there when you define pointers just so that Visual C++ will know that the variable is a pointer and not a regular variable. The * is not part of the pointer variable's name.

Definition—An *overloaded operator* performs two different operations depending on its context of use.

The purpose of pointer variables is to point to other variables. When you define a pointer variable, you must tell Visual C++ what type of data the pointer will point to. In the previous definition, iPtr is a pointer to integer data. iPtr can't point to anything other than integers. If you wanted to define a pointer to a floating-point variable, you could do so like this:

```
float * fPtr;   // A pointer to a floating-point variable
```

You can define pointer variables for all of Visual C++'s data types. In the next lesson, you'll learn how to define your own data types. Visual C++ even lets you define pointers to data types that you define.

UNIT

16

Pointers Simplified

You can give pointer variables any name you want. Often, programmers develop special naming conventions for their pointer variables so that they can more easily distinguish between pointers and regular variables without having to refer often to the program's definition section.

As with all variables, defining pointer variables is only half your job. You also must initialize pointer variables before you can do anything with them. When you define a pointer variable, initializing it with a value, the value you store in the pointer variable is always the address of another variable. Pointers don't hold data in the normal sense of the word. The data that a pointer variable holds is always an address.

To store the address of another variable, you must learn about one additional operator. The address of operator, &, returns the address of (good name, huh?) other variables. After you define a pointer variable named fPtr, as done earlier, you can store the address of a floating-point variable named aFloat like this:

```
fPtr = &aFloat;    // Link the pointer to the floating-point variable
```

The following code defines an integer variable named count. The value 135 is stored in count as count is defined. Immediately after that integer is defined, a pointer to an integer variable named iPtr is defined. The third line then stores the address of count in iPtr:

```
int count = 135;
int * iPtr;
iPtr = &count;    // Make iPtr point to count
```

Figure 16.3 shows what the memory would look like after these three lines execute. This figure assumes that count appears at the address of 456212, but the address probably would be something else, of course, depending on the makeup of the PC's memory. The important thing to know is that whatever address count is stored at is assigned to iPtr.

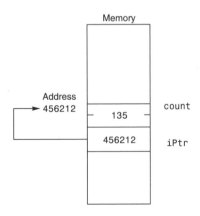

Figure 16.3.
iPtr points to count.

Notice that you don't use the * again when assigning the address of count to iPtr. The second line contains the * just to tell Visual C++ that iPtr is a pointer variable. If you want to, you can initialize the pointer variable at the time you define it. The following variable definitions are equivalent to the previous code:

```
int count = 135;
int * iPtr = &count;   // Initialize iPtr and make iPtr point to count
```

After you've defined a pointer, what can you do with it? Well, through the pointer, you can manipulate the variable being pointed to. Given the count and iPtr definitions just shown, the following statement stores a 7 in count:

```
count = 7;
```

That's no big deal. However, now that the iPtr pointer points to count, the following statement also puts a 7 in count:

```
*iPtr = 7;   // Stores a 7 in the variable pointed to
```

Perhaps you can now see why the * operator, when used with pointers, is called the dereference operator. The pointer variable iPtr is dereferenced so that the address pointed to by iPtr gets the 7. Without the *, what would have happened? Visual C++ would think that you wanted to store the address 7 in iPtr! Always keep in mind that pointers hold only addresses. When you assign to a pointer, you will assign only addresses. However, when you assign to a dereferenced pointer, you assign data that you want to go in the pointer's pointed-to location.

You've now seen three uses of the * operator:

▶ A multiplication operator, such as ans = p * u;

▶ A pointer definition operator, such as char * cPtr;

▶ A dereference operator, such as *cPtr = 'X';

Note The * is called the dereference operator both when you use it to define pointer variables and when you use it to store data in memory pointed to by the pointer.

If you want to use the value pointed to by a pointer variable, you can. Given the previous variable definition, both of the following cout statements are equivalent:

```
cout << count;   // Print the value of count
```

```
cout << *iPtr;   // Print the value of count
```

The first cout prints the contents of the variable count. The second cout prints the same value by dereferencing the iPtr variable.

UNIT

16

Pointers Simplified

You can now define pointer variables and work with variables pointed to by pointer variables. Right now, you might wonder why there's any need to use pointer variables. After all, it's a lot easier to work directly with a specific variable by name than to dereference a pointer to that variable. You're right that variable names are easier to use than dereferenced variables. In the next lesson, however, you'll learn how to store data in unnamed memory locations! The only way to get to those locations is through pointer variables. Therefore, you should learn all about pointers now. In the next lesson, you'll be glad you did.

STOP&TYPE Listing 16.1 contains a program that defines several variables and pointers to those variables. Different values are then printed using dereferenced pointer variables.

Review
What You Have Learned

Pointers point to other data values. Pointers always hold addresses of other variables, and you store only addresses in pointers. When you define a pointer, using *, you must also tell Visual C++ what data type that pointer variable will point to. You also use the * to store and retrieve data values in the memory pointed to by pointer variables.

▼ INPUT   LISTING 16.1. WORKING WITH POINTERS.

```
 1:// Filename: DEFPNTS.CPP
 2:// Defines several variables and pointers to those variables
 3:#include <iostream.h>
 4:
 5:void main()
 6:{
 7:    int     i1 = 14;     // Define and initialize an integer
 8:    int*    ip1;         // Define a pointer to an integer
 9:    int     i2 = 20;
10:    int*    ip2 = &i2;   // Define and initialize the pointer
11:    float   f = 92.345;
12:    float*  fp = &f;
13:    double  d;
14:    double* dp;
15:
16:    ip1 = &i1;
17:
18:    cout.precision(3);
19:    cout.setf(ios::showpoint);
20:    cout.setf(ios::fixed);
21:
22:    cout << "i1 is " << i1 << " and *ip1 is also "
23:        << *ip1 << endl;
24:
```

```
25:    cout << "i2 is " << i2 << " and *ip2 is also "
26:         << *ip2 << endl;
27:
28:    cout << "f is " << f << " and *fp is also "
29:         << *fp << endl;
30:
31:    *fp = 1010.10;
32:
33:    cout << "After changing f through fp, " << endl;
34:    cout << "f is now " << f << " and *fp is also "
35:         << *fp << endl;
36:
37:    dp = &d;
38:    *dp = 83949443.54333;    // Change dp
39:
40:    cout << "d is now " << d << " and *dp is also "
41:         << *dp << endl;
42:    return;
43:}
```

▼ OUTPUT

```
i1 is 14 and *ip1 is also 14
i2 is 20 and *ip2 is also 20
f is 92.345 and *fp is also 92.345
After changing f through fp,
f is now 1010.100 and *fp is also 1010.100
d is now 83949443.543 and *dp is also 83949443.543
```

▼ ANALYSIS

This program simply defines and assigns variables and pointers to those variables. In lines 7 and 8, integer i1 is defined and assigned the value 14, and the pointer to an integer named iPtr1 is defined. iPtr1 isn't assigned anything until later in the program. Line 9 defines another integer named i2 and stores 20 in the variable. Line 10 defines and links the iPtr2 pointer to i2.

Lines 11 and 12 define and initialize a floating-point variable named f and a pointer to that floating-point variable named fPtr. Line 13 defines a double variable without initializing it. Line 14 defines a pointer that can point to a double, but no address is placed there yet.

Line 16 links iPtr1 to the address of i1. Although this could be done in line 8, the initialization occurs here for your review. The couts that follow in lines 22 through 29 print both the regular variable and the regular variable's value using the pointer.

Line 37 finally connects dPtr to d, and line 38 stores a value in d, indirectly, through a dereferenced dPtr. A subsequent cout prints the result.

UNIT

16

Pointers Simplified

It wouldn't make a lot of sense to print the contents of a pointer variable unless you needed access to internal memory addresses because you were writing system-level programs such as operating system utilities. The actual address stored in a pointer isn't a meaningful number. Due to a sectioned addressing scheme that the PC uses, the address appears in hexadecimal. From one run of a program to another, the address might change as the program might be put into a different bit of memory by the operating system.

▶ The Marriage of Arrays and Pointers

Concept   **What You Will Learn**

Arrays share common storage methods with pointers. As this section explains, an array is nothing more than a special kind of pointer.

Often, Visual C++ programmers use array subscript notation and pointer notation interchangeably. This is possible because Visual C++ stores both arrays and pointers in the same way. After you master the similarities between arrays and pointers, you'll be able to understand how to represent an array of string values, something not possible in Visual C++ without pointers.

Until now, an array was considered a list of values. That's still what an array is conceptually, but internally an array name is a pointer to the first element in the array. Such a pointer is a fixed pointer (called a constant pointer). Unlike with a pointer variable, you can't change the contents of an array name pointer.

When you define an array such as this:

```
int ages[] = {32, 45, 42, 19, 67};
```

Visual C++ really stores six values in memory. Visual C++ stores the five data values in the array, as you already know. It's important to realize that Visual C++ stores every array element in back-to-back memory. In other words, ages[0] always comes right before ages[1], ages[1] always comes right before ages[2], and so on.

The sixth value that Visual C++ stores—a value that you didn't need to know about until now—is the array name itself. The array name is a separate variable that is always a pointer to the array's first element. A picture is worth a thousand words (although I'll give you both!). Figure 16.4 shows how Visual C++ stores the ages array in memory.

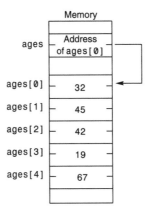

Figure 16.4.

When Visual C++ stores an array, it stores the data and a pointer to the array.

Suppose that you want to print the array's first element. The following cout does the trick:

```
cout << "The first element is " << ages[0] << endl;
```

The following cout also prints the array's first element:

```
cout << "The first element is " << *ages << endl;
```

If you want to change the contents of the array's first value, you can do so using either array or pointer notation. For example, you can do this:

```
ages[0] = 24;   // Store a new value in the first element
```

This also does the same thing:

```
*ages = 24;   // Store a new value in the first element
```

The array name is nothing more than a pointer. The only limitation is that you can't change where an array name points because its value is always a fixed constant. (Perhaps now you can see why you can't put an array name on the left side of an equal sign!) Given the pointer definition

```
int i = 9;
int j = 10;
int *pt = &i;
```

you can change where pt points:

```
pt = & j;   // pt now points to j
```

You can never switch an array name to another value, however. Given the previous ages array definition, the following is not allowed:

```
ages = &j;   // Invalid! Arrays must keep pointing to their first value
```

You can use the pointer notation to step into the array elements, accessing the remaining elements, without using the actual array notation. For example, you can print the contents of the ages array using the familiar subscript notation:

```
cout << "ages[0] is " << ages[0] << endl;
cout << "ages[1] is " << ages[1] << endl;
cout << "ages[2] is " << ages[2] << endl;
cout << "ages[3] is " << ages[3] << endl;
cout << "ages[4] is " << ages[4] << endl;
```

You also can print them by adding to and dereferencing a pointer:

```
cout << "*(ages + 0) is " << *(ages + 0) << endl;
cout << "*(ages + 1) is " << *(ages + 1) << endl;
cout << "*(ages + 2) is " << *(ages + 2) << endl;
cout << "*(ages + 3) is " << *(ages + 3) << endl;
cout << "*(ages + 4) is " << *(ages + 4) << endl;
```

The parentheses are important because the dereferencing operator, *, has higher precedence than the addition operator, +, as shown in Appendix C. To print the second array element, you want Visual C++ to first add one integer memory location to the address stored in ages before dereferencing that location to print its value.

Of course, astute Visual C++ programmers would never print the five elements one at a time when a for loop does more work in less code:

```
for (c = 0; c < 5; c++)
{   cout << "ages[c] is " << ages[c] << endl; }
```

The same for loop will print the array using pointer notation also:

```
for (c = 0; c < 5; c++)
{   cout << "*(ages + c) is " << *(ages + c) << endl; }
```

The whole key to being able to point into an array is that all array elements are stored back-to-back with no padding between them. Even though most data types require more than one byte of memory, when you add one to a subscript or a pointer's value, Visual C++ adds one data type location and not just 1. ages[2] is two bytes away from ages[3]; therefore, *(ages + 2) is also two bytes away from *(ages + 3) even though they lie back-to-back in sequential array element locations.

STOP&TYPE Listing 16.2 contains a program that defines a floating-point array and then uses lots of pointer notation to print various values from the array. You'll see that you can use some strange notation to get to individual array elements using pointers. If you keep in mind that a pointer contains an address, you'll be able to figure out how the program works.

Tip Keep in mind the following equivalent notations:

ara[3], *(ara + 3), and *(ara + 1)[2] all reference the same value! Just do the math and then subscript accordingly from the answer, and you'll see for yourself.

Review **What You Have Learned**

You can reference arrays as if they were pointers. However, you can't change where an array name points. An array name always points to the array's first element.

▼ INPUT   LISTING 16.2. REFERENCING AN ARRAY THROUGH POINTER NOTATION.

```
 1:// Filename: FLOTARPT.CPP
 2:// Defines a floating-point array and then
 3:// accesses elements from the array using
 4:// pointer notation
 5:#include <iostream.h>
 6:
 7:void main()
 8:{
 9:   float ara[6] = {11.1, 22.2, 33.3, 44.4, 55.5, 66.6};
10:   int ctr;   // for-loop counter
11:
12:   // First, print the array using subscripts
13:   cout << "Here is the array using subscripts:" << endl;
14:   cout.precision(1);
15:   cout.setf(ios::showpoint);
16:   cout.setf(ios::fixed);
17:   for (ctr = 0; ctr < 6; ctr++)
18:     { cout << ara[ctr] << ' '; }
19:
20:   // Print the array using simple pointer notation
21:   cout << endl << endl
22:        << "Here is the array using pointers:" << endl;
23:   for (ctr = 0; ctr < 6; ctr++)
24:     { cout << *(ara + ctr) << ' '; }
25:
26:   // You can even combine pointer and array notation!
27:   cout << endl << endl
28:        << "Here is the array using a combination:" << endl;
29:   cout << (ara + 0)[0] << ' ';   // ara[0]
30:   cout << (ara + 1)[0] << ' ';   // ara[1]
31:   cout << (ara + 0)[2] << ' ';   // ara[2]
32:   cout << (ara + 0)[3] << ' ';   // ara[3]
33:   cout << (ara + 3)[1] << ' ';   // ara[4]
34:   cout << (ara + 2)[3] << ' ';   // ara[5]
35:   return;
36:}
```

UNIT

16

Pointers Simplified

▼ OUTPUT

```
Here is the array using subscripts:
11.1  22.2  33.3  44.4  55.5  66.6

Here is the array using pointers:
11.1  22.2  33.3  44.4  55.5  66.6

Here is the array using a combination:
11.1  22.2  33.3  44.4  55.5  66.6
```

▼ ANALYSIS

Familiar subscript notation in line 17's for loop prints the contents of the floating-point array as you're used to. Then the fun begins.

Lines 23 and 24 print the same array using pointer notation. Being able to reference the array as *(ara + 1) instead of ara[1] proves beyond a shadow of a doubt that an array is nothing more in Visual C++ than a pointer to the first element in the array. The expression *(ara + 1) tells Visual C++ to add one floating-point memory location (which takes four bytes) to the address stored in ara. That references the array's second element, which the * then dereferences to print the value stored there.

This program uses some strange notation to print the array in lines 29 through 34, but as you can see from the output, the array elements appear as if you used subscripts to print them. An array name is nothing more than an address, so you can add to that name, as in ara + 2, and subscript from there instead of from the start of the array (ara) like this: (ara + 2)[1]. To bring the expression back down to simple subscript notation, just do the math. In other words, the expression (ara + 2)[1] references the same element as ara[3] (2 plus 1 is 3). Likewise, an expression such as (ara - 25)[27] references nothing more than ara[2] (–25 plus 27 is 2).

Although this program doesn't change any of the array elements using pointer notation, it could do so. All of the following assignments store 8.9 in ara[4]:

```
ara[4] = 8.9;

*(ara + 4) = 8.9;

 (ara + 4)[0] = 8.9;

 (ara + 2)[2] = 8.9;

 (ara + 3)[1] = 8.9;
```

Tip You'll never use the dereference operator and a subscript at the same time. `*(ara + 4)`, `ara[4]`, `(ara + 4)[0]`, and `(ara + 1)[3]` all refer to `ara[4]`, but notice that the `*` is never used when a subscript in brackets is used also. The subscript is a sort of dereference too.

Master pointer notation now because, in the next lesson, you'll be defining data that has no variable or array name. Sometimes, the only way to access data is to use pointer notation.

▶ **Pointers to Characters**

Concept **What You Will Learn**

Using pointers to characters, you can assign string literals directly to variables.

Never before could you assign a string literal to a variable in Visual C++. Before this unit, the only variables you knew of that held strings were character arrays, and an array name can never appear on the left side of an equal sign. In Visual C++ terminology, an array name isn't an `lvalue` (left value) and therefore can't be changed. You learned in this unit that an array name is a constant. Thus, you see why an array name can't appear on the left side of an equal sign.

A pointer variable, however, doesn't have that limitation. Pointers are variables, and variables can appear on the left side of equal signs. Consider the following character array definition:

```
char name[] = "I like Visual C++!";
```

Nothing is new here. A pointer constant, `name`, points to the array's first value, `I`. Now consider how the following variable definition differs from the preceding one:

```
char * nameP = "I like Visual C++!";
```

In this case, `nameP` is also a pointer that points to the first letter, `I`. The difference is that `nameP` is a variable. Therefore, if you want to change the string pointed to by `nameP`, you can do so like this:

```
nameP = "I love Visual C++!";
```

UNIT

16

Pointers Simplified

To change the `name` array, you have two choices:

▶ Use `strcpy()`:

```
strcpy(name, "I love Visual C++!";
```

▶ Change the array one character at a time:

```
name[3] = 'o';    // Change "like" to "love"
name[4] = 'v';
name[5] = 'e';
```

Note   You got lucky here, because only three letters needed to be changed. Usually, it's not so easy because you have to change many more over several assignment statements just to put a new string value in an array.

Changing arrays is tedious. Changing strings pointed to by pointer variables is extremely easy with a simple assignment statement. Keep in mind that you assigned the address of a string into the `nameP` variable; you did not overwrite the storage that was pointed at.

Note   As long as the character pointer's string ends with a terminator, all the string functions work for both arrays and character data pointed to with pointers. You can use `strcpy()` to make pointer variables point to new strings with some limitations, as described in next.

An array is nothing more than a pointer, and you print strings in character arrays. The following `cout` prints the contents of `nameP`:

```
cout << nameP;
```

Visual C++ always replaces string literals in memory with the address where they're stored. In other words, the assignment

```
nameP = "I love Visual C++!";
```

stores a null-terminated `I love Visual C++!` in memory and then assigns that string literal's address to `nameP`.

Some warnings are in order before you go any further. Only string literals work in assignments such as the ones just shown. If you use any of the array-changing functions, such as `get()` or `strcpy()`, you must treat the character pointer as if it is an array because those functions all assume that they're working with an array.

Consider what happens if you define a character pointer like this:

```
char *myName;
```

And then you assign it a string literal like this:

```
myName = "Sam";
```

Visual C++ finds the address of Sam and stores that address in myName. Everything is fine. However, what if, instead of using that assignment, you *initialized* myName like this:

```
char * myName;
cin.get(myName, 20);    // Oops!
```

You must use some value for the maximum length of the string. The 20 used here was arbitrarily chosen but no value will work properly. The user might enter a long name or a short name, but whatever she enters, something bad will probably happen! get() knows that you might pass it a character array that lives in a fixed place in memory. Therefore, get() knows that it should never change the address of myName. Even though, in this case, myName happens to be a character pointer, Visual C++ doesn't bother about the difference between arrays and pointers. Therefore, Visual C++ stores the user's name wherever myName points. myName could have anything in it, even an address that's pointing to part of the operating system. Remember that Visual C++ doesn't initialize variables for you, so the definition char * myName; simply reserves a character pointer that points to an unknown location.

If you want to use a character pointer inside character array functions, the easiest way is to reserve a character array and assign a character pointer to the first element of that array:

```
char largeArray[101];      // Can hold a string as long as 100 bytes
char *cPtr = largeArray;   // cPtr now points to the
// array's first element
```

You can now store strings up to 100 bytes long in cPtr using get() and strcpy() because the data will go to the memory already reserved for the array.

STOP&TYPE Listing 16.3 contains a program that demonstrates what you can and can't do with pointers to characters. Remember that none of the string functions changes its argument's address because the functions might be working with arrays.

Review

What You Have Learned

You can directly assign string literals to character pointers. You can also use character pointers in all string functions as long as the character pointer is already pointing to a string that is long enough to hold the result.

UNIT **16** Pointers Simplified

▼ **INPUT   LISTING 16.3. USING CHARACTER POINTERS AND ARRAYS.**

```
 1:// Filename: CHARFUNS.CPP
 2:// Uses character arrays and character pointers
 3:#include <iostream.h>
 4:#include <string.h>
 5:
 6:void main()
 7:{
 8:  char c;
 9:
10:  char * cpt0;    // A stand-alone character pointer
11:  char * cpt5 = "abcd";           // Points to 5 bytes
12:  char * cpt12 = "Programming";   // Points to 12 bytes
13:  char   ara27[27];               // Points to 27 bytes
14:  char * cpt27 = ara27;           // Points to 27 bytes
15:
16:  cpt0 = "cpt0 is pointing to this string";
17:  cout << cpt0;   // No problem
18:  cpt0 = "A new string for cpt0";   // Still no problem
19:  cout << endl << cpt0 << endl;
20:  // You couldn't
21:  // strcpy(cpt0, "This is a string for cpt0 that is too long")
22:  // though!
23:
24:  cout << "Please type your name (up to 12 characters): ";
25:  cin.get(cpt12, 12);   // Okay because of get() 12-char limit
26:  cout << "You typed " << cpt12 << endl << endl;
27:
28:  // cin.get(cpt5, 12) wouldn't work either because
29:  // all characters after the fifth one would overwrite
30:  // memory not pointed to by cpt5
31:
32:  // Fill the 27-character array
33:  for (c = 'A'; c <= 'Z'; c++)
34:    { ara27[c - 65] = c; }   // ASCII A is equivalent to decimal 65
35:  ara27[26] = '\0';
36:
37:  strcpy(cpt27, ara27);   // Okay because they point to
38:                          // the same number of bytes
39:  // strcpy(cpt12, ara27) would NOT be okay
40:  cout << "cpt27 contains: " << cpt27;
41:  return;
42:}
```

▼ **OUTPUT**

```
cpt0 is pointing to this string

A new string for cpt0

Please type your name (up to 12 characters): Derek Prince
```

```
You typed Derek Prince

cpt27 contains: ABCDEFGHIJKLMNOPQRSTUVWXYZ
```

▼ ANALYSIS

The numbers at the end of this program's character pointers indicate the maximum number of bytes each character pointer can point to. Remember that once you assign a string literal to a character pointer, or once you make a character pointer point to the starting location of a character array, you can never make the pointer point to more bytes than it already points to, except by assigning a string literal to the pointer.

Lines 16 and 18 show an uninitialized character pointer being assigned two different string literals. Everything works fine. Note the comment starting on line 21. Although you can assign a string literal of any length to cpt0, you can't use strcpy() to assign a string longer than what cpt0 already holds at the time. If you do, Visual C++ stores the longer string directly over the existing one, overwriting other data or code that might appear behind the existing string. It does not produce an error or warning while doing so either.

It's okay to use get() to enter strings into character pointers as done on line 25 because get() ignores any characters longer than get()'s second argument. cpt12 already points to a string 12 bytes long, so there's no problem using get() to get a string up to 12 bytes long.

The for loop on lines 33 and 34 stores the letters A through Z in ara27, adding the terminator at the end of the letters to turn the data into a 26-byte string. Notice how the character variable c is used as the character data (holding A, B, and so on), as the loop counter, and as part of line 34's subscript expression. Visual C++ lets you interchange char data and int expressions to create such a loop.

Line 37's strcpy() has no problem copying the array to the character pointer because both happen to be pointing to data that's the same length. You also could use strcpy() to assign an array to a pointer that's pointing to a longer string, but not to a shorter string.

▶ Arrays of Pointers

Concept

What You Will Learn

When you need lots of pointers, define an array of pointers.

You can define an array that holds any data type, including pointers. When you want a list of pointers, you'll want to use an array to hold that list of pointers. Figure 16.5 gives you a general idea of what such an array looks like. A pointer contains addresses to other memory locations. When you have an array of pointers, you have an array that acts like the one in Figure 16.5.

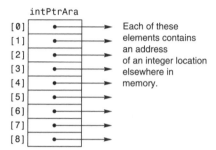

Figure 16.5.

You can define an array of pointers!

Figure 16.5 shows an array of nine integer pointers. The array is named `intPtrAra`, and each element in the array is a pointer to an integer somewhere else in memory. The arrows indicate that each element holds an address of another value somewhere.

Defining such an array is easy. As long as you keep in mind the difference between a nonpointer definition and a pointer definition, you can remember how to define an array of pointers. You define a nonarray integer like this:

```
int i;
```

You define a pointer to an integer like this:

```
int * iPtr;
```

You define an array of nine integers like this:

```
int iAra[9];
```

Finally, you define an array of nine pointers to integers like this:

```
int * intPtrAra[9];    // Defines an array of 9 pointers to integers
```

 Tip   Reading all variable definitions from right to left makes understanding them easier. The preceding definition defines an array of nine elements. That array is named `intPtrAra`. The array contains pointers (indicated by the *). The pointers can point only to integers.

To write advanced programs, you'll need to be able to define several pointer variables at once. Although you could define several nonarray pointers with different names such as

```
int *iPtr1, *iPtr2, *iPtr3, *iPtr4, *iPtr5, *iPtr6, *iPtr7, *iPtr8, *iPtr9;
```

you already know that an array gives you much more power than separately named variables because you can use a `for` loop to step through an array.

We'll return to numeric pointers in the next lesson. For now, it's important to learn how to store an array of pointers to characters. There's really nothing different about pointers to characters, except that you can now hold an array of strings! (Well, you can simulate holding an array of strings.)

Study the following definition. See whether you can figure out what's being defined (remember to read from right to left):

```
char * cities[5];
```

This definition builds a memory layout similar to that in Figure 16.5, with these two exceptions:

▶ Only five elements are defined.

▶ Each element points to character data.

Here is how you could initialize such an array at the same time that you define it:

```
char * cities[5] = {"San Diego", "Miami", "New York",
"Oklahoma City", "St. Louis"};
```

Remember that Visual C++ treats all string literals as an address. In other words, Visual C++ stores the five city names somewhere in free memory. Visual C++ then assigns the address of each of those string literals to each element of the cities array. The end result is that each element in cities points to one of the cities.

Note The array named cities doesn't end in a null zero because the array holds pointers, not strings. However, the strings pointed to by each element in cities do end in null zeros, as all strings do.

Figure 16.6 shows what the cities array looks like in memory. Each element, cities[0] through cities[4], holds an address to a city name. You can print each of the names using the %s format code.

Figure 16.6.
The cities array.

STOP&TYPE Listing 16.4 defines the array of pointers to five cities and prints the cities on-screen.

Review

An array of character pointers lets you work with lists of strings as if those strings were stored inside the array.

▼ INPUT   LISTING 16.4. STORING AND PRINTING DATA IN AN ARRAY OF CHARACTER POINTERS.

```
1:// Filename: CITYNAME.CPP
2:// Stores and prints a list of city names
3:#include <iostream.h>
4:
5:void main()
6:{
7:   int ctr;
8:
9:   char * cities[5] = {"San Diego", "Miami", "New York",
10:                      "Oklahoma City", "St. Louis"};
11:
12:   // Print the cities
13:   // Anywhere a character array can appear, so can the
14:   // elements from the cities array of pointers
15:   cout << "Here are the stored cities:" << endl;
16:   for (ctr = 0; ctr < 5; ctr++)
17:     { cout << cities[ctr] << endl; }
18:   cout << endl;
19:
20:   // Change the cities with literals
21:   // These assignments store the address of
22:   // the string literals in the elements
23:   cities[0] = "Tulsa";
24:   cities[1] = "Boston";
25:   cities[2] = "Indianapolis";
26:   cities[3] = "Las Vegas";
27:   cities[4] = "Dallas";
28:
29:   // Print the cities again using pointer notation
30:   cout << endl << "After changing the pointers:" << endl;
31:   for (ctr = 0; ctr < 5; ctr++)
32:     { cout << *(cities + ctr) << endl ; }
33:   cout << endl;
34:
35:   return;
36:}
```

▼ OUTPUT

```
Here are the stored cities:
San Diego
Miami
New York
```

```
Oklahoma City
St. Louis

After changing the pointers:
Tulsa
Boston
Indianapolis
Las Vegas
Dallas
```

▼ ANALYSIS

After assigning pointers to the city names in lines 9 and 10, the for loop in line 16 prints the five cities using a subscript notation.

Lines 23 through 27 then assign new strings to the array. In reality, the addresses of the new strings are assigned to each array element. A strcpy() function wouldn't work reliably in place of the assignment if the new string literal were longer than the string being pointed to at the time by each element.

Notice that the for loop body in line 32 prints the names of the five new cities using pointer dereferencing instead of subscript notation.

▶ Pointers and C++ Type Safety

Concept   **What You Will Learn**

The types of pointers have to match the data that they point to and other pointers in assignments.

A pointer to a float can't be used to access an integer value. There is a very practical reason for this restriction. Different types take up different amounts of storage, and if pointers were mixed up, the data underneath would get confused. To avoid this, C++ insists that pointers to different types are not interchangeable, even though the pointers themselves all hold memory addresses.

There are a couple of exceptions to the rule. First, you can have a special pointer type of void *. A void * counts in bytes of memory. This means a pointer to an undefined type. You can't do much with such a pointer, but it is a useful representation for when you need to mess around with some memory whose type you have not yet determined. You can always assign into a void*, but you cannot assign a void* into any other type. Second, there is the C++ *casting* mechanism. By casting a pointer, you can assign it into a different type.

Given the declarations

```
int   i[5] = {0x1,0x22,0x333,0x4444,1000};
long  l[5] = {0x1,0x22,0x333,0x4444,1000};
char  c[5] = {'1','2','3','4','5'};
```

this is what a memory printout might look like. (The source is on the disk as SHOWHEX.CPP if you want to look at this further. However, it is a little confusing because it uses quite a bit of fiddling to get to the data character by character.)

```
Array of ints
[ 0] 01 [ 1] 00 [ 2] 22 [ 3] 00
[ 4] 33 [ 5] 03 [ 6] 44 [ 7] 44
[ 8] e8 [ 9] 03
Array of longs
[ 0] 01 [ 1] 00 [ 2] 00 [ 3] 00
[ 4] 22 [ 5] 00 [ 6] 00 [ 7] 00
[ 8] 33 [ 9] 03 [10] 00 [11] 00
[12] 44 [13] 44 [14] 00 [15] 00
[16] e8 [17] 03 [18] 00 [19] 00
Array of chars
[ 0] 31 [ 1] 32 [ 2] 33 [ 3] 34
[ 4] 35
```

Look carefully at the data. You can see that an int is two characters long, but the long values are four characters long. Can you see that

```
long longValue = ((long*)i)[0];
```

produces the hexadecimal value 0x00220001, not 1, the value of i[0]? It has read the first element of a long array as the first *two* values of the int array. The correct way to read that very tricky assignment expression is "cast the pointer i to a long pointer before using it to get the first (long) element pointed at." Operator precedence means that without the extra parentheses, C++ would interpret the subscript before the cast. You can also see that character data has a very different value from the number it represents.

▶ **Homework**
General Knowledge

1. What is an address?

2. What is a pointer?

3. What is the & operator called?

4. What does a pointer variable hold?

5. What are the three uses of *?

6. What is * called when it's used with pointer variables?

7. What do arrays have in common with pointers?

8. Assume that `iPtr` is a pointer to an integer and that integers take two bytes in Visual C++. How many bytes does Visual C++ really add to `iPtr` in the following assignment? Hint: Remember that pointer arithmetic adds enough for each data type when you increment a pointer.

```
iPtr += 2;
```

9. Which of the following are equivalent, assuming that `iAry` is an integer array and that `iPtr` is an integer pointer pointing to the start of the array?

A. `iAry` and `iPtr`

B. `iAry[3]` and `iPtr + 3`

C. `iAry[2]` and `*iPtr + 2`

D. `*iAry` and `*iPtr[0]`

E. `iAry[5]` and `(iPtr + 4)[1]`

10. How does Visual C++ simulate holding arrays of string data?

11. Explain what kind of data the following definition defines:

```
float * measures[250];
```

12. Given the following floating-point array and pointer to a `float` definition

```
float fAra[] = {1.1, 2.2, 3.3, 4.4, 5.5, 6.6, 7.7, 8.8};
float * fPtr1, *fPtr2;
```

which of the following assignments are allowed?

A. `iPtr1 = fAra;`

B. `iPtr2 = iPtr1 = &fAra[2];`

C. `fAra = 19.45;`

D. `*(iPtr2 + 2) = 19.45;`

13. True or false: Two or more memory locations can have the same address.

14. True or false: A pointer variable can point to floating-point values only.

15. True or false: An array name is nothing more than a pointer variable.

What's the Output?

16. What is in `i` after the following executes?

```
int i = 18;
int *ip = &i;
*ip = 99;
```

17. Describe what is in `ip` after the preceding code executes.

Find the Bug

18. Given the variable definitions

```
int i;
long int j;
int * ip1;
int * ip2;
```

why will the following not work?

```
ip1 = &i;
ip2 = &j;
```

19. Given the array definition

```
int num[5] = {1, 2, 3, 4, 5};
```

why doesn't the following cout produce a 3?

```
cout << (*num + 2);   // Tries to print num[2]
```

Write Code That...

20. Write two couts that print the first value in a double array named values. Use subscript notation for the first cout and use pointer notation for the second.

21. Write a program that stores the names of your all-time favorite movies in an array of character pointers. Print the names of the movies.

22. Write a program that stores your favorite temperature for each of the four seasons in an array of floating-point pointers. Print the array forward, and then backward, using only pointer notation.

Extra Credit

23. Pretend that you're a teacher who just gave 15 students a hard pop quiz. Write a program that defines an array of 15 pointers to float values that you initialize when you define the array. Print the values for your grade sheet. Search the array for the highest score and the lowest score and print both. Step through the array again and compute the average test score. Use only pointer notation.

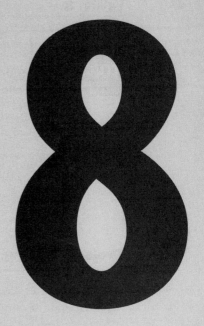

Lots of Data

STOP&TYPE In this lesson, you learned about advanced variable access techniques. You saw the following:

▶ How to define and access numeric arrays.

▶ How to search arrays to find key values.

▶ Storing data in a series of parallel arrays advances the kinds of programs you write so that you can search tables of information.

▶ Each memory location in your PC resides at a unique address.

Project 8 Listing. Searching through arrays for property data.

```
1:// Filename: PROJECT8.CPP

2:// A simple in-memory property database program. Through a menu,

3:// the user decides if he or she wants to see a property

4:// database on the screen or search for a specific property.

5:#include <iostream.h>

6:#include <string.h>    // For strcmp()

7:

8:void DisplayMenu();

9:int  GetAnswer();

10:void DisplayProps(char * code[], float price[],

11:                  char * addr[], float commPer[]);

12:void SearchProps(char * code[], float price[],
```

▶ Using pointer variables, you can access data by its address instead of through the variable's name.

▶ Arrays are nothing more than pointer constants. You can access arrays with pointer notation, and you can access pointers with array notation.

▶ After you learn to define arrays of pointers, you can keep track of lists of string data.

Description

1: A C++ comment that includes the program's filename.

2: A C++ comment that contains the program's description.

3: The program's description continues.

4: The program's description continues.

5: `cout` and `cin` need information in the IOSTREAM.H header file.

6: The `strcmp()` function requires STRING.H.

7: Place blank lines throughout your code to improve your program's readability.

8: The functions written by the programmer are prototyped. `DisplayMenu` takes no parameters.

8: Prototype all your functions.

9: The second prototyped function, `GetAnswer`, takes no parameters.

10: The third prototyped function, `DisplayProps`, takes four parameters.

11: The third prototype continues here to make the parameter list readable.

12: The fourth prototyped function. `SearchProps` takes four parameters.

Project 8 Listing. continued

```
13:                    char * addr[], float commPer[]);

14:

15:// Eight properties maximum due to next constant

16:int const NUM = 8;

17:

18:void main()

19:{

20:   int ans;

21:   // Define the program's data in parallel arrays

22:   // A code that uniquely identifies each property

23:   char * code[NUM] = { "231DV", "821WQ", "1990I", "294JU",

24:                        "901RE", "829BN", "483LQ", "778AS" };

25:   // The price of each property

26:   float price[NUM] = { 89432.34, 123029.34, 321293.95,

27:                        214293.20, 68402.92, 421034.53,

28:                        232456.54, 432123.40};

29:   // The address of each property
```

Description

13: The fourth prototype continues here to make the parameter list readable.

14: A blank line helps separate the prototypes from the rest of the program.

15: Comments the defined constant that follows.

16: Defines a named integer constant that holds the number of properties in the database.

17: A blank line helps separate the opening code from `main()`.

18: `main()` begins.

19: All functions begin with an opening brace.

20: An integer variable that will hold the user's menu response.

21: Comments that describe the data.

22: Comments that describe the data.

23: The first of four parallel arrays that hold property data. `code` contains a unique code number for each property.

23: All data is assigned in advance.

24: The `code` array's values are still being initialized.

25: Place comments throughout your code.

26: The parallel array that holds the price of each property.

27: The `price` array's values are still being initialized.

28: The `price` array's values are still being initialized.

29: Place comments throughout your code.

continues

Project 8 Listing. continued

```
30:   char * addr[NUM] = { "919 N. Elm", "2202 West Sycamore",

31:                       "7560 E. 26th Pl.", "213 W. 104th Ave",

32:                       "123 Willow Rd.", "5629 S. 188th",

33:                       "45 North Harvard", "17093 Lansford" };

34:   // The broker's commission on each property

35:   float commPer[NUM] = {.072, .07, .065, .091,

36:                       .078, .0564, .102, .0834 };

37: do

38: {

39:    DisplayMenu();

40:    ans = GetAnswer();

41:

42:    switch (ans)

43:    { case (1) : { DisplayProps(code, price, addr, commPer);

44:                   break; }

45:      case (2) : { SearchProps(code, price, addr, commPer);

46:                   break; }
```

Description

30:	The parallel array that holds the address of each property.
31:	The addr array's values are still being initialized.
32:	The addr array's values are still being initialized.
33:	The addr array's values are still being initialized.
34:	Place comments throughout your code.
35:	The parallel array that holds the broker's commission.
36:	The commPer array's values are still being initialized.
37:	Start of the loop that displays a menu.
38:	All loop bodies should contain braces.
39:	Displays a menu for the user.
40:	Gets the user's menu response from the GetAnswer() function.
41:	A blank line to help separate the switch statement.
42:	switch will determine what code executes in response to the user's answer.
43:	If the user entered a 1, calls the property-displaying function and passes the parallel arrays to the function to be printed.
44:	break keeps the rest of the case code from executing.
45:	If the user entered a 2, calls the property-searching function and passes the parallel arrays to the function to be printed.
46:	break keeps the rest of the case code from executing.

30: Squeezing too much data on one line makes your programs harder to read.

39: The code in main() is kept simple.

continues

Project 8 Listing. continued

```
47:        case (3) : { return;

48:                    break; }    // "unreachable code"

49:    }    // If user entered bad value, while loop will repeat

50: } while (ans != 3);    // Keep looping until return takes over

51: return;

52:}

53://************************************************************

54:void DisplayMenu()

55:{    // Display a menu for the user

56: cout << endl << endl;

57: cout << "\t\t** Property Database Menu **" << endl << endl;

58: cout << "Here are your choices:" << endl << endl;

59: cout << "\t1. Look at the property listing" << endl;

60: cout << "\t2. Search for a property by its code" << endl;

61: cout << "\t3. Quit the program" << endl;

62: cout << endl << "What is your choice? ";

63: return;
```

Description

47: If the user entered a 3, terminates the program.

48: This `break` is for completeness. If `return` executes, execution will never get here.

49: Close all `switch` statements with a right brace.

50: Keeps displaying the menu as long as the user doesn't enter a 3.

51: Returns to QuickWin, even though the `return` in line 47 actually keeps this `return` from ever executing.

52: All functions end with a closing brace.

53: The asterisk comment helps separate functions from each other.

54: The definition line for the menu-displaying function.

55: All functions begin with an opening brace.

55: Although this code is trivial, splitting into functions clarifies `main()`.

56: Prints the menu text.

57: Prints the menu text.

58: Prints the menu text.

59: Prints the menu text.

60: Prints the menu text.

61: Prints the menu text.

62: Prints the menu text.

63: Returns to calling program, in this case, `main()`.

continues

Project 8 Listing. continued

```
64:}

65://****************************************************

66:int GetAnswer()

67:{   // Get the user's menu choice

68:   int ans;   // Local variable also named ans

69:   cin >> ans;   // Answer to menu

70:   cin.ignore(80,'\n');

71:   return (ans);

72:}

73://****************************************************

74:void DisplayProps(char * code[], float price[],

75:                   char * addr[], float commPer[])

76:{   // Display a list of properties

77:   int ctr;   // for-loop control variable

78:   cout.precision(2);

79:   cout.setf(ios::showpoint);

80:   cout.setf(ios::fixed);
```

Description

64: All functions end with a closing brace.

65: The asterisk comment helps separate functions from each other.

66: The definition line for the menu-answer function.

66: Each function should perform a single task.

67: All functions begin with an opening brace.

68: A local variable is defined for the function's answer.

69: Gets the user's answer.

70: Throws away any garbage typed in after the first number.

71: Returns the answer to main()'s line 40.

72: All functions end with a closing brace.

73: The asterisk comment helps separate functions from each other.

74: The definition line for the property-displaying function. A loop in the body of this function prints all the property data.

75: The rest of the function's parameter list, neatly aligned.

76: All functions begin with an opening brace.

77: A for loop always needs a control variable.

78: Ensures that two decimal places print.

79: Always show the decimal point.

80: Guards against scientific notation.

continues

Project 8 Listing. continued

```
81:  for (ctr = 0; ctr < NUM; ctr++)

82:    {

83:      cout << endl << "Code: " << code[ctr]

84:           << "\t Price: $" << price[ctr] << endl;

85:      cout << "Address: " << addr[ctr] << endl;

86:      cout << "Commission percentage: "

87:           << commPer[ctr] * 100.0 << "%" << endl << endl;

88:      if (ctr == 3)   // Don't scroll off too fast

89:        {

90:          cout << "Press enter to continue...";

91:          cin.ignore(80,'\n');

92:        }

93:    }

94:  cout << "Press enter to continue...";

95:  cin.ignore(80,'\n');

96:

97:  return;
```

Description

81: Starts the counting through the property's parallel values.

82: Multistatement `for` loops need a compound statement.

83: Prints the first line of property-data output with the property code and price.

84: Line 83's `cout` concludes.

85: Prints the second line of property-data output with the property address.

86: Prints the third line of property-data output with the commission percentage.

87: The commission is stored as a decimal, so the percentage is multiplied by `100.0` to display the value as a decimal.

88: If three properties are on-screen, temporarily pauses the output to give the user a chance to read the screen's contents.

89: Multiple action `if` clauses need compound statements.

90: Tells the user how to proceed.

91: Waits for the user's keystroke.

92: Closes the `if` compound statement.

93: All `for` loops end with a closing brace.

94: When the list is finished displaying, gives the user another chance to read the screen's contents.

95: Waits for the user's keystroke.

96: Blank lines help separate parts of the program.

97: Returns to `main()`'s line 43.

continues

Project 8 Listing. continued

```
98:}

99://************************************************************

100:void SearchProps(char * code[], float price[],

101:                  char * addr[], float commPer[])

102: {   // Ask the user for a property code and display match

103:    int ctr;         // for-loop control variable

104:    int found = 0;    // Initially not found

105:    char buf[6];       // Code plus null zero size

106:    // Get the search key

107:    cout << "I'll now search for a specific property." << endl;

108:    cout << "What is the property's code? ";

109:    cin.getline(buf, 6);

110:    for (ctr = 0; ctr < NUM; ctr++)

111:    {

112:        if (!strcmp(code[ctr], buf))

113:        {

114:            cout << endl << "Code: " << code[ctr]
```

Description

98: All functions end with a closing brace.

99: The asterisk comment helps separate functions from each other.

100: The definition line for the property-searching function.

101: The parameter list continues.

102: All functions begin with an opening brace.

103: The `for` loop control variable.

104: Until a match is found, the `found` trigger variable will remain false.

105: Reserves a place for the user's search code (the key).

106: Place comments throughout your code.

107: Tells the user what is happening.

108: Prompts the user for the search code.

108: The user's property code will be asked for, and a search for that property will be made.

109: Gets no more than six characters from the user for the search code. Uses `getline()` to remove Enter keystroke.

110: Starts the loop that begins the property search.

111: The `for` loop starts with an opening brace.

112: Compares the user's search code to each code in the parallel arrays. `strcmp()` compares strings and returns 0 if they match.

112: `strcmp()` tests strings for equality.

113: The `if` statement needs a compound statement for multiple actions.

114: If the search code is found, starts printing the property data.

continues

Project 8 Listing. continued

```
115:                << "\t Price: $" << price[ctr] << endl;

116:        cout << "Address: " << addr[ctr] << endl;

117:        cout << "Commission percentage: "

118:                << commPer[ctr]*100.0

119:                << "%" << endl << endl;    // Show as a percent

120:        found = 1;

121:        break;

122:            }

123:        }

124:    if (!found)

125:        {

126:        cout << endl << "* I'm sorry, but I don't find code "

127:                << buf;

128:        }

129:    return;

130: }
```

Description

115: Continues printing the found property's data.

116: Continues printing the found property's data.

117: Continues printing the found property's data.

118: Continues printing the found property's data.

119: Continues printing the found property's data.

120: Sets the `found` variable to true because a match was made.

121: Stops the search because the match was found.

122: `if` tests end with a closing brace if opened with a brace.

123: `for` loops end with a closing brace if opened with a brace.

124: In case no match was made, prepares to apologize to the user.

125: The `if` statement can use braces even enclosing a single statement.

126: Prints the message telling the user no match was made.

127: Continues the message.

128: Ends the `if` with a closing brace.

129: Returns to `main()`'s line 45.

126: All functions end with a closing brace.

▼ OUTPUT

```
                  ** Property Database Menu **
Here are your choices:
        1. Look at the property listing
        2. Search for a property by its code
        3. Quit the program
What is your choice? 1
Code: 231DV       Price: $89432.34
Address: 919 N. Elm
Commission percentage: 7.20%
Code: 821WQ       Price: $123029.34
Address: 2202 West Sycamore
Commission percentage: 7.00%
Code: 1990I       Price: $321293.95
Address: 7560 E. 26th Pl.
Commission percentage: 6.50%
Code: 294JU       Price: $214293.20
Address: 213 W. 104th Ave
Commission percentage: 9.10%
Press any enter to continue...
Code: 901RE       Price: $68402.92
Address: 123 Willow Rd.
Commission percentage: 7.80%
Code: 829BN       Price: $421034.53
Address: 5629 S. 188th
Commission percentage: 5.64%
Code: 483LQ       Price: $232456.54
Address: 45 North Harvard
Commission percentage: 10.20%
Code: 778AS       Price: $432123.40
Address: 17093 Lansford
Commission percentage: 8.34%
Press any enter to continue...
                  ** Property Database Menu **
Here are your choices:
        1. Look at the property listing
        2. Search for a property by its code
        3. Quit the program
What is your choice? 2
I will now search for a specific property.
What is the property's code? 483LQ
Code: 483LQ       Price: $232456.54
Address: 45 North Harvard
Commission percentage: 10.10%
                  ** Property Database Menu **
Here are your choices:
        1. Look at the property listing
        2. Search for a property by its code
        3. Quit the program
What is your choice? 3
```

Lesson ▶

9

Consolidating Items

Unit 17: Structure with *struct*

Unit 18: Allocating Memory

Lesson 9 Project

17

Structure with *struct*

dot operator

member

structure

structure assignment operator

structure pointer operator

▶ **What You'll Learn**

> ▶ Grouping in a structure
>
> ▶ Initializing structure variables
>
> ▶ Accessing members of a structure
>
> ▶ Passing structures as parameters

This unit teaches you how to build your own data types! In addition to the regular data types such as int, float, and double, you can now have data types called George, Paul, and Ringo if you want.

The most important reason for defining your own data types is to group other data types together. As a matter of fact, in a nutshell, that's what this unit is all about. Visual C++ gives you primary data types from which you can represent virtually any low-level value such as a single number, character, or string (through an array). After you finish this unit, you'll be able to define data types that are aggregate collections of Visual C++'s fundamental data types.

> *Tip*   Sometimes, defining your own data types eliminates the need to program using parallel arrays. Instead of a parallel array that represents several types of data, you can define an array of your own data types that represents data. However, your excursion through parallel arrays was not in vain. Advanced Visual C++ programmers often create parallel arrays of their own data types to perform high-level data access.

▶ **Grouping in a Structure**

Concept   **What You Will Learn**

Use the struct statement to define your own data types. struct tells Visual C++ to treat a collection of fundamental data types as a single data type from which you can define variables and arrays of variables.

Structures are a very important part of C++. In C, structures provided a way to represent a collection of data. In C++, structures are far more important because they are a fundamental building block to representing an object. A structure represents the data needed to describe an object. In the next lesson, you will explore the concepts behind object-oriented programming. But first, you will explore the mechanics of structures.

Arrays (and also pointers to data lists) are a powerful method of grouping a lot of data together, but they have one drawback: All data elements must be of the same data type. You can't create a 10-element array in which half the elements are integers and half are floating-point values.

There might be times, however, when such a mixed data-typed array would come in handy. A local television station wants to track its weekday broadcast audience (an int or long int) and the cost of each average airtime hour per day (a float). You'd need five integer values and five floating-point values, and you would pair two at a time for each day of the week. Two parallel arrays are the only means that you know of right now for achieving such a database.

Such combined data almost always works better and makes for easier coding when you store it in structures instead of parallel arrays. One of the easiest ways to begin thinking about structure data is to picture the 3×5 cardfiles you've seen or used. Such cardfiles usually contain names of contact people, their phone numbers, possibly their ages, and all sorts of other related but differently formatted data.

Definition—A *structure* is a programmer-defined collection of other data types.

Note   Structures are often called *records* in other programming languages and in database systems.

Another good example of the perfect data for Visual C++ structures is a stack of rental applications for an apartment. Each application contains the same format and collection of information: the prospective tenant's name, address, income, Social Security number, and so on. Each application contains completely different facts and figures, but they all have the same format.

When you define a structure, you define the format (similar to a blank form) of the data you want the structure to hold. When you ask Visual C++ to define a structure variable, Visual C++ makes a place in memory that combines all the data types in each structure member. The members in the structure correspond to each blank on a form. Through assignment statements, user input, and file input, programs initialize structure variables with unique data in each of the structure variable's fields.

Note   Members are often called *fields* in other programming languages and in database systems.

Members of structures should have something in common with each other; they always should describe the same thing or *object*. This might be a real object or something imaginary. If you have several things you need to hold data for in your program, each of these things should have its own structure. If you own a car rental company and you want to have records describing your cars and your customers, you should have a structure for a car and a structure for your customer. If you had one structure, thinking that only one customer can rent a car at a time, you would soon run into trouble when a customer rented two cars. You would need to have the information about the customer in two places at once. What would you do with structures for cars that weren't rented? Hey, this isn't a data analysis course! Let's get on with structures. Just remember that a structure is more than just a convenient way of putting several data items together.

The *struct* Statement

When you define a structure, you tell Visual C++ exactly what format you want that structure to take. For example, suppose that your company currently keeps its inventory on 3×5 cards that look like the one in Figure 17.1. It would be your job to convert that card-file system to a Visual C++ program.

Figure 17.1.
Each cardfile contains the same structure.

Definition—A *member* is an individual data value within a structure.

Each card in the cardfile has the same format. In other words, each card has a place for a product description, a retail price, and so on. Each card shares a uniform format, or structure, with the other cards. Each card contains the same details. Therefore, each card could be considered a structure variable, and each data item on each card would be a member of that structure variable. Your job is to convert the card into a structure, convert the card's items into members, and convert each card's facts and figures into data for the structure variables.

The first thing you must do to convert the cardfile to a program using Visual C++ structures is to determine the data types for each of the members. Table 17.1 lists good data type suggestions for the card inventory. If a data type is char *, that can mean either a character array holding a string or a character pointer pointing to a string.

Warning You must decide in advance how much space to allow for each text member that will hold string data. You'll store each string member in an array, so you must decide in advance how long that array will be. Make the array long enough to hold the longest but most reasonable data value you expect. In other words, don't make the array too short, because you won't be able to hold needed descriptions, but at the same time, don't allow for a lot of unused space by making the array too large.

Table 17.1. The parts inventory members.

Member Name	Data Type	Length of String	Description
partID	char *	4	Unique part ID. No duplicates are allowed.
descrip	char *	15	Description of the item.
quant	int		Quantity in inventory currently.
retPrice	float		Retail price.
whoPrice	float		Wholesale price.
reorder	int		Reorder quantity. When the quantity gets to this level, the item should be reordered.

If you were defining the data in Table 17.1 in separate variables, you might do so like this:

```
char partID[5];    // Leave room for the terminator
char descrip[16];
int quant;
float retPrice;
float whoPrice;
int reorder;
```

Instead of using separate variables, it would be nice to be able to refer to these items as a whole. When you pick up one of the 3×5 inventory cards, you're manipulating all the data at once. If you were to define a structure variable from these items, you could manipulate the single structure variable and treat the collection as a single entity instead of as six separate variables.

The struct statement defines structures. As mentioned earlier, when you define a structure, you don't actually define variables at that time. (Technically, there's a way to define both the structure and variables at once, but it's rarely done.) Defining structure variables requires two steps:

1. Define the structure so that Visual C++ knows what the collection of data types in the structure looks like.

2. Define one or more structure variables from that structure.

Definition—A *structure name* is a name you can assign to a structure's format.

Here is the format of the struct statement that you must use when defining the format of data:

```
struct [structureName]
  {
    member definition;
    member definition;
    // One or more member definitions can follow
    member definition;
  };    // Remember the required semicolon!
```

Putting the inventory items in a structure definition is easy. All you have to do is take the separate variable definitions shown earlier and surround them with the opening and closing lines of the struct statement. You don't have to supply a structure name. The brackets around structureName in the format indicate that the name is optional. However, in C++ it is normal to use a name, and a name is required if you define the structure format in one place and a structure variable in another. You can think of a structure name as a data type name from now on. In C, structure names are called tags, so you might see this terminology elsewhere.

Here is an example of a structure definition for the inventory described earlier:

```
struct Invent           // Defines a new data type named invent
  {
    char partID[5];     // A part ID code. Leave room for the null zero.
    char descrip[16];   // A description of the item
    int quant;          // The number of items in the inventory
    float retPrice;     // Retail price
    float whoPrice;     // Wholesale price
    int reorder;        // Level reached before reordering
  };                    // The semicolon is required
```

Remember that this struct statement defines only the format of the structure, not the structure variable. After this struct statement executes, the program can define int variables, float variables, and also Invent variables. Before this struct, Visual C++ knew about the built-in data types, but it had no idea what an Invent data type was.

 Tip   Put comments to the right of members to describe the data each member holds.

One thing to note about the `struct` statement is that it looks quite like a function definition without any code. However, a `struct` declaration is a statement in its own right, and it must have that final semicolon that all C++ statements have. Structure data types have their first letter capitalized to help distinguish them from variables.

Now that Visual C++ recognizes the `Invent` data type, you can use the structure tag `Invent` to define variables. The following statement defines three inventory structure variables:

```
Invent item, item2, item3;
```

When you define an integer variable, you precede the variable name with `int` like this:

```
int i;
```

When you define a structure variable, you precede the variable name with *structureName*, as done for the three inventory parts. Figure 17.2 shows what the variable `item1` looks like. The boxes next to the members represent how many bytes of memory each member consumes using the Visual C++ compiler.

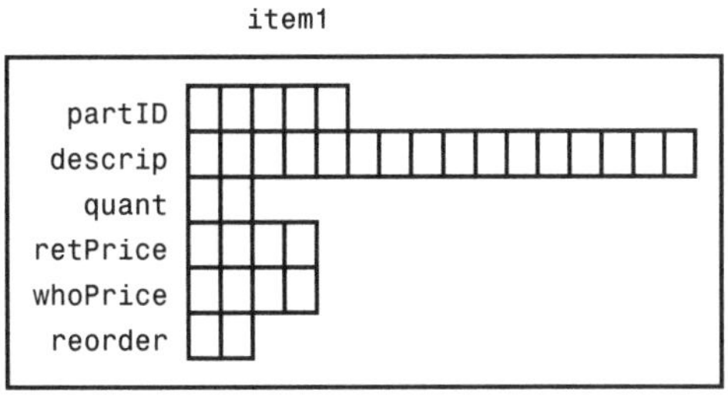

Figure 17.2.
The format of the `item1`
structure variable.

What does Visual C++ put in the structure variable's members? The answer is the same as for any other kind of variable: Visual C++ doesn't put anything in the structure automatically. The structure will contain garbage. If you want data in the structure variable members, you have to put data in the structure variable, as described in the next section.

One nice advantage that C++ offers over C is that you don't have to use the `struct` keyword when defining structure variables. The following C-like definition is identical to the previous one:

```
struct Invent item, item2, item3;
```

STOP&TYPE Listing 17.1 doesn't contain a complete program, but it demonstrates how to define a structure for a radio station's listener database. Instead of defining individual, separately named structure variables, this program defines an array of structure variables.

Review   **What You Have Learned**

The struct statement defines a structure and gives the structure a name used for defining variables from structures.

▼ INPUT   LISTING 17.1. DEFINING AN ARRAY OF STRUCTURE VARIABLES.

```
 1:  // Filename: RADIOST.CPP
 2:  // Defines a structure for a radio station listener
 3:  // database and defines an array of structure
 4:  // variables for that database
 5:
 6:  // Before defining structure variables,
 7:  // you must define the structure's format
 8:  struct RadioList
 9:    {
10:      char listName[25];    // Listener name
11:      char dateFirst[9];    // Date first tuned in (i.e., 11/02/93)
12:      int age;
13:      char sex;
14:      int progSegment;      // Favorite daily program segment number
15:    };
16:
17:  void main()
18:    {
19:      struct RadioList listeners[100];   // Define 100 variables
20:      RadioList *owner;                  // A pointer to a structure
21:                                         // variable
22:  // Rest of program would follow
```

Note   There is no output because this program is incomplete.

▼ ANALYSIS

You'll see the pattern in Listing 17.1 throughout your career as a Visual C++ programmer. Most Visual C++ programmers define their structures globally before the main() function. Remember that the structure definition doesn't define variables, so you won't be defining global variables just because the structure definition appears before main().

 Tip   If you use the same structure definitions often, put them in their own header files and include them at the top of whatever programs need to define structure variables. If you must make a change to the structure definition, you can do so in one place without changing all the source code files that use the structures.

Line 19 uses the structure definition to define 100 occurrences of the `listener` variables in an array. (Of course, you could define 100 separately named variables, but that wouldn't be useful, as you already know.) Keep in mind, however, that line 19 defines a lot of data! Not only does line 19 define 100 variables, but each variable is actually a collection of five other member variables, two of which are also arrays. A single element of the `listeners` array, such as `listeners[16]`, takes approximately 39 bytes of data!

 Warning   You can't predict by adding individual data sizes exactly how much memory a structure variable will consume. Visual C++ might add hidden padding between members to help with memory organization. There is always only one way to determine the size of any data in Visual C++—by using the `sizeof` operator.

Figure 17.3 shows what the `listeners` array looks like. Each element in the array contains an individual set of five members that look like the `RadioList` structure's format.

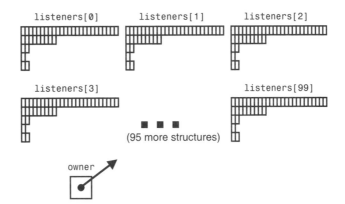

Figure 17.3.
The organization of the
`listeners` array.

Line 20 of Listing 17.1 defines a pointer to a structure. Not only can you define pointers to the built-in data types, but you can also define pointers to the data types that you define. (You must first define the structure before defining a pointer to a structure that is not built-in.) You won't see the full advantage of using pointers to structures in this unit, but in the next unit you'll fully understand how pointers to your structures can help you manage memory effectively. If line 20 included the `struct` keyword, the results would be the same.

 Warning   A pointer to a structure can point only to data with that particular format. In other words, if Listing 17.1 defined a second structure in addition to the `listener` structure, `owner` couldn't point to variables defined from that second structure; `owner` could point only to variables defined from the `listeners` structure.

▶ Initializing Structure Variables

Concept

The dot operator and structure pointer operator access data of the members of structure variables.

There are two places in a program that you can initialize structure variables. You can initialize structure variables when you define them, and also in the body of the program through the usual mechanisms of assignment, user input, and file input.

Rarely will you initialize structures when you define them, but for completeness, you should know how to put data in structure variables at definition time. You'll see a pattern here, because you initialize structure variables the same way you initialize array data—using braces. The following struct defines a simple structure that contains a float, an int, and a char array:

```
struct S
  {
    float f;
    int i;
    char name[15];
  };   // Define the structure
```

To define a structure variable without initializing the data, you already know that this will work:

```
S aVar;
```

To assign and initialize at the same time you define the variable, do this:

```
S aVar = {10.5, 14, "Paul Jones"};
```

The order of the data in the braces must match the order of the members. This kind of assignment is available only at the time you define the structure variable, just as assigning a list of values to arrays is possible only when you define arrays.

If you want to define and initialize an array of structures, list the data values consecutively:

```
S aVars[3] = { {10.5, 14, "Paul Jones"},
               {73.4, 8, "Kim London"},
               {19.5, 56, "William Meck"}
             };
```

Each group of inner braces initializes a new structure variable.

Warning You can't initialize structure variables directly using the literal braces once you've defined the variables.

Inside the program's body, assigning data to structures takes just a little more effort. You must learn about two new operators before you put data in structure variables. They are the dot operator and the structure pointer operator. Table 17.2 describes each of these operators.

Table 17.2. The structure access operators.

Operator	Description
.	Accesses data in a member of an individual structure variable.
->	Accesses data in a member of a structure pointed to by a pointer.

The dot operator and the structure pointer operator access data one member at a time. Therefore, if the structure variable contains 15 members, you'll need 15 statements to assign data to the entire structure variable.

Here is the format of the dot operator's usage:

```
structureVariableName.memberName
```

Here is the format of the structure pointer operator's usage:

```
pointerToStructure->memberName
```

You'll never see a structure variable on the left of the -> operator, only a pointer to a structure. That's how you know which to use. If you want to store data in a specific structure variable's member, use the dot operator. If you want to store data in a member of a structure that's pointed to by a structure pointer, use the -> operator.

Newcomers to Visual C++ programming often feel that the dot operator is easier to understand than the structure pointer operator. Part of the reason they feel this way is that they don't see the need for pointers to structures until they learn about dynamic memory allocation (which you'll learn about in the next unit). Until you get to the next unit, leave the -> alone and concentrate on the dot operator.

Here is the s structure definition:

```
struct S
  {
    float f;
    int i;
    char name[15];
  };  // Define the structure
```

Given this definition, if you were to define three nonarray variables like

```
S aVar1, aVar2, aVar3;   // Define three nonarray variables
```

you then could put data in the members of aVar1 like this:

```
aVar1.f = 12.34;   // Fills up the first member
aVar1.i = 23;      // Fills up the second member
strcpy(aVar1.name, "Sally Lake");   // Fills up the third member
```

When you grab the correct structure variable by putting it on the left side of the dot operator, the right side of the dot operator tells Visual C++ exactly which member from that particular operator is to be assigned. As usual, if you want to store data in character arrays, you'll have to use the strcpy() function, because you can't assign to arrays directly.

Here's some code that would fill the other two variables:

```
aVar2.f = 84.5;
aVar2.i = 3;
strcpy(aVar2.name, "Tim Deer");
aVar3.f = 56.3;
aVar3.i = 16;
aVar3.name[0] = 'A';
aVar3.name[1] = 'n';
aVar3.name[2] = 'n';
aVar3.name[3] = ' ';
aVar3.name[4] = 'H';
aVar3.name[5] = 'u';
aVar3.name[6] = 'f';
aVar3.name[7] = 'f';
aVar3.name[8] = '\0';
```

Do you understand the last few assignments? You don't have to assign strings to character arrays using strcpy(). If you like, you can store one character at a time. Just because the character array is part of a structure variable, that doesn't affect what you can do with the array. The existence of the structure variable simply affects how to get to the data, because you must preface the data with the name of the structure variable using the dot operator.

If an array of s variables was defined instead of separately named nonarray variables, the dot operator would work exactly as it does with nonarray variables. The only thing you must be sure of is to put the variable's subscript to the left of the dot, because the subscript goes with the structure variable and not with the member. For example, the following definition defines an array of three s variables:

```
S aVar[3];   // An array of three variables
```

The following code assigns each of these array elements the same data just assigned to the individual variables. However, the subscripts determine which structure variable is being assigned:

```
aVar[0].f = 12.34;     // Fills up the first member
aVar[0].i = 23;        // Fills up the second member
strcpy(aVar[0].name, "Sally Lake");    // Fills up the third member
aVar[1].f = 84.5;
aVar[1].i = 3;
strcpy(aVar[1].name, "Tim Deer");
aVar[2].f = 56.3;
aVar[2].i = 16;
aVar[2].name[0] = 'A';
aVar[2].name[1] = 'n';
aVar[2].name[2] = 'n';
aVar[2].name[3] = ' ';
aVar[2].name[4] = 'H';
aVar[2].name[5] = 'u';
aVar[2].name[6] = 'f';
aVar[2].name[7] = 'f';
aVar[2].name[8] = '\0';
```

Note   Yikes! The last few assignments show subscripts on both sides of the dot operator. Nothing is really new here. The left side of the dot indicates which of the array structure variables is being assigned to, and the subscript on the right of the dot operator determines the member's individual element you're assigning to.

Just in case you're following this, I'll now confuse you further! There is nothing stopping you from having a structure that contains another structure in C++. You have already seen that a structure name can be thought of as a data type. Consider the following code:

```
struct Point
  {
    int x;
    int y;
  };
struct Rectangle
  {
    Point topLeft;
    Point bottomRight;
  };

Rectangle rect = {{10,10},{100,200}};
int left = rect.topLeft.x;
rect.bottomRight.y = 300;
rect.topLeft = rect.bottomRight; // !!! What does this do?
```

To access each level, you use the dot operator. So the first assignment reads "Using the variable rect, get me the member topLeft, and then using that member, get me the member x." In real programs, you might even have arrays of structures. The important thing to note is that you perform each member access in a right-to-left fashion, evaluating the result before going to the next level of member access. Note the braces in the initialization of the rect variable. Each level of structure can be initialized as a separate unit.

Review

The dot operator lets you access the data of individual members of structure variables.

▶ Structure Assignment

Concept

Structures can be assigned to other structures of the same type.

We have talked about structures being used as data types. You can do all sorts of operations with standard Visual C++ data types. With structures, you can see that you can't add and subtract them sensibly. Visual C++ does allow you to use the assignment operator (=) with them. So the following is sensible and acceptable:

```
struct S
  {
    char name[30];
    int  number;
  }
...
S iAmNotANumber = {"The Prisoner",6};
S numberOne;
numberOne = iAmNotANumber;
```

However, the following code is not allowed:

```
if (numberOne == iAmNotANumber)
```

Visual C++ always creates a default assignment operator if you do not create one (defining operators is beyond the scope of this book). On the other hand, Visual C++ does not create an equality operator for you. In fact, most operations are not allowed on structures by default; only assignment and copying (which are not quite the same thing in C++) are allowed. As far as you are concerned, the default assignment operator works by assigning each member, one by one. For simple data this is just what you need. Sounds like there is a catch, right? There is! What happens if you assign a structure that contains a pointer? The pointer gets copied, not the data that the pointer points to. This means that you have two structures with a pointer pointing to the same data. In the next unit, you will explore some code that shows the problem.

▶ Passing Structures As Parameters

Concept

What You Will Learn

Structures can be passed as parameters in the same way as any other data type.

A structure can be passed by value, by address, or by reference:

```
struct S
  {
    int x;
    int y;
  };
void AValueFunction(S s);
void AnAddressFunction(S *s);
void AReferenceFunction(S &s);
...
void main()
  {
    S sArg = {1,2};
    AValueFunction(sArg);
    AnAddressFunction(&sArg); // address of
    AReferenceFunction(sArg);
```

This code fragment shows that the parameters work just like any other standard data type. It is important to remember that a structure can hold a lot of data. Recall that pass by value creates a copy of the variable passed so that the called function can't change the original value. Creating a copy of a large structure will be inefficient. In fact, C++ invents a special operation to copy a structure. (By the way, I'm being pedantic here; there is a subtle difference between the assignment operator that I mentioned earlier and the copy function. You'll learn about how C++ does the copying in Lesson 10.) As you can see, if you have a structure with a pointer in a structure, the data accessed by the pointer *can* be changed, even when passed by value.

To avoid processing large amounts of data on the parameter list, you should always pass a structure by reference. Remember that *by reference* means that the called function is given the actual data of the argument, not a copy. Similarly, you can use the address operator. Lazy C++ programmers don't like typing all those pointers rather than dots, so they often prefer by reference. Once passed, the data would be accessed as follows for each of the previous functions:

```
void AValueFunction(S s)
  {
    int x = s.x;
```

```
       }
void AnAddressFunction(S *s)
  {
    int x = s->x;
  }
void AReferenceFunction(S &s)
  {
    int x = s.x;
  }
```

Note   Remember that you can use the `const` keyword to ensure that reference or address parameters are not changed in the called function.

Those examples show you something else about scope. Note that C++ can tell the difference between the local variable x in the called functions and the x that belongs to the structure. The structure xs belong only to the structure and can't be accessed without reference to the structure name. C++ calls this new scope *class scope* because a structure is a special sort of a C++ class, which you will learn about in the next lesson.

STOP&TYPE   Listing 17.2 contains a simple example of capturing data into a record and then displaying it, which explores the joys of structure passing and access.

▼ INPUT   LISTING 17.2. A SIMPLE PHONE NUMBER DATABASE.

```
 1:// Filename: CONTACT.CPP
 2:// Store and show contacts
 3://
 4:#include <iostream.h>
 5:
 6:struct Contact
 7:  {
 8:     char name[50];
 9:     int  age;
10:     char phoneNo[15];
11:  };
12:
13:// Maximum number of contacts
14:const int MAXCONTACTS = 10;
15:
16:// Prototypes
17:int AddContact(Contact& contact);
18:void DisplayContact(const Contact& contact);
19:void DisplayAllContacts(const Contact contacts[MAXCONTACTS],int count);
20:
21:void main()
22:  {
23:     Contact contacts[MAXCONTACTS];
24:     int count = 0;
25:     while( count < MAXCONTACTS )// while more room
26:       {
```

```
27:          if (AddContact(contacts[count]))
28:            count++;
29:          else
30:            break;
31:       }
32:     DisplayAllContacts(contacts,count);
33:  }
34://
35:// DisplayContact displays a single name
36://
37:void DisplayContact(const Contact& contact)
38:  {
39:    cout << endl;
40:    cout << "Name    : " << contact.name << endl;
41:    cout << "Age     : " << contact.age << endl;
42:    cout << "phone no: " << contact.phoneNo << endl;
43:    cout << endl;
44:  }
45://
46:// DisplayAllContacts calls DisplayContact to show
47:// all entered names
48:void DisplayAllContacts(const Contact contacts[MAXCONTACTS],
49:                         int count)
50:  {
51:    for (int i = 0; i < count; i++)
52:      {
53:         DisplayContact(contacts[i]);
54:      }
55:  }
56://
57:// Add contact asks for one contact
58://
59:int AddContact(Contact& contact)
60:  {
61:    char answer;
62:    cout << "Do you want to add a contact [Y]es/[N]o: ";
63:    cin >> answer;
64:    cin.ignore(80,'\n'); // skip rubbish
65:
66:    if (answer == 'y' || answer == 'Y')
67:      {
68:        cout << "Name: ";
69:        cin.getline(contact.name,30);
70:        cout << "Phone no: ";
71:        cin.getline(contact.phoneNo,15);
72:        cout << "Age ";
73:        cin >> contact.age;
74:        cin.ignore(80,'\n');
75:        return 1;   // Added name ok
76:      }
77:    else
78:      return 0;     // Did not add name
79:  }
```

▼ OUTPUT

```
Do you want to add a contact [Y]es/[N]o: y
Name: Stanley B. Lippman
Phone no: 0-201-54848-8
Age 20
Do you want to add a contact [Y]es/[N]o: y
Name: Robert Arnson
Phone no: 0-679-7921-3
Age 70
Do you want to add a contact [Y]es/[N]o: y
Name: Matthias Hansen
Phone no: +44 123 4567
Age 30
Do you want to add a contact [Y]es/[N]o: n

Name    : Stanley B. Lippman
Age     : 20
phone no: 0-201-54848-8


Name    : Robert Arnson
Age     : 70
phone no: 0-679-7921-3


Name    : Matthias Hansen
Age     : 30
phone no: +44 123 4567
```

▼ ANALYSIS

This program consists of a few very simple routines. For a start, notice how the structure makes it easy to pass around large amounts of data. The Contact structure defined in lines 6 through 11 contains three variables, but the parameter list of AddContact in line 17 only needs a single parameter. Structures do make it easy to handle large amounts of information.

The main program in lines 21 through 33 simply asks for as many contacts as possible, up to the maximum it can store. When the user has entered the maximum, or the user has entered all the data, the loop stops and the information is displayed. Note that line 27 uses the return value of AddContact (which only adds a single contact) to decide whether to increment the stored contact's count. It is very important to keep counts and arrays in synchronization. The clever part of C++ is that a reference can refer to an individual array member as well as a single declared value. This means that the code in AddContact in lines 68 to 73 that accesses the members does not need to know that there is an array of contacts. The routine would work well however you chose to store the contacts—even if it was part of another structure.

DisplayAllContacts passes the maximum number of items to be shown. With arrays, you must be careful to keep track of which members are valid. C++ cannot tell which elements have entries and which do not by default. You could put an indicator to show which entries are present and check each one. Again, in line 53, the routine takes advantage of the reference parameter to pass an individual contact to the DisplayContact function. By breaking the function up in this way, the code for displaying is much simplified and could be reused if you changed your mind about how the contact data was to be held.

AddContact and DisplayContact are good examples of simple *object-oriented* functions. They understand about the one object—the contact—and know how to perform a task with that object. In the next lesson, you'll see how you can associate data not only with structures, but also with functions.

▶ Homework
General Knowledge

1. What is a structure?

2. What's one advantage of a structure over a parallel array?

3. What are the individual names of a structure called?

4. Answer the next five questions based on this structure definition:

```
struct S
{
  int i;
  char * c;
  char c2[100];
  float x;
  long int l;
};
```

   A. How many structures are being defined?

   B. How many members are being defined?

   C. How many structure variables are being defined? If any, what are their names?

   D. How many structure names are being defined? If any, what are their names?

   E. Would you probably place this code locally or globally?

5. Which two operators perform structure assignment?

6. What's the advantage of defining a structure globally?

7. What always appears on the right side of . or ->?

8. What always appears on the left side of .?

9. What always appears on the left side of ->?

10. True or false: A struct statement defines the format of a structure but not a variable name.

11. True or false: You can initialize a structure format when you define it.

12. True or false: You can initialize a structure name when you define it.

13. True or false: You can initialize a structure variable when you define it.

What's the Output?

14. Answer the next five questions based on this structure definition and initialization. Some have no valid answer, so be careful.

```
struct Astruct
{
    char c[10];
    char c2;
    int i;
    float x;
};
AStruct aVar = {"abc", 'X', 4, 34.3};
```

A. What is the value of c?

B. What is the value of aVar.c[2]?

C. What is the value of aVar.x?

D. What is the value of aVar[1].c?

E. What is the value of aVar[1].c[4]?

Find the Bug

15. Study the following struct definition closely. What's missing?

```
struct Book
{
    char title[25];
    char author[16];
    int quant;
    float retPrice;
    float whoPrice;
}
```

16. After you fixed the preceding struct, John J. Johnson decided to write a program using the structure. He defined a Book variable like this:

```
Book myBook;
```

John then decided to store data in the variable one member at a time. However, he ran into a problem with this statement:

```
strcpy(title.myBook, "A Thousand Tales");
```

See if you can help him.

Write Code That...

17. Add error checking to the CONTACT.CPP program in Listing 17.2 so that the user has to enter a sensible age in response to the `AddContact` age query. As it now stands, the program doesn't contain error checking for the age.

18. Write a program that keeps track of Olympic skaters' names and scores. Use an array of eight structure variables to keep track of the eight competitors. Initialize the information when you define the variables. Print the average scores (assume that the scores can range from 0.0 to 10.0), the name of the skater with the highest scores, the name of the skater with the lowest scores, and the name of the skater who makes the most from television movies about her life (just kidding!).

Extra Credit

19. Rewrite the parts inventory system described in Listing 15.2 (INVENT.CPP) using an `Inventory` structure, like one described in this unit, rather than parallel arrays. Before letting the user add an item to the inventory, check to see whether that part ID already exists. If it does, display an error message and redisplay the menu. By checking for duplicate part IDs, you disallow duplicate keys in the array.

18

Allocating Memory

delete

dynamic

heap

new

static

▶ What You'll Learn

- ▶ Dynamic memory
- ▶ The dynamic memory commands
- ▶ Check new for errors
- ▶ The scope of pointers versus the scope of pointed to data
- ▶ Multiple allocations

This unit explores the memory-management power of Visual C++. Storing data in variables is extremely important, but variables are not the only way to store data in memory. Through the techniques that you learn in this unit, you will be storing data in unnamed memory locations. You won't have to keep track of memory addresses. You'll access the memory through pointers.

Some of the pointer discussion up to this point might have seemed, well, pointless. Visual C++ pointers are far from pointless, however. Without pointers, you would not be able to write the kinds of programs that the commercial software developers write all the time. Named variables are simply too limiting to do everything you need to do when writing programs such as word processors. Variables are practical and needed, as you've seen throughout this book, but they can't handle all data requirements alone.

The most important thing to realize about the material in this unit is that you will soon be able to request memory any time your program wants extra memory. When your program is through with that memory, your program can put the data right back where it found it and give the memory back to the system to dole out later or to give to other tasks.

▶ Dynamic Memory

What You Will Learn

Learn what dynamic memory is and how to control it.

Definition—The *heap* is your PC's unused memory.

The heap is your computer's leftover memory. In other words, the heap would be any memory left after the following tasks consume their share:

- ▶ The operating system
- ▶ Any resident programs that you or your AUTOEXEC.BAT file might have loaded
- ▶ Any windowing environment, such as Windows, that you might be running

- ▶ Device drivers such as the ones you must load before using a mouse or CD-ROM
- ▶ Your Visual C++ compiler
- ▶ The Visual C++ program you are running
- ▶ The variables used by your Visual C++ program

How much memory will be left? Under Windows the answer is *a lot*! With Windows, you have not only the memory that is your RAM, but also memory invented by Windows and its swap files (called *virtual memory*). Typically, that means megabytes. This compares with a very limited amount that is available for local variables (often limited to around 30KB).

> ***Note*** With QuickWin, you are not writing Windows programs, but you still have access to all that Windows memory. A QuickWin program is really an emulation of a DOS program that is normally limited to a miserly 640KB. However, the programs in this book are tiny and under DOS would only need a few kilobytes in which to run, so they would still not be affected if you built them with a compiler that ran DOS programs.

Think for a moment about the implications of this discussion. First of all, you might not even think it matters to your Visual C++ program whether there is a little or a lot of memory left. After all, according to the previous list, there's already room for your Visual C++ program and its data. Why would a Visual C++ program need more memory from this free area called the heap? You might have a 16MB PC, but your customers might be putting up with a 4MB machine. How could you write a program to run on both machines, taking advantage of the extra memory if it was there?

C++ uses the heap to provide dynamic memory allocation. No program in this book has used heap memory yet. As a clue, if a program contains only variables and pointers to variables, the program does not use the heap.

MORE MEMORY WON'T SOLVE ANYTHING

As memory grows and as operating environments continue to provide more and more memory, your memory problems will not be solved. It seems that ample memory today is not enough for tomorrow (the same holds true for processor speeds).

As memory grows, the programs we use get bigger, we use more windowed operating environments, and we're more likely to connect to a network of some kind. As your memory increases, you'll begin to load more and more programs at once within your windowed environment, perhaps printing a word processor document while calculating a spreadsheet. The more memory we get, the more we use it.

You should not think of your PC as a stand-alone, one-task machine. Even if you never plan to network with another user, you're still going to be loading more and more programs, and you'll be demanding that your computer keep track of more and more data at the same time. These days, a background fax is common. It's easy to receive a fax while writing a Visual C++ program or balancing your checkbook.

The bottom line is that you are going to be adding to that memory crunch with your own programs. When your program defines a variable, that variable will take memory away from another process that could have put that memory to good use. You've got to become more environmentally aware, but that environment is within your PC's memory chips!

All this discussion leads us to the following important point: The heap might be big or small, but it is important. The heap, the available memory after everything running gets what it needs, is constantly being eroded by the operating system and other environments. Luckily, most programs that use memory from the heap put the memory back. That's what this unit is really all about: Use memory when you need it and use as much as you need, but when you are done, put the memory right back on the free heap storage so that other tasks can have access to that memory.

When you begin to use memory as if it is an accordion, growing as you need more memory and shrinking as you put memory back, you'll be optimizing your computer's memory use. Your programs will be able to give more to Windows when Windows needs it (Windows continually grabs and returns heap memory), and give more to other tasks that you might be running in Windows.

Dynamic Memory is Critical for Software Developers

Programmers can't predict how much memory their users will need. When you write a program to work with a specific amount of data, such as the previous year's temperature readings, you know at programming time how much memory is going to be required and you can define your arrays and variables accordingly. However, when you write a program such as a word processor, you have no idea just how much memory the user will consume. The user doesn't even know until he or she writes a document.

You could reserve a tremendous amount of space ahead of time, in a huge array, and the user could fill only the portion needed. However, most of the time—in fact, probably all of the time—the user will never fill all of your reserved memory. Therefore, when you define more than enough space, you waste too many memory resources that could be better utilized by the user's operating system, network, and windowing environment.

The goal of dynamic memory usage is to use only what the user needs. If the user begins typing a document into a word processor program that is based on the heap, the word processor can begin with very little memory reserved. As the user types more and more, the word processor can grab more memory from the heap. If the user deletes a bunch of pages, that memory can be sent back to the heap so that other programs can use the memory.

Getting the Terms

When your program uses only named variables and arrays to hold data, the program is not taking advantage of dynamic memory. The memory sits there, perhaps being used by other tasks but not by your programs.

Before learning how to work with the heap, you must understand some important terms associated with the heap. Table 18.1 lists the terms most often used.

Table 18.1. Terms associated with the heap.

Term	Definition
Allocate	To request memory from the heap. Once a program successfully allocates memory for data, the operating system makes sure that no other tasks can access that allocated memory. In other words, when you define heap storage, the available heap shrinks in size by that many bytes.
Available heap	The amount of memory on the heap at any one time.
Deallocate	Releasing heap memory from your program's use and returning the memory to the available heap.
Dynamic memory allocation	The process of allocating and deallocating heap memory from within a program.
Free	Same as deallocate.
Free heap	Same as available heap.
Free store	Same as available heap.
Heap management	Making sure that you utilize the heap properly, checking for errors when you allocate, and freeing heap memory that you no longer need.
Unallocated heap	Same as available heap.

When you read other literature about Visual C++ programming, you'll run across these terms. Despite the long list of terms, the entire process of using the heap boils down to these two steps:

▶ Grab more heap memory when your program needs it.

▶ Put that heap memory back when your program is through with it.

The accordion-like growth and shrinkage of the heap produces dynamic memory allocation. Instead of defining all your variables in advance, you allocate memory dynamically, on the fly, when you need it.

Definition—*Dynamic* means changing, as opposed to *static*, which means constant.

Many times, a program you write needs a lot of memory, but only for a small portion of the program. For example, a customer processing program might track customers as they purchase items throughout the day. The program runs all day. However, at any one time, the program needs very little memory because, as each customer finishes paying, the program stores that customer's data to the disk. The program does not need to be able to hold more than one customer's structure at any one time until the end of the day when the store manager selects the menu option to produce the evening reports. The day's customer data is then read into memory, statistics are computed, and reports are produced. Only at the end of the day does the program need to allocate a lot of memory. There is simply no reason to keep that memory allocated throughout the day, especially if the PC is connected to a network in which memory is even more dear than on a stand-alone computer.

Note   Local variables are not part of the heap even though they disappear when their block ends as described in Lesson 7. The memory for local variables comes from a section of memory known as the stack, and you can't control the size of the stack in any way. A local variable's value disappears once its block ends, but the memory reserved for that variable does not automatically become available to other tasks in the same way that the heap memory becomes available.

Review   **What You Have Learned**

You now know the importance of using dynamic memory. When a program needs memory, it should get that memory from the heap. When the program is finished, the program should free the memory back to the heap. The heap does not replace the named variables that you've seen so far. Often, variables are needed to hold totals, counters, and even data. The heap, however, is a better holding place when you must work with large amounts of data, or varying amounts of data, because the heap can grow and shrink as you use it.

Note There is no Stop and Type part here due to this section's textual nature.

▶ The Heap Commands

UNIT

Concept

What You Will Learn

The new command allocates heap memory for your Visual C++ programs while delete deallocates memory by sending unwanted memory back to the heap's control.

18

Allocating Memory

From now on, when you think of dynamic memory, forget about the notion of sequential memory. In other words, think of the heap as just a pile of memory locations heaped on top of each other! This analogy is important if you are to use dynamic memory effectively. When you allocate dynamic memory two times in a row, the second chunk of dynamic memory might not be close to the first. You can't predict just where from dynamic memory your next allocation request will come. Likewise, when you deallocate memory, you don't know what Visual C++ will do with that memory. After the memory is deallocated, forget about it because you have no idea where the memory went.

You must keep track of allocated heap space with pointers. You can't name dynamic memory because allocated memory contains no variables to name. Allocated bytes might be located anywhere, and if you store data in that memory and then free that memory back to the heap, those values aren't necessarily still in the heap memory. When it is freed, you must forget all about the memory. Again, the pile of heap memory analogy helps keep your management of dynamic memory better focused. As Figure 18.1 shows, when you allocate from the heap, Visual C++ might go anywhere to get memory; when you deallocate, you must act as if you don't know where that memory came from.

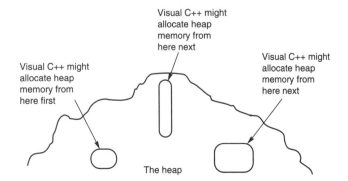

Figure 18.1.
Who knows where Visual C++ will grab the next chunk? Who knows where Visual C++ will put it back? Only Visual C++ knows!

Visual C++ might allocate heap memory from here next

Visual C++ might allocate heap memory from here first

Visual C++ might allocate heap memory from here next

The heap

Warning   So far, this discussion might sound strange, but it is important, so heed its warnings. When you free memory, forget about it. If you need a value from that memory later, don't free it! Some Visual C++ programmers deallocate the heap but expect to still use their pointers to read values they stored on the heap. Those Visual C++ programmers soon find lots of bugs. Always keep in mind that you share the heap with other tasks, especially the operating system. As soon as you free memory, that memory is available for another task to grab immediately, so whatever you put there is usually long gone if you try to read the value later.

Rarely will you allocate one byte from dynamic memory at a time. Doing so would be tremendously inefficient and would take too much work. Usually, you'll allocate a chunk of memory at once and your application will determine how many bytes that chunk should be. For example, if you were writing a word processing program, you wouldn't want to allocate a new byte each time the user typed a new character into the document. Instead, you might allocate 100 or 250 bytes at a time, and then let the user fill that memory up. If the user needs more, allocate another chunk.

Although you don't know the address where Visual C++ will get its next allocation, and although you can't rely on Visual C++'s next allocated memory falling directly behind the memory you last allocated, you can rely on Visual C++ to give you contiguous memory within each allocation. Whether you allocate 10 or 100 bytes of memory, Visual C++ might go anywhere on the heap to get that memory, but those 10 or 100 bytes will all appear back-to-back, sequentially in memory. You can rely on the memory being contiguous. As a matter of fact, you have to rely on the memory being contiguous or the heap would not offer much advantage to the programmer.

Figure 18.2 shows you what Visual C++ does when you request eight bytes from the heap. Visual C++ goes to the heap and finds where it wants to grab those eight bytes. When Visual C++ gets the eight bytes, however, those bytes are always together, with the first address of the first byte appearing exactly eight bytes before the address of the last byte.

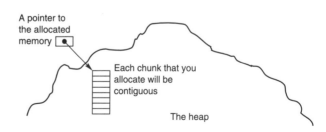

Figure 18.2.
The memory that you allocate will always be contiguous.

If you understand the rest of this paragraph, you will already have garnered a full under-standing of the heap: When you allocate heap memory, you also provide a pointer vari-able. When the allocation is completed, Visual C++ makes sure that the pointer variable points to the first byte of the memory you just allocated. The rest of the allocated memory will appear right behind that address. You end up with a contiguous set of new memory pointed to by a pointer. You then can use array notation or pointer notation on that memory. In other words, even though the allocated memory has no variable name, you can access the memory via the pointer as if it is an array that you defined. Unlike your program's defined arrays, however, this allocated array did not begin taking up memory until you allocated it! Also, this array's memory will go back to the system as soon as you deallocate the array, even though your program will not be over yet.

The `new` command allocates memory. The `delete` command frees memory. `new` always returns a pointer. Look again at Figure 18.2 and you'll see that the heap memory is shown pointed to by a pointer. Therefore, when you execute `new`, you must supply a pointer that `new` can make point to the allocated memory.

`new` will always allocate data based on the number of bytes that you want allocated. You don't allocate characters, you don't allocate integers, and you don't allocate floating-point values, but you do allocate bytes. The end result is that you'll eventually store characters, integers, and floating-point values on the heap, but when you execute `new`, you must tell `new` how many bytes to allocate before `new` can properly allocate.

There are two formats of the `new` command that your Visual C++ programs will execute:

```
aPointerVar = new dataType;
```

```
anotherPointerVar = new dataType[num];
```

The first version allocates a piece of memory big enough to hold a single `dataType`. The second version allocates a piece of memory to hold an array of `dataType`.

As you can see, you must assign the return value of `new` to a pointer variable. The pointer variable must be the same data type as the kind of data you want to store on the heap. If you want to store a `double` value on the heap, you must assign `new` to a `double` pointer. If you want to store an array of 18 `double` values on the heap, you still need a `double` pointer:

```
double *dPtr = new double;
double *dPtrs = new double[18];
```

Recall that a pointer variable is just like an array in that once you have allocated your storage to a pointer, you can treat it using the array syntax or the pointer syntax.

Let's look at a specific `new` example. If you are trying to allocate 50 integers on the heap, you first need an integer pointer. The following definition defines an integer pointer:

```
int * hPtr;    // Defines a pointer to integers
```

The following `new` command call defines 50 integers on the heap and assigns the `hPtr` pointer to point to the first of those integers:

```
hPtr = new int [50];
```

The format of `new` makes sense. This command tells `new` to allocate 50 integers. How many bytes does this `new` allocate? The answer is `50 * sizeof(int)`. In Visual C++, that's exactly 100 bytes because 50 integers consume 100 bytes at two bytes each. The data type following `new` tells Visual C++ what kind of data you want allocated, and the value inside the brackets tells Visual C++ how many of those values to allocate. If you omit the bracketed value, Visual C++ allocates a single value on the heap.

After you allocate memory, you can treat that memory as if it is an array. That's the good news! After you execute `new`, the allocated memory is just like an array, and you can treat the memory as if it is an array because an array is nothing more than a pointer to a list of contiguous data, which is what you get from `new`.

When you are done with the memory, be sure to put the memory back on the heap. Other tasks will then have access to your freed memory. There are two formats of `delete`:

```
delete aPointerVar; // delete

delete [] anArrayVar;
```

To free the memory that was allocated earlier, you pass `hPtr` to `delete` like this:

```
delete hPtr;    // Deallocates the allocated memory

delete [] dPtr; // Deallocates an array of allocated memory
```

 Warning   It is up to you as the programmer to ensure that you match an array `new[]` with an array `delete[]`.

When you free the memory, keep these things in mind:

1. You can never use that memory again through the pointer that you had originally allocated with.

2. `hPtr` is still visible but its value is meaningless. Although the actual address in `hPtr` will not change, keep in mind that when Visual C++ deallocates memory, you must assume that you don't know where that memory will be put back. Right after your `delete` command, your operating system, network, or windowing environment might have decided to allocate some dynamic memory. If so, another task might be using the address held in `hPtr`.

3. `hPtr` is still an active visible variable, at least until its block ends. You can use `hPtr` for an integer pointer to hold addresses of other integers, and you can use `hPtr` for another allocation. `delete` frees the allocated memory but does not change the life of `hPtr`.

4. You must use the correct version of `delete`. C++ will not report an error. It can't track how you have manipulated memory pointers.

5. It is sensible to set to zero a pointer that is invalid. This means you can easily test to see whether a pointer points to valid memory elsewhere in your code. You can't examine a pointer value in any other way to decide whether it is valid. There is another advantage: If you have difficulty in your code keeping track of whether a pointer is valid, you can safely delete a zeroed pointer and no damage to memory will occur.

6. You must never delete memory twice. Your program, and possibly Windows, will go very wrong.

> ***Note*** When you allocate memory with `new`, Visual C++ keeps track through an internal table of how many bytes you allocated. When you free the pointer pointing to those bytes, Visual C++ remembers exactly how many bytes it allocated to that pointer and deallocates exactly that many bytes.

You can allocate your own structure data with dynamic memory. If you had defined a structure named `Customer`, you could define as many heap locations for as many `Customer` structures as your program needs. The following `new` defines 150 `Customer` structures on the heap, assuming that `custPtr` is a defined pointer to your structure:

```
custPtr= new Customer [150];
```

The `struct` keyword can be added after the `new`, but it is optional. After you allocate structures on the heap, you're left with a pointer to a structure, not a structure variable. Therefore, you must use the structure pointer operator, `->`, not the dot operator to store and retrieve members within that structure. The following assignments would store four values in four of the `Customer` members:

```
custPtr->purchase = 65.27;
strcpy(custPtr->name, "Sam Kane");
custPtr->balance += custPtr->purchase;
custPtr->code = 'X';
```

STOP&TYPE Listing 18.1 contains a program that totals the checks written by the user in the previous month. Instead of defining a big array, the program allocates memory based on the number of checks the user actually wrote.

Review
_____
What You Have Learned

`new` dynamically allocates memory when your program needs it, and `delete` sends that memory back to the heap.

▼ INPUT   LISTING 18.1. ALLOCATE AN ARRAY BASED ON THE USER'S INPUT.

```
1:// Filename: ALCHECK.CPP
2:// Asks the user for the number of checks written
3:// last month, then allocates that many floating-point
4:// values. The user then enters each check into the
5:// allocated array and the program prints the total
6:// after all checks are entered.
7:#include <iostream.h>
8:
9:int    HowMany();
10:void  GetChecks(int noOfChecks, float * theChecks);
11:float GetTotal(int noOfChecks, const float * theChecks);
12:
13:void main()
14:{
15:   int noOfChecks;
16:   float total;
17:   float * theChecks;  // Will point to allocated memory
18:
19:   cout << "** Monthly Checkbook Program **" << endl << endl;
20:
21:   noOfChecks = HowMany();            // Ask the user how many checks
22:
23:   // Allocate the memory, 1 float per check
24:   theChecks = new float [noOfChecks];
25:   GetChecks(noOfChecks, theChecks);         // Get the values
26:   total = GetTotal(noOfChecks, theChecks);  // Add them up
27:   cout.precision(2);
28:   cout.setf(ios::showpoint);
29:   cout.setf(ios::fixed);
30:   cout << endl << endl << "Your total was $" << total
31:        << " for the month." << endl;
32:   delete [] theChecks;
33:   return;
34:}
35://********************************************************
36:int HowMany()
37:{
38:   int ans;  // To hold the cin value
39:   cout << "How many checks did you write last month? ";
40:   cin >> ans;
41:   return (ans);
42:}
43://********************************************************
44:void GetChecks(int noOfChecks, float * theChecks)
45:{
46:   int ctr;
47:   // No need or vehicle for passing allocated memory. The
48:   // memory does not go away between functions or blocks.
49:   cout << endl << "You now must enter the checks, one at a time."
50:        << endl << endl;
51:   for (ctr=0; ctr< noOfChecks; ctr++)
```

```
52:  {
53:    cout << "How much was check " << (ctr+1) << " for? ";
54:    cin >> theChecks[ctr];  // Store value on the heap
55:  }
56:  return;
57:}
58://*************************************************************
59:float GetTotal(int noOfChecks, const float * theChecks)
60:{
61:  // Add up the check totals
62:  int ctr;
63:  float total = 0.0;
64:  for (ctr=0; ctr<noOfChecks; ctr++)
65:  {
66:    total += theChecks[ctr];
67:  }
68:  return total;
69:}
```

▼ OUTPUT

```
** Monthly Checkbook Program **

How many checks did you write last month? 6

You now must enter the checks, one at a time.

How much was check 1 for? 17.82
How much was check 2 for? 109.28
How much was check 3 for? 536.49
How much was check 4 for? 9.80
How much was check 5 for? 3.73
How much was check 6 for? 84.08

Your total was $761.20 for the month.
```

▼ ANALYSIS

As you can see, the only thing new about this program's code is the new on line 24 and the delete on line 32. main() only defines three variables: noOfChecks, total, and theChecks. theChecks is a pointer variable that will be used to point to the allocated memory. After you allocate the floating-point values on line 24, the program treats theChecks as if theChecks is a defined array.

The GetChecks() function uses a for loop in lines 51 through 55 to get its check values. As the user enters check values on line 54, those values go directly to dynamic memory. There is no reason to pass the dynamic memory between functions because the memory is neither local nor global. The dynamic memory is memory that's separate from the variables' memory. As long as you keep track of the pointer to the allocated memory, you can access the allocated memory from anywhere in the code.

Warning If you ever lose track of the value stored in the allocation pointer, you'll never again have access to that allocated memory. You can't use the allocated memory, and you can't free the allocated memory! Be sure that you pass the pointer to dynamic memory between functions because the pointer is the key to getting to the allocated memory.

▶ Check *new* for Errors

Concept   **What You Will Learn**

In rare circumstances, there might not be enough memory to allocate. new's return value tells you whether the allocation worked or failed.

There are many reasons that a new might fail. You might have too many device drivers and other programs loaded. You might be requesting far more than new can deliver given your computer's memory limits. Whatever the reason, don't execute new without checking its return value for an error.

new returns 0 if new fails. Even if new could allocate 99 percent of your requested memory, the entire allocation process is a failure if you can't allocate every byte that you need to allocate. After an allocation attempt like

```
hPtr = new float [2500];
```

hPtr holds one of two values:

▶ The value of the allocated memory in dynamic memory.

▶ The value 0, which indicates that the allocation failed.

To check hPtr for an error, you simply need to compare it against 0 like this:

```
if (hPtr == 0)
  {
    cout << "The allocation failed.";
    return (ERROR_CODE);
  }
// Rest of program can assume the allocation worked
```

Given the fact that hPtr contains false (0) if the allocation failed, the following code is a little more efficient (and easier to read for a C++ programmer) because the extra == does not have to be tested:

```
if (!hPtr)
  {
```

```
        cout << "The allocation failed.";
        return (ERROR_CODE);
    }
// Rest of program can assume the allocation worked
```

Warning If you fail to check for an allocation error and an error does occur, you will be storing data in memory that is not allocated using a zero-based pointer, and the results will be less than satisfactory (such as your computer freezing up at just the wrong moment or the infamous General Protection Exception of Windows).

▶ Local Scope and Dynamic Memory Scope

Concept ▪▪▪▪▪▪▪▪▪▪▪▪▪▪▪▪▪▪▪▪▪▪▪▪▪▪▪▪ **What You Will Learn**

Keeping track of dynamic memory requires care to avoid nasty bugs.

When using allocated memory with pointers, you need to remember that the allocated memory does not belong to the pointer; it just happens to be at the end of it. You can pass the memory from one pointer to another, and C++ does not mind. However, the operating system does mind. You should always tidy up memory when you're finished with it or it will be lost. If the only pointer that owns the allocated memory goes out of scope, the memory will be lost. When a pointer is destroyed, the memory it points to still exists. Also, you can destroy memory pointed to by more than one pointer, and you can check the code of the other pointer and never spot that it is a different pointer deleting the shared memory.

If you think I'm laboring the point, you're right! The biggest cause of program bugs in C++ (perhaps after copying long strings into short string arrays) is getting the management of allocated memory wrong.

STOP&TYPE Listing 18.2 explores some of the issues of pointers, dynamic memory, and scope.

▼ **INPUT   LISTING 18.2. THE PERILS OF SCOPE.**

```
1:// Filename : JellyB1.CPP
2:// Demonstration of pointer scope issues
3://
4:#include <iostream.h>
```

continues

```
 5:#include <string.h>
 6:
 7:struct JellyBean
 8:  {
 9:    int i;
10:    int j;
11:    char* str;
12:  };
13:
14:void main()
15:  {
16:    JellyBean red = {1,2,0};
17:    red.str = new char[30];
18:
19:    strcpy(red.str,"A red jelly bean");
20:
21:    JellyBean anotherRed = red;
22:
23:    // But now both red.str and anotherRed
24:    // point to str
25:
26:    cout << anotherRed.i << ", "
27:         << anotherRed.j << ", "
28:         << anotherRed.str;
29:
30:    strcpy(red.str,"A blue jelly bean");
31:
32:    // Is this a surprise?
33:    cout << endl << "After assignment to red:" << endl;
34:    cout << anotherRed.i << ", "
35:         << anotherRed.j << ", "
36:         << anotherRed.str;
37:
38:    delete [] red.str;
39:    red.str = 0; // Good practise
40:    // What does anotherRed.str equal?
41:    //
42:    // Another small experiement
43:    //
44:    {
45:      char newString[30] = "Oh! no! not the comfy chair!";
46:      red.str = newString;
47:    } // newString no longer exists
48:    {
49:      char anotherNewString[30] =
               "No one expects the Spanish Inquisition!";
50:      cout << endl << red.str;  // red.str should point to newString???
51:    }
52:  }
```

▼ OUTPUT

```
1, 2, A red jelly bean
After assignment to red:
1, 2, A blue jelly bean
No one expects the Spanish Inquisition!
```

▼ ANALYSIS

Wow! That is one tricky program for such a few lines of code.

In the JellyBean structure declared in lines 7 through 12, there is a pointer to a character string, but no memory allocated. In line 17, we allocate some dynamic memory and use the strcpy function to copy the data from the literal into the dynamic memory. This is normal practice to make sure that the structure owns the memory.

In line 21, the default assignment operator of C++ copies the contents of the structure into anotherRed. The numbers are copied individually, but something nasty happens with the string. It seems all right (the printout from line 28 tells us so), but in line 34 the contents of anotherRed have changed. There is no mention of anotherRed in lines 29 to 33, so how did that happen? The memory allocated to red is shared with anotherRed. The correct way to copy a structure with pointers is as follows:

```
anotherRed = red; // ignore pointers for the moment
anotherRed.str = new char[strlen(red.str + 1)];
strcpy(anotherRed.str,red.str);
```

This code does something different. It finds out how much space is required to hold the string using strlen and then allocates a new separate piece of dynamic memory. It then copies the data from one piece of dynamic memory to the other. Now anotherRed is entirely independent of red and unaffected by any code using red alone. Of course, when anotherRed is done being used, the memory for anotherRed.str needs to be deleted.

Going back to the original code, if you accessed anotherRed.str in line 40, there is no telling what data you would get because the memory pointed to by both strings was removed in line 38 with the array delete keyword. In line 39, I set the pointer to zero. This means that I can test to see whether it owns any memory before I use it again.

Lines 42 to 51 are really another program. They are an experiment with scope. The string array newString in line 45 only exists until line 47. In line 46, the red.str pointer stores the address of the characters that newString stores. (Note that because this is an array, not a character pointer, the initialization copies the data into the newString array. It does not point newString to the literal.) In the theory of C++, the data only exists within the local block, although the pointer exists for longer. At line 47, the character array disappears, leaving red.str pointing nowhere. A new local block starts on line 48 and goes to line 51. This makes up anotherNewString. This time, red.str is not assigned the new string.

It tries to print out the old value. Surprise! Although nothing at all references anotherNewString, its contents appear in the output of line 50. The trick is that local variables appear on the stack. At the end of a block, the stack is rolled back, throwing away the variables. You can guarantee that the next block will be placed in the same place on the stack, and by making the local declarations identical, I tricked C++ into seeing the other variables.

This program worked. Imagine what the output would be if the second local block declared some floats instead. The output would be garbage. Worse, the stack also is the place where the statement address of a function call is placed so the program can then get back to the calling function. Get a memory pointer wrong and you could destroy that "address," and the program could jump into virtual reality midair.

 Warning   Warning! The experiment on lines 44 to 51 is just that—an experiment. It is highly dependent on the way Visual C++ looks after local variables. I engineered the coincidence of the strings. You must never assume how the compiler really works, and other compilers might produce different results.

▶ **Multiple Allocations**

Concept   **What You Will Learn**

You can allocate more than one group of dynamic memory, just as you can define several arrays. As long as you define more than one pointer, you can allocate more than one chunk of dynamic memory.

In the same program, you could define three pointer variables like this:

```
char * cPtr;
int * iPtr;
float * fPtr;
```

Then, you could allocate three different chunks of memory with these news:

```
cPtr = new char [150];
iPtr = new int [45];
fPtr = new float [188];
```

To be complete, you'd also want to check the return value of each new just to make sure that all three allocations work before you attempt to store data in dynamic memory.

One of the most powerful data storage routines you can create is an array of pointers with each pointer pointing to dynamic memory. An array of dynamic memory pointers is fairly common in advanced Visual C++ programs. Perhaps the programs need to keep track of several sets of data, with each set being pointed to by a different pointer in the array.

When you allocate several times using an array of pointers, the rest of your program does not get any harder to code than if you had defined a lot of arrays ahead of time. Yet, you gain the memory-saving techniques through dynamic memory usage. The array of pointers gives you a means to step through (via a for loop) several lists of data values.

STOP&TYPE Listing 18.3 contains a program that tracks the sales people for five cities, with each city having three sales people. Unlike the previous program, it tries to manage memory properly!

Review **What You Have Learned**

An array of pointers lets you store several lists of allocated data on the heap.

▼ **INPUT   LISTING 18.3. ALLOCATING AN ARRAY OF POINTER DATA.**

```
1:// Filename: ARRHEAP.CPP
2:// Allocates an array of heap pointers
3:#include <iostream.h>
4:
5:void  AllMemory(float * cities[5]);
6:void  GetCity(float * cities[5]);
7:float CalcCity(float * cities[5]);
8:void  FreeAll(float * cities[5]);
9:
10:void main()
11:{
12:  float * cities[5];     // Five city's worth of data
13:  float avg=0.0;
14:  AllMemory(cities);
15:  cout.precision(2);     // Ensure that dollar
16:  cout.setf(ios::fixed); // amounts display
17:  cout.setf(ios::showpoint);
18:
19:  GetCity(cities);
20:  avg = CalcCity(cities);// Total each city
21:  avg /= 15.0F;          // Calculate average from total
22:  cout << endl << "The average is $" << avg << endl;
23:
24:  FreeAll(cities);       // Why not a simple delete[]?
25:
26:}
27://****************************************************
28:void AllMemory(float * cities[5])
29:{
30:  // Allocate each array's three values
```

UNIT 18 Allocating Memory

continues

```
31:  int ctr;
32:  for (ctr=0; ctr<5; ctr++)
33:    { cities[ctr] = new float [3]; }
34:}
35://**********************************************************
36:void GetCity(float * cities[5])
37:{
38:   // This function gets the total number
39:   // of values for each city. Each city has 3
40:   // salespeople covering the territories.
41:   int ctr1, ctr2;
42:   // Use a nested for-loop to get each city's values
43:   for (ctr1=0; ctr1<5; ctr1++)
44:     {  cout << "City #" << (ctr1+1) << ":" << endl;
45:       for (ctr2=0; ctr2<3; ctr2++)
46:        {
47:           cout << "What is value #" << (ctr2+1) << "? ";
48:           cin >> cities[ctr1][ctr2];
49:        }
50:     }
51:}
52://**********************************************************
53:float CalcCity(float * cities[5])
54:{
55:   // Add up the total sales in each city
56:   int ctr1, ctr2;
57:   float totalCity=0.0, total=0.0;
58:   cout << endl;
59:   for (ctr1=0; ctr1<5; ctr1++)
60: {
61:     for (ctr2=0; ctr2<3; ctr2++)
62:       {
63:         float* &tempCity = cities[ctr1];
64:         totalCity+= tempCity[ctr2];
65:       }
66:     cout << "City #" << (ctr1+1) << " total is $"
67:          << totalCity << endl;
68:     total += totalCity; // Add to grand total
69:     totalCity = 0.0;    // Zero for next city
70: }
71: return total;
72:}
73://**********************************************************
74:void FreeAll(float * cities[5])
75:{
76:   // Free each array's three values
77:   int ctr;
78:   for (ctr=0; ctr<5; ctr++)
79:     { delete cities[ctr]; }
80:   return;
81:}
```

▼ OUTPUT

```
City #1:
What is value #1? 434.56
What is value #2? 554.21
What is value #3? 231.78
City #2:
What is value #1? 765.45
What is value #2? 392.12
What is value #3? 439.24
City #3:
What is value #1? 1021.34
What is value #2? 604.54
What is value #3? 375.58
City #4:
What is value #1? 778.09
What is value #2? 605.77
What is value #3? 542.23
City #5:
What is value #1? 435.70
What is value #2? 835.32
What is value #3? 302.34

City #1 total is $1220.55
City #2 total is $1596.81
City #3 total is $2001.46
City #4 total is $1926.09
City #5 total is $1573.36

The average is $554.55
```

▼ ANALYSIS

The AllMemory() function (lines 28 through 34) allocates all the city dynamic memory, with five cities and three values per city. Each of the three elements in the cities array points to a different set of three floating-point values. The rest of the program lets the user fill these heap values with 15 sales numbers.

The GetCity() function in lines 46 through 50 contains a nested for loop. The outer loop steps through each of the five cities in line 43, and the inner loop in line 45 steps through each of the three sales figures in each city.

Line 47 requires a little more discussion than a typical cin requires. Although we have not covered it previously, you can have arrays of arrays. Compare the code here to that in lines 61 through 65 of CalcCity, which needs the same access. This is an opportunity to use a reference to make the code more understandable. You can't reference an array, but you can reference a pointer. The slightly tricky line 63 says "make me a reference to a float pointer" (the order of the * and the & are very important). The other trick here is that the reference is created and destroyed in every loop. You can only initialize a reference once, and scope comes to the rescue.

When the city values are in memory, CalcCity() (in lines 53 through 72) calculates each city's total sales (printed in lines 70 and 71 at each iteration of the outer loop) and calculates a running grand total of all the city sales.

After main() prints the grand total, the FreeAll() function steps through each of the city addresses, deallocating them before the program ends.

Note   If you don't free your allocated memory, the operating system might free the memory for you when you return from QuickWin. However, if you rely on Windows to do your job, you might as well not go to the trouble of using dynamic memory allocation because your data will remain allocated and unavailable to the rest of the system—at least while your program is running.

▶ Homework
General Knowledge

1. What is the heap?
2. What is dynamic memory allocation?
3. What is the advantage of using the heap over using defined variables?
4. What command allocates memory?
5. What command deallocates memory?
6. What is the return value of new?
7. How does delete know how many bytes to deallocate?
8. How do you access heap memory once you allocate it?
9. Why must you use the -> operator when accessing structure members on the heap?
10. How does your use of the heap improve memory for other tasks that might need memory?
11. How can you ensure that new works properly?
12. What happens to allocated memory values when you call delete?
13. Does memory allocation require a header file?
14. True or false: You can name allocated memory.
15. True or false: An integer variable can point to heap memory.
16. True or false: If new can't allocate all of the requested memory, at least new allocates as much as possible.

17. True or false: If you fail to deallocate memory, the PC will free the memory for you when your program terminates.

18. True or false: When you use `new` to allocate a chunk of memory, all bytes in that allocated memory will be contiguous.

19. True or false: When you deallocate an array of pointers' dynamic memory, an array of pointers also goes away.

Find the Bug

20. What is wrong with the following `new` call?

```
int values;
values = new int [200];
```

21. After allocating a structure like

```
aStructPtr= new AStruct [10];
```

Linda tries to store a string value in the structure's member named `firstName`, like this:

```
strcpy(aStructPtr.firstName, "Linda");
```

Please help Linda find the problem with her code.

Write Code That...

22. Write a `new` command that allocates 300 characters on the heap pointed to by the `pChar` character pointer.

23. Write a `delete` command that deallocates the `pChar` pointer you used to allocate in the preceding question.

24. Write a program to allocate an array of 10 country names. Allocate 15 letters for each country's name on the heap. Be sure to perform error-checking in case the allocation fails. With a `for` loop, store a different country on the heap in the 10 spaces that you allocate. Print the names in backward order, from the last country name in the list to the first. Then deallocate the list of names before your program terminates.

Extra Credit

25. Write a program that stores three parallel arrays on the heap. The first array is to hold your friends' names (in a heap array of no more than 20 characters each). The second array is to hold your friends' age. The third array is to hold your friends' gender in a single character (as M or F). Print a list of your friends and their data, and at the bottom of the list print the average age. Deallocate all the data when you're done.

26. Rewrite the program from question 25 by using allocated structures instead of parallel arrays.

Consolidating Items

STOP&TYPE In this lesson, you learned about storing data using the advanced data techniques of structures and dynamic memory allocation.

▶ Structures are aggregate collections of data.

▶ You must define a structure, naming that structure with a structure tag, before you can define structure variables.

▶ A structure's members, its individual data parts, hold fundamental data types such as ints and chars.

▶ The dot operator and structure pointer operators access the members of a structure variable.

Project 9 Listing. Allocating an array of structures on the heap.

```
1:// Filename: PROJECT9.CPP

2:// A stockbroker's program that lets the broker enter a client's

3:// stock portfolio into an array of pointers. Each of the

4:// pointers in the array points to nothing when the program

5:// begins but the program allocates each pointer's structure

6:// when needed for the next stock.

7:

8:#include <iostream.h>

9:

10:const int NUM = 150;

11:
```

- ▶ The heap is your computer's free memory.
- ▶ When you allocate heap memory, your program then uses only as much memory as it needs at any one time.
- ▶ Allocate memory with `new` and deallocate memory with `delete`.

Description

1: A C++ comment that includes the program's filename.

2: A C++ comment that contains the program's description.

3: Continues the program description.

4: Continues the program description.

5: Continues the program description.

6: Continues the program description.

7: Blank lines make your programs more readable.

8: `cin` and `cout` need information in the IOSTREAM.H header file.

9: Blank lines make your programs more readable.

10: Define a constant to limit the number of stocks to be analyzed, such as if you convert this to a disk file input program later.

11: Blank lines make your programs more readable.

continues

Project 9 Listing. continued

```
12:struct Stock

13: {

14:    char  stockID[4];

15:    float price;

16:    float dividendRate;

17:    int   peRatio;

18: };

19:

20:int  GetStockCount();

21:int  CreateStocks  (Stock * stocks[],int stockCount);

22:void GetStocks      (Stock * stocks[],int stockCount);

23:void CalculateStats(Stock * stocks[],int stockCount);

24:void DeleteStocks  (Stock * stocks[],int stockCount);

25:

26:

27:void main()

28:{
```

Description

12: Define the stock structure format.

13: Structs start with an opening brace.

14: Keeps track of a 3-character string (leaves room for terminator).

15: The stock price.

16: The dividend rate.

17: The Price/Earnings ratio.

18: struct definitions end with a brace and a semicolon.

19: Blank lines help make your program more readable.

20: You should prototype all functions.

21: Prototype of another function.

22: Prototype of another function.

23: Prototype of another function.

24: Prototype of another function.

25: Blank lines help make your program more readable.

26: Blank lines help make your program more readable.

27: main() begins.

28: All functions begin with an opening brace.

continues

Project 9 Listing. continued

```
29:   int stockCount = 0;   // Total number of stocks entered

30:   Stock * stocks[NUM];   // For use with larger arrays

31:

32:   cout << "** Stock Analysis**" << endl << endl << endl;

33:   // Ask broker how many stocks are in portfolio

34:   stockCount = GetStockCount();

35:

36:   if (!CreateStocks(stocks,stockCount))   // Allocate the stocks

37:     return;                                // Exit if error

38:   GetStocks(stocks,stockCount);       // Get the data from the broker

39:   CalculateStats(stocks,stockCount);// Print statistics

40:   DeleteStocks(stocks,stockCount);   // Deallocate the stocks

41:}

42://**********************************************************

43:int GetStockCount()

44:{

45:   int stockCount = 0;
```

Description

29: Define a local variable that exists for the life of the program.

30: `main()` defines a local array of pointers to the stock structures.

31: Blank lines help make your program more readable.

32: Prints a title.

33: Comments make the program more readable.

34: Calls a function that asks the broker how many stocks are in the portfolio.

35: Blank lines help make your program more readable.

36: Calls a function that allocates memory for each of the broker's stocks.

37: If an error occurred in dynamic memory allocation, end the program.

38: Calls a function that loops until the broker's stock data is entered.

39: Calls a function that computes statistics from the stock data.

40: Always deallocate your program's allocated memory.

> 40: Deallocate all data that you allocate when you're done with dynamic memory.

41: A final brace ends all `main()` functions.

42: A line of asterisks helps to separate functions.

43: The definition (first line) of `GetStockCount()`.

44: All functions begin with an opening brace.

45: Declare a temporary variable to receive input.

continues

Project 9 Listing. continued

```
46:  cout << "How many stocks to analyze? ";

47:  cin >> stockCount;

48:  cout << endl;    // Blank line

49:  return stockCount;

50:}

51://************************************************************

52:int CreateStocks(Stock * stocks[],int stockCount)

53:{

54:  // Allocate memory needed for the broker's stocks

55:  for (int count=0; count<stockCount; count++)

56:  {

57:    stocks[count]= new Stock;

58:    if (!stocks[count])

59:    {

60:      cout << endl << endl

61:            << "The memory allocation failed.";

62:      return 0;
```

Description

46: Ask the user how many stocks there are.

47: Get the number of stocks.

48: Print a blank line for subsequent output.

49: Return to the `main()` function.

50: A final brace ends all functions.

51: A line of asterisks helps to separate functions.

51: Notice that you don't have to specify a subscript when you receive an array. You must pass the array of pointers to `allocMemory()` because the array is local to `main()`.

52: Defines the function that dynamically allocates memory.

53: All functions begin with an opening brace.

54: Place comments throughout your code.

55: Steps through the stocks.

56: Always use braces in the body of `for` loops.

57: Allocates memory for each pointer in the array.

57: You must allocate each pointer's data in the array.

58: Always check for allocation errors!

59: A brace starts a compound statement.

60: Print an error message if the allocation failed.

61: The message continues.

62: Return zero if an error occurred.

continues

Project 9 Listing. continued

```
63:       }

64:  }

65:  return 1;

66:}

67://*************************************************************

68:void GetStocks(Stock * stocks[],int stockCount)

69:{   // Get the stock data from the broker

70:  for (int count=0; count<stockCount; count++)

71:  {

72:    cin.ignore(80,'\n');

73:    cout << "Stock #" << (count+1) << endl;

74:    cout << " What is the 3-letter ID of the stock? ";

75:    cin.get(stocks[count]->stockID, 4);

76:    cout << " What is the price? ";

77:    cin >> stocks[count]->price;

78:    cout << " What is the dividend rate? ";

79:    cin >> stocks[count]->dividendRate;
```

Description

63: Closes the body of the `if` loop.

64: Closes the `for` loop body.

65: Returns to `main()` with 1 to indicate success.

66: All functions require a closing brace.

67: A line of asterisks helps to separate functions.

68: Defines the function that will get the stock data. Pass `main()`'s local array of pointers and the count of stocks.

69: Place comments throughout your code.

70: Steps through the stocks.

71: Always use braces in the body of `for` loops.

72: Gets rid of any unwanted characters from the input buffer.

72: The previous request for the number of stocks could have left an Enter keypress on the buffer.

73: Tells the user which stock he or she is entering.

74: Asks for the three-letter stock ID of the next stock.

75: Gets a three-character string from the user.

75: Use the structure pointer, `->`, with pointers to structures.

76: Asks for the price.

77: Gets the stock's price.

78: Asks for the stock's dividend rate.

79: Gets the dividend rate.

continues

Project 9 Listing. continued

```
80:    cout << " What is the integer P/E ratio? ";

81:    cin >> stocks[count]->peRatio;

82: }

83: return;

84:}

85://**********************************************************

86:void CalculateStats(Stock * stocks[],int stockCount)

87:{

88: // Calculate and print stock statistics

89:    float highPrice, lowPrice;

90:    int highIndex=0, lowIndex=0;

91:    highPrice = stocks[0]->price;  // Set the initial values

92:    lowPrice = stocks[0]->price;

93:    float avgDiv=0.0, avgPE = 0.0;

94:    for (int count=0; count<stockCount; count++)

95:       {

96:        if (stocks[count]->price > highPrice)
```

Description

80:	Asks for the price/earnings ratio.
81:	Gets the P/E ratio.
82:	The brace that closes the body of the `for` loop.
83:	Return to `main()`.
84:	All functions end with a closing brace.
85:	A line of asterisks helps to separate functions.
86:	Defines a function that will calculate stock statistics based on `main()`'s local pointer array.
87:	All functions begin with an opening brace.
88:	Places comments throughout your code.
89:	Defines variables that will keep track of the statistics.
90:	Defines index of high and low price.
91:	Initializes the high stock subscript with the first stock.
92:	Initializes the low stock subscript with the first stock.
93:	Defines two more variables that will hold statistics.
94:	Steps through the stocks.
95:	The brace begins the body of the `for` loop.
96:	If the current loop's stock is more than the highest stock price so far...

continues

Project 9 Listing. continued

```
97:        {

98:            highIndex = count;

99:            highPrice = stocks[count]->price;

100:       }

101:    if (stocks[count]->price < lowPrice)

102:        {

103:            lowIndex = count;

104:            lowPrice = stocks[count]->price;

105:        }

106:    avgDiv += stocks[count]->dividendRate;

107:    avgPE += stocks[count]->peRatio;

108:    }

109: avgPE /= stockCount;

110: avgDiv /= stockCount;

111: cout.precision(3);

112: cout.setf(ios::showpoint);

113: cout.setf(ios::fixed);
```

Description

97: Braces start a compound statement.

98: Updates the high stock index with the current stock index.

99: Stores the highest price for the next test.

100: Brace ends a compound statement.

101: If the current loop's stock is less than the lowest stock price so far...

102: Braces start a compound statement.

103: Updates the low stock index with the current stock index.

104: Stores the lowest price for the next test.

105: Brace ends a compound statement.

106: Adds to the dividend total for a subsequent average calculation.

107: Adds to the price/earnings total for a subsequent average calculation.

108: Closes the `for` loop.

109: Divides the price/earnings total for a P/E average.

110: Divides the dividend total for a dividend average.

111: Outputs three decimal places.

112: Ensures that the decimal point shows.

113: Guards against scientific notation.

continues

Project 9 Listing. continued

```
114:  cout << endl;

115:  cout << "The average P/E ratio is " << avgPE << endl;

116:  cout << "The average dividend rate is " << avgDiv

117:      << "%" << endl;

118:  cout << "The highest priced stock ID is "

119:      << stocks[highIndex]->stockID << endl;

120:  cout << "The lowest priced stock ID is "

121:      << stocks[lowIndex]->stockID << endl;

122:  return;

123:}

124://*************************************************************

125:void DeleteStocks(struct Stock * stocks[],int stockCount)

126:{

127:  // Allocate memory needed for the broker's stocks

128:  for (int count=0; count<stockCount; count++)

129:  {

130:    delete stocks[count];
```

Description

114: Prints a blank line.

115: Prints the average P/E ratio.

116: Prints the average dividend rate.

117: Continues printing the dividend rate.

118: Begins printing of the highest stock price ID.

119: Continues the ID's printing.

120: Begins printing of the lowest stock price ID.

121: Continues the printing.

122: Returns to `main()`.

123: Closes the function body.

124: A line of asterisks helps to separate functions.

125: Defines the function that will deallocate the dynamic memory.

126: All functions begin with an opening brace.

127: Scatter comments throughout your code.

128: Steps through the stocks.

129: The opening brace of the `for` loop body.

130: Deallocates each of the memory chunks pointed to by `main()`'s array of pointers.

130: Free each pointer's heap memory.

continues

Project 9 Listing. continued

```
131:   }

132:   return;

133:}
```

Description

131: Closes the `for` loop.

132: Returns to `main()`.

133: Closes the function.

▼ OUTPUT

```
* Stock Analysis**

How many stocks to analyze? 3

Stock #1
 What is the 3-letter ID of the stock? BQS
 What is the price? 22.75
 What is the dividend rate? 2.31
 What is the integer P/E ratio? 4

Stock #2
 What is the 3-letter ID of the stock? WWC
 What is the price? 32.50
 What is the dividend rate? 5.39
 What is the integer P/E ratio? 19

Stock #3
 What is the 3-letter ID of the stock? XRU
 What is the price? 58.00
 What is the dividend rate? 6.21
 What is the integer P/E ratio? 13

The average P/E ratio is 12.000
The average dividend rate is 4.637%
The highest priced stock ID is XRU
The lowest priced stock ID is BQS
```

10

Object-Oriented Programming

Unit 19: Object-Oriented Programmnig

Unit 20: Making and Breaking Classes

Lesson 10 Project

19

Object-Oriented Programming

classes

encapsulation

inheritance

polymorphism

▶ **What You'll Learn**

- ▶ OOP buzzwords
- ▶ Moving from structures to classes
- ▶ Member functions
- ▶ Scope and classes
- ▶ Access to members

Until now, the programming you have done has been "traditional" programming. In the last lesson, you saw that working with structures and memory allocation started to get complicated, especially when keeping track of all that memory. In this lesson, you'll see that C++ provides you with a number of useful tools to help you contain this complexity.

The gathering of a number of special techniques has come to be called *object-oriented programming* (OOP). In this unit, you will see what this really means and start learning some new C++ tricks.

▶ **OOP Buzzwords**

When working with computers, it is very important to be fashionable! In the 1960s, the new fashion was what were called *high-level languages* such as FORTRAN and COBOL, in which the programmer did not have to understand the machine instructions. In the 1970s, people realized that there were better ways to program than with a jumble of GOTO statements, and the structured programming languages such as PASCAL were invented. (PASCAL looks and works much like the C++ you have seen so far.) In the 1980s, much time was invested in trying to get good results out of *fourth-generation languages* (4GLs), in which complicated programming structures could be coded in a few words (if you could find the right words with so many words to choose from). There were also schemes such as Analyst Workbenches, which made systems analysts into highly paid and overqualified programmers. The fashion of the 1990s is most definitely object-oriented programming.

Read any book on object-oriented programming, and the first things you will read about are three words:

- ▶ Encapsulation
- ▶ Inheritance
- ▶ Polymorphism

Well, that's enough to scare you away from OOP before you start! Don't panic, though. Before you do the spelling test at the end of the unit, take comfort in the fact that only the most difficult to spell, polymorphism, is a really novel programming language feature. As you will see, there is not much in OOP that isn't common sense, although it might seem to be black magic at first.

Let's take a look at each one of those words and find out what they really mean.

Encapsulation

Definition—*Encapsulation* means hiding away the workings of your code.

Encapsulation means that you hide away the inner workings of your system and present a well-defined interface to the rest of the world that tells it only what it needs to know.

A good real-world example of encapsulation is a wristwatch. It is important to know what the time is. The way your watch keeps time—whether it is battery-powered or has a spring and lots of cogs—is not important as long as the accuracy is there. You look at the face, and that tells you all you need to know.

Writing good code means not only that it is fast and does what it is supposed to do (bug-free), but also that it can easily be maintained and amended. Over the years, programmers have come to recognize that hiding the workings of one piece of code away from another helps the programmer change code, fix errors, or improve its workings without breaking some piece elsewhere in the program.

Another example of encapsulation is the PC that you've been doing battle with over the lessons in this book. IBM-compatible PCs are examples of a set of encapsulated hardware systems. You can buy screens, printers, and disk drives from different sources and plug them together, and they work. You might have spent three weeks trying to install your sound card last month, but normally it is simple. When a standard interface has been defined to the rest of the electronic jungle that is your PC, you have a fighting chance. You can buy a bigger screen and a laser printer to replace your dot-matrix printer, plug them together, and they talk. The different units know how to talk to each other; you don't need to wire your disk drive into your screen and your printer into the sound card to make everything work. (That might seem like a stupid remark, but real programmers often write code that does the software equivalent of just that.) When the workings of a device have not been successfully encapsulated, your troubles begin.

Inheritance

Definition—*Inheritance* is the capability to borrow pieces of code to reuse.

Inheritance is the process of taking an object that does most of the job that you want it to do and adding some extra bits to do a more useful or specialized job. For instance, in the example of the wristwatch, you could take an ordinary wristwatch and add a date display to it. The world of consumer durables does this all the time—taking a basic model and adding extra features that give lots of added value for very little effort on the manufacturer's part.

It is a lot easier to build a car with an automatic gearbox by throwing away the old manual gearbox and adding a new automatic box, than it is to design a complete car from scratch. You might need to throw away some old parts, but usually the car designer has taken the option into account in the first place. The extra benefit is that if the designer wants to change features of the two "different" cars, he can change a single design and both versions are updated. In the world of programming, Visual C++ gives you some tools to easily borrow some code you have already written and add or change parts. If the underlying way it works is changed, only one set of code needs changing.

Polymorphism

Definition—*Polymorphism* is the capability to ask different objects to perform the same task and have the object know how to achieve that task in its own way.

Polymorphism is the most novel idea in OOP. It is easiest to explain by an example. You can press the Play button on a CD player, VCR, or cassette player and each will play some sound (one will also give you a picture). You don't have to understand how they work; you just understand the interface.

In Visual C++, this is implemented so that you can ask an object to perform a function, and depending on what type of object you ask, the function responds in a different way. The classic programming example is that of a graphics program in which you create objects such as circles, rectangles, and triangles. The drawing program is written to store shapes and know where the shapes should be placed on the drawing. When it is time to print, it only has the code to tell the object where to print, and it asks each object to draw itself in the right place. By defining the right interface, the program can be provided with more and more shapes and the main program does not need to change.

Why Is OOP Important?

Definition—*Object-oriented programming* is a productivity tool.

So you have read about all of these wonderful concepts. Why choose these features? Each of these features is a step on the road to reliable and productive programming. By using prebuilt libraries of code, you can save time and still have the flexibility of altering the way that they work to suit your own needs. Comparing C++ with C, you will find that there are lots of extra features that encourage putting thought into structuring programs so that they are more maintainable. By gathering code into what C++ calls classes, the language helps you divide large programs into small manageable sections, in the same way that you divide small programs into functions. This is very important, because the difficulty of understanding pieces of code increases exponentially (in other words, a lot!) as the pieces of code get bigger and bigger. C++ does not guarantee productivity and maintainability, but it provides you with some tools to help you along the path.

> **Note**   There is no Stop and Type here due to the textual nature of this section.

▶ Moving from Structures to Classes

Concept **What You Will Learn**

The class is the cornerstone of object orientation in Visual C++.

Cast your mind back to when we looked at structures. Do you remember the comment about a structure being a gathering of related data items? With a quick change in terminology, you can change a structure into a class and a structure variable into an object. An object needs two things:

▶ data

▶ function

You already know how to make class data. In C++, a structure is a special case of a class. To make a class, change the `struct` keyword to `class` and add a special extra label, `public`, and you've done it!

```
class C
  {
    public:
      int   i;
      float f;
      char  str[30];
  };
```

Remarkable! It is almost identical to a dull old structure, but now it is a shiny new object-oriented class. Don't worry about that `public` word yet; we'll deal with that before the end of the unit. Just don't miss it. What's the catch? There isn't one! Let's define an object:

```
C anObjectOfTypeC;
```

So you've created an object called `anObjectOfTypeC`. All the rules for accessing data members are the same as for `struct`s. Let's not labor the point and move straight to what's new about classes.

▶ Member Functions

Concept   **What You Will Learn**

A *class* can hold functions as well as data.

Recall, back in Lesson 9, that you built a program dealing with contacts (Listing 17.2). There were two functions in this program that were prototyped like this:

```
int AddContact(Contact& contact);
void DisplayContact(const Contact& contact);
```

Both of these functions had the sole purpose of taking a Contact struct (or a contact object) and providing a function that used that object. All they need to know is what Contact they are operating on. You want to tidy up your program so that all the code is encapsulated and related. At the moment, these functions are available globally, but they are useless without a Contact object. Visual C++ provides a way of declaring the function so that it is only available when there is a class object to use it with.

> *Note*   A function that is part of a class is called a *member function*, in the same way that a variable is called a *data member*.

```
class Contact
  {
    public:
      char name[50];
      int  age;
      char phoneNo[15];
      void AddContact();
      void DisplayContact();
  };
```

The only odd thing about these declarations is that the Contact object has been removed. This is because, to use member functions, you use the member access operators—the dot operator (.) and the pointer operator (->)—to tell Visual C++ which data to work on. In main() the code could look like this:

```
Contact contact;
contact.Add();
contact.Display();
```

> *Note*   That looks familiar! Now you understand what those funny cout.precision() calls were about.

The class definition only declares the member function; it does not define how the function works. It is time to meet a new operator, ::, which is called the scope operator. If you try to define the functions as before, Visual C++ lets you, but all sorts of problems will arise because Visual C++ doesn't realize that you meant to define the member functions. You tell Visual C++ the class that the function belongs to by adding the class name and scope operator to the function name.

```
void Contact::Display()
  {
    // body of function
```

Note The class name precedes the function name, *not* the return type.

Now that you have taken away the Contact parameter, you need to access the members in a different way. In a member function, Visual C++ knows which object was used when calling the function, so member access is easy. Within a member function, you can access all the class data members and member functions directly, and you get the data for the object that calls that member function:

```
void Contact::Display()
  {
    cout << "Name : " << name << endl;
    cout << "Age  : " << age << endl;
```

You can access member functions in the same way that you access the data members.

STOP&TYPE We've covered enough to look at an example. Let's turn the contact program into an object-oriented version in Listing 19.1.

▼ **INPUT   LISTING 19.1. AN OBJECT-ORIENTED CONTACT PROGRAM.**

```
1:// Filename: CONTACTO.CPP
2:// Allow the display and entry of contacts
3:// using OOP techniques
4://
5:#include <iostream.h>
6:
7:class Contact
8:  {
9:    public:
10:      char name[50];
11:      int  age;
12:      char phoneNo[15];
13:
14:      // Member function declarations (prototypes)
15:      void AddContact();
16:      void DisplayContact() const;
17:  };
18:
19:// Maximum number of contacts
20:const int MAXCONTACTS = 10;
```

continues

```
21:
22://  Global Prototypes
23:void DisplayAllContacts(const Contact contacts[MAXCONTACTS],int count);
24:
25:void main()
26:  {
27:    Contact contacts[MAXCONTACTS];
28:    char answer;
29:    int count = 0;
30:    while( count < MAXCONTACTS )// while more room
31:      {
32:        // Ask the user if they want to continue
33:        cout << "Do you want to add a contact [Y]es/[N]o: ";
34:        cin >> answer;
35:        cin.ignore(80,'\n'); // skip rubbish
36:
37:        if (answer == 'y' |¦ answer == 'Y')
38:          {
39:            // Add the information
40:            contacts[count].AddContact();
41:            count++;
42:          }
43:        else
44:          break;
45:      }
46:
47:    DisplayAllContacts(contacts,count);
48:
49:  }
50://
51://  DisplayContact displays a single name
52://
53:void Contact::DisplayContact() const
54:  {
55:    cout << endl;
56:    cout << "Name    : " << name << endl;
57:    cout << "Age     : " << age << endl;
58:    cout << "phone no: " << phoneNo << endl;
59:    cout << endl;
60:  }
61://
62://  DisplayAllContacts calls DisplayContact to show
63://  all entered names
64://
65:void DisplayAllContacts(const Contact contacts[MAXCONTACTS],int count)
66:  {
67:    for (int i = 0; i < count; i++)
68:      {
69:         contacts[i].DisplayContact();
70:      }
71:  }
72://
73://  Add contact asks for one contact
```

```
74://
75:void Contact::AddContact()
76:  {
77:    cout << "Name: ";
78:    cin.getline(name,30);
79:    cout << "Phone no: ";
80:    cin.getline(phoneNo,15);
81:    cout << "Age ";
82:    cin >> age;
83:    cin.ignore();
84:  }
```

▼ OUTPUT

```
Do you want to add a contact [Y]es/[N]o: y
Name: Ian Spencer
Phone no: 0-672-30600-X
Age 36
Do you want to add a contact [Y]es/[N]o: y
Name: Konrad Borkowy
Phone no: Ex-directory
Age 41
Do you want to add a contact [Y]es/[N]o: y
Name: Wendy Smith
Phone no: 111-1111
Age 40
Do you want to add a contact [Y]es/[N]o: no

Name     : Ian Spencer
Age      : 36
phone no: 0-672-30600-X


Name     : Konrad Borkowy
Age      : 41
phone no: Ex-directory


Name     : Wendy Smith
Age      : 40
phone no: 111-1111
```

▼ ANALYSIS

The program works much the same as it did last time. Let's go through the special OOP differences. Lines 7 to 17 declare the class. The only differences are the public label on line 9 and the member functions in lines 15 and 16. These function declarations are similar to the global declarations. There is an extra feature on DisplayContact. In the original CONTACT.CPP, DisplayContact() took a constant parameter. Because there is no parameter, C++ needs a new way to say "I will not change the object I'm operating on." This is done by adding an extra `const` keyword after the function name (in both the declaration in line 16 and the definition in line 53).

Note that the definition in line 53 uses the scope operator (`::`) to tell C++ which class this function definition belongs to. This means that you can have the same function in different classes and C++ can tell them apart.

The `main()` code is very similar to the original program. Notice that the `main()` code does not reference any of the object's data items. All the data items are referenced in the member code of `AddContact()` and `DisplayContact()`. The interesting part of the code in the member functions is that within a member function, the function has access to the class member data items without qualification—for example, `name` in line 56.

There is nothing stopping the code in `main()` from directly accessing the data members of the class. This is a source of great danger, and you haven't gained a great deal of safety from putting the code into the class.

*N**ote*** In this book, I have not used header files for the code. Normally, a C++ programmer places the class definition (such as lines 7 to 17 in the previous code) in a header file called CONTACT.H. Then the definition is included by using `#include "contact.h"` in the main code. The quotation marks mean that C++ should look for the file in the current directory first. This enables you to split code that uses the class into many CPP files rather than having one long file. You can build several files into one executable by using the Visual Workbench's project facility. (Projects are explained in a comprehensive section in the Visual Workbench online help, which you can easily find from the help contents page.)

► **Access to Members**

Concept   **What You Will Learn**

Classes have a new sort of scope: class scope.

When writing code within a member function, the code can access all the members of the current object as if they are local variables. How does Visual C++ decide which object's members the function is working with when there is more than one member? The access to members is always with the object that the function is called with, as in the following example:

```
class A
  {
```

```
    public:
      int x;
      void SetX(int X);
      int GetX();
  };
void A::SetX(int X)
  {
    x = X;
  }
int A::GetX()
  {
    return x;
  }
void main()
  {
    A a1;
    a1.SetX(5);
    A a2;
    a2.SetX(10);
    int y = a1.GetX();
    int z = a2.GetX();
  }
```

In each access of the class member function, the programmer specifies which object the member function is associated with. So although GetX() only refers to x inside the function, C++ knows to access a1.x or a2.x because the function, when called, remembers which object was referred to.

Even though you have class functions, you can still access the members in the normal way. Outside member functions (or outside *class scope*), you need the member access operators; inside the class, access is given automatically.

However, you need to remember one of our long words, *encapsulation*. If everyone can get at data members, there is no advantage to classes over structures. To control access to both data members and function members, Visual C++ provides the access labels public, protected, and private to declare what is available to the world outside the member functions. public means that the members are available for access by the class member access operators; private and protected are only available to member functions. A class can contain as many of these access labels as you like.

The reason for having private members is that the class can ensure that only sensible values are set. For example, a Person class might have an age member. If age was a public member, any programmer could set the age to an unreasonable amount. If age is private, the only functions that can access age are the classes own functions. This doesn't mean that the age can't be set from outside the class, only that it has to be set by passing a parameter of a member function and then assigning it into the member. Similarly, to get a private member out, another accessing function is provided. This provides two benefits:

▶ Hiding the way the class holds data

▶ Protecting the data from data errors

If age has a wrong value, only the class member functions need to be looked at to understand how this could happen. Correcting this might mean adding code into the access functions to validate the data passed to the class by the function. After the access functions are provided, the class can change the way the data member is held, and the outside world need not be aware of the change. For example, your Person class might hold a date of birth. Externally, it might be convenient to pass this as a character array; internally, it might be better to hold it as a number for calculations. The outside world never needs to know that the date is held as a number, as long as the access functions know how to convert the data.

Note   Member functions provided just for giving and receiving data are known as *access functions*.

A struct is not really a separate mechanism in C++. It is a special case of the class. The difference between a struct and a class is that in a struct, the default access without a label is public, and the default access for a class is private. By convention, structs are only used to represent a data-only class.

STOP&TYPE   The final listing of this section, Listing 19.2, shows a simple class for handling retirement ages.

▼ INPUT   LISTING 19.2. LOOKING FORWARD TO A QUIET LIFE.

```
 1:// File name: PERSON.CPP
 2:// A simple class for handling age of a person
 3://
 4:#include <iostream.h>
 5:#include <string.h>
 6:
 7:// Class declaration
 8:class Person
 9:  {
10:          // Public - available like a struct member
11:    public:
12:          // Set up data
13:      int AskForPerson();
14:      void SetRetirementAge(int year);
15:          // Get the name, but const char * stops the
16:          // pointer being used to change the name
17:          // and the following const after GetName means
18:          // that the class will not be changed by calling
19:          // this function
20:      const char * GetName() const;
```

```
21:        int GetAge() const;
22:        int YearsToRetirement() const;
23:            // Private - only member functions of this class
24:            // can see the following members
25:    private:
26:        char name[30];
27:        int  age;
28:        int  retirementAge;
29:    };
30:
31:int MoreNames();
32:
33:
34:void main()
35:    {
36:      // Array to hold up to 20 people - initialized to 0 pointers
37:      Person * people[20] = {0};
38:      int more = 1;
39:      int count = 0;
40:
41:      while (more)
42:        {
43:          more = MoreNames();  // Ask whether more input
44:          if (more)
45:            {
46:              people[count] = new Person;
47:              if (people[count]->AskForPerson())
48:                count++;
49:              else
50:                {
51:                  cout << "** Invalid input - rejected **" << endl;
52:                  delete people[count]; // Tidy up problem
53:                }
54:            }
55:        }
56:
57:      //
58:      // Output collected data
59:      //
60:      cout << endl << endl
61:          << "Name                          Age"
62:          << "     Years to Retirement" << endl;
63:
64:      for (int i = 0; i < count; i++)
65:        {
66:          cout << people[i]->GetName();
67:          for (int j = strlen(people[i]->GetName()); j < 31; j++)
68:            cout << ' ';
69:          cout << people[i]->GetAge();
70:          if (people[i]->YearsToRetirement())
71:            cout << "        " << people[i]->YearsToRetirement() << endl;
72:          else
```

continues

```
73:               cout << "         " << "Retired" << endl;
74:          }
75:
76:      for (i = 0;i < count; i++) // Tidy up dynamic data
77:        delete people[i];
78:  }
79://****************************************************************
80://
81://  Global functions
82://
83:
84:int MoreNames()
85:  {
86:    char temp;
87:    cout << endl << endl << "Do you want to add more names? ";
88:    cin >> temp;
89:    cin.ignore();
90:    if (temp == 'y' || temp == 'Y')
91:      return 1;
92:    else
93:      return 0;
94:  }
95://****************************************************************
96://
97://  Person functions
98://
99:int Person::AskForPerson()
100:  {
101:    cout << endl << "Name: ";
102:    cin.getline(name,30);
103:    if (strlen(name) == 0)
104:      return 0;
105:    cout << "Age : ";
106:    cin >> age;
107:    cin.ignore();
108:    if (age < 0 || age > 120)
109:      return 0;
110:    cout << "Retirement age [0 for default]: ";
111:    cin >> retirementAge;
112:    if (retirementAge <= 0 || retirementAge > 120)
113:      retirementAge = 65;
114:    return 1;
115:  }
116:
117:const char * Person::GetName() const
118:  {
119:    return name;
120:  }
121:
122:int Person::GetAge() const
123:  {
124:    return age;
125:  }
```

```
126:
127:int Person::YearsToRetirement() const
128:  {
129:    if (age >= retirementAge)
130:      return 0;
131:    else
132:      return retirementAge - age;
133:  }
```

▼ OUTPUT

```
Do you want to add more names? y

Name: Phill Dorrell
Age : 29
Retirement age [0 for default]: 0


Do you want to add more names? y

Name: Neil Hoskins
Age : 33
Retirement age [0 for default]: 0


Do you want to add more names? y

Name: Stefan Winman
Age : 28
Retirement age [0 for default]: 60


Do you want to add more names? y

Name: Trevor Cox
Age : 124
** Invalid input - rejected **


Do you want to add more names? n


Name               Age    Years to Retirement
Phill Dorrell      29     36
Neil Hoskins       33     32
Stefan Winman      28     32
```

▼ ANALYSIS

The program is similar to the Contact program listed earlier. In this program, the class protects its own data. The class definition in lines 8 through 29 divides up its functions and members. The labels in lines 11 and 25 tell Visual C++ how to treat the following declarations. In this case, no outside function is allowed to see any of the data of class Person declared in lines 26 through 28 after the private label.

The main loop knows nothing about the class and how the data is held. Line 37 takes advantage of the initialization feature to initialize each element of the array to zero.

The class provides the functions GetName(), GetAge(), and YearsToRetirement() to allow nonmember functions to see the information. Because the return type is a copy of the data, the nonmember functions can't change the internal data. GetName() returns a const char *, which you'll recall was used for parameters to ensure that the data pointed to by a character pointer was not allowed to be changed.

The const after the parameter list of the functions for getting the data (for example line 117) does not mean that you can't change the returned data. Instead, it means that you are guaranteeing that the function will not change the data inside the class when the function executes. Visual C++ can't tell this for itself. This allows Visual C++ to let you call functions against data items that are constant:

```
const Person p;
p.AskForPerson(); // Invalid, updates Person
p.GetName();      // Valid, does not change Person
```

The storage of name in line 26 limits the class to a maximum of 29 characters for a name. In fact, there is no need for the limit. In AskForPerson() (lines 99 through 115) you could get the input into a temporary character string, dynamically allocate a string of the length to match the input, and hold a pointer to the string as a class member. Although you can do this to create the string and no external program needs to be aware of the change in the way the string is stored, you would need to introduce a function to tidy up the data, deleteing the character string before deleteing the Person structure. This is very important because without such a function, the application loses memory. The need to tidy up a class before it is deleted is a common and important problem—so important that we will look at it in the next unit.

The other problem with this class occurs if a new Person object is created, but the AskForPerson() function is not called. Following functions could go seriously wrong because the string and age data would not have been initialized. Because the data is private, there is no way that the main() function can initialize the data, and in any case the user of the class should not know how the data is held. This is another important hole to fill if you want to ensure that your classes are robust and error free.

The simple function in lines 127 through 133 shows how you can start to protect external functions from errors. For a start, line 132 knows how to calculate retirement ages. If Person was a simple structure, the user would have to remember that was the calculation. Furthermore, in line 129, the program ensures that it does not give negative numbers back to the calling function. In future revisions of the program, it might be useful to change the default logic of retirement ages to take into account different rules for different types of employees. Although some changes might be needed to get this information, other programs that just use the `YearsToRetirement()` function would not need to be changed to account for the new rules. This means that you've started to succeed in your objective of encapsulation, keeping all the code that is specific to the class hidden away inside member functions.

▶ Homework
General Knowledge

1. What sort of language is C++?
2. Name (and spell!) the three important things that C++ provides, which other languages do not.
3. How does encapsulation help stop programming errors?
4. What buzzword is used to mean reusable code?
5. What are functions belonging to a class called?
6. How does Visual C++ know which class variable should be used by a member function?
7. What label(s) can you use in a class declaration to stop external functions from accessing the data members of a class.
8. What label(s) can you use in a class declaration to stop external functions from accessing the function members of a class?
9. What label(s) can you use in a class declaration to stop member functions from accessing data members of a class?
10. True or false: OOP is useful because it makes programs harder to understand and protects (encapsulates) programmers jobs.
11. True or false: OOP programs run 10 times faster on average than other programs.
12. True or false: Visual C++ programs are easier to maintain than standard C programs.
13. True or false: The default access of a `struct` is `public`.
14. True or false: The default access of a `class` is `protected`.

What's the Output?

Given the code

```
class A
  {
    public:
```

```
      int a;
      int b;
      void Update(int a);
   };
void main()
   {
     A a;
     a.Update(3);
     a.b = a.a;
     a.b++;
     int c = a.a;
   }
void A::Update(int A)
   {
     a = A;
     b = 0;
   }
```

what is the value of the following:

15. Class member a at the end of the program?

16. Class member b at the end of the program?

17. main() variable a at the end of the program.

Find the Bug

18. Grizwald is having trouble with his code. Why won't his code compile?

```
class A
   {
     int GetA();
     void SetA(int a);
     int a;
   };
void main()
   {
     A a;
     a.SetA(5);
     int b = a.GetA();
   }
int GetA()
   {
      return a;
   }
void SetA(int A)
   {
      a = A;
   }
```

19. What is wrong with this code snippet?

```
class B
   {
```

```
    private:
      char b[30];
    public:
      void SetB(const char B);
  }

void main()
  {
    B b;
    b.SetB("Hello there!");
  }
```

20. Grizwald really isn't very good at this Visual C++ programming. He needs your help again to find another problem.

```
class C
  {
    public:
      int a;
      void SetA(int a);
  };
void main()
  {
    int a;
    SetA(a);
  }
```

Write Code That...

21. Change the code in PERSON.CPP in Listing 19.2 to dynamically allocate the name string. Use the strlen() function to determine how long the string is. Remember the comment about deleting the string at the end. For the time being, write a new member function called CleanUp(), which is called just before deleting a Person. Aside from adding the CleanUp() function, how many lines of code did you change that were not in the Person() class?

22. Add code to PERSON.CPP to print a number alongside each entry. After displaying the listing, allow the user to enter the number to update the details of any entry. Add a new function to the class that allows the user to be shown the existing entry and decide whether it is to be changed. To keep input handling simple, allow the user to enter zero to indicate the age or retirement date is not to be changed.

Extra Credit

23. Write a program that allows you to enter the type, brand, and cost of each component of the PC that you are sitting in front of. The type should be entered as a code, and as the user enters the code, you should check that the code is valid. When the listing of the PC is displayed, you should show a description of the code.

20

Making and Breaking Classes

constructor

the copy constructor

destructor

▶ **What You'll Learn**

- ▶ Making a class: the default constructor
- ▶ Breaking a class: the destructor
- ▶ Other constructors
- ▶ Copying a class
- ▶ Classes can be members of other classes

There are a number of special events in the life-cycle of a class, the most important ones being the creation of a class object and the deletion of a class object. These events are so important that Visual C++ provides some special functions to help.

▶ **Making a Class: The Default Constructor**

Concept   **What You Will Learn**

Whenever a class is made, a special function called the *constructor* is called.

When you declare a variable, it is a good practice to initialize its value so that if you do not set it again in the program, the rogue value it has does not cause problems later. The same is true of variables inside a class. When a new class object is declared, it is best if all the members of the class are set up correctly. You could write a function, Initialize(), which would set up the correct values. However, you are now depending on the programmer remembering to write the correct code. If the Initialize() function is not called, the class code might not work properly.

Visual C++ can call a function automatically when a class object is made, either by declaration or dynamically by calling new. This function is called the constructor. So that Visual C++ and the programmer know which member function is meant to be called, there is a special convention for constructor functions: They are called exactly the same name as the class, and they have no return type. Look at the following example:

```
include <iostream.h>
class Example
  {
    public:
      Example();
};
Example::Example()
  {
    cout << "An example has been made!";
```

```
  }
void main()
  {
    Example e;
  }
```

This would output the following:

```
An example has been made!
```

It will seem very strange that a program with only a declaration can output data. A constructor is just like any function except that it is called automatically. Normally, you write code to ensure that values are correctly set and any memory required is allocated. Typically, you set pointers to zero if you are not going to use them immediately. Then, in functions called later, you can check to see whether any memory has been allocated.

Definition—When you declare a constructor with no parameters, it is called the *default constructor*.

▶ Breaking a Class: The Destructor

Concept   **What You Will Learn**

Visual C++ calls another special member function, the *destructor*, when an object is destroyed.

If you think about the typical sequence of events in the simple programs you've seen so far, they consist of main functions that do the following:

▶ Initialize

▶ Do some work

▶ Tidy up

Sometimes the tidy up step is not necessary, or rather Visual C++ does it for us. The same three steps are required for a class. You have seen how to initialize. You have also seen how to do work, by calling member functions. Now you need to see how to tidy up. Visual C++ automatically calls another function just before an object is destroyed. This function is called a destructor. It is declared almost exactly like the default constructor, except you place a ~ (tilde) in front of the class name. (There is no magic here. Visual C++ simply looks in the class definition for this name when looking to see whether a destructor has been provided.) Again, a destructor has no return value, and it receives no parameters.

```
include <iostream.h>
class Example
  {
    public:
      Example();
      ~Example();
};
Example::Example()
  {
    cout << "An example has been made!" << endl;
  }
Example::~Example()
  {
    cout << "An example has been destroyed!" << endl;
  }
void main()
  {
    Example e;
    cout << "The program does some work" << endl;
  }
```

This code would output the following:

```
An example has been made!
The program does some work
An example has been destroyed!
```

Now this is getting extremely confusing. You can see the line of code that makes the example object and the place where main outputs its line, but where does An example has been destroyed! come from?

Remember, way back in the early units, you learned that declared data items have a lifetime of the block they are declared in. At the end of a block, Visual C++ looks for all the data items that are no longer required. For each data item, it looks to its class definition and checks whether there is a destructor. If there is a destructor, it will be called.

 Warning   You should never directly call a constructor or destructor yourself. If you have code that you want to happen at construction time and at some other time, extract it into a separate member function and call it from the constructor and anywhere else.

The main importance of destructors is in deallocating dynamic memory. Destructors are normally very simple pieces of code because the class will no longer exist after the destructor is called. However, sometimes you invent a class in which other pieces of code expect the object to be present. The destructor is an opportunity to sort out objects that are linked together without relying on the programmer remembering to call the code.

STOP&TYPE A very common use of destructors is to tidy up dynamically allocated strings. In Listing 20.1, the program shows how constructors and destructors cooperate to correctly manage storage. In the program, you will also put in some *debugging* code to see when these magic calls occur.

▼ **INPUT   LISTING 20.1. DISPLAYING CONSTRUCTION AND DESTRUCTION OF OBJECTS.**

```
1:// File name: CONDEST.CPP
2:// Shows construction and destruction
3:// of objects and simple memory management
4://
5:#include <iostream.h>
6:#include <string.h>
7:
8:class Name
9:  {
10:    public:
11:      // Constructor
12:      Name();
13:      // Destructor
14:      ~Name();
15:      void SetName(const char * newName);
16:      const char * GetName() const;
17:    private:
18:      char * name;
19:  };
20:void main()
21:  {
22:    cout << "-- First line of main() --" << endl;
23:    Name firstName;
24:    firstName.SetName("firstName");
25:    Name * secondName = new Name;
26:    secondName->SetName("secondName");
27:    cout << "-- Before block --" << endl;
28:    // New block
29:      {
30:        cout << "-- First line of block --" << endl;
31:        Name thirdName;
32:        Name fourthName;
33:        thirdName.SetName("thirdName");
34:        cout << "-----------------" << endl;
35:        cout << "Contents of objects" << endl;
36:        cout << firstName.GetName() << endl;
37:        cout << secondName->GetName() << endl;
38:        cout << thirdName.GetName() << endl;
39:        cout << fourthName.GetName() << endl;
40:        cout << "-----------------" << endl ;
41:        cout << "-- Last line of block --" << endl;
42:      } // Block ends - third & fourth name destroyed
```

continues

UNIT

20

Making and Breaking Classes

```
43:      cout << "-- After block --" << endl;
44:      delete secondName;
45:      cout << "-- Last line of main() --" << endl;
46:  }        // firstName goes;
47://***********************************************************
48://
49:// Name   class function definitions
50://
51:
52:// Constructor
53:Name::Name()
54:  {
55:      cout << "Constructor called" << endl;
56:      name = 0;
57:  }
58:
59:// Destructor
60:Name::~Name()
61:  {
62:      cout << "Destructor called ";
63:      cout << "name is " << GetName() << endl;
64:      delete [] name; // Delete on zero pointer is safe
65:  }
66:
67:// Member function to store a name
68://
69:void Name::SetName(const char* newName)
70:  {
71:      // First, remove any name that might already exist
72:      // Use zero pointer to inidicate no name stored
73:      // C++ will not destroy storage on a zero pointer
74:      // "if (name)"
75:      delete [] name;
76:      // Create new storage
77:      name = new char[strlen(newName) + 1]; // add 1 for
78:                                       // terminator
79:      strcpy(name,newName);  // Copy data into new name
80:  }
81:
82:// Member function to get the stored name
83:// Coded to always return a safe value
84:const char * Name::GetName() const
85:  {
86:    if (name)
87:      return name;
88:    else
89:      return "No name exists";
90:  }
```

▼ OUTPUT

```
-- First line of main() --
Constructor called
Constructor called
-- Before block --
-- First line of block --
Constructor called
Constructor called
------------------
Contents of objects
firstName
secondName
thirdName
No name exists
------------------
-- Last line of block --
Destructor called name is No name exists
Destructor called name is thirdName
-- After block --
Destructor called name is secondName
-- Last line of main() --
Destructor called name is firstName
```

▼ ANALYSIS

This skeleton program lets you see the timing of the creation and deletion of objects. By the way, there is nothing special about the timing of the class constructor and destructor. The same applies to standard C++ data types such as char or int.

The simple class Name manages a single dynamically allocated string. It allows the string to be set using SetName() (line 15) and retrieved using GetName() (line 16). The actual method of holding the string is hidden to the outside world. (When using a class that has been created for you, you should imagine that you can't see anything marked protected and private.)

When an instance of Name is created, the constructor (line 12 and lines 53 through 57) initializes the name member to zero in line 56. Zero is an important value for a pointer. delete can be called on a zero pointer and Visual C++ knows that there is no storage to be deleted. It is the safest value to set a pointer to when not in use. Also, in line 55, the constructor outputs some text to trace when it is called.

When an instance of Name is destroyed—either by delete or by going out of scope—its destructor (lines 60 through 65) is called. The destructor only deletes the name member, remembering that name might not have been set to point to some dynamic memory, so it should then be zero. Again, the destructor identifies when it has been called by outputting some text.

SetName(), in lines 69 through 80, allocates storage just sufficient to hold the name provided. Before it places the new name, it deletes name in case a name has already been stored. It then tests the size of the supplied string and allocates enough memory for the string and the string terminator. Finally, it copies the input string into its newly created area of storage.

GetName() demonstrates an advantage of encapsulation. It always returns a valid string, even if it has not stored a name. In line 86, it tests name to see whether a value has been stored. If something has been stored, the value is returned. If no value has been stored, GetName() returns an error string. This means that the class can be used, and code using it can never retrieve an invalid string. This relies on the constructor having set an initial value and the GetName() function having the extra code in place. Furthermore, because SetString() cleverly checks the length of the string that is passed to it, it can never overwrite another variable's storage as might happen with a simple character array.

The main program simply declares and dynamically allocates some objects. Look at the output. Notice that the constructor gets called at exactly the line in the code where the declaration of the object takes place (lines 23, 25, 31, and 32). Then look at the destructor. If delete is used, the destruction takes place at that point (line 44). If the object is locally declared (firstName, thirdName, and fourthName), the destructor takes place at the end of the block (lines 42 and 46). In the case of the main block, the destructor call is after the last line of code (line 46). In the inner block, the destruction takes place after the last line of code of the inner block (line 42) and before the next line of code in main() (line 43).

▶ **Other Constructors**

Concept   **What You Will Learn**

Visual C++ allows constructors to have parameters for objects that have to be supplied with information before they can be used.

Default constructors are often used in Visual C++, but quite often it is important to be able to set an initial value. A constructor can have any parameter list that other functions have. In the case of the Name class from Listing 20.1, it is useful to be able to set an initial string value:

```
class Name
  {
    public:
      Name();                  // default constructor
      Name(const char * name); // char * constructor
```

```
   ... and so on
};
```

In the code, there is no need to have separate lines to make and then initialize the Name variables:

```
Name name1("Paddy McGinty"); // Explicit construction
Name name2;                  // Use default constructor
name2.SetName("and his goat");
```

It is also quite all right to use default parameters:

```
class RetirementAge
  {
    public:
      RetirementAge(int age = 65);
      int retirementAge;
  };
void main()
  {
    RetirementAge ra;
    cout << ra.retirementAge;
    // prints 65
  }
```

Recall that this is called function overloading. You can overload member functions in the same way as global functions. There is a trap to be wary of, though. If no constructor is declared for a class, Visual C++ invents one for itself (it does nothing). If you declare a constructor yourself, Visual C++ doesn't invent a default (parameterless) constructor, as in the following example:

```
class A
  {
    public:
      int a;
  };
class B
  {
    public:
      B(int bb);
      int b;
  };
```

The declaration A a; would be valid. The default constructor that Visual C++ creates would be used. The declaration B b(5); is also valid, but B b; would be invalid because there is already an explicitly defined constructor for B and no default parameterless constructor has been declared. A constructor with parameters for which all can be defaulted can be used as the default.

UNIT

20

Making and Breaking Classes

It is tempting to explicitly define that you want to call the default constructor by using parentheses. This is wrong because C++ thinks you are declaring a function with no parameters and a return type of the class:

```
A a;      // calls the default constructor
A a();    // Wrong! declares a parameterless function called a
          // with a return type A
A a(1);   // OK, calls constructor taking an int
```

Although you can create constructors with any parameter lists you like, you can never have parameters for a destructor. In other words, there are many ways of making an object, but there is always only one way of deleting an object.

Here's a final note: In Visual C++, it is useful to remember that the language designers wanted user-defined classes to be just like the built-in data types such as int and char. These built-in types have a few extra goodies, but generally the designers succeeded. Until now, you might not have realized that in defining an int or a char, you are using the same idea of constructors and destructors that you see in classes. Here are constructors that you can call for an int and a float:

```
int i(5);
float f(98.7F);
```

▶ Copying a Class

Concept   **What You Will Learn**

A special form of constructor takes another object of the class as a parameter to allow it to be copied.

A special case of constructor is called the copy constructor. This special constructor always looks like this:

```
ClassName(const ClassName& name)
```

This is a constructor that takes a reference to the class object itself as a parameter. This constructor allows an object to be copied to another object of the same type at the time of construction.

STOP&TYPE Let's look at why you would want such a thing. The easiest way to understand this is to look at another program that shows the automatic calls that C++ does. Listing 20.2 shows that Visual C++ will use a copy constructor not only when you ask it to, but also when you do a pass by value call to a function with a class object as a parameter.

```
1:// File name: NAMENAME.CPP
2:// Demonstration of implicit use of constructors
3:// by Visual C++
4:
5:#include <iostream.h>
6:#include <string.h>
7:
8://
9:// Name - a trivial class
10://
11:class Name
12:  {
13:   public:
14:     // Constructors
15:     Name();                    // Default
16:     Name(const Name& n);       // Copy
17:     Name(const char * newName); // Normal
18:     // Destructor
19:     ~Name();
20:     // Access function
21:     const char * GetName() const;
22:   private:
23:     // Data member
24:     char * name;
25:  };
26:
27:// Default constructor - ensure name is initialized
28:Name::Name()
29:  {
30:   name = 0;
31:   cout << "Default constructor used" << endl;
32:  }
33:
34:// Copy constructor - ensure string is duplicated
35:Name::Name(const Name& n)
36:  {
37:   if (n.name)
38:     {
39:        name = new char[strlen(n.name) + 1];
40:        strcpy(name,n.name);
41:     }
42:   else
43:     name = 0;
44:   cout << "Copy constructor used - "
45:        << (name != 0?name : "") << endl;
46:  }
47:
48:// Make a name for myself
49:Name::Name(const char * newName)
50:  {
51:   if (newName)
```

continues

```
52:      {
53:          name = new char[strlen(newName) + 1];
54:          strcpy(name,newName);
55:      }
56:    else
57:      name = 0;
58:    cout << "const char* constructor used - "
59:          << (name != 0?name : "") << endl;
60:  }
61:
62:// Destructor
63:Name::~Name()
64:  {
65:    cout << "Destructor - " << (name != 0?name : "") << endl;
66:    delete name;
67:  }
68:
69:// Provide access
70:const char * Name::GetName() const
71:  {
72:    return name;
73:  }
74:
75:// Global function with pass by value
76:void PrintName(Name n)
77:  {
78:    cout << "In PrintName  - " << n.GetName() << endl;
79:  }
80:
81:// main() function to excercise the class
82:void main()
83:  {
84:    cout << "-- Start of main() --" << endl;
85:    Name n("Norman Lamont");
86:
87:    cout << "-- Before PrintName --" << endl;
88:    PrintName(n);
89:
90:    cout << "-- Before n1 declaration --" << endl;
91:    Name n1(n);
92:
93:    cout << "-- Before n2 declaration --" << endl;
94:    Name n2;
95:
96:    cout << "-- Before n2 = n1 --" << endl;
97:    n2 = n1; // Unsafe !!!
98:
99:    cout << "-- End of main() --" << endl;
100: }
```

▼ OUTPUT

```
-- Start of main() --
const char* constructor used - Norman Lamont
-- Before PrintName --
Copy constructor used -
In PrintName  - Norman Lamont
Destructor - Norman Lamont
-- Before n1 declaration --
Copy constructor used - Norman Lamont
-- Before n2 declaration --
Default constructor used
-- Before n2 = n1 --
-- End of main() --
Destructor - Norman Lamont
Destructor - ¬·'5t= Lamont
Destructor - Norman Lamont
```

ANALYSIS

In this case, to let you follow the class more easily, all the class members are grouped at the top.

The class declares three different constructors in lines 15 to 17. The constructor in line 17 is just used to let the class have some value of interest. In line 15 the default constructor is declared, and in line 16 the const Name& parameter tells C++ that this is a copy constructor.

The class needs a copy constructor to duplicate the class because otherwise the pointers will get mixed up (as we will see!). To properly copy a pointer member, it is necessary to duplicate the data pointed to by the pointer, or both pointers will point to the same object. Then, at destruction time, C++ will have two separate dynamic objects owned by the pointers so that C++ will not try to delete the same dynamic storage twice.

The difficult thing to follow here is the code for the copy constructor itself, coded in lines 35 through 46. How does this function tell the two Names apart? The Name that is being made requires no qualification of its member variables. The Name that is the copy parameter needs the parameter variable to access the class members to be copied. The name accessed in line 37 belongs to the Name to be copied. There is something fishy here! Wasn't name private? It was, but here is code accessing a private member from outside a member function. Well, that isn't the case. A class member function has access to all the members of a class, not just all the members of the current object. The restriction is that the class object does not have any automatic means of finding other objects of the same class, so normally the members are safe from getting mixed up.

Follow the output as you step through the main() code of lines 82 through 100. The variable n is initialized using the special const char * constructor, which means that it can be directly initialized with a character literal. The output shows that the appropriate constructor is called. The next task is to call the global routine `PrintName()` in line 88. `PrintName` takes a single `Name` parameter passed by value. Recall that this means C++ must take a copy of the variable to stop the called argument from being accidentally changed. Looking to the output, see that the copy constructor is called.

 Warning   It is vital to understand that if you do not explicitly declare a copy constructor, Visual C++ will invent one for itself. It does this by copying each individual data member, but it treats a pointer as a data item and does not duplicate the data pointed to. You can stop the compiler from accidentally using the copy constructor by declaring one as a private member function (you do not have to write the body of this dummy function).

Consider what would have happened if a copy constructor had not been declared. Visual C++, trying to be helpful, would automatically try to copy the `Name` class, but it would then simply copy the pointer and not the data. At the end of the function (line 79), the destructor would be called and delete the character array at the end of the `name` pointer of the temporary variable. Unfortunately, that data also belonged to the original argument n. Fortunately, we *have* coded the copy constructor, so it has copied the string itself, and the copy gets deleted. The important lesson is that the copy constructor is called by C++ itself when passing a class by value. There are other times that C++ will call it, too. To be safe with C++, you should always declare a copy constructor when your class can't simply be copied by copying each data member individually.

Look for the output -- `Before n1 declaration` --. The next action is to copy the variable n into the new variable n1 in line 91. This time, the copy constructor is explicitly called. In line 94, n2 is declared. (Remember, no parentheses for the default constructor.)

In line 97, there is a seemingly harmless line of code. Visual C++ kindly makes an assignment operator for our class. It is important to know that an assignment is not the same as a copy constructor. Look at the output. Although it seems like you should be copying the class, the copy constructor is not used. There is a good reason that C++ does not use the copy constructor: The copy constructor is only for new class instances with no data in them. What would a constructor do with existing data owned by the `name` pointer? In the next lesson, you will see how to fix this problem. Because of this error, at the end of the program (line 100) when all the destructors are called, n2 and n1 both have a pointer to the same piece of memory. n2 is deleted first, and n1 is deleted second. The output shows some gobbledygook, but in fact you are lucky the program worked at all. It could have completely failed. Variable n survives due to n1 having been properly copied.

This is a difficult business! Don't be disheartened because you do not follow this at the moment. I hope you will at least remember that this chapter is here. When you gain more experience, you will remember that odd things happen with classes and refer back here. It's better than being surprised later on.

▶ Classes Can Be Members of Other Classes

What You Will Learn

Classes can contain other classes. Class data types can be used in exactly the same way as the standard Visual C++ data types.

The examples used so far have been quite simple. One of the design aims of Visual C++ was to allow programmers to define their own types that work just like the built-in data types such as int and char. In the previous example, you saw a hint that Visual C++ even lets you make a class use operators (even though the example used the assignment operator wrongly in line 97). Before you go on to these exciting features of Visual C++, it is worth reviewing some of the simple things you can do with classes.

Having invented the Name class, you are starting to have a useful string handling class. (I should warn you that 99.5 percent of all C++ books end up doing examples on string handling classes!) You can now easily create a string, copy a string, and set a string to a new value with a function call. This is so useful that you could add it into the contact program you wrote earlier:

```
class Contact
  {
    public:
      Contact();           // Default
      Contact(const char * Name, const char * Phone, int Age);
      // Other functions here
    private:
      Name name;
      Name phoneNo;  // must rename the class to something better!
      int  age;
  };
```

Then, in the constructor, you can initialize all the variables:

```
Contact::Contact(const char * Name, const char * Phone, int Age)
  {
    name.SetName(Name);
    name.SetName(Phone);
    age = Age;
  }
```

Something is not quite right here. Really, you should call the constructor to make sure that the values are set up properly from the very beginning. You can't simply call the constructor, because the declaration has already been written in the class declaration. C++ does not let you put initialization into the class declaration. Instead, there is a special way of initializing class members: the initialization list. This is simply a list of constructors called for each member that you want to initialize. The list follows the parameters and lives just before the opening brace, with a colon (:) thrown in for good measure. This list can see all the parameters of the constructor that the list is associated with. You don't have to use parameters; they could be set to fixed values. The initialization list finds which variable it is constructing by matching the member name.

```
Contact::Contact(const char * Name, const char * Phone, int Age)
        : name(Name),phoneNo(Phone),age(Age)
   {
   }
```

In this case, the initialization list was all you needed, but you still have to put in the function braces just so Visual C++ knows what it is looking at. Recall that standard data types had constructors. This shows why it is useful to know that the standard data types also have constructors.

One of the very useful things about initialization lists is that they can be used to set constant and reference variables in a class. It is the only way that they can be set. After the constants or references have been made, they can't be assigned to. The initialization list is in a special place (just before the constructor begins), which allows constant members to be defined before any class code can use them.

▶ **Homework**
General Knowledge

1. Which function automatically gets called when a class object is deleted?
2. What is the name of the function that gets called when a class object is declared but not initialized?
3. How many constructors can be declared for a class?
4. How many destructors can be declared for a class?
5. For class Excellent, give the member function of the default constructor.
6. For class Way, give the member function of the destructor.
7. Declare a copy constructor for class WeAreNotWorthy.
8. Declare a single constructor for class String that can be a default constructor and can be used to initialize the class with a constant character string.
9. Name three functions that Visual C++ can provide automatically for a class.
10. True or false: A constructor must be defined in a class declaration to make an instance of a class.

11. True or false: You can only have a single constructor in a class.

12. True or false: You can only have a single destructor in a class.

13. True or false: The copy constructor and the assignment operator are the same thing.

14. True or false: A member constant must be initialized in a class initialization list.

What's the Output?

Given the following class, answer the subsequent questions:

```
class A
  {
    public:
      A();
      ~A();
      void Print();
  }
A::A()
  {
    cout << "Constructor called" << endlL
  }
A::~A()
  {
    cout << "Destructor called" << endlL
  }
void A::Print()
  {
    cout << "Print called " << endl;
  }
```

15. What does the following code produce?

```
{
  A a;
  a.Print();
}
```

16. What does the following code produce?

```
{
  A* a = new A;
  a->Print();
  delete a;
}
```

17. What does the following code produce?

```
{
  A* a = new A;
  a->Print();
}
```

UNIT

20

Making and Breaking Classes

Find the Bug

18. What is wrong with the following code?

```
class Telephone
  {
    Telephone();
    ~Telephone();
    private:
      char number[15];
  };

void main()
{
  Telephone t;
  cout << t.number;
}
```

19. Why won't this compile?

```
class A
  {
    public:
      A(int a1);
    private:
      int a;
  };
A::A(int a1)
  {
    a = a1;
  }

a a;
```

20. What is missing from the following class declaration?

```
class String
  {
    public:
      String();
      void Assign(const char * s);
      const char * GetString() const;
    private:
      char * string;
  };
```

Write Code That...

21. Add a member to the Name class of Listing 20.1 that allows the value of the name to be set at the time of construction. This change must still allow the existing code to work.

22. Add a copy constructor to the Name class of Listing 20.1. Prove that it works by adding a global function call using a Name as a parameter.

Extra Credit

23. Write a class to store the titles of the books on your bookshelf, along with their authors and ISBN numbers, minimizing the amount of storage that the class uses. Provide functions to set and display the data. Allow the programmer to directly construct a book, copy a book, or set up a blank book.

24. If you have not already done so, write a simple string class to allocate just enough storage to hold a string and convert the class you wrote in question 23 to use it for the character array members.

10

Object-Oriented Programming

STOP&TYPE In this lesson, you learned about how a class is defined, and you covered the basic features of all C++ classes. You learned about these features of classes:

▶ There are three important concepts in object-oriented programming: encapsulation, inheritance, and polymorphism.

▶ Classes are similar to structures but also contain functions.

▶ Functions that are part of a class are called member functions and can only be used with a class object.

▶ There is another scope called class scope, which restricts the visibility of objects to within a class.

▶ Access to members is controlled via access labels that restrict to private, protected, and public access.

Project 10 Listing. A simple class-based program.

```
1:// File name: PROJCT10.CPP

2:// An OOP program to list favorite radio stations

3://

4:#include <iostream.h>

5:#include <string.h>

6:

7://***********************************************************

8:// String - a class to manage strings

9://

10:class String

11:  {
```

- ▶ The default constructor is used to define the settings of variables when a class is declared.
- ▶ Copy constructors can be used to control the C++ mechanism of duplicating objects and also a constructor can have the same parameter list as any normal function.
- ▶ The destructor is called by Visual C++ when a class object is deleted.
- ▶ Classes can be members of other classes and are used just like standard Visual C++ data types.

Description

1: A comment to identify the program source file.

2: A comment to describe the program's purpose.

3: Empty comments enhance the appearance of the program.

4: Include the header for the cout functions.

5: Include the header required for strcpy and strlen().

6: Blank lines make the program more readable.

7: A bold comment separates each class.

8: A comment to describe the following class.

9: Empty comments enhance the appearance of the code.

10: Declare a class called String.

11: All class definitions start with an opening brace.

continues

Project 10 Listing. continued

```
12:    public:

13:      // Constructors

14:      String();                    // Default

15:      String(const String& n);      // Copy

16:      String(const char * newString); // Normal

17:      // Destructor

18:      ~String();

19:      // Access functions

20:      const char * Get() const;

21:      void Set(const char * newString);

22:      int Length() const;

23:    private:

24:      // Data member

25:      char * string;

26: };

27:

28:// Default constructor - ensure string is initialized
```

Description

12:	All members following this label will be public.
13:	A comment to identify the following functions.
14:	A default constructor is declared.
15:	A copy constructor, which takes a reference to its own class.
16:	A general constructor.
17:	Comment to identify following functions.
18:	The ~ in front of the class name and no return type identifies this function as a destructor.
19:	Comment to identify following functions.
20:	Get() is provided solely to access a private data member safely.
21:	A function Set will be provided in this class, and a definition will follow.
22:	An information function that provides the length of the string.
23:	All members following this label will be public.
24:	A comment to identify the following definition.
25:	A pointer to a character string is defined as a class data member.
26:	All class definitions end with a closing brace and a semicolon.
27:	Blank lines help to make the program more readable.
28:	A comment to identify the following function.

14: A constructor can always be identified because it has no return type and has the same name as the class.

16: A constructor that takes a single parameter can also be used as a type converter.

continues

Project 10 Listing. continued

```
29:String::String()

30:  {

31:    string = 0;

32:  }

33:

34:// Copy constructor - ensure string is duplicated

35:String::String(const String& n)

36:  {

37:    if (n.string)

38:      {

39:        string = new char[strlen(n.string) + 1];

40:        strcpy(string,n.string);

41:      }

42:    else

43:    string = 0;

44:  }

45:
```

Description

29: This line identifies that a member function of String is to be defined and that the function is the default constructor.

30: All functions start with an opening brace.

31: Ensure that the pointer is marked with zero for empty.

> 31: A pointer with valid storage can never be zero.

32: All functions end with a closing brace.

33: Blank lines make the code more readable.

34: A comment to describe the following code.

35: The definition of the class copy constructor starts.

36: All functions start with an opening brace.

37: If the passed string to be copied contains data, do the following:

38: Start a compound statement with an opening brace.

39: Create a new character array as long as the string to be copied plus an extra character for the terminator.

40: Copy the actual string into the new class storage.

41: End a compound statement with a closing brace.

42: If the string pointer does not point to data, do the following.

43: Set the new string pointer to zero so that C++ can later identifiy that no memory is allocated to this pointer.

44: Function definitions always end with a closing brace.

45: Blank lines make the program more readable.

continues

Project 10 Listing. continued

```
46:// Make a string from C string

47:String::String(const char * newString)

48:  {

49:    if (newString)

50:      {

51:          string = new char[strlen(newString) + 1];

52:          strcpy(string,newString);

53:      }

54:    else

55:      string = 0;

56:  }

57:

58:// Destructor

59:String::~String()

60:  {

61:    delete [] string;

62:  }

63:
```

Description

46: A comment to describe the following function.

47: Define the class constructor that accepts a `const char*` parameter.

48: All functions start with an opening brace.

49: If a non-zero string is passed, do the following:

49: When accepting pointers, it is a good idea to check that a value has been passed.

50: Compound statements start with an opening brace.

51: Create a new character storage that is long enough to contain the string passed in.

52: Copy the string.

53: Compound statements end with a closing brace.

54: If the string pointer does not point to data, do the following:

55: Set the new string pointer to zero so that C++ can later identifiy that no memory is allocated to this pointer.

56: All functions end with a closing brace.

57: Blank lines help to make the program more readable.

58: A comment to describe the following function.

59: A function with the same name as the class name and a ~ in front declares a destructor.

60: Function definitions always start with an opening brace.

61: An array is deleted with the array deletion operator.

62: C++ functions are typically very short, as this closing brace shows.

63: Blank lines make the program more readable.

continues

Project 10 Listing. continued

```cpp
64:// Provide access to stored string

65:const char * String::Get() const

66: {

67:    return string;

68: }

69:// Replace contents with new string

70:void String::Set(const char * newString)

71: {

72:    delete [] string;

73:    if (newString)

74:      {

75:        string = new char[strlen(newString) + 1];

76:        strcpy(string,newString);

77:      }

78:    else

79:      string = 0;

80: }

81:// Get length of stored string
```

Description

64: Comments explain the actions of the code.

65: Define a function that retrieves a pointer to a string that cannot be used to update.

66: All function definitions start with an opening brace.

67: Returning a non-const value causes the return value to be automatically cast into const by the compiler.

68: All functions end with a closing brace.

69: Use comments to explain the workings of the code.

70: Define a function with no return value, which accepts a literal (or variable) string.

71: All functions start with an opening brace.

72: Remove the existing contents of the string pointer. `delete` does not operate on a zero pointer.

72: `delete` does not operate on a zero pointer.

73: If the parameter passes an actual string, do the following:

74: Compound statements start with an opening bracket.

75: Create a dynamic allocation as long as the passed string plus the terminator.

76: Copy the parameter into the allocated storage.

77: Compound statements are ended with a closing brace.

78: If no string was passed, a zero pointer is received. Perform the following step.

79: Set the pointer to zero.

79: `delete` does not reset the pointer to zero.

80: All functions end with a closing brace.

81: Comment to explain the workings of the program.

continues

Project 10 Listing. continued

```cpp
82:int String::Length() const

83: {

84:    if (!string)

85:      return 0;

86:    return strlen(string);

87: }

88://************************************************************

89://

90://

91:class RadioStation

92: {

93:    public:

94:       RadioStation(const char * Name, const char * City,

95:                  float Frequency);

96:       void Print() const;

97:    private:

98:       String name;

99:       String city;
```

Description

82: Declare a function that returns an `int` and takes no parameters.

83: All functions start with an opening brace.

84: If no string is stored by the class, do the following:

85: Return a zero length, avoiding checking a missing string.

86: Return the length found by a library function.

87: All functions end with a closing brace.

88: A comment helps delimit sections of code.

89: Empty comments can enhance the appearance of the program.

90: Empty comments can enhance the appearance of the program.

91: Declare a class called `RadioStation`.

92: All class definitions start with an opening brace.

93: All functions following this label will be public.

94: Declare a constructor for the class.

95: Long declarations are best split over a number of lines.

96: Declare a public member function.

97: All members following this label will be private.

98: Declare a member that is a class of your own making.

99: Declare a `String` data member.

continues

Project 10 Listing. continued

```
100:      float  frequency;

101:  };

102:

103:RadioStation::RadioStation(const char * Name, const char * City,

104:                  float Frequency)

105:              : name(Name),

106:                city(City),

107:                frequency(Frequency)

108:  {

109:  }

110:

111:void RadioStation::Print() const

112:  {

113:    int i;

114:    cout << name.Get();

115:    // Line up printout

116:    for (i = name.Length(); i < 20; i++)

117:      cout << ' ';
```

Description

100: Declare a data member of type float.

101: All class definitions end with a closing brace and a semicolon.

102: Blank lines enhance the appearance of the program.

103: Define the radioStation constructor.

104: Long parameter lists are best split over a number of lines.

105: Members are very efficiently initialized using class constructors in an initialization list.

106: Initialize the city String with the String constructor.

107: Standard classes also have constructors that can be directly called.

108: All function definitions must start with an opening brace even though they might do nothing.

109: All function definitions must end with a closing brace even if they do nothing.

110: Blank lines make the program more readable.

111: Define a function that has been declared part of the RadioStation class.

112: All functions start with an opening brace.

113: Declare a variable i for later use.

113: It is a tradition from FORTRAN and BASIC that integer counters are named i.

114: Output a character string obtained from the string name.

115: Comments explain the workings of the program.

116: Do the following statement for the number of characters in the string up to 19.

117: Output a space to line up the list for names of different lengths.

continues

Project 10 Listing. continued

```
118:     cout << city.Get();

119:     for (i = city.Length(); i < 20; i++)

120:       cout << ' ';

121:     cout.precision(2);          // NB cout is a class

122:                                 // precision is a function

123:     cout.setf(ios::showpoint);// as is setf

124:     cout.setf(ios::fixed);

125:     cout.width(6);

126:     cout << frequency;

127:   }

128://*************************************************************

129:// Some global functions (they are still allowed in OOP!)

130://

131:int MoreInput();

132:RadioStation* NewRadioStation();

133:void PrintTitle();

134://*************************************************************

135:// The main function
```

Description

118: Print the `city` name retrieved from the string member.

119: Do the following statement for the number of characters in the string up to 19.

120: Output a space to line up the list for city names of different lengths.

121: Use built-in class member function of `cout` to set the number of decimal places printed.

122: Comments explain the working of the program.

123: Ensure that the decimal place is always shown.

124: Stop numbers from being displayed in floating-point format.

125: Limit the number of characters for displaying the number to six.

126: Output the number according to the previous formatting.

127: All functions end with a closing brace.

128: Bold comments help divide the sections of the program.

129: Attempts at witty comments become irritating over time.

130: Blank comments enhance the appearance of your code.

131: Prototype a global function.

132: Prototype a global function.

132: Of course, global functions can still see and use class object definitions.

133: Breaking up large functions into several routines makes the program easier to follow.

134: Bold comments help divide the sections of the program.

135: A comment can title the following code.

continues

Project 10 Listing. continued

```
136://

137:void main()

138: {

139:     RadioStation* stations[20]; // There are better ways to

140:                                 // store lists, but this is

141:                                 // good enough for this example

142:     int count = 0;

143:     while (MoreInput())

144:       {

145:         stations[count] = NewRadioStation();

146:         if (!stations[count])

147:           cout << "*** Error! Input rejected! ***" << endl;

148:         else

149:           count++;

150:       }

151:

152:     PrintTitle();               // Should this be global or part

153:                                 // of RadioStation?
```

Description

136: Blank comments enhance the appearance of your code.

137: Define the `main()` function where the program starts executing.

138: A function definition always starts with an opening brace.

139: A declaration of an array of 20 `RadioStation` pointers.

140: A comment to explain the way the program has been coded.

141: A comment to explain the way the program has been coded.

142: A counter to record the number of stations entered.

143: `while` the user requests further input.

143: This should test for the array bound. How would you code that?

144: Multiple statements repeated by a `while` loop need to be enclosed in a compound statement.

145: Allocate a new radio station using a function defined later.

146: If the program was not able to allocate a new radio station...

147: Report the error to the user.

148: If the program was able to allocate the new radio station...

149: Increment the count of successfully added radio stations.

150: This closing brace marks the end of a `while` loop.

151: Blank lines help to make the program more readable.

152: Call a global routine to output the title of the report.

153: Use comments to note places where the code might be improved in the future.

continues

Project 10 Listing. continued

```
154:

155:    for (int i = 0; i < count; i++)

156:      {

157:        stations[i]->Print();   // Call member function via pointer

158:        cout << endl;

159:        delete stations[i];

160:      }

161:    }

162:

163://********************************************************

164:// Globals

165://

166:int MoreInput()

167:  {

168:    char temp;

169:    cout << endl << endl << "Do you want to add more stations? ";

170:    cin >> temp;

171:    cin.ignore();
```

Description

154: Blank lines help to make the program more readable.

155: For each radio station stored, do the following:

156: Loops requiring multiple statements need compound statements.

157: Call the member function of RadioStation using the pointer access operator.

158: Output a newline sequence.

159: Delete the allocated memory when it is no longer required.

160: The closing brace marks the end of the for loop.

161: Closing braces also mark the end of function definitions.

162: Blank lines make programs more readable.

163: Bold comments separate sections of the program.

164: A comment is used to title the following code.

165: Blank comments can enhance the appearance of your program.

166: Define a global function that returns true (nonzero) or false (zero).

167: Function definitions always start with an opening brace.

168: A variable to test the user input.

169: Prompt the user for an answer with a question.

170: Get the first character of input.

171: Ignore all input after the first character.

165: Many libraries of code and new ANSI draft of C++ declare a type BOOL or bool with values of TRUE and FALSE or true and false.

continues

Project 10 Listing. continued

```
172:    if (temp == 'y' || temp == 'Y')

173:        return 1;

174:    else

175:        return 0;

176:  }

177:

178:RadioStation* NewRadioStation()

179:  {

180:    char tempName[81];

181:    char tempCity[81];

182:    float tempFrequency;

183:    cout << endl << "Name: ";

184:    cin.getline(tempName,81);

185:    if (strlen(tempName) == 0)

186:        return 0;

187:    cout << "City: ";

188:    cin.getline(tempCity,81);

189:    if (strlen(tempCity) == 0)
```

Description

172:	If the answer is lower- or uppercase Y...
173:	Return true
174:	Otherwise...
175:	Return false.
176:	All function definitions end with a closing brace.
177:	Blank lines help to make your programs more readable.
178:	Declare a function that returns a pointer to a `RadioStation`.
179:	All function declarations start with an opening brace.
180:	Declare a temporary character string big enough for any response.
181:	Declare a temporary character string big enough for any response.
182:	Declare a temporary variable for the frequency of the station.
183:	Prompt the user to enter the name of the station.
184:	Get the name of the station.
185:	If name is zero length...
186:	Reject the input.
187:	Prompt for city name.
188:	Get the city name entered by the user.
189:	If name is zero length...

184: Using `getline()` allows the name to contain blanks.

continues

Project 10 Listing. continued

```
190:      return 0;

191:    cout << "Frequency : ";

192:    cin >> tempFrequency;

193:    cin.ignore(80,'\n');

194:    if (tempFrequency < 0)

195:      return 0;

196:    return new RadioStation(tempName,tempCity,tempFrequency);

197:  }

198:

199:void PrintTitle()

200:  {

201:    cout << endl << "--------------------";

202:    cout << "--------------------";

203:    cout << "----------" << endl;

204:    cout << "Station            ";

205:    cout << "City               ";

206:    cout << "Frequency" << endl;

207:  }
```

Description

190: Reject the input.

191: Prompt the user to enter the frequency.

192: Get the frequency from the user.

193: Ignore any extra characters entered after the user enters the frequency.

194: If frequency is nonsense...

195: Reject the input.

196: If the input is acceptable, return a new `RadioStation` object via a temporary hidden pointer.

196: If the function can't allocate memory, zero will be returned.

197: All functions end with a closing brace.

198: Blank lines make the program more readable.

199: Define the `PrintTitle()` global function.

200: All function definitions start with an opening brace.

201: Output a newline sequence and text.

202: Output text.

203: Output text and a newline.

204: Output text.

205: Output text.

206: Output text and a newline.

207: All functions end with a closing brace.

▼ OUTPUT

```
Do you want to add more stations? y

Name: Capital
City: London
Frequency : 95.8


Do you want to add more stations? y

Name: Picadilly
City: Manchester
Frequency : 97.6


Do you want to add more stations? y

Name: BRMB
City: Birmingham
Frequency : 98.8


Do you want to add more stations? y

Name:
*** Error! Input rejected! ***


Do you want to add more stations? n

— — — — — — — — — — — — — — — — — — — — — —
Station          City             Frequency
Capital          London           95.80
Picadilly        Manchester       97.60
BRMB             Birmingham       98.80
```

11

Inheritance and Virtual Functions

21

Inheritance

base class

derived class

private

protected

public

▶ **What You'll Learn**

- ▶ Making a new class from an existing class
- ▶ Adding and replacing functions
- ▶ Initialization of an inherited class
- ▶ Pointers to classes
- ▶ Data access under inheritance
- ▶ Which function gets called

After encapsulation comes inheritance. In this unit, you will see how Visual C++ uses classes to enable you to make new code from old.

You'll see why there is a difference between protected and private members, and you'll see some of the magic that makes Visual C++ different from any language you've previously seen.

▶ **Making a New Class from an Existing Class**

Concept   **What You Will Learn**

Visual C++ needs to be told in the class definition from which other class the new class is to be made.

So far, you've seen some of the simpler features of classes. You might be wondering whether all the effort of classes is worth it, compared to simpler ways of coding the programs you have developed. By the end of this unit, you will start seeing some of the real bonuses of classes.

Definition—A *base class* is a class that stands on its own and is not derived from any other class.

Definition—A *derived class* is a class that is made by inheriting the characteristics of another class.

Let's look first at an example of a set of classes that you will develop. To make a set of classes that work well, a plan is required. Imagine that you want to write a system to look after the vehicles owned by the Wheels-U-Like rental company. It can own cars, buses, and trucks. These vehicles have lots of things in common: mileage, cost, whether they are currently rented. There are also things that are special to each of them: The number of seats is irrelevant to a truck rental, but the carrying capacity of a truck is important. The plan in writing a set of objects is to make a *base class*, which covers all the common information. Then, for each specific case, invent a *derived class*, which takes the base class and adds extra information.

The starting point will be a vehicle. First, define the data you want to hold and some simple functions you know you'll need.

```
class Vehicle
  {
    public:
      Vehicle();
      ~Vehicle();
      void Print();
      void Set();
      void Rent();
      void Return();
    protected:
      long    mileage;
      date    dateRented;
      date    dateReturned;
      string make;
      string model;
  };
```

Pretend that you have written a date handling class. Dates are always a tricky thing to handle in programs. You'll work out what the functions really look like later.

Wheels-U-Like rents cars. On top of the basic data, you will need a group for rental and a group for whether it is auto or manual; everything else will be the same as for a vehicle. In Visual C++, a class is derived from another simply by placing the class name of the base class and the `public` keyword after a colon (:) and before the body of the class. (You can use other than public derivation, but then you are starting to get into the tricky parts of the language that you are unlikely to come across.)

```
Car : public Vehicle
  {
  };
```

The preceding declaration is complete in itself but not very useful. It works exactly like the `Vehicle` class you designed before. Just like the other classes you have declared, you can add more data items:

```
Car : public Vehicle
  {
    protected:
      int  catagory;
      int  isAutomatic;
  };
```

Now you have the data made up of all the `Vehicle` data and all the `Car` data.

► Adding and Replacing Functions

Concept   **What You Will Learn**

New functions can be added easily. Changing the way original functions work needs more care.

You can easily add functions to get and set the category and whether the car has a manual or automatic gear shift:

```
Car : public Vehicle
  {
    public:
      void SetAuto(int Auto);
      int GetAuto();
      // and so on...
```

However, you really are interested in making use of code that you already have. When Print() is called for a Vehicle, you would expect it to tell all about the data in the Vehicle class, and you need the same function for the Car class. It should be no surprise that you can use the same function name in the Car class as the Vehicle class. How does Visual C++ tell the functions apart? If you did not give a Car printing function, the Vehicle Print() function would be called. Quite simply, when there are two identical functions in the original class and the derived class, Visual C++ decides which to call by looking at the class of the calling object:

```
Vehicle v;
Car c;
v.Print();  // calls Vehicle::Print()
c.Print();  // calls Car::Print()
```

Normally, this is just what you need. However, the Car version will not do anything clever with the Vehicle function it replaces. Often, you will want a replacement function to do just what the base class function did, and then do some extra code to do the special things that the derived class needs. Within a member function, you can call other member functions, but these will still look to the current class. To say that you want to execute a different version of the function, you need to use the scope operator (::) and tell Visual C++ which version you want to call:

```
void Car::Print()    // Normal function signature
  {
    Vehicle::Print();// Call a base class version
    cout << "Automatic? " << automatic?'Y' : 'N';
    // and so on
  }
```

The `Vehicle::` in front of `Print()` is vital. Without it, Visual C++ would call `Car::Print()`, which would rapidly result in a very serious loop calling itself over and over again. As you can see, inheriting a function is straightforward and consists of these steps:

▶ Design a base function, knowing it will be called by other functions.

▶ In a derived class, add a function of the same name.

▶ If the function replaces the base function, write a complete function.

▶ If the function does something more than the base function does, put a call to the base function using the scope operator to make sure that the correct version is called.

Visual C++ lets you derive further classes from an already derived class. The mechanism works in just the same way:

```
class SportsCar : public Car
   {
   protected:
      int openTop;
   };
```

Definition—The class from which a new class has been derived is called the *immediate base class* to distinguish it from any other classes that the new class might be derived from.

In this case, `SportsCar` can use all the functions of `Car` and `Vehicle`. Where the new class does not replace a function, it will see the function of the most derived class.

▶ Initialization with Inheritance

There is a special trick for constructors. Instead of calling the constructor in the body of the code, you must use the initialization list:

```
Car::Car() : Vehicle()
   {
   }
```

Use this if there are parameters:

```
Car::Car(long Mileage) : Vehicle(Mileage)
   {
   }
```

If you do not specify the base class constructor to call, Visual C++ will call the default constructor for you. For a class that has been derived several times, there is no need to call all the base classes' constructors because the previous base class has already called the next base class.

Destructors work differently. A derived class always automatically calls any base class destructors. You never need to put any code to call base class destructors. Visual C++ does it all automatically. (I thought that was worth saying twice.)

STOP&TYPE Time for a listing! Listing 21.1 makes a simple version of your rental classes. To keep things from getting too complicated, you will just store dates as character strings and not use the string class that you've developed. But when you develop classes, you should look to use classes within classes, rather than rewriting all the string and date management features in every class you use.

▼ INPUT   LISTING 21.1. WHEELS-U-LIKE HITS THE ROAD.

```
 1:// File name: WHEELSUL.CPP
 2://
 3:// A simple set of rental classes
 4://
 5:#include <iostream.h>
 6:#include <string.h>
 7:
 8:
 9:// Base class
10:class Vehicle
11:  {
12:    public:
13:      Vehicle(long Mileage, const char * Model);     // Constructor
14:      void Print() const;
15:      void Rent(const char * ReturnDate);
16:    protected:
17:      long mileage;
18:      char model[21];
19:      char returnDate[9];
20:  };
21:
22:class Car : public Vehicle     // Car is derived from Vehicle
23:  {
24:    public:
25:                               // Constructor
26:      Car(long Mileage, const char * Model,char Category);
27:      void Print() const;     // Override Vehicle::Print
28:    protected:
29:      char category;          // Only in Car not Vehicle
30:  };
31:
32:class Truck: public Vehicle    // Truck is derived from Vehicle
33:  {
34:    public:
35:                               // Constructor
36:      Truck(long Mileage, const char * Model,float MaxLoad);
37:      void Print() const;     // Override Vehicle::Print
38:    protected:
39:      float maxLoad;          // Only in Truck
40:  };
41:
42:// Global function
43:void GetRentalDate(char * date)
```

```
44:  {
45:    cout << "When are you returning the vehicle?";
46:    cin.getline(date,9);
47:  }
48:
49://-------------------------------------------------------------
50://           Main is here!
51://-------------------------------------------------------------
52:void main()
53:  {
54:    char type;
55:    char rentalDate[9];
56:    // Ask what type of rental
57:    cout << "Rent car (c) or truck (t)? ";
58:    cin >> type;
59:    cin.ignore();
60:    if (type == 't' || type == 'T')
61:      {
62:        // truck rental
63:        // Make a truck (for simplicity - hard coded)
64:        Truck truck(4000,"Dodge",3.5F);
65:        // Normal function
66:        GetRentalDate(rentalDate);
67:        // Truck does not have Rent - calls Vehicle::Rent
68:        truck.Rent(rentalDate);
69:        // Truck does have Print - calls Truck::Print
70:        truck.Print();
71:      }
72:    else
73:      {
74:        // Car rental
75:        Car car(2500,"Buick",'B');   // W.U.L. only has 1 car!
76:        GetRentalDate(rentalDate);
77:        // Car does not have Rent - calls Vehicle::Rent
78:        car.Rent(rentalDate);
79:        // Car has Print - calls Car::Print
80:        car.Print();
81:      }
82:  }
83://-------------------------------------------------------------
84:// Vehicle class functions
85://
86:Vehicle::Vehicle(long Mileage, const char * Model)
87:  {
88:    mileage = Mileage; // could have used intialization list
89:    strcpy(model,Model);
90:    returnDate[0] = '\0'; // zero length string
91:  }
92:
93:void Vehicle::Print() const
94:  {
95:    cout << "Model  :    " << model << endl;
96:    cout << "Mileage:    " << mileage << endl;
```

continues

```
97:     cout << "Rented till: " ;
98:     if (returnDate[0]) // a test to see if first char is
99:                        // a terminator
100:       cout << returnDate;
101:    else
102:       cout << "Not rented";
103:    cout << endl;
104:  }
105:
106:void Vehicle::Rent(const char * RentalDate)
107:  {
108:    strcpy(returnDate,RentalDate);
109:  }
110:
111://------------------------------------------------------------
112://  Car class functions
113://
114:Car::Car(long Mileage, const char * Model, char Category)
115:     : Vehicle(Mileage,Model)    // calls base constructor
116:  {
117:    category = Category;
118:  }
119:
120:void Car::Print() const          // Overrides Vehicle::Print()
121:  {
122:     cout << "Car Rental" << endl;
123:     Vehicle::Print();           // Calls base class Print
124:     cout << "Category : " << category << endl;
125:  }
126:
127://------------------------------------------------------------
128://  Car class functions
129://
130:Truck::Truck(long Mileage, const char * Model, float MaxLoad)
131:     : Vehicle(Mileage,Model)
132:  {
133:    maxLoad = MaxLoad;
134:  }
135:
136:void Truck::Print() const
137:  {
138:     cout << "Truck Rental" << endl;
139:     Vehicle::Print();
140:     cout << "Max load : " << maxLoad << endl;
141:  }
```

▼ **OUTPUT**

First run:

```
Rent car (c) or truck (t)? c
When are you returning the vehicle?10/10/95
```

```
Car Rental
Model  :    Buick
Mileage:    2500
Rented till: 10/10/95
Category : B
```

Second run:

```
Rent car (c) or truck (t)? T
When are you returning the vehicle?09/09/95
Truck Rental
Model  :    Dodge
Mileage:    4000
Rented till: 09/09/95
Max load : 3.5
```

▼ ANALYSIS

The Vehicle class declared in lines 10 to 20 contains the code and data to be shared between all the different types of rental classes. The data is declared as protected (line 16) so that derived classes can directly access it if need be (which does not happen in this program). In fact, it is often better to use access functions to get and set the data in a safe way.

In line 22, a Car is derived from the class Vehicle. Typical of a derived class, the constructor needs all the parameters of the base class (compare lines 13 and 26) and any extra data for the new class. In lines 114 to 118, the derived class calls the base class constructor (line 115) in the initialization list, passing on the parameters that belong to the Vehicle class. This means that Car does not need to know how to set up the Vehicle part of the data. In line 117, the rest of the class is initialized.

The Truck class is very nearly identical. Although Truck is derived from the same class as Car, the classes can't see each other.

When the program runs, if Truck is chosen, the program calls the Truck constructor (line 64), which in turn calls the Vehicle constructor. When the program calls Rent(), it must look for the definition of the function. It is not declared in the Truck class, so Visual C++ looks to see whether it could be anywhere else. Visual C++ looks in the base class and finds a matching function, which it then calls. Although the calling object is a Truck, the function executes as if the calling object type was a Vehicle. This is an important point, because even though the calling class is Truck, Vehicle can't see any data or functions that belong to Truck.

Next, in line 70, there is a call to Print(). This time, Print() has been overridden. Visual C++ looks to Truck's class definition and finds that there is a matching function. The function in lines 136 through 141 executes as if the other functions did not exist. Then, in line 139, it wants to output the data belonging to the base class. Fortunately, the base class Print() has been designed so that the data will fit in with a standard listing. The call to the base class (line 139) needs the scope operator and class to tell Visual C++ which version of the function must be executed. (If Vehicle was derived from another class that contained Print(), and Vehicle did not contain it, Visual C++ is clever enough to still use the base class version, even with the explicit class scope being called.)

The Car class works in exactly the same way as Truck, except that it has its own data to work with. Car can't see Truck.

▶ **Pointers to Classes**

Concept   **What You Will Learn**

Visual C++ uses the type of the calling object to decide which version of the function to use.

When a derived class is given to a pointer, the pointer can be of the type of the derived class or of any base class, as in the following example:

```
Vehicle * v = new Car("Ford",3000,'A');
```

Something strange happens when you use an object via the Vehicle pointer. Instead of working like the Car class, it only appears to be a vehicle:

```
v->Print();
```

This code would print the following:

```
Model  :    Ford
Mileage:    3000
Rented till: Not Rented
```

However, somewhere in the heart of Visual C++, the class always remembers its ancestry. If it is known that the base class pointer really points to a Car, you can turn it back into one with a cast:

```
((Car*)v)->Print();
```

This code would print the following:

```
Car Rental
Model  :    Ford
Mileage:    3000
Rented till: Not rented
Category : A
```

This strange collection of brackets is required because of operator precedence: Casting is a low precedence, and without the brackets, it would be applied to the return value of

`Print()`. An easier to follow expression—though not in the "all in one breath" style so beloved by your fellow C++ programmers—would be the following:

```
Car* c = (Car*)v;
c->Print();
```

You can always make a derived class into a base class without so much as a hiccup. You can never safely make a base class into a derived class. The cast will work, but there is not a way in Visual C++ of checking that the cast is valid. One workaround solution is to store the type of object yourself in the base class, and then implement an `IsA()` function that you can use to run different versions of code depending on the type. This solves the problem, but has the downside of being error-prone and a maintenance problem as new derived classes are added. (Fortunately, in the next unit, you'll see that Visual C++ has an extremely clever mechanism to deal with this problem.)

Note In the latest versions of C++ as defined by the ANSI committee, there is a new feature called `dynamic_cast`, which allows the checking of the type as the cast is made. However, this is not available in this version of Visual C++, and it only solves the problem of detecting an error, not determining the type of class.

```
Vehicle * v = new Vehicle("Ford", 3500);
((Car*)v)->Print()
```

The preceding code will compile, but it won't work. Figure 21.1 gives a clue as to why. You can imagine (but not rely on the fact) that the storage of a derived class is added to the end of the base class as C++ makes the structure. Imagine that accessing the storage is like using a cardboard cutout placed over the storage. As you can see from Figure 21.1, going toward the base class, you'll always see a valid storage area; but trying to look at a base class with a derived class cutout, you'll see bits of storage that don't belong.

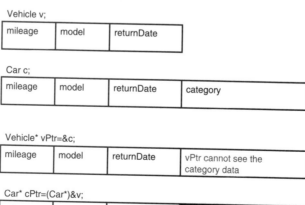

Figure 21.1
Viewing class storage via pointers.

The same is true for using references, aside from the different access operator. This is important because quite often you'll want to store collections of objects. For example, Wheels-U-Like wants to expand from renting one truck and one car (even though the owner is extremely lazy, he wants to make money one day). Therefore, the program needs to store lots of vehicles. The program could store one array for cars and another for trucks. But then, for reports such as vehicles on rental today, the program would have to look through two lists, even though the program is not interested in the type of vehicle.

The program could hold an array of `Vehicle` pointers, and then use the appropriate class depending on the new rentals to create the objects.

Care must be taken when using `delete`. This only deletes the class that is pointed to. It will not remove any storage or perform any other tidying up, which is required by a more derived class type than the type of the object that is being operated on by `delete`.

▶ Accessing Members When Using Inheritance

The `Vehicle` class uses `protected` rather than `private`. To the world outside the class, they are identical; neither `protected` nor `private` can be accessed. To a derived class, there is a difference. The base class designer can decide to allow a derived class to access the data. If it is safe, the data is declared `protected`, and to the code within member functions, it is as if the data is public. Here's an example:

```
class A
  {
    public:
      int a;
    protected:
      int b:
    private:
      int c:
  };

class B: public A
  {
    void Bfunction();
  };

void main()
  {
    B b;
    b.a = 5;  // ok, public
    b.b = 5;  // Illegal - protected
    b.c = 5;  // Illegal - private
  }
```

```
B::Bfunction()
  {
    a = 5; // ok, public
    b = 5; // ok, protected appears as public to
           // derived classes
    c = 5; // Illegal - private cannot be seen
  }
```

To understand why there is a difference, notice that the access requirements for a derived class are different from the access requirements for a base class. To improve a class by derivation means that the derived class is likely to need privileged access to class members. The target is still to create a public interface for both the base and derived classes in which only safe functions and variables can be accessed.

The derived class can be allowed to be trusted by the designer of a base class. There might be some complicated code that the base class designer needs to look after carefully. The members and functions to run this code would be private. There might be certain variables and (especially) functions that the designer knows a derived class should be able to access in order to write a good class. For example, the Print() function of vehicle might not be adequate on its own. It does not put out a title. The base class designer might decide that it is not a suitable part of the public class, but it does need to be made available for the derived classes to use. In this case, declaring Print() protected would allow any derived class to use the function without restriction. But any coder using the Vehicle class would not be allowed to use Print().

The following should complete your understanding of the three classes of access:

▶ Private: For use in this class only. Private functions are to ensure good structured code within the class. Private data is to ensure that only controlled access to data is allowed.

▶ Protected: For use in this class and any derived classes. Protected functions are usually provided to allow derived classes to be implemented—for example, to allow these classes to access otherwise private data. Protected data implies that derived classes can safely change the data.

▶ Public: Global access. This applies to data for which the value does not matter. For functions, it defines the functions that are meant to be used.

The choice between public and private is normally easy. Trying to decide which data is protected and which is private is more difficult. The dilemma for the novice programmer is that providing lots of access functions seems tedious, so it's very tempting to make everything protected or even public. If you look at professional C++ classes, they are nearly always made up of lots of very small functions. This means that the code is normally very easy to follow. The downside is that working out when the functions execute can be a little complicated at times.

▶ **Making Function Calls Faster**

Before you go on to the final listing, there is a different way of coding class functions. Because a class tends to lead to writing small one-line functions, the overhead of the C++ calling mechanism could make your programs inefficient. By adding the modifier `inline`, you can suggest to the compiler that, instead of using a function call, it could replace the call in the calling function with all the code in the called function:

```
void inline A::DoIt(int a)
   {
     b = a * 5;
   }
void main()
   {
     A a;
     int i = 2;
     a.DoIt(i);
   }
```

This code becomes the following:

```
void main()
   {
     A a;
     int i = 2;
     tempi = 2; // pass by value assume not optimized
                // tempi some internal variable invented
                // by the compiler
     a.b = tempi * 5;// compiler looks after access itself
   }
```

Normally, you need not worry about this finesse in your early coding days. Worry about getting the code right first! However, there is a shortcut way of writing class functions. You can put the code within the class declaration, and then it automatically becomes inlined:

```
class A
   {
     public:
       int GetA()
         {
             return a;
         }
     private:
       a;
   };
```

The temptation is to write all your classes like this because it is compact. This is fine for routines of a few lines (less than five is a rule of thumb). However, there are certain instructions that C++ can't inline, so the compiler might warn that it won't inline the code after all. Also, too much code in the class definitions makes them difficult to read.

STOP&TYPE Listing 21.2 uses this method to keep the listings small and manageable.

```
 1:// File name : PETS.CPP
 2:// Object oriented pet program to manage
 3:// a simple list of different types of
 4:// pets
 5://
 6:#include <iostream.h>
 7:
 8://------------------------------------------------------------
 9:// Pet class
10://
11:const int nameLength = 21;
12:
13:class Pet
14:  {
15:    public:
16:      enum PetType {cat, dog, fish};
17:      void Print()
18:        {
19:          cout << name;
20:        }
21:      PetType GetType()
22:        {
23:          return type;
24:        }
25:      void Query();
26:    protected:
27:      Pet(PetType pt)       // protected -
28:                            // do not make Pets
29:        {
30:          type = pt;
31:          name[0] = '\0';
32:        }
33:    private:
34:      PetType type;
35:      char name[nameLength];
36:  };
37:
38:void Pet::Query()
39:  {
40:    cout << "What is your pet's name? ";
41:    cin.getline(name,nameLength);
42:  }
43:
44://------------------------------------------------------------
45:// Cat class - derived from Pet
46://
```

continues

```
47:class Cat : public Pet
48: {
49:   public:
50:     Cat(int Scratches = 1)
51:       : Pet(cat)        // can see protected constructor
52:       {
53:         scratches = Scratches;
54:       }
55:     void Print();      // Overrides Pet::Print
56:     void Query();      // Overrides Pet::Query
57:   private:
58:     int scratches;
59: };
60:
61:void Cat::Print()
62: {
63:    cout << "Cat: " ;
64:    Pet::Print();
65:    cout << endl << "Scratches: " << (scratches? "Yes":"No")
66:         << endl;
67: }
68:
69:void Cat::Query()
70: {
71:    char yn;
72:    Pet::Query();
73:    cout << "Does your cat scratch? ";
74:    cin >> yn;
75:    cin.ignore(80,'\n');
76:    if (yn == 'Y' || yn == 'y')
77:      scratches = 1;
78:    else
79:      scratches = 0;
80: }
81:
82://------------------------------------------------------------
83:// Dog class - derived from Pet
84://
85:
86:class Dog : public Pet
87: {
88:   public:
89:     Dog(int Barks = 1)
90:       :  Pet(dog)
91:       {
92:         barks = Barks;
93:       }
94:     void Print();
95:     void Query();
96:   private:
97:     int barks;
98: };
99:
```

```
100:void Dog::Print()
101:  {
102:    cout << "Dog: " ;
103:    Pet::Print();
104:    cout << endl << "Barks: " << (barks? "Yes":"No")
105:         << endl;
106:  }
107:
108:void Dog::Query()
109:  {
110:    char yn;
111:    Pet::Query();
112:    cout << "Does your dog bark? ";
113:    cin >> yn;
114:    cin.ignore(80,'\n');
115:    if (yn == 'Y' || yn == 'y')
116:      barks = 1;
117:    else
118:      barks = 0;
119:  }
120:
121://------------------------------------------------------------
122:// Fish class - derived from Pet
123://
124:class Fish : public Pet
125:  {
126:    public:
127:      Fish(int ColdWater = 0)
128:        : Pet(fish)
129:        {
130:          coldWater = ColdWater;
131:        }
132:      void Print();
133:      void Query();
134:    private:
135:      int coldWater;
136:  };
137:void Fish::Print()
138:  {
139:    cout << "Fish: " ;
140:    Pet::Print();
141:    cout << endl << "Water: " << (coldWater? "Cold":"Tropical")
142:         << endl;
143:    cout << "You can't take a goldfish for walks" << endl;
144:  }
145:
146:void Fish::Query()
147:  {
148:    char yn;
149:    Pet::Query();
150:    cout << "Is your fish tropical? ";
151:    cin >> yn;
152:    cin.ignore(80,'\n');
```

continues

```
153:      if (yn == 'Y' || yn == 'y')
154:        coldWater = 0;
155:      else
156:        coldWater = 1;
157:  }
158:
159://-----------------------------------------------------------
160:// main procedure
161://
162:
163:void main()
164:  {
165:      char type;
166:      Pet * pets[20] = {0};
167:      int count = 0;
168:
169:      while (1)    // Do forever
170:        {
171:          // Where do you want to go today?
172:          cout << "Pet type, [C]at, [D]og, [F]ish, [Q]uit: ";
173:          cin >> type;
174:          cin.ignore(80,'\n');
175:
176:          // Stop forever loop
177:          if (type == 'q' || type == 'Q')
178:            break;
179:
180:          switch (type)
181:            {
182:              case 'C': // Cat
183:              case 'c':
184:                {
185:                  pets[count] = new Cat; // Looses "Catness"
186:                  ((Cat*)pets[count])->Query(); // nasty cast
187:                  break;
188:                }
189:              case 'D': // Dog
190:              case 'd':
191:                {
192:                  Dog * d = new Dog; // Use Dog pointer to
193:                  d->Query();        // keep dogginess
194:                  pets[count] = d;   // automatic type conversion
195:                  break;
196:                }
197:              case 'F': // Fish
198:              case 'f':
199:                {
200:                  pets[count] = new Fish; // Looses Fish
201:                  Fish * f = (Fish*)pets[count]; // Get Fish back
202:                  f->Query();                // f points to same place(!)
203:                                             // as pets[count]
204:                  break;
205:                }
```

```
206:                default:
207:                   count--;
208:             }
209:          count++;
210:       }
211:
212:    // List pets - don't need derived classes for this
213:     cout << endl << "Pet Names" << endl;
214:     for (int i = 0; i < count; i++)
215:        {
216:          pets[i]->Print();
217:          cout << endl;
218:        }
219:
220:    // List characteristics - need exact types
221:     cout << endl << "Characteristics" << endl;
222:     for (i = 0; i < count; i++)
223:        {
224:          switch (pets[i]->GetType())
225:             {
226:               case Pet::dog: // Use access to get at class enum
227:                 ((Dog*)pets[i])->Print(); // nasty cast
228:                 break;
229:               case Pet::cat:
230:                  {
231:                    Cat* c = (Cat*)pets[i]; // still nasty
232:                    c->Print();
233:                    break;
234:                  }
235:               case Pet::fish:
236:                 ((Fish*)pets[i])->Print();// no escape from cast
237:                 break;
238:             }
239:        }
240:    // Tidy up storage
241:     for (i = 0; i < count; i++)
242:        {
243:          switch (pets[i]->GetType())
244:             {
245:               case Pet::dog:
246:                 delete (Dog*)pets[i];
247:                 break;
248:               case Pet::cat:
249:                 delete (Cat*)pets[i];
250:                 break;
251:               case Pet::fish:
252:                 delete (Fish*)pets[i];
253:                 break;
254:             }
255:        }
256:  }
```

▼ **OUTPUT**

```
Pet type, [C]at, [D]og, [F]ish, [Q]uit: c
What is your pet's name? Tibbles
Does your cat scratch? no
Pet type, [C]at, [D]og, [F]ish, [Q]uit: dog
What is your pet's name? Ross
Does your dog bark? Yes
Pet type, [C]at, [D]og, [F]ish, [Q]uit: f
What is your pet's name? Bubbles
Is your fish tropical? n
Pet type, [C]at, [D]og, [F]ish, [Q]uit: q

Pet Names
Tibbles
Ross
Bubbles

Characteristics
Cat: Tibbles
Scratches: No
Dog: Ross
Barks: Yes
Fish: Bubbles
Water: Cold
You can't take a goldfish for walks
```

▼ **ANALYSIS**

This program makes use of the common base class Pet, declared in lines 13 through 36, to make the basic operations required for the pet handling. Most of its functions—except Query() defined in line 38—are inlined (declared within the class) because they are small and simple.

The class uses an enumerated constant, defined in line 16, to record the allowed derived types. A Visual C++ purist would frown on this because it shows that you need to know what types you are going to derive from the class. This makes the class subject to amendment in the future.

The designer of the Pet class has decided that the class is not meant to be used on its own. To stop anyone from using a class, the constructor is made protected. This means that only a derived class can call it. Any attempt to declare a Pet object will result in a compile-time error. The constructor simply takes the class type, stores it, and terminates the name storage to ensure that nothing nasty happens if a program tries to print the name before a value is set.

The three derived classes all work in a similar way. Let's look at the Cat class in detail. Line 47 shows C++ that a Cat is a Pet. That is a very important sentence. When you make a class, should it have another class as a member or be derived? If you can say "class *a* is a class *b*," you can derive a new class. If you say "class *a* has a class *b*," you should not derive but simply make the class a member of the new class.

Lines 50 and 51 show C++ how to make a Cat. Cat has a constructor that is used to initialize its own private member. But this is defaulted, so this constructor can do double time as a default constructor. In line 51, it calls the base class constructor to set the class type of Pet. This setting is very important to the correct working of the classes, so only derived classes are allowed to get at the constructor. Protected objects can be accessed by derived classes.

Lines 55 and 56 tell us that Cat has two functions that replace the base Pet functions. In lines 61 through 67, the way the Cat::Print() works is defined. In line 64, it calls the base class Print() to get the base class information. The base class function did not need to be called Print() to be called from the derived class function. In fact, you could argue that the two functions do something different and that it would have been clearer if the base class function was called PrintName() instead.

Jumping down to main() in lines 163 to 256, this program simply loops until the user has finished putting in the list. (A more professional programmer would have made sure the array bounds of pets were not exceeded!)

The test to stop the loop in lines 177 and 178 can't make use of the switch statement because the break would only exit the switch statement and not the complete loop.

All of the pets are stored in a single array. This array has to be declared as the common base type to be able to store the pointers. This can be trouble because when a particular class is needed, the special features can't be accessed. The calling type (that is, the type of the array) is used by default. To work around this, casts must be used to make the calling type into the right type. In line 186, a tricky cast expression is used. Recall that you saw that casting has a low precedence. You need to use two sets of parentheses—the inner set around the type name to represent the cast operator, and a second set around the expression for which you need to change the type. So the second closing parenthesis has to be placed where the Pet pointer, not the array itself, is retrieved from the array.

To do the same thing with Dog, this time you can plan ahead and make a temporary Dog pointer. Now the calls can be made without any casting, and the Dog pointer can simply be assigned into the pets array at the end of any special processing.

Just to drive the point home, the Fish method explicitly makes a Fish pointer. This is a waste of code because you have to make the Fish pointer using a cast on the array; the type was lost on assigning the pointer into the array. Out of the three methods, the Dog method is the best.

The lines 207 and 209 ensure that the store is correctly incremented. In case of an error, the counter is decremented to correct the following increment.

The two reports at the end have different requirements. The first report, simply lists the names. Because this is all held in the Pet class, there is no need to do any casting. All the objects are treated as Pet objects, as in line 216.

In line 224, the special Pet function to decide what sort of class is held is needed. Then, in each case, the casting method is used to get the right information out.

You can see how careful you need to be with the typing, because even the delete needs special care. The correct delete is called by using the casting operator again.

▶ Homework
General Knowledge

1. How does inheritance help a C++ programmer?
2. Which needs to be defined first, the base class or the derived class?
3. How do you tell C++ which class you want another class to be made out of?
4. What is the word used to describe a derived class function that replaces a base class function?
5. How do you specify which version of a function you need when it appears in both the base and derived class?
6. What happens if you don't specify which version of a function you use when calling a base function in an overloaded function?
7. How do you call a base class constructor from a derived class constructor?
8. How do you call a base class destructor from a derived class destructor?
9. Which type determines which version of the function is called when a pointer is used to a derived object, the object type or the calling pointer type?
10. Which type of access label needs to be used to allow derived classes to see members, but not allow users of the class to see members?
11. True or false: When a class has been derived from, it can't be used in a program by itself.
12. True or false: Member functions can be overloaded just like global functions.
13. True or false: A private member function is available only to derived classes.
14. True or false: delete must use the same class type as the matching new.

What's the Output?

Given the class definitions in Listing 21.2, what do the following lines output?

15.
```
Pet * p = new Cat(1);
p->Print();
```

16.
```
Cat * c = new Cat(1);
c->Print();
```

17.
```
Pet * p = new Cat(1);
((Cat*)p)->Print();
```

Find the Bug

18. Given the class definitions of Listing 21.2, why won't this compile?
```
Pet * p = new Pet(Pet::cat);
((Cat*)p->Print();
```

19. What's wrong here? What sort of complaint will the compiler make?
```
class A
  {
    int a;
    void Print()
      {
        cout << a;
      }
  };
void main()
  {
    A a;
    a.Print();
  }
```

20. Ozwald hasn't got the hang of casts. Help him correct the following:
```
Pet* p = new Cat;
((Dog*)p->Print();
```

Write Code That...

21. Class `Bicycle` is derived from class `Transportation`. Write a statement to change a pointer to a `Bicycle` into a pointer to `Transportation`.

22. Class `MotorCycle` is also derived from class `Transportation`. Write a statement to change a `MotorCycle` pointer into a `Bicycle` pointer.

23. Write a class declaration for `Bicycle`, `MotorCycle`, and `Transportation` containing a constructor, a destructor, a copy constructor, and a data member. Do not write the body of the code, but consider what access is appropriate to each member.

Extra Credit

24. Add function(s) to the program in Listing 21.2 to contain life expectancy of each type of pet.

25. Add function(s) to the program in Listing 21.2 to set the number of lives each type of pet has and an output function to report the number lives. (Hint: Add two functions to cover the three classes for the input.)

22

Polymorphism: Calling the Right Function

polymorphism

virtual functions

▶ What You'll Learn

▶ The limitations of inheritance and how to overcome them

▶ Virtual functions

▶ Access type versus object type

▶ Virtual destructors

▶ The this pointer

▶ The Limitations of Inheritance

Concept   **What You Will Learn**

Inheritance becomes difficult to manage when using multiple types.

The mechanism of inheritance is very useful for making a new class out of an existing one. Quite often as you progress into Visual C++, you'll want to write a program that needs a class similar to one you have already written, but with a few changes. Inheritance works very well for this. Listing 21.2 in the previous unit showed that when you try to mix up your classes, the system of inheritance gets rather messy. The problems included the following:

▶ Needing to record the type in the base class

▶ Casting to call the correct version of the function

▶ Care required over the deletion of objects

All in all, these problems probably confused you quite a bit!

In Visual C++, a new calling mechanism has been invented to ensure that the right function is called. This mechanism is what provides our third buzzword—polymorphism. What you need is a system in which the called object remembers what it is, so that when an overloaded function is called, the right version is called without all the casting.

There is another limitation, though. Consider a very simple function to print out your pets from the base class. It would be nice to write a function that prints out the type of food that the pet eats. You could do something like this:

```
void Pet::PrintType()
  {
    PrintHeadings();
    select (type)  // declared in Pet
    {
```

```
    case dog:
      // Print Pet::Food string
    case cat:
      // Print Pet::Food string
    }
  PrintFooter();
}
```

This is very unsatisfactory. The base class needs to know all about the type of class. If you change things around so that the derived classes do the printing, you get two problems: First, the calling program needs to call the correct version; and second, each version needs to remember to call the `PrintHeadings()` and `PrintFooter()` code.

Visual C++ provides a mechanism to enable you to call functions that belong to derived classes from the base class. This is a clever thing to do because when a base class is written, it does not know about the derived classes. Visual C++ needs to wait until the program is running to know the actual type of an object that is currently associated with a pointer. Until now, Visual C++ has had all the information it needs at the time of compilation. Until now, when the program used a base class pointer to access a derived class, you told C++ which derived class to use with a cast. With the new mechanism, C++ hides away some information about the class so that when it is running, it knows what type it is—similar to the type information you stored in the pet program.

▶ Virtual Functions

Concept   **What You Will Learn**

A virtual function enables you to call a function depending on the type of class object.

To use this special mechanism, you simply use the keyword `virtual` in front of the function signature, as in this example:

```
class A
  {
    public:
      virtual void Print()
        {
            cout << "A printed" << endl;
        }
  };

A a;
a.Print();
```

This code appears to work exactly like previous versions that you have written, and it prints out A printed.

You can now add a new class:

```
class B : public A
  {
    virtual void Print()
      {
          cout << "B printed" << endl;
      }
  };

B b;
b.Print();
```

This also prints what you might expect, B printed. However, let's now mix up the types:

```
A * aPtr = new B;  // aPtr points to a B
aPtr->Print();
```

This prints B printed. So, even though the pointer is of type A, the object remembers what type it really is. As a class object is created, Visual C++ stores a secret piece of information about the object. When it executes a virtual call, it looks up the information about the object and only then decides which version to call.

Note   There is a common trap in declaring functions as virtual. When a base class has declared a function virtual, all derived class functions that override that function will also be declared virtual. So the following class definition of B is identical to the previous definition:

```
class B : public A
  {
    void Print()  // Implicitly virtual
      {
          cout << "B printed" << endl;
      }
  };
```

STOP&TYPE   Things become more interesting when you put a virtual function call into a class member. In Listing 22.1, you run a little exercise to follow the different ways in which virtual and nonvirtual functions work.

▼ INPUT   LISTING 22.1. A PROGRAM TO SHOW THE DIFFERENCE BETWEEN VIRTUAL AND NONVIRTUAL FUNCTIONS.

```
1:// File name : VIRTUAL.CPP
2:// Program to demonstrate the difference between
3:// standard and virtual function calls
4://
5:#include <iostream.h>
```

```
 6:
 7:class BaseClass
 8:  {
 9:    public:
10:      void Plain()
11:        {
12:          cout << "BaseClass::Plain()" << endl;
13:        }
14:      virtual void Virtual()
15:        {
16:          cout << "BaseClass::Virtual()" << endl;
17:        }
18:      void CallVirtual()
19:        {
20:          Virtual();
21:        }
22:  };
23:
24:class DerivedClass : public BaseClass
25:  {
26:    public:
27:      void Plain()
28:        {
29:          cout << "DerivedClass::Plain()" << endl;
30:        }
31:      virtual void Virtual()
32:        {
33:          cout << "DerivedClass::Virtual()" << endl;
34:        }
35:  };
36:
37:void main()
38:  {
39:    BaseClass baseClass;
40:    DerivedClass derivedClass;
41:
42:    baseClass.Plain();
43:    baseClass.Virtual();
44:    baseClass.CallVirtual();
45:    cout << endl;
46:
47:    derivedClass.Plain();
48:    derivedClass.Virtual();
49:    derivedClass.CallVirtual();
50:    cout << endl;
51:
52:    BaseClass * basePointer = &baseClass;
53:    BaseClass * derivedPointer = &derivedClass;
54:    // NB type of pointer is base class
55:
56:    basePointer->Plain();
57:    basePointer->Virtual();
58:    basePointer->CallVirtual();
```

UNIT

22

Polymorphism: Calling the Right Function

continues

```
59:        cout << endl;
60:
61:        derivedPointer->Plain();
62:        derivedPointer->Virtual();
63:        derivedPointer->CallVirtual();
64:        cout << endl;
65:    }
```

▼ **OUTPUT**

```
BaseClass::Plain()
BaseClass::Virtual()
BaseClass::Virtual()

DerivedClass::Plain()
DerivedClass::Virtual()
DerivedClass::Virtual()

BaseClass::Plain()
BaseClass::Virtual()
BaseClass::Virtual()

BaseClass::Plain()
DerivedClass::Virtual()
DerivedClass::Virtual()
```

▼ **ANALYSIS**

This is a very simple program that shows which version of the function gets called. First, it makes two objects—one for each class in lines 39 and 40. In lines 42 to 44, the base class is called, and as you might expect, all the base class output appears after these calls.

Next, in lines 47 through 49, the derived class object is used to call all three functions. This time, you might be less certain as to what you were expecting to happen, but calling Plain() and Virtual() results in the derived class being called. Look at CallVirtual(). This has not been overridden in DerivedClass. From what you've seen in earlier units, you know that this will execute the base class version. What happens now might seem surprising. Although you are executing BaseClass::CallVirtual(), the call to Virtual() inside this calls DerivedClass::Virtual(). That is a clever trick because when you wrote BaseClass, you did not make any mention of DerivedClass at all!

Next, you'll use a BaseClass pointer to do the same calls. Unsurprisingly, the code works just the same for a BaseClass pointer as for a BaseClass variable.

Finally, you access the DerivedClass through a BaseClass pointer, accessing exactly the same object as before because you used the address of operator to assign the pointer. As you've seen before, the Plain() function is called because the access is by the BaseClass pointer. In a virtual function call, something different happens. C++ only apparently calls `BaseClass::Virtual()`; in fact, because it is virtual, it still uses the `DerivedClass::Virtual()`. Then, in the final call, C++ still calls the derived `Virtual()` even from the `BaseClass` pointer.

Tip　If, in the future, you are confused about the way Visual C++ calls functions, quickly write a little program like this to see how Visual C++ works. You can easily step through the code with the debugger to see in detail what gets executed.

▶ Access Type Versus Object Type

Concept　　　　　　　　　　　　　　**What You Will Learn**

When a virtual function is executed, the type of the object determines which version of a function executes, not the type of the calling object.

As you saw in the previous example, the type of the object that is made decides which version of a virtual function gets called. This is true both of calls from objects outside the class and of calls from within the class hierarchy (either base or further derived classes). Compared with standard functions, both of these call the same function:

```
baseClassPointer->Virtual()
```

```
((DerivedClass*)baseClassPointer)->Virtual()
```

You must be very careful in spotting when an object can lose its type. If you assign or copy a derived class into a base class object (that is not using an address or pointer but an actual object copy or assignment), the data of the object gets copied and not the object type. A simple example shows the difference:

```
void ThreeObjects(BaseClass bc, BaseClass& bcr, BaseClass* bcp)
  {
    bc.Virtual();
    bcr.Virtual();
    bcp->Virtual();
  }
```

When this code is called by

```
ThreeObjects(derivedClass,derivedClass,&derivedClass);
```

it produces the following:

```
BaseClass::Virtual()
DerivedClass::Virtual()
DerivedClass::Virtual()
```

This occurs because when a parameter is passed by value, the passing mechanism makes a copy of the object, but the temporary object is actually of the type of the parameter, not of the type of the argument passed. The same applies when passing a return value that is not a reference or pointer. Therefore, care is needed when passing objects around where you are hoping to use virtual functions. If in doubt, try to use a reference parameter rather than passing by value—and use the const keyword where sensible.

When do you use virtual functions? It seems so useful that the classes automatically run the right function that it is tempting to always use them. However, virtual functions are not as efficient as standard functions, and there is no point in using virtual functions for private functions or functions that are not intended to be overridden.

 Warning   You can't use virtual functions in constructors because the derived class has not yet been made.

Think about your Vehicle class again from Unit 21. Wheels-U-Like needed to maintain a database of vehicles, and you used derived classes to represent the different types of vehicles. When a vehicle is to be rented, you need to get general information and then specific information. Instead of relying on the derived classes to repeat the work of remembering to call the base class functions, you can turn the program inside out and ask the derived class to provide information at specific points in the program. For example, Vehicle::PrintRental() could work like this:

```
class Vehicle
  {
    //... the rest of the class
    public:
      void PrintRental();
    protected:
      virtual void PrintAdditionalDetails();
  };

void PrintRental()
  {
    cout << "Rental Title" << endl;
    // cout the vehicle details
    PrintAdditionalDetails();
  }
```

The preceding snippet will print out the common information about a class and then call a version of PrintAdditionalDetails() that is appropriate to the class.

What should PrintAdditionalDetails() do in the base class? The answer depends on whether the class designer wants the vehicle class to be usable in its own right. There is a trick you can use to stop the class from being usable and to force the person who uses the class to provide a function. If the virtual function

```
virtual void PrintAdditionalDetails() = 0;
```

is declared, the class won't be usable. (In the difficult words that seem to always appear with C++, this makes the class an *abstract base* class). C++ will reject a program that tries to define a class in which such a function has not been overridden.

You can still force a specific version of a function to be called. A derived class virtual function replaces the base class function, so the derived class still might need to call the base class to make the function work. It would be very inconvenient if the virtual mechanism came into play, so the call

```cpp
void DerivedClass::Virtual()
  {
    BaseClass::Virtual();
    cout << "DerivedClass::Virtual()";
  }
```

still calls the base class version as its first action.

It's tricky to decide what version executes when a virtual function calls a nonvirtual member function. The answer is that the class used is determined by the class of the executing function (which might be of neither the calling class nor the object class):

```cpp
class A
  {
    public:
      void Print()
        {
          cout << "A";
        }
      virtual void CallPrint()
        {
          Print();
        }
  };
class B : public A
  {
    public:
      void Print()
        {
          cout << "B";
        }
      virtual void CallPrint()
        {
          Print();
        }
  };
class C : public A
  {
    public:
      void Print()
        {
          cout << "C";
        }
  };
```

```
A * a = new C;
a->CallPrint();
```

This looks to class C to decide which virtual function to call. Finding no virtual function there, it looks back to the base class (to class B) and executes B::CallPrint(). Then B::CallPrint() looks for Print(). Because Print() is not virtual, it uses the current type of the call (which is now B not C) to decide which version of Print() it uses. So when you write a function, you know that the following are true:

▶ If the function you call is virtual, the type of the function called will be the object type.

▶ If the call is nonvirtual, the type of the call is the calling object when called by an object.

▶ A special case of the last point is that a call to a nonvirtual function within a member function—either virtual or nonvirtual—will use the version of the member function being executed.

▶ Virtual Destructors

Concept   **What You Will Learn**

Virtual destructors ensure that a matching destructor is called for any object.

The last hole in your code for Wheels-U-Like was trying to sort out a way of calling the right destructor. By using the virtual mechanism on the destructor, you can leave this up to Visual C++. Visual C++ knows the type of the object, so it can call the right virtual destructor. This derived class still automatically calls all the destructors of the base class.

The rule on whether to declare a base class destructor as virtual is pretty simple: Always declare a base class destructor as virtual unless you are absolutely certain that any derived class will only be handled by objects of its own class.

STOP&TYPE Listing 22.2 shows a much cleaner implementation of the Wheels-U-Like system. By using virtual functions, the code becomes much easier.

▼ INPUT   LISTING 22.2. WHEELS-U-LIKE GOES INTO VIRTUAL REALITY.

```
1:// File name: WHEELSVL.CPP
2://
3:// A simple set of rental classes using virtuals
4://
5:#include <iostream.h>
6:#include <string.h>
7:
```

```
 8:
 9:// Base class
10:class Vehicle
11:  {
12:    public:
13:      virtual ~Vehicle()     // Virtual destructor
14:         {}                  // does nothing but safe
15:      void Print() const;    // Never overridden
16:      virtual void Rent(const char * ReturnDate); // Could be
17:    protected:
18:      Vehicle(long Mileage, const char * Model); // Not needed public
19:      virtual const char * GetRentalType() const = 0;
20:      virtual void PrintAdditionalDetails() const = 0;
21:    private:
22:      long mileage;
23:      char model[21];
24:      char returnDate[9];
25:  };
26:
27:class Car : public Vehicle     // Car is derived from Vehicle
28:  {
29:    public:
30:      Car(long Mileage, const char * Model,char Category);
31:    protected:
32:     const char * GetRentalType() const     // Still virtual
33:        {
34:          return "Car";
35:        }
36:      void PrintAdditionalDetails() const;  // still virtual
37:    private:
38:       char category;           // Only in Car not Vehicle
39:  };
40:
41:class Truck: public Vehicle    // Truck is derived from Vehicle
42:  {
43:    public:
44:      Truck(long Mileage, const char * Model,float MaxLoad);
45:    protected:
46:      virtual const char * GetRentalType() const
47:        {
48:          return "Truck";
49:        }
50:      virtual void PrintAdditionalDetails() const;
51:    private:
52:       float maxLoad;           // Only in Truck
53:  };
54:
55:// Global function
56:void GetRentalDate(char * date)
57:  {
58:    cout << "When are you returning the vehicle?";
59:    cin.getline(date,9);
60:  }
```

continues

```
61:
62://--------------------------------------------------------------
63://            Main is here!
64://--------------------------------------------------------------
65:void main()
66:  {
67:    char type;
68:    char rentalDate[9];
69:    Vehicle * vehicle;
70:    // Ask what type of rental
71:    cout << "Rent car (c) or truck (t)? ";
72:    cin >> type;
73:    cin.ignore(80,'\n');
74:    if (type == 't' || type == 'T')
75:        // truck rental
76:        vehicle = new Truck(4000,"Dodge",3.5F);
77:    else
78:        // Car rental
79:        vehicle = new Car(2500,"Buick",'B');
80:    // Normal function
81:    GetRentalDate(rentalDate);
82:    vehicle->Rent(rentalDate); // Not overridden
83:    vehicle->Print();
84:    delete vehicle;
85:  }
86://--------------------------------------------------------------
87://  Vehicle class functions
88://
89:Vehicle::Vehicle(long Mileage, const char * Model)
90:  {
91:    mileage = Mileage; // could have used intialization list
92:    strcpy(model,Model);
93:    returnDate[0] = '\0'; // zero length string
94:  }
95:
96:void Vehicle::Print() const
97:  {
98:    cout << GetRentalType() << " Rental" << endl;
99:    cout << "Model   :    " << model << endl;
100:    cout << "Mileage:     " << mileage << endl;
101:    cout << "Rented till: " ;
102:    if (returnDate[0]) // a test to see if first char is
103:                       // a terminator
104:        cout << returnDate;
105:    else
106:        cout << "Not rented";
107:    cout << endl;
108:    PrintAdditionalDetails();
109:  }
110:
111:void Vehicle::Rent(const char * RentalDate)
112:  {
113:    strcpy(returnDate,RentalDate);
```

```
114:   }
115:
116://---------------------------------------------------------
117://  Car class functions
118://
119:Car::Car(long Mileage, const char * Model, char Category)
120:      : Vehicle(Mileage,Model)     // calls base constructor
121:   {
122:      category = Category;
123:   }
124:
125:void Car::PrintAdditionalDetails() const
126:   {
127:      cout << "Category : " << category << endl;
128:   }
129:
130://---------------------------------------------------------
131://  Truck class functions
132://
133:Truck::Truck(long Mileage, const char * Model, float MaxLoad)
134:      : Vehicle(Mileage,Model)
135:   {
136:      maxLoad = MaxLoad;
137:   }
138:
139:void Truck::PrintAdditionalDetails() const
140:   {
141:      cout << "Max load : " << maxLoad << endl;
142:   }
```

▼ **OUTPUT**

First run:

```
Rent car (c) or truck (t)? Car
When are you returning the vehicle?10/10/95
Car Rental
Model  :    Buick
Mileage:    2500
Rented till: 10/10/95
Category : B
```

Second run:

```
Rent car (c) or truck (t)? t
When are you returning the vehicle?11/11/95
Truck Rental
Model  :    Dodge
Mileage:    4000
Rented till: 11/11/95
Max load : 3.5
```

▼ **ANALYSIS**

Comparing this listing with the original, you should see two things: First, it is shorter. Second, it is simpler but it does the same job as last time.

This is a successful class structure. The only significant function of the classes is `Print()` in lines 96 to 109. This is not a virtual function. It is designed to do the printing for any derived class. To do this, it needs to ask two things of the derived classes: how they would like the rental titled (`GetRentalType()`), and if there is any additional information they would like printed (`PrintAdditionalDetails()`). `Vehicle` forces derived classes to provide both of these functions by declaring them abstract (that is `=0`) in lines 19 and 20. It also declares them protected, because they are only intended to be helper routines, rather than for general use.

It is worth taking a look at the `Car` and `Truck` classes. Both have been reduced to very simple classes. They have a constructor that just needs to look after their own data members and pass on the rest to the base class (line 120). Then the type description is a one-liner (lines 32 to 35—not quite one line, but you get my drift). The additional details are again trivial: another one-liner, lines 125 through 128. You can see that it would be very simple to add further rental classes derived from `vehicle` that looked after specific data. By leaving the right blanks in the base class in the right place, it is easy to make code very general using virtual functions. Notice that the base class designer has planned from the start to allow the class to be derived from. This is typical. Classes are not just written to fill one job; from the beginning, they will be designed to be borrowed from.

This example does not exaggerate the power of a well-designed class. When you use library code, you often need to derive from a standard class. The objective of a code library class is to do all the hard work for you and just get the derived class to fill in any specific gaps. You'll normally find that to use a professional class to make your own specific objects, you write a few simple functions according to some simple rules, and often you're able to copy another example. You do not need to be an expert coder of C++ to make use of sophisticated prewritten classes.

▶ **The *this* pointer**

There is one important, though occasionally used, feature that should be covered before closing this lesson. At times, you want to get a pointer to the current object within a member function. For example, you could write a function to search an array of pointers to a class to find out which array index holds the object. Although you could do this outside of a member function, you might want to encapsulate the code. You can get a pointer to the current object within a member function by using the `this` keyword. `this` returns a pointer of the type of the current class. The code

```
Vehicle::Print()
  {
    cout << this->mileage;
```

. . .

is equivalent to this code:

```
Vehicle::Print()
  {
    cout << mileage;
    . . .
```

Normally, you don't need to use the this pointer because C++ always implies it within member functions. There are some special cases in which the this pointer becomes important, such as when an object needs to identify itself to a function that it calls. If you build linked lists of objects, you might need to store a pointer to the new object in another object, and if the processing is within a member function, this is an easy way to access the current object.

STOP&TYPE The code in Listing 22.3 shows a simple example of how you might use this.

▼ INPUT LISTING 22.3. USING THE this POINTER TO IDENTIFY AN OBJECT WITHIN A MEMBER FUNCTION.

```
 1:// Filename : THIS.CPP
 2:// A simple demonstration of using the this pointer
 3://
 4:#include <iostream.h>
 5:
 6:class Search
 7:  {
 8:    public:
 9:      int IsTheSameAs(Search * s)
10:        {
11:          if (s == this)
12:            return 1;
13:          else
14:            return 0;
15:        }
16:  };
17:
18:void main()
19:  {
20:    Search s[5];
21:    Search * test = &s[3];
22:    for (int i = 0; i < 5; i++)
23:      {
24:        if (s[i].IsTheSameAs(test))
25:          {
26:            cout << "The index is " << i;
27:            break;
28:          }
29:      }
30:  }
```

▼ **OUTPUT**

```
The index is 3
```

▼ **ANALYSIS**

The code creates the objects in an array in line 20. The objects don't do anything useful. In line 21, the program saves a pointer to the fourth object in the array.

In lines 22 through 29, the array is searched by calling a member function against each array member. (Note that the code could just as easily have called the member function from the test pointer and passed the address of each array member.) For each member, the IsTheSameAs test is applied. IsTheSameAs receives the pointer and compares it in line 11 to the this pointer, which is the pointer to the current object. If the object is the same, the pointer values will match.

▶ **Homework**
General Knowledge

1. How does a virtual function call decide which member function to execute?

2. What is the main reason for needing a polymorphic class rather than simple inheritance?

3. If you did not use virtual functions, what would you need to do to call the correct version of a member from a base class pointer pointing to a derived class?

4. What does a base class need to know about a derived class when using virtual functions?

5. How can a base class force a programmer to provide certain member functions?

6. What is the difference in timing between how a virtual function is called and a standard function is called?

7. Give two ways in which a program might lose track of an object's type information during the execution of the program.

8. How can you make a base class access data members of a derived class?

9. Given a class, Vehicle needs to describe the engine powering the vehicle. Should Engine be a base class of Vehicle? Why?

10. True or false: A class containing a virtual function is known as an abstract base class.

11. True or false: A virtual function can call a nonvirtual function.

12. True or false: A nonvirtual function can call a virtual function.

13. True or false: A virtual function can be overridden by a nonvirtual function.

14. True or false: If a call is made to a virtual function and there is no member function of that class, Visual C++ will execute a base class function instead.

What's the Output?

Given the following class definitions, answer the subsequent questions:

```
class A
  {
    public:
    virtual ~A()
      {
        cout << "A deleted ";
    void Print()
      {
        cout << "A";
      }
      virtual void CallPrint()
      {
        Print();
      }
  };
class B : public A
  {
    public:
      void Print()
      {
        cout << "B";
      }
      virtual void CallPrint()
      {
        Print();
      }
  };
class C : public B
  {
    public:
      ~C()
      {
          cout << "C deleted ";
      }
      void Print()
      {
        cout << "C";
      }
};
```

15. What does this print?

```
A a;
```

16. What does this print?

```
C c;
```

17. What does this print?

```
A * a = new C;
((B*)a)->CallPrint();
delete a;
```

Find the Bug

18. Why does the derived class sometimes leak memory?

```
class A
  {
    public:
      A()
       {}
      ~A()
       {}
  };
class B : public A
  {
    public:
      B()
       {
         b = new char[21];
       }
      ~B()
       {
         delete [] b;
       }
      char * b;
  };
void main()
  {
    A * a = new B;
    delete a;
  }
```

19. Why won't this compile (it's one of Ozwald's I'm afraid)?

```
#include <iostream.h>
class A
  {
    public:
     virtual ~A()
        {
          cout << "A deleted ";
        void Print()
          {
            cout << "A";
          }
        virtual void CallPrint() = 0;
  };
class B : public A
  {
    public:
```

```
        void Print()
        {
          cout << "B";
        }
};
void main()
  {
    B b;
  }
```

Write Code That...

20. Add function(s) to the WHEELSUV.CPP program (Listing 22.2) to allow users to change the name of the vehicle they are renting.

21. Add function(s) to the WHEELSUV.CPP program (Listing 22.2) to allow users to upgrade the rental to a higher class for a car or a heavier truck.

Extra Credit

22. Write a program to take airline bookings. Depending on the class (First, Club, or Cattle Wagon), allow the traveler to select a seat and prebook his meal. There is a different menu in each class. (The cheap seats only need to ask the question "Do you like grits?" The First Class has a five course menu.)

11

Inheritance and Virtual Functions

STOP&TYPE In this lesson, you learned about the advanced features of Visual C++. You learned how to make one class out of another and how to change the way a function is called to depend on either the calling type or the object type.

In this lesson, you saw the following:

▶ Deriving a class

▶ Access to class members under derivation

▶ Calling constructors and destructors of base classes

Project 11 Listing. An object-oriented pet care program.

```
1:// File name : PROJCT11.CPP

2:// Object oriented pet program to manage

3:// a simple list of different types of

4:// pets

5://

6:#include <iostream.h>

7:#include <string.h>

8:

9://----------------------------------------------------------

10:// Pet class

11://

12:class Pet
```

▶ Calling the correct version of an overridden function

▶ Declaring a member function to be virtual

▶ How virtual functions are called depending on the type of the object.

Description

1: Comment refers to the source filename.

2: Comment to describe the program.

3: The program description continues.

4: The program description continues.

5: Blank lines help to make the program more readable.

6: Include the header for the library of stream output functions.

7: Include the header for the library of string-handling functions.

8: Blank lines help to make the program more readable.

9: A comment helps separate the different classes.

10: A title for the following class.

11: A blank comment can also be used for appearance.

12: A line to declare a class called Pet.

continues

Project 11 Listing. continued

```
13:  {

14:   public:

15:     virtual ~Pet()              // Destructor

16:     {

17:       delete [] name;

18:     }

19:     void Print() const;         // Print all about pet

20:     void Query();               // Get details

21:     const char * GetName() const// Provide name string

22:     {

23:       if (name)

24:         return name;

25:       else

26:         return "";

27:     }

28:   protected:

29:     virtual void PrintDetails() const = 0;// Print details
```

Description

13: All classes start with an opening brace.

14: All members after this label will be declared `public`.

15: The destructor for `Pet` is shown with the ~ character. It is declared virtual.

16: The destructor function is coded inline. The function starts with an opening brace.

17: Delete the character string pointed to by `name`.

18: All functions end with a closing brace.

19: A function `Print()` is declared that will not change the class members.

20: A function `Query()` is declared. This is allowed to change class members.

21: A function `GetName()` is declared that will not change class members.

22: All functions start with opening braces. This is declared inline.

23: `name` might not have a string attached, but the constructor ensures it is zeroed.

24: If `name` did have a string, return it.

25: A single statement `if-else` does not need braces surrounding the statement.

26: Return a blank string if no name has been set.

27: A closing brace ends all functions.

28: All members following this label will be protected.

29: This virtual function has not been defined and is known as a pure virtual function.

29: Classes containing pure virtual functions are known as abstract classes.

continues

Project 11 Listing. continued

```
30:        virtual void QueryDetails() = 0;        // Ask for details

31:        virtual const char * GetPetType() const = 0;

32:        Pet()      // protected -

33:               // do not make Pets

34:        {

35:          name = 0;

36:        }

37:    private:

38:      char * name;

39:  };

40:void Pet::Print() const

41:  {

42:    cout << GetPetType()  << " : ";

43:    if (name)

44:      cout << name << " - ";

45:    PrintDetails();

46:    cout << endl;
```

Description

30: `QueryDetails()` is also a pure virtual function.

31: There is no definition for `GetPetType()`.

32: The default constructor for the `Pet` class.

33: A comment helps explain an unusual coding feature.

34: An inline function starts with a closing brace.

35: Pointers should always be initialized. A valid pointer can never be zero.

36: Functions always end with closing braces.

37: All members following this label will be private.

38: A pointer to a character string initially does not own any storage.

39: All class declarations end with both a closing brace and a semicolon.

40: The function `Print()` belonging to the `Pet` class is defined.

41: All functions start with an opening brace.

42: Output the type of pet, using a virtual function so that each class can output its name.

43: Check the validity of a character pointer before using.

44: `name` is a member of this class, so it needs no special function to access it.

45: Call a virtual function to get details that differ by derived type.

46: Output a newline sequence.

continues

Project 11 Listing. continued

```
47:  }

48:

49:void Pet::Query()

50:  {

51:     char tempName[81];

52:     cout << "What is your pet " << GetPetType() <<"'s name? ";

53:     cin.getline(tempName,81);

54:     if (name)

55:       delete [] name;

56:     name = new char[strlen(tempName) + 1];

57:     strcpy(name,tempName);

58:     QueryDetails();

59:  }

60:

61://------------------------------------------------------------

62:// Cat class - derived from Pet

63://
```

Description

47: All functions end with a closing brace.

48: Blank lines help you make the code more readable.

49: Define the nonvirtual function `Query`.

50: All functions start with an opening brace.

51: Declare a temporary character string much bigger than expected input.

52: Ask for user input, using a virtual function to customize the request for each class.

53: Get the `name` into a temporary string.

54: If the `name` already points at a string, delete it.

55: Delete the current string to recover the memory.

56: Create a dynamic memory allocation just big enough to hold the string and its terminator.

57: Copy the temporary name into the class storage.

58: Call a virtual function to get details specific to the actual class.

59: All functions end with a closing brace.

60: Blank lines help to make the program more readable.

61: A comment to mark the start of a new class.

62: A comment to identify which class is now being defined.

63: Empty comments can enhance the appearance of the program.

continues

Project 11 Listing. continued

```
64:class Cat : public Pet

65:  {

66:    public:

67:      Cat(int Scratches = 1)

68:        {

69:          scratches = Scratches;

70:        }

71:    protected:

72:      virtual void PrintDetails() const;

73:      virtual void QueryDetails();

74:      const char * GetPetType() const

75:        {

76:          return "Cat";

77:        }

78:    private:

79:      int scratches;

80:  };
```

Description

64: Class Cat builds the functionality of class Pet.

65: Class definitions start with an opening brace.

66: All members following this label will be public.

67: The constructor for cat can optionally take a parameter.

68: A function always starts with an opening brace.

69: A constructor should always initialize the members.

69: If no base constructor is explicitly called in the initialization list, the default base constructor is called.

70: A function always ends with a closing brace.

71: All the functions following this label will be protected.

71: Protected members are only visible to this class and derived classes.

72: This class is going to define the PrintDetails() function.

73: This class is going to define the QueryDetails() function.

74: This class defines the GetPetType() function.

75: All functions start with an opening brace.

76: This function returns the literal string Cat.

76: Visual C++ can't access the actual class name.

77: All functions end with a closing brace.

78: All members following this label will be private.

79: A private data member that is an integer.

80: All class definitions end with a closing brace and a semicolon.

continues

Project 11 Listing. continued

```
81:

82:void Cat::PrintDetails() const

83:  {

84:     cout << "Scratches: " << (scratches? "Yes":"No");

85:  }

86:

87:void Cat::QueryDetails()

88:  {

89:     char yn;

90:     cout << "Does your cat " << GetName() << " scratch? ";

91:     cin >> yn;

92:     cin.ignore(80,'\n');

93:     if (yn == 'Y' || yn == 'y')

94:        scratches = 1;

95:     else

96:        scratches = 0;

97:  }
```

Description

81: Blank lines make the program more readable.

82: Define the function `PrintDetails()`. This version belongs to `Cat`.

83: All functions start with an opening brace.

84: Output extra details of the `Cat` class.

85: All functions end with a closing brace.

86: Blank lines help to make the program more readable.

87: Define the function `QueryDetails()`.

88: All functions start with an opening brace.

89: Declare a character variable to test the input.

90: Query the user for information. Customize the output with a call for base class information.

91: Ask for an answer that takes just the first character.

92: Ignore the input until the newline character.

93: If the answer is yes...

94: Set the member flag to true.

95: If the answer is no...

96: Set the member flag to false.

97: All functions end with a closing brace.

continues

Project 11 Listing. continued

```
98:
99://----------------------------------------------------------
100:// Dog class - derived from Pet
101://
102:
103:class Dog : public Pet
104: {
105:    public:
106:       Dog(int Barks = 1)
107:          {
108:             barks = Barks;
109:          }
110:    protected:
111:       virtual void PrintDetails() const;
112:       virtual void QueryDetails();
113:       const char * GetPetType() const
114:          {
```

Description

98:	Blank lines help to make the program more readable.
99:	A comment to mark the start of a new class.
100:	A comment to identify which class is now being defined.
101:	Empty comments can enhance the appearance of the program.
102:	Blank lines help to make the program more readable.
103:	Class Dog builds the functionality of class Pet.
104:	Class definitions start with an opening brace.
105:	All members following this label will be public.
106:	The constructor for Dog can optionally take a parameter.
107:	A function always starts with an opening brace.
108:	A constructor should always initialize the members.
109:	A function always ends with a closing brace.
110:	All functions following this label will be protected.
111:	This class is going to define the PrintDetails() function.
112:	This class is going to define the QueryDetails() function.
113:	This class defines the GetPetType() function.
114:	All functions start with an opening brace.

continues

Project 11 Listing. continued

```
115:          return "Dog";

116:        }

117:    private:

118:       int barks;

119:  };

120:

121:void Dog::PrintDetails() const

122:  {

123:    cout << "Barks: " << (barks? "Yes":"No");

124:  }

125:

126:void Dog::QueryDetails()

127:  {

128:    char yn;

129:    cout << "Does your dog " << GetName() << " bark? ";

130:    cin >> yn;

131:    cin.ignore(80,'\n');
```

Description

115: This function returns the literal string `Dog`.

116: All functions end with a closing brace.

117: All members following this label will be private.

118: A private data member that is an integer.

119: All class definitions end with a closing brace and a semicolon.

120: Blank lines make the program more readable.

121: Define the function `PrintDetails()`. This version belongs to `Cat`.

122: All functions start with an opening brace.

123: Output extra details of `Dog` class.

124: All functions end with a closing brace.

125: Blank lines help to make the program more readable.

126: Define the function `QueryDetails()`.

127: All functions start with an opening brace.

128: Declare a character variable to test the input.

129: Query the user for information. Customize the output with a call for base class information.

130: Ask for an answer that takes just the first character.

131: Ignore the input until the newline character.

continues

Project 11 Listing. continued

```
132:    if (yn == 'Y' || yn == 'y')

133:      barks = 1;

134:    else

135:      barks = 0;

136:  }

137:

138://-----------------------------------------------------------

139:// Fish class - derived from Pet

140://

141:class Fish : public Pet

142:  {

143:    public:

144:      Fish(int ColdWater = 0)

145:        {

146:          coldWater = ColdWater;

147:        }

148:    protected:
```

Description

132: If the answer is yes...

133: Set the member flag to true.

134: If the answer is no...

135: Set the member flag to false.

136: All functions end with a closing brace.

137: Blank lines help to make the program more readable.

138: A comment to mark the start of a new class.

139: A comment to identify which class is now being defined.

140: Empty comments can enhance the appearance of the program.

141: Class Fish builds the functionality of class Pet.

142: Class definitions start with an opening brace.

143: All members following this label will be public.

144: The constructor for Fish can optionally take a parameter.

145: A function always starts with an opening brace.

146: A constructor should always initialize the members.

147: A function always ends with a closing brace.

148: All the functions following this label will be protected.

continues

Project 11 Listing. continued

```
149:      virtual void PrintDetails() const;

150:      virtual void QueryDetails();

151:      const char * GetPetType() const

152:         {

153:          return "Fish";

154:         }

155:    private:

156:       int coldWater;

157:  };

158:void Fish::PrintDetails() const

159:  {

160:    cout << (coldWater? "Cold water":"Tropical");

161:  }

162:

163:void Fish::QueryDetails()

164:  {

165:    char yn;
```

Description

149: This class is going to define the `PrintDetails()` function.

150: This class is going to define the `QueryDetails()` function.

151: This class defines the `GetPetType()` function.

152: All functions start with an opening brace.

153: This function returns the literal string `Fish`.

154: All functions end with a closing brace.

155: All members following this label will be private.

156: A private data member that is an integer.

157: All class definitions end with a closing brace and a semicolon.

158: Define the function `PrintDetails()`. This version belongs to `Fish`.

159: All functions start with an opening brace.

160: Output extra details of the `Cat` class.

161: All functions end with a closing brace.

162: Blank lines help to make the program more readable.

163: Define the function `QueryDetails()`.

164: All functions start with an opening brace.

165: Declare a character variable to test the input.

continues

Project 11 Listing. continued

```
166:    cout << "Is your fish " << GetName() << " tropical? ";

167:    cin >> yn;

168:    cin.ignore(80,'\n');

169:    if (yn == 'Y' || yn == 'y')

170:       coldWater = 0;

171:    else

172:       coldWater = 1;

173: }

174:

175://------------------------------------------------------------

176:// main procedure

177://

178:

179:void main()

180: {

181:    const int maxPets = 20;

182:    char type = ' ';
```

Description

166:	Query the user for information. Customize the output with a call for base class information.
167:	Ask for an answer that takes just the first character.
168:	Ignore the input until the newline character.
169:	If the answer is yes...
170:	Set the member flag to true.
171:	If the answer is no...
172:	Set the member flag to false.
173:	All functions end with a closing brace.
174:	Blank lines make the program more readable.
175:	A comment to divide the code.
176:	A comment to tell the programmer that he has found the main procedure.
177:	Blank comments can enhance the appearance of the program.
178:	Blank lines make the program more readable.
179:	The start of the main procedure.
180:	All functions start with an opening brace.
181:	Define a constant for the maximum number of entries.
182:	Initialize a temporary input character.

continues

Project 11 Listing. continued

```
183:    Pet * pets[maxPets] = {0};

184:    int count = 0;

185:

186:    while (count < maxPets)

187:       {

188:         // Where do you want to go today?

189:         cout << "Pet type, [C]at, [D]og, [F]ish, [Q]uit: ";

190:         cin >> type;

191:         cin.ignore(80,'\n');

192:

193:         // Stop loop early

194:         if (type == 'q' || type == 'Q')

195:            break;

196:

197:         switch (type)

198:            {

199:               case 'C': // Cat
```

Description

183: Define an array of pointers to the Pet class.

183: An array of pointers takes up a small amount of space compared to the classes, and derived classes might take up much more storage than a base class.

184: A counter to record how many pets have been entered.

185: Blank lines make the program more readable.

186: Do the following statements as long as the number of entries do not exceed the array capacity.

187: A while loop of multiple statements is delimited by an opening brace.

188: Not all comments serve a useful purpose.

189: Prompt the user for a selection.

190: Store the first character of a user's answer.

191: Ignore any spare input after the first character.

192: Blank lines make the program more readable.

193: Comments can explain why code is written.

194: Test the input to see whether the user has finished.

195: Leave the loop if the if test is true.

196: Blank lines make the program more readable.

197: Avoid complex if statements by using the switch statement.

198: switch statements are enclosed in braces.

199: Execute from here if type is 'C'.

continues

Project 11 Listing. continued

```
200:        case 'c':
201:            {
202:                pets[count] = new Cat;
203:                break;
204:            }
205:        case 'D': // Dog
206:        case 'd':
207:            {
208:                pets[count] = new Dog;
209:                break;
210:            }
211:        case 'F': // Fish
212:        case 'f':
213:            {
214:                pets[count] = new Fish;
215:                break;
216:            }
```

Description

200: Execute from here if type is `'c'`. The first case will fall through.

201: case statements can be enclosed in a block.

201: case statements must be enclosed in braces if they declare a variable.

202: Make an object of type Cat and store it in a general Pet pointer.

203: Break out of the rest of the switch statement.

203: Meeting a case statement does not cause a branch out of the switch statement.

204: End of case block.

205: case for Dog.

206: case for Dog.

207: case statements can be enclosed in a block.

208: Make an object of type Dog and store it in a general Pet pointer.

209: Break out of the rest of the switch statement.

210: End of case block.

211: case for Fish

212: case for Fish

213: case statements can be enclosed in a block.

214: Make an object of type Fish and store it in a general Pet pointer.

215: Break out of the rest of the switch statement.

216: End of case block.

continues

Project 11 Listing. continued

```
217:              default:

218:                  continue; // can be used in switch

219:          }

220:          pets[count]->Query();

221:        count++;

222:      }

223:

224:    // List pets - don't need derived classes for this

225:    cout << endl << "Pet Names" << endl;

226:    for (int i = 0; i < count; i++)

227:      {

228:          cout << pets[i]->GetName();

229:          cout << endl;

230:      }

231:

232:    // Print characteristics - rely on virtual functions

233:    cout << endl << "Characteristics" << endl;
```

Description

217: If the input does not match any planned `case`, do the following.

218: Executing `continue` will go around the loop, skipping the remaining code.

219: End the switch `statement`.

220: Call the input function for the new object. Because it contains virtual function calls, different code for each type will be called.

221: Increment the number of valid objects count.

222: End the `while` loop compound statement.

223: Blank lines help make the program more readable.

224: Comment to help understand the following processing.

225: Output a title.

226: `for` as many items in the container.

226: The scope of local variable `i` is the block containing `for`, not the `for` loop itself. Note the following `for` loops.

227: `for` loops performing multiple statements enclose them in braces.

228: Output the pet's name by using a nonvirtual function belonging to the base class.

229: A newline character sequence is output.

230: End of the `for` loop is denoted by the closing brace.

231: Blank lines make the program more readable.

232: A comment to explain the following processing.

233: Output a title.

continues

Project 11 Listing. continued

```
234:    for (i = 0; i < count; i++)

235:        pets[i]->Print();

236:

237:    // Tidy up storage

238:    for (i = 0; i < count; i++)

239:        delete pets[i];

240: }
```

Description

234: for all the items in the container.

235: A for loop can execute a single statement.

235: Print() contains virtual functions that will execute code specific to each object's class.

236: Blank lines make the code more readable.

237: A comment to explain the following processing.

238: for each item in the container.

239: Delete the storage associated with the pointer.

240: The main function ends with a closing brace.

239: Because the base class destructor is virtual, the correct destructor will be called even though the pointer belongs to the base class.

▼ OUTPUT

```
Pet type, [C]at, [D]og, [F]ish, [Q]uit: cat
What is your pet Cat's name? Tibbles
Does your cat Tibbles scratch? no, never has
Pet type, [C]at, [D]og, [F]ish, [Q]uit: d
What is your pet Dog's name? Ross
Does your dog Ross bark? Yes
Pet type, [C]at, [D]og, [F]ish, [Q]uit: f
What is your pet Fish's name? Wanda
Is your fish Wanda tropical? yes
Pet type, [C]at, [D]og, [F]ish, [Q]uit: p
Pet type, [C]at, [D]og, [F]ish, [Q]uit: q

Pet Names
Tibbles
Ross
Wanda

Characteristics
Cat : Tibbles - Scratches: No
Dog : Ross - Barks: Yes
Fish : Wanda - Tropical
```

Lesson ▶ 12

Using Disk Files

23

Visual C++ Library of Functions

`isalpha()`

`toupper()`

▶ **What You'll Learn**

- ▶ Character functions
- ▶ String functions
- ▶ Numeric functions
- ▶ Time and date functions
- ▶ Using class libraries

The nice thing about Visual C++ is that Microsoft has already written lots of code for you! For example, you don't have to write the code needed to copy a character string character by character. Visual C++ has done that for you in strcpy(). strcpy() is one of several library functions that you've seen so far. Visual C++ provides several more library functions (often just called functions in this unit) that do work for you.

To use any library function, you need to include the proper header file and know the name of the function that you want to use and the type and number of parameters. For example, instead of writing the code needed to determine the length of a string, you can include the STRING.H header file and request the strlen() function.

In addition to library functions, Visual C++ provides several library classes as well. You have used two library classes—cin and cout—in just about every program in this book.

This unit teaches you several string, character, and numeric functions that do work for you. There are a lot more library functions included with Visual C++, but the ones described here are some of the most common.

▶ **Character Functions**

Concept   **What You Will Learn**

The character functions let you change and test character variables for specific values.

This section explores many of the character functions available in Visual C++. Generally, you pass character arguments to the functions, and the functions return values that you can store or print. By using these functions, you offload much of your work to Visual C++ and allow it to perform the more tedious manipulations of character and string data.

This book gives you a feel for the sort of functions you can expect to find in Visual C++. If there is some task for which you feel lots of programmers might need a function, look in the online help. Choose Help | C/C++ Language from the Visual C++ Workbench. The contents will point you to runtime library functions, and you can browse around looking for functions under the appropriate category.

Character-Testing Functions

Several functions test for certain characteristics of your character data. You can determine whether your character data is alphabetic, digital, uppercase, lowercase, and much more. You must pass a character variable or a literal argument to the function (by placing the argument in the function parentheses) when you call it. These functions return a True or False result so that you can test their return values inside an `if` statement or a `while` loop.

> ***Note*** All character functions presented in this section are prototyped in the CTYPE.H header file. Be sure to include CTYPE.H at the beginning of any programs that use these functions.

Testing Letters and Numbers

The following functions test for alphabetic conditions:

- ▶ `isalpha(c)`: Returns True (nonzero) if *c* is an uppercase or lowercase letter. Returns False (zero) if *c* is not a letter.

- ▶ `islower(c)`: Returns True (nonzero) if *c* is a lowercase letter. Returns False (zero) if *c* is not a lowercase letter.

- ▶ `isupper(c)`: Returns True (nonzero) if *c* is an uppercase letter. Returns False (zero) if *c* is not an uppercase letter.

Remember that any nonzero value is True in Visual C++, and zero is always False. If you use the return values of these functions in a relational test, the True return value is not always 1 (it can be any nonzero value), but it is always considered True for the test.

The following functions test for digits:

- ▶ `isdigit(c)`: Returns True (nonzero) if *c* is a digit 0 through 9. Returns False (zero) if *c* is not a digit.

> ***Note*** Although some character functions test for digits, the arguments are still character data and can't be used in mathematical calculations unless you calculate using the ASCII values of characters.

- ▶ `isxdigit(c)`: Returns True (nonzero) if *c* is any of the hexadecimal digits 0 through 9 or A, B, C, D, E, F, a, b, c, d, e, or f. Returns False (zero) if *c* is anything else.

The following function tests for numeric or alphabetical arguments:

▶ `isalnum(c)`: Returns True (nonzero) if *c* is a digit 0 through 9 or an alphabetic character (either uppercase or lowercase). Returns False (zero) if *c* is not a digit or a letter.

> *Note*   You can pass to these functions only a character value or an integer value holding the ASCII value of a character. You cannot pass an entire character array to character functions. If you want to test the elements of a character array, you must pass the array one element at a time.

Special Character-Testing Functions

A few character functions become useful when you have to read from a disk file, a modem, or another operating system device from which you route input. These functions are not used as much as the character functions you saw in the preceding section, but they are useful for testing specific characters for readability. The character-testing functions do not change characters.

The remaining character-testing functions are as follows:

▶ `iscntrl(c)`: Returns True (nonzero) if *c* is a control character (any character from the ASCII table numbered 0 through 31). Returns False (zero) if *c* is not a control character.

▶ `isgraph(c)`: Returns True (nonzero) if *c* is any printable character (a noncontrol character) except a space. Returns False (zero) if *c* is a space or anything other than a printable character.

▶ `isprint(c)`: Returns True (nonzero) if *c* is a printable character (a noncontrol character) from ASCII 32 to ASCII 127, including a space. Returns False (zero) if *c* is not a printable character.

▶ `ispunct(c)`: Returns True (nonzero) if *c* is any punctuation character (any printable character other than a space, a letter, or a digit). Returns False (zero) if *c* is not a punctuation character.

▶ `isspace(c)`: Returns True (nonzero) if *c* is a space, newline (\n), carriage return (\r), tab (\t), or vertical tab (\v) character. Returns False (zero) if *c* is anything else.

Some people program in Visual C++ for years and never need any of these functions. Programmers often use them to parse, or interpret, lines of input. Specialized applications such as language translators need special character-testing functions such as these. Other times, a programmer produces a file that contains many control characters, and the programmer needs to strip out any data that is not a text or numeric character.

Character Conversion Functions

The two remaining character functions are handy. Rather than testing characters, these functions convert characters to their lowercase or uppercase equivalents.

▶ `tolower(c)`: Converts `c` to lowercase. Nothing changes if you pass `tolower()` a lowercase letter or a nonalphabetic character.

▶ `toupper(c)`: Converts `c` to uppercase. Nothing changes if you pass `toupper()` an uppercase letter or a nonalphabetic character.

These functions return their changed character values.

These functions are also useful for user input. Suppose that you ask users a yes-or-no question, such as the following:

```
Do you want to print the checks (Y/N)?
```

Before `toupper()` and `tolower()` were developed, you had to check for both a Y and a y to print the checks. Instead of testing for both conditions, you can convert the character to uppercase, and test for a Y.

STOP&TYPE Listing 23.1 contains a program that uses `toupper()` for character conversion.

Review **What You Have Learned**

The character testing and conversion functions give you the ability to check character data for certain conditions.

▼ **INPUT   LISTING 23.1. USING `toupper()` TO CHECK FOR AN UPPERCASE ANSWER.**

```cpp
1:// Filename: GB.CPP
2:// Determines whether the user typed a G or a B.
3:#include <iostream.h>
4:// toupper is in ctype.h
5:#include <ctype.h>
6:
7:void main()
8:{
9:  char ans;   // Holds user's response
10:
11:  cout << "Are you a girl or a boy (G/B)? ";
12:  cin >> ans;   // Gets answer
13:
14:  cout << endl;
15:
16:  ans = toupper(ans);   // Converts answer to uppercase
```

```
17:  switch (ans)
18:  {    case ('G'): { cout << "You look pretty today!" << endl;
19:                      break; }
20:       case ('B'): { cout << "You look handsome today!" << endl;
21:                      break; }
22:       default :   { cout << "Your answer makes no sense!" << endl;
23:                      break; }
24:  }
25:  return;
26:}
```

▼ **OUTPUT**

```
Are you a girl or a boy (G/B)?b

You look handsome today!
```

▼ **ANALYSIS**

Listing 23.1 prints an appropriate message if the user is a girl or a boy. The program tests for the uppercase G or B after converting the user's input to uppercase in line 16. No check for lowercase has to be done due to the `toupper()` function call.

As you have seen with the string and I/O functions throughout the book, you needed to add the appropriate header file, CTYPE.H, in line 5 to get the program to compile. When you use library functions, you do not include the entire body of the functions in the compilation. Visual C++ keeps a ready-made collection of code in a library, and when the compiler moves on to the linking phase, it spots that you have used a library function and adds the extra bit of code needed by your program into the final executable. The Options | Project | Linker controls the list of libraries Visual C++ uses, but normally you do not need to worry about this.

▶ **String Functions**

What You Will Learn

The string functions combine and check strings for certain conditions.

Some of the most powerful built-in Visual C++ functions are the string functions. They perform much of the tedious work for which you have been writing code so far, such as inputting strings from the keyboard and comparing strings.

As with the character functions, there is no need to reinvent the wheel by writing code, when built-in functions do the same task. Use these functions as much as possible.

Now that you have a good grasp of the foundations of Visual C++, you can master the string functions. They enable you to concentrate on your program's primary purpose rather than spend time coding your own string functions.

Useful String Functions

You can use a handful of useful string functions for string testing and conversion. In earlier lessons, you saw the `strcpy()` string function, which copies a string of characters to a character array.

Note All string functions in this section are prototyped in the STRING.H header file. Be sure to include STRING.H at the beginning of any program that uses the string functions.

The string functions work on string literals or on character arrays that contain strings.

The following are string functions that test or manipulate strings:

Definition—To *concatenate* means to merge one string onto the end of another.

▶ `strcat(s1, s2)`: Concatenates the s2 string to the end of the s1 character array. The s1 array must have enough reserved elements to hold both strings.

If st1 is a character array for which you've reserved 25 characters, and it currently holds the string `"First"`, it will hold `"First National"` if you perform the following `strcat()` function call:

```
strcat(st1, " National");
```

▶ `strcmp(s1, s2)`: Compares the s1 string with the s2 string on an alphabetical, element-by-element basis. If s1 alphabetizes before s2, `strcmp()` returns a negative value. If s1 and s2 are the same strings, `strcmp()` returns 0. If s1 alphabetizes after s2, `strcmp()` returns a positive value.

Note The following code tests to see whether two strings (strings stored in character arrays) hold the same value:

```
if (!strcmp(s1, s2))
   { cout << "They are the same"; }
```

This is a time when the NOT operator (!) is clear. Because `strcmp()` returns 0 or False if the strings compare, you must test for NOT False in order to perform the comparison and print if they truly do compare.

▶ `strlen(s1)`: Returns the length of s1. Remember that the length of a string is the number of characters, not including the null terminator. The number of characters defined for the character array has nothing to do with the length of the string.

Note The following code stores the length of the string in n:

n = strlen("A string");   // Stores 8 in n

Before using strcat() to concatenate strings, use strlen() to ensure that the target string (the string being concatenated to) is large enough to hold both strings.

Converting Strings to Numbers

Sometimes you have to convert numbers stored in character strings to numeric data types. Visual C++ provides three functions that enable you to do this:

▶ atoi(s): Converts s to an integer. The name stands for alphabetic to integer.

▶ atol(s): Converts s to a long integer. The name stands for alphabetic to long integer.

▶ atof(s): Converts s to a floating-point number. The name stands for alphabetic to floating-point.

Note These three ato() functions are prototyped in the STDLIB.H header file. Be sure to include STDLIB.H at the beginning of any program that uses the ato() functions.

The string must contain a valid number. Here is a string that can be converted to an integer:

"1232"

The string must hold a string of digits short enough to fit in the target numeric data type. The following string could not be converted to an integer with the atoi() function:

"-1232495.654"

It could, however, be converted to a floating-point number with the atof() function.

Visual C++ can't perform any mathematical calculation with such strings, even if the strings contain digits that represent numbers. Therefore, you must convert any string to its numeric equivalent before performing arithmetic with it.

Note If you pass a string to an ato() function and the string does not contain a valid representation of a number, the ato() function returns 0.

The following code fragment gets a number from the user as a string and converts that string to a floating-point number:

```
float fv;    // Will hold the converted number
char cnum[20];    // Will hold the user's number
cout << "How much was your check? ";
cin >> cnum;    // Gets the number into the character
                // array
fv = atof(cnum);    // Converts the string to a
                    // floating-point
```

The conversion functions will become more useful to you after you learn about disk files in the last unit.

STOP&TYPE Listing 23.2 contains a program that uses three string functions.

Review

What You Have Learned

`strcat()`, `strcmp()`, `strlen()`, and the `ato()` functions give you added string power.

▼ **INPUT   LISTING 23.2. USING THE STRING FUNCTIONS.**

```
1:// Filename: STRPGM.CPP
2:// Program that uses string functions to
3:// work with string input
4:#include <iostream.h>
5:#include <string.h>
6:#include <stdlib.h>
7:
8:void main()
9:{
10:   char name[31];
11:   char age[4];      // Will hold a string of integer digits
12:   int intAge;
13:
14:   cout << "What is your name? ";
15:   cin.getline(name, 30);
16:   cout << "How old are you? ";
17:   cin.getline(age, 3);
18:
19:   // Make into one string if room for comma, space, and null
20:   if ((strlen(name) + strlen(age) + 3) <= 30)
21:     {
22:        strcat(name, ", ");
23:        strcat(name, age);
24:        cout << "Your name and age: " << name << endl;
25:     }
```

```
26:  else
27:   { // Here if name cannot hold entire string
28:      cout << endl << "Thanks, " << name << endl;
29:   }
30:
31:  // Convert the age string to an integer
32:  intAge = atoi(age);  // Convert the age to an integer
33:  intAge += 10;
34:  cout << "In ten years, you'll be " << intAge << endl;
35:  return;
36:}
```

▼ OUTPUT

```
What is your name? Alan Reardon
How old are you? 41

Your name and age: Alan Reardon
In ten years, you'll be 51
```

▼ ANALYSIS

Notice that this program includes three header files in lines 4 through 6 to handle all the functions needed in the body of the code. Lines 15 and 17 accept string input from the user. Line 16's cout asks for an integer, but line 17 grabs the user's response (the age) and stores the integer age in a character array as a zero-terminated string.

Line 20 checks to see whether there is enough room in name to hold both the name and the string age, separated by a comma and a space. Therefore, line 20's if determines whether name is long enough to hold the entire concatenated string. If so, line 22 appends a comma and a space to the name, and then line 23 appends the age string. Line 24 prints the results of the concatenated string.

 Warning If you don't check to see whether the target string is long enough to hold the fully concatenated string, Visual C++ will not issue an error but will overwrite an unprotected area of memory to complete the concatenation. The results of this overwriting of memory are unpredictable.

If there is not enough room to hold the entire concatenated string, line 28 prints a simple message that includes only the name.

Line 32 simply shows the atoi() function in action by converting the integer stored as a string to a numeric integer and placing that integer in the variable named intAge. Line 33 adds 10 to intAge just to show that intAge holds a numeric value.

▶ Numeric Functions

Concept

Thank goodness for the numeric functions! With them, you can perform common calculations without having to write formulas or understand the internals of the math involved.

The following sections present many of the built-in Visual C++ numeric functions. As with the string functions, these functions convert and calculate numbers. They save you time because you don't have to write functions that do the same thing. Many of these are trigonometric and advanced mathematical functions. You might use some of these numeric functions only rarely, but they are there if you need them.

These sections conclude the discussion of Visual C++'s standard built-in functions. As you develop more skills in Visual C++, you might find yourself relying on these I/O, string, character, and numeric functions when you write more powerful programs.

Trigonometric and Logarithmic Functions

The following functions are available for trigonometric and logarithmic applications:

- ▶ `cos(x)`: Returns the cosine of the angle x, expressed in radians.
- ▶ `sin`: Returns the sine of the angle x, expressed in radians.
- ▶ `tan(x)`: Returns the tangent of the angle x, expressed in radians.
- ▶ `exp(x)`: Returns e, the base of the natural logarithm, raised to a power specified by x (e^x). e is the mathematical expression for the approximate value of 2.718282.
- ▶ `log(x)`: Returns the natural logarithm of the argument x, mathematically written as $\ln(x)$. x must be positive.
- ▶ `log10(x)`: Returns the base-10 logarithm of argument x, mathematically written as $\log 10(x)$. x must be positive.

Note   All mathematical and trigonometric functions are prototyped in the MATH.H header file. Be sure to include MATH.H at the beginning of any program that uses the numeric functions.

UNIT

23

Visual C++ Library of Functions

For many programmers—especially business programmers—these are probably the least-used Visual C++ functions because of the functions' highly technical nature.

 Tip   Visual C++ supplies additional trigonometric functions, including hyper-bolic equivalents of these three functions. Search the online help (via Help Topic Search within C/C++ Help from the help menu) for math functions to see all the Visual C++ mathematical functions.

If you are confused, you're probably in good company. Trigonometric functions are not used in everyday applications. If you don't have a need for them, leave them alone and you'll be just fine.

If you have to pass an angle that is expressed in degrees to these functions, convert the angle's degrees to radians by multiplying the degrees by pi/180.0. (pi equals approximately 3.14159.)

Common Mathematical Functions

Several built-in numeric functions return results based on numeric variables and literals passed to them. Even if you write only a few science and engineering programs, some of these functions are useful. These numeric functions return double-precision values. Here are the functions and their descriptions:

▶ `ceil(x)`: The `ceil()`, or ceiling, function rounds numbers up to the nearest integer.

Note   The following statement

```
cout << ceil(11.2);
```

prints 12 to the screen.

▶ `fabs(x)`: Returns the absolute value of *x*. The absolute value of a number is its positive equivalent.

Note   The following statement

```
cout << fabs(-412);
```

prints 412 to the screen.

 Tip   Absolute value is used for distances (which are always positive), accuracy measurements, age differences, and other calculations that require a positive result.

▶ `floor(x)`: The `floor()` function rounds numbers down to the nearest integer.

▶ fmod(x, y): The fmod() function returns the floating-point remainder of (x/y) with the same sign as x, and y can't be zero. Because the modulus operator (%) works only with integers, this function is used to find the remainder of floating-point number divisions.

▶ pow(x, y): Returns x raised to the y power, or x^y. If x is less than or equal to zero, y must be an integer. If x equals zero, y can't be negative.

▶ sqrt(x): Returns the square root of x. x must be greater than or equal to zero.

Tip You can find the *n*th root of any number by raising that number to the power of 1 divided by *n*. In other words, you could find the fourth root of 256 with this function call: fourth = pow(256, (1.0/4.0));

STOP&TYPE Listing 23.3 contains a program that uses fabs() to compute a difference between people's ages.

Review **What You Have Learned**

The mathematical and trigonometric functions give you lots of calculating power. By calling these functions by name, you eliminate a lot of code that you would normally have to write.

▼ INPUT   LISTING 23.3. THE FUNCTION IN ACTION.

```
1:// Filename: ABS.CPP
2:// Computes the difference between two ages
3:#include <iostream.h>
4:#include <math.h>
5:void main()
6:{
7:  float age1, age2, diff;
8:  cout << endl << "What is the first child's age? ";
9:  cin >> age1;
10:  cout << "What is the second child's age? ";
11:  cin >> age2;
12:
13:  // Calculates the positive difference
14:  diff = age1 - age2;
15:  diff = fabs(diff);   // Determines the absolute value
16:
17:  cout << endl << "They are " << diff << " years apart.";
18:  return;
19:}
```

UNIT

23

Visual C++ Library of Functions

▼ OUTPUT

```
What is the first child's age? 10
What is the second child's age? 12

They are 2 years apart.
```

▼ ANALYSIS

Due to the use of fabs() in line 15, the order of the ages doesn't matter. Without absolute value, this program would produce a negative age difference if the first age was less than the second. Because the ages are relatively small numbers, floating-point variables are used in this example. Visual C++ automatically converts floating-point arguments to double precision when passing them to fabs(), although the compiler gently reminds you of the conversion back from double to float in case the answer might be too big for a float.

▶ Time and Date Functions

Concept   **What You Will Learn**

Your programs can access the PC's internal clock and calendar through functions supplied by Visual C++.

The header file TIME.H includes necessary definitions for handling time and date values in your Visual C++ programs. There are two new data types that you should know when dealing with time and its types. They are

```
time_t
```

and

```
struct tm
```

time_t is defined in the TIME.H header file. Be sure to include TIME.H when you want to work with date or time functions. Although time_t is defined as nothing more than an unsigned long int, any variable you define with time_t, such as

```
time_t rightNow;   // Defines a time variable
```

can hold a time value. In Visual C++, a time variable holds the number of seconds since midnight, January 1, 1970. That is when Visual C++ thinks that time began. Because you know the number of seconds, this is both a time and a date function. Depending on how you calculate from those seconds, you can determine the proper time and even the date.

Consider the program that follows:

```
 1:// Filename: TIME1.CPP
 2:// Tests the time() function
 3:#include <time.h>
 4:#include <iostream.h>
 5:
 6:void main()
 7:{
 8:  time_t lt;
 9:  // Passing time() a NULL pointer makes it
10:  // return the time in seconds
11:  lt = time(NULL);   // NULL is defined in stdio.h
12:  cout << "The number of seconds since 1-1-1970: " << lt;
13:  return;
14:}
```

Here is the program's output:

```
The number of seconds since 1-1-1970: 804361926
```

Note You will get a different output depending on the time and date that you run the program.

Passing `time()` the NULL value (defined in STDIO.H) makes `time()` return a value, as shown in TIME1.CPP. You can then calculate from the seconds (by converting the seconds into hours, days, or months by dividing by the appropriate value) to get the date or time needed. (Can you write a program to work out when I ran this example? Don't try yet!)

Definition—The *broken-down time structure* is a special data value that holds time and date information.

Another time-related variable is a structure variable. The broken-down time structure variable is defined in the TIME.H header file, so be sure to include TIME.H when you work with the date or time.

You can access helpful values from the time structure with a function named `localtime()`. `localtime()` returns a pointer to a `tm` structure. Accessing a structure requires the pointer operator, just as you have seen with structures and classes.

STOP&TYPE Listing 23.4 contains a program that fills the broken-down time structure, letting the rest of the program access various elements of the date and time.

Review

The TIME.H header file supplies several time and date access functions that you can use to work with the PC's time and date values.

▼ INPUT   LISTING 23.4. USING THE BROKEN-DOWN TIME STRUCTURE TO DISPLAY TIME AND DATE VALUES.

```
 1:// Filename: TIME2.CPP
 2:// Printing date and time values
 3:#include <iostream.h>
 4:#include <time.h>
 5:
 6:void main()
 7:{
 8:  struct tm *local;   // Pointer to the time structure
 9:  time_t t;
10:  t = time(NULL);   // Store seconds time in t
11:  local = localtime(&t);   // Fills the structure-pointed data
12:
13:  cout << "The current seconds are " << local->tm_sec << endl;
14:  cout << "The current minutes are " << local->tm_min << endl;
15:  cout << "The current hours are " << local->tm_hour << endl;
16:  cout << "The current day is " << local->tm_mday << endl;
17:  cout << "The current month is " << local->tm_mon << endl;
18:  cout << "The current year (since 1900) is "
19:       << local->tm_year << endl;
20:  cout << "The current weekday is " << local->tm_wday << endl;
21:  cout << "The current day of year is "
22:       << local->tm_yday << endl;
23:  cout << "The current Daylight Savings Flag is "
24:       << local->tm_isdst << endl;
25:  // DST is 0 in during winter months, 1 otherwise
26:  return;
27:}
```

▼ OUTPUT

```
The current seconds are 34
The current minutes are 56
The current hours are 10
The current day is 28
The current month is 5
The current year (since 1900) is 95
The current weekday is 3
The current day of year is 178
The current Daylight Savings Flag is 1
```

The program uses the `time` function to get the time from the system. Passing to `time` the `localtime()` function via a pointer returns the results of several time calculations into the `tm` structure. The sort of time required is then easily accessed from the structure, as in line 13 for example.

When you are ready for a date or time value, look at TIME2.CPP, define the time variables as it does in lines 8 and 9, and call the `time` and `localtime()` functions. You can then print any of the remaining values or use them in your own calculations by referencing them as this program does. See how powerful library functions are? How long would it take you to write a program to find out when I ran the earlier example now?

▶ Using Class Libraries

Concept

What You Will Learn

The real power of classes comes from class libraries, which save you from writing a lot of code.

So far, you have looked at library functions, but the world of C++ provides you with access to another set of prewritten code—class libraries.

Standard C++ really only provides one set of classes for you to play with—the stream library of code. You've used these so often that you don't need to look through how to use them. The only thing that you have used with `cin` and `cout` that has not been covered elsewhere is the `<<` and `>>` operators. These are special operators that work a bit like an assignment operator, moving data from one side of the operator to another. Although the syntax looks a bit strange, there is nothing magic about these provided classes. You can use them and derive from them yourself. In the next unit, you will work a lot with the file handling variations of the stream library.

You can buy libraries of classes that you can then use in your programs. There are classes to work with databases, draw graphs, and store large amounts of data easily in your programs.

The version of Visual C++ that you have with this book contains a very exciting class library called the *Microsoft Foundation Class* (MFC), which is an obscure way of saying that it is a library of classes for writing Windows programs. I hope you're not too disappointed that we haven't done any Windows programming. There are a few reasons why we haven't tried to cover it: It has taken a whole book just to learn about programming in C++; you'll need another whole book to learn about how Windows works and how to program in that. Any commercial Windows program developed now is likely to have been written at least in part using a class library, whether it is a commercially available class library or a manufacturer's own internal version. So there is little point in trying to learn how to write Windows programs without using a class library.

Although it is interesting to write complicated programs, if you write the code, you have to sort out getting it to work and maintaining it as things change. In most professional environments, you need to write code quickly. A class library will most likely have thousands of users who will have found any problems before you start to use the code. On PCs, complex class libraries often cost less than $200, which is often less than it costs a company to employ a programmer for one day. Programs that you see on PCs today are more complicated than the ones around five years ago mainly because program writers are able to borrow code from previous versions. If the previous code was OOP, borrowing the code is very easy.

Class libraries are often supplied with source code, because you are encouraged to write new classes based on the provided classes. Although (hopefully) the documentation provided with the classes is good, when writing complex classes, you sometimes need that extra information to see exactly how a class works. The most accurate documentation of a program is its source!

Definition—*API* stands for *Application Programming Interface*, which is the set of function calls provided to allow users of a system to access it within a program.

STOP&TYPE As the last exercise in this unit, in Listing 23.5 you'll see a simple Windows program written using MFC. Don't expect to understand the program; just look to see how a class library is used to hide away the complications of Windows programming and its thousands (literally) of API functions. The MFC comes with some extra goodies, one of which is the CString class.

Warning To run this program, do not try to write it yourself. Use the project file provided so that the Workbench options are properly set. Do the following:

Choose Project I Open I MFC.MAK. This opens a project file that has lots of special options set and knows how to make Windows programs. When you make the project, the Workbench uses the *make file*, rather than the default QuickWin settings, to decide how to build the project.

```
 1:// File Name : MFC.CPP
 2:// A very simple Windows program
 3://
 4:// To compile and run this, you will need to
 5:// use the MFC.MAK project included with the
 6:// source. Choose Project ¦ Open ¦ MFC.MAK
 7://
 8:#include<afxwin.h> // This lives in a different include
 9:                   // directory
10:
11://-------------------------------------------------------
12:// SimpleApp is a class that hides the Windows equivalent
13:// of main()
14://
15:class SimpleApp:public CWinApp
16: {
17:   public:
18:   BOOL InitInstance() // A virtual function - trust me!
19:      {
20:        CString title("Hello World");  // A string class
21:        title += "!"; // Classes can define operators too.
22:                      // Define the addition to concatenate
23:                      // a string.
24:      // Make a window object with a frame border
25:      CFrameWnd* mainWindow = new CFrameWnd;
26:      // Tell Windows to make a window
27:      mainWindow->Create(0,title);
28:      // Assign the window to the application
29:      m_pMainWnd = mainWindow;
30:      // Tell Windows to show the window
31:      m_pMainWnd->ShowWindow(m_nCmdShow);
32:      // Tell Windows to make sure that the window
33:      // is properly drawn.
34:      m_pMainWnd->UpdateWindow();
35:      // Tell the base application that we successfully
36:      // made a window
37:      return TRUE;
38:      }
39:
40:   };
41:
42:
43:SimpleApp SimpleApp;  // This makes a global object
44:                      // which includes a main()
45:                      // that Windows can find
```

▼ **OUTPUT**

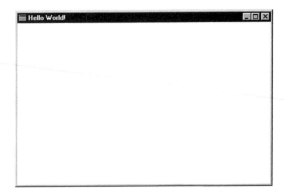

▼ **ANALYSIS**

For a start, you are not expected to understand how the program really works because Windows programming is really quite complicated. But let's look through the listing and see what you can understand.

The code uses three library classes. The first is CWinApp, which is a Windows Application class (as is meant to be implied by the name). All MFC classes start with C for class. In line 15, to make a new Windows application, you derive a new class SimpleApp from the provided CWinApp.

The second provided class that is very useful is the CString class. As you might expect, all programmers need better string handling functions than Visual C++ provides. Rather than everybody writing their own class, Microsoft has provided the CString class. This not only manages storage, but adds a lot of useful extra features.

Note You can read about the CString member functions by pressing F1 with the edit cursor on the CString word in an edit window.

In line 20, a new CString object is created and initialized with a string. In line 21, the overridden += operator is used to provide string concatenation. Without the need for spare characters, allocating new memory, or length checks, you can easily add character strings together by thinking of concatenation as string addition (you wouldn't want to add each character up).

In line 25, the third class is used. Without getting drowned in the details of MFC, you can create a frame window class that knows about the many lines of code and API calls needed to operate a Windows window. You first make an MFC frame window object (line 25), ask MFC to make a Windows window (line 27), and then perform some other standard functions to show the window (lines 31 through 34). If you learn MFC, you need lessons on the correct calls to make things happen. It's a bit like learning to drive a car: providing a gear shift and steering wheel does not mean you can drive it. For example, you won't find a matching delete for the new CFrameWnd, but the code is correct. You rely on MFC deleting the window for you.

How does the InitInstance function in line 18 get called? The magic is in the SimpleApp object declared in line 43. Hidden in the CWinApp class are all the function calls needed to start a Windows application. Somewhere in the heart of the class, when starting the application, the base class calls the virtual function InitInstance(). Because the call is virtual, it executes the object version, which you have overridden. This is a very important concept and it is just like using a class you derive yourself. It means that a class written perhaps thousands of miles away from your PC knows how to call your code. A well-written library provides enough of these virtual functions so that in every place you might need to do your own processing, you can replace the library code with your own.

When the application runs, notice that it does not run in the familiar QuickWin window but is a real application in its own right. It knows how to draw itself on the screen and put a title on the box, and you can resize it. It even has a system menu and responds to the commands. What you are seeing is a combination of Windows code being called and class library code that asks Windows to create the application and work in a particular way. The few lines of code in your application are actually making use of tens, if not thousands, of lines of code when it runs. Can you imagine how hard it would be to write a program that talked directly to the computer hardware to do the same as the few lines of code you have just written? This shows the power of OOP. Although you can write libraries of code without using classes, managing functions without the aid of classes soon becomes difficult.

▶ Homework
General Knowledge

1. What class and operator can you use to put output to the screen?
2. What is the class library used to write Windows programs with Visual C++?
3. Which keypress releases the buffered input to the program?
4. If the character array str1 contains the string Peter and the character array str2 contains Parker, what does str2 contain after the following line of code executes?

   ```
   strcat(str1, str2);
   ```

5. Which function enables you to get a string with spaces from the keyboard?
6. What is the difference between floor() and ceil()?

7. What does the following nested function return?

```
isalpha(islower('s'));
```

8. True or false: Library functions are for programmers who do not know how to code properly.

9. True or false: The header file contains all the code that Visual C++ needs to run a library function.

10. True or false: You can test the user's character input to see whether it is a letter, number, or space.

11. True or false: The `isxdigit()` and `isgraph()` functions could return the same value, depending on the character passed to them.

12. True or false: The following statements print the same results.

```
cout << pow(64.0, (1.0/2.0)) ;
cout << sqrt(64.0);
```

What's the Output?

13. What is the output of the following `cout`?

```
cout << floor(8.5) << " " << ceil(8.5);
```

14. What is this program's output?

```
// Filename: AD1.CPP
#include <iostream.h>
#include <ctype.h>

void main()
{
  if (isalpha('2'))
    { cout << "Yes"; }
  else
    { cout << "No"; }
  return;
}
```

15. What is this program's output?

```
// Filename: AD2.CPP
#include <iostream.h>
#include <ctype.h>

void main()
{
  char ch = 'a';
  if (islower(ch))
    { cout << "Yes"; }
  else
    { cout << "No"; }
  return;
}
```

16. What is this program's output?

```
// Filename: AD3.CPP
#include <iostream.h>
#include <ctype.h>

void main()
{
  char ch = 'a';
  if (isupper(ch))
    { cout << "Yes"; }
  else
    { cout << "No"; }
  return;
}
```

17. What is this program's output?

```
// Filename: AD4.CPP
#include <iostream.h>
#include <ctype.h>

void main()
{
  char ch = 'a';
  if (isdigit(ch))
    { cout << "Yes"; }
  else
  { cout << "No"; }
  return;
}
```

Find the Bug

18. What is wrong with the following program?

```
#include <ctype.h>
#include <iostream.h>

void main()
{
  char first[30];
  cout << "What is your first name? ";
  cin >> first;
  if (isalpha(first))
    { cout << "Nice job, " << first << endl; }
  else
    { cout << "That is not a name!" << endl; }
  return;
}
```

19. How could you improve the output of the following program?

```
#include <string.h>
#include <iostream.h>

void main()
{
  char full[10] = "\0";    // Will hold both names
  char first[10];
  char last[10];
  cout << "What is your first name? ";
  cin >> first;
  cout << "What is your last name? ";
  cin >> last;
  strcat(full, first);
  strcat(full, last);
  cout << "Your full name is " << full << endl;
  return;
}
```

Write Code That...

20. Write a program that tests user input to count the words entered. The program will look through a character array read in and look for spaces and punctuation. If a set of characters is not separated by a space and the punctuation is an apostrophe, it is not a separate word. (You need only code for a single line of input.)

21. Write a program that prints the letters of the alphabet to the screen and the printer forward and backward. Use loops for getting the next character in sequence.

22. Write a program that asks users for their first and last initials. If a user types anything other than two letters, display an error message. If the user enters the initials in lowercase, print them to the screen in uppercase.

Extra Credit

23. Write a program that rounds up and rounds down the numbers –20.51, –5.75, and 9.00.

24. Write a program that tells the user today's date and the date exactly 30 days from now. Hint: You will have to first calculate the number of seconds in 30 days.

25. A palindrome is a word or a phrase spelled the same forward and backward. Three sample palindromes are

Draw pupil's lip upward!

Was it a rat I saw?

Tut, tut. Star Comedy by Democrats, tut, tut.

Write a Visual C++ program that asks the user for a phrase. Build the input, one character at a time, using the standard input methods of cin. When you have the full string (store it in a character array), determine whether the phrase is a palindrome. You have to filter special (nonalphabetic) characters, storing only alphabetic characters to a second character array. You also must convert the characters to uppercase as you store them. The first palindrome would become

DRAWPUPILSLIPUPWARD

Using one or more for or while loops, you now can test the phrase to determine whether it is a palindrome. Print the result of the test on the printer. Sample output should look like this:

```
"Draw pupil's lip upward!" is a palindrome.
```

24

Storing Data in Files

append

field

`read()`

record

`seekg()`

`write()`

random file access

sequential file access

▶ **What You'll Learn**

- ▶ Data on the disk
- ▶ Sequential and random access
- ▶ Using sequential files
- ▶ Opening and closing files
- ▶ Writing data
- ▶ Appending to files
- ▶ Reading from files
- ▶ Random-access records
- ▶ Opening random-access files
- ▶ Jumping with seekg()
- ▶ More I/O functions

Most "real-world" computer applications need to hold data long after the computer is turned off. So far, all the programs in this book have used data that was either placed in literals or entered through the keyboard. You've used expressions to move the data around inside the program and the standard input and output classes, cin and cout, to converse with the user.

Nearly all useful programs remember data from previous times they have been run, or they can read data from other programs. In the PC world, nearly all the data is held in the form of disk storage. This unit looks at how you can use files.

Having used the standard input and output routines, you will be surprised how easy it is to read and write data to and from disk in a very similar way.

Random file access enables you to read or write any data in your disk file without having to read or write every piece of data that precedes it. You can quickly search for, add, retrieve, change, and delete information in a random-access file. Although you need to learn a few new functions to access files randomly, the extra effort pays off in flexibility, power, and the speed of disk access.

This unit ends the basics of programming in Visual C++. When you began reading this book, you might have been a beginning programmer. After this unit, you will be past the rank of beginning programmer and can begin writing extremely powerful programs.

▶ Data on the Disk

What You Will Learn

Disks hold lots of data for a long time.

Nearly all computers have much less memory (RAM) than hard disk storage. Your disk drives hold much more data than your computer can hold in RAM. Also, if you turn off your PC, the disk memory is remembered, whereas RAM is lost and the data is forgotten.

Disk is the perfect place to store programs. That's where all of your code is stored. It's also a good place to hold data. You can have several disks if you want, so you can increase your storage to massive amounts. Hard disk memory is relatively cheap: A gigabyte (1,000,000,000 characters) of disk costs roughly the same as 8 megabytes (1,000,000) of memory—and one hundred times cheaper is worth worrying about!

When you run lots of programs, they all must share RAM, which is limited. The more you can keep on disk, the better the PC can run your programs and efficiently share memory between them. If you can keep most of your data on disk, there is less for the PC to hold in RAM. If you need lots of data, you can always throw some data away out of RAM and get it back from disk a bit later when you need it again.

Review

What You Have Learned

Disks are not as limited as RAM for memory. You can store vast amounts of data and it will still be there after you have switched off the PC.

Note There is no Stop and Type section due to the textual nature of this section.

▶ Sequential and Random Access

Concept

What You Will Learn

Sequential data is read from start to finish in order, but you can read random files in any order you like.

UNIT

24

Storing Data in Files

You can access files in two ways: using sequential access or random access. What your application needs to do determines the method you will use. The access mode of a file determines how you are allowed to read, change, and delete data from a file. Most files can be accessed in both ways as long as the data lends itself to both kinds of access.

Sequential files have to be accessed in the same order as they were written. This is like cassette tapes: You play music in the same order as it was recorded. You can skip forward or backward, ignoring the music, but the order of the songs on the tape dictates how you have to wind through the tape. You can't insert new songs in between songs already on the tape. The only way to add or remove data is to copy the data to a new file.

It might seem that sequential files are limiting, but their ease of processing means that they can be used effectively in many applications. In fact, in C++ the screen and the keyboard are treated as sequential files because that is an easy model to process.

You can access random-access files in any order you like. In some ways, they are much more like a compact disc or an old-fashioned record because you can hop around playing parts of a track, switching to another part nearly instantaneously. The order of play is not limited to the order of recording. Random-access files take more effort to program, but the result can be a more flexible system.

Review
What You Have Learned

The type of file you use—sequential or random—depends on your application's requirements. Not all programs need random-access files.

▶ Using Sequential Files

Concept
What You Will Learn

There are two basic operations you can do to a sequential file: read it and write it. A special form of writing is adding to an existing file.

Only three operations are possible with sequential files.

- ▶ Creating disk files
- ▶ Adding to disk files
- ▶ Reading from disk files

If you are making a file for the first time, you first create the file, and then you add the data to it. Suppose you want to create a customer data file. You create a new file and write your current customers to that file. The data might be in arrays or structures, or in lots of variables. Over time, as your customer list grows, you could add them to the file. When you add to the end of a file, it is called appending to the file. As the customers contact you, you could read the file to look for information about the customer.

A sequential file is like that music cassette. You can't easily change the music in the middle of the tape. Likewise, not all applications are good for sequential processing. If you need to change the customer's details, you need to copy the whole file. Similarly, if you want to delete a customer, you need to copy the whole file but skip over that customer. Unlike a music cassette, because the data is digital, you can copy a file over and over and it is still as good as the original.

Note The primary approach to sequential file updating is to create a new file from the old one. Don't worry about updating a file directly until you review random-access files later in this section.

▶ Opening and Closing Files

Concept
What You Will Learn

Programs must open files before they can access data. After your program has accessed the data, your program should close them.

Before you can use a file, you must open it. This is like opening a book before reading it. When you are finished with the book, you close it again. You must also close a file when you have finished with it.

When you open a file, you must tell Visual C++ what the file is called, regardless of whether you are reading it or creating it. Visual C++ uses the operating system to help it prepare the file for use, making sure that there is an entry on the disk's index of files and a space for the file to occupy. When a file is closed, any remaining data is written to disk and the file information is updated.

File accessing in C++ is done with *streams*. To make a stream, you make an object. There are two ways to make a stream. You can make a stream without a name and then open it, or you can open a stream with a filename.

There are two kinds of sequential file streams: input file streams (or `ifstream`), and output file streams (or `ofstream`). The file streams live in the `fstream.h` header. You don't need to worry too much about the inner workings of streams. You use various member functions to find out about them, such as `eof()` to find whether you are at the end of an input file and `is_open()` to find whether you successfully opened the file. Here is a statement to open file `vc.txt` for input:

```
ifstream input("vc.txt");
```

Here is a snippet of code to open a file for output and check that it was opened correctly:

```
ofstream output("vcout.txt");
if (output.is_open())
```

Files can be opened to work in different ways. The default file type is a text file. You can make the file a binary file. If you write a number to a text file, it appears as it would if you wrote it to `cout`. In fact, `cout` is a special case of a text file, so anything you write to a screen will appear in the same way in a text file. If you open a binary file such as

```
ofstream output("binary.out",ios::binary);
```

Visual C++ writes the characters in a different way (especially numbers). The binary format is more compact, but it is specific to the program. You can't guarantee that other programs can read your data. It mainly differs in the handling of numbers. In the next program, you'll see that if you write a number to a text file, it gets converted. To a binary file, Visual C++ writes the bytes of data that represent the number—such as two bytes for an integer—instead of five characters for 12345.

The second parameter of the stream constructor or `open` member function sets the access mode of the file. Table 24.1 lists them.

Table 24.1. Possible access modes.

Mode	Description
ios::app	Opens a file for appending (adding to)
ios::ate	Seeks to end of file on opening it
ios::in	Opens a file for reading
ios::out	Opens a file for writing
ios::binary	Opens a file in binary mode
ios::trunc	Discards the contents if the file exists
ios::nocreate	If file does not exist, open fails
ios::noreplace	If file exists, open fails unless appending or seeking to the end of file on opening

Note To combine these flags (in order to have a binary file with no create), you need to use the bitwise OR operator (¦). Here's an example:

```
ifstream input("infile.bin",ios::nocreate ¦ ios::binary);
```

You can combine as many as flags as you like in this way. If you want to know more about bitwise operators, refer to the bonus chapter, "Advancing with Bitwise Operators," on the disk.

When you try to open a file, you should always check whether you have been successful by using is_open() or testing that the stream variable is nonzero. (A clever thing with C++ is that the class can be made to return different types of values.) When the file is open, you never need to refer to the filename again.

Because the input and output is a stream, the same rules apply as for screen input. You use the >> and << operators for input and output respectively. If you use these, each variable is delimited by whitespace. (The following program might help you clarify what goes on with screen input.) Whitespace is not automatically added to output. (You can change the delimiter to a special character if you like, using the fill() function.) You can also use get (get a single character), put (put a single character), getline, and putline to more carefully control the characters written.

Often, you develop a class that owns a file, normally as a data member. Rather than performing low-level reading and writing, you will develop functions to write out structures of data. To successfully use stream input, you should know what has been written. If you can predict the data types on the input stream (they must have been written in a particular order), you can read into the correct data type as you go. If you don't know what is coming, normally you will read the input into a character string using getline (or read for binary data) and then examine it, perhaps using the library functions of the previous unit.

Tip There is not a function that checks for a file's existence. To do this, open a file for input with the ios::nocreate flag set. This will fail if the file does not exist. If the file does exist, you can immediately close the file again.

Files should be closed as soon as they are finished being used. A file will automatically be closed by the stream destructor (by using delete or by the object going out of local scope) or by explicitly calling close():

```
output.close();
```

Closing does more than just close the file. It first ensures that any data loitering about in the program is written out too.

UNIT

24

Storing Data in Files

You can use as many files as you like in your program. (That is not strictly true. Different operating systems have limits on the number of files they can handle once.)

STOP&TYPE Listing 24.1 shows a program that reads itself onto the screen.

▼ INPUT   LISTING 24.1 READING A TEXT FILE INTO A PROGRAM.

```
 1:// File name: PROGREAD.CPP
 2:// A simple text reading program
 3://
 4:#include <fstream.h>
 5:void main()
 6:  {
 7:    char buffer[255];  // A place to read into
 8:    char inputFile[]="PROGREAD.CPP";   // The file name
 9:
10:    ifstream input(inputFile);   // Declare an input stream
11:
12:    if (!input)                        // Has it opened OK?
13:      cout << "Error in file name";    // Oops!
14:    else
15:      {                                // Ok
16:        cout << "File: " << inputFile << endl;
17:        while (!input.eof())           // While more data
18:          {
19:            input.getline(buffer,255); // Get line of input
20:            cout << buffer << endl;     // Output input(!)
21:          }
22:      }
23:  } // input closes here due to scope & destructor
```

▼ OUTPUT

```
File: PROGREAD.CPP
// File name: PROGREAD.CPP
// A simple text reading program
//
#include <fstream.h>
void main()
  {
    char buffer[255];  // A place to read into
    char inputFile[]="PROGREAD.CPP";   // The file name

    ifstream input(inputFile);   // Declare an input stream

    if (!input)                        // Has it opened OK?
      cout << "Error in file name";    // Oops!
    else
      {                                // Ok
        cout << "File: " << inputFile << endl;
        while (!input.eof())           // While more data
```

```
          {
            input.getline(buffer,255); // Get line of input
            cout << buffer << endl;    // Output input(!)
          }
      }
   } // input closes here due to scope & destructor
```

▼ ANALYSIS

Aside from being a quick way to fill a few pages of this book (just joking, honest!), this shows how easy file handling is now that you're used to screen output.

In line 10, the program finds the file and opens it in one simple statement. In line 12, the file variable is tested to see whether the file opened correctly. If the file did open, you want to output the contents to the screen line by line. Text files have the same concept of lines that the screen has. Therefore, you can simply read a whole line—not to exceed 255 characters—into a character string, and then immediately output it again. This demonstrates an important principle. This program could handle a file of thousands of lines, but it only needs the RAM to hold a few work variables and 255 characters of the file at a time.

Note   To specify a DOS path name, you need to use the double backslash, because \ is a special character to C++. So, to print AUTOEXEC.BAT from any directory or drive would require the following:

```
ifstream auto("C:\\AUTOEXEC.BAT");
```

Line 17 contains a very significant statement. The while test uses the function eof() to find out whether there is any more file to be read. Inside the stream processing, when C++ reads the file and finds that there is no more data to be read, it sets the eof status, which is one of several status flags maintained for a stream. By using the eof() function, the program can retrieve the setting of this status to decide when to stop. After a status is set, it is not automatically unset. Therefore, if further processing is required on the file, clear() needs to be called in order to reset the status. Another test you can make is to check the value of bad(), which returns a nonzero value if there has been a severe I/O error (such as removing a floppy disk from the drive halfway through an executing program).

Definition—eof stands for *end of file*.

▶ **Writing Data**

Concept   **What You Will Learn**

It's a snap to write to an output file. You've been doing it for the whole book!

UNIT

24

Storing Data in Files

STOP&TYPE   As was mentioned earlier, the commands you use with cout work just the same with a file stream, except the result ends up on the disk. You can overwrite an existing file or append to a file. You control this by setting the ios::app flag for appending. The program in Listing 24.2 adds some data to a file every time it is run.

▼ INPUT   LISTING 24.2. WRITING DATA TO A FILE.

```
 1:// Filename: WR1.CPP
 2:// Writes names to a file
 3:#include <fstream.h>
 4:
 5:void main()
 6:{ //Create or append to a file
 7:   ofstream fp("C:\\NAMES.DAT", ios::app);
 8:
 9:   if (!fp) // Exit on error
10:     return;
11:   fp << "Kim Spencer" << endl;
12:   fp << "Michael Spencer" << endl;
13:   fp << "Derek Spencer" << endl;
14:   fp << "Jane Spencer" << endl;
15:   fp << "-------------" << endl;
16:} // Close file automatically
```

▼ OUTPUT

After three runs, the file looks like this:

```
Kim Spencer
Michael Spencer
Derek Spencer
Jane Spencer
-------------
Kim Spencer
Michael Spencer
Derek Spencer
Jane Spencer
-------------
Kim Spencer
Michael Spencer
Derek Spencer
Jane Spencer
-------------
```

▼ ANALYSIS

The file is opened in line 7. The flag tells it to append to an existing file; hence the output is tripled by running three times. (You can check the output by opening the file with the Visual C++ Workbench editor.)

Note that the only reason that the output has one name per line is that you wrote the newline (endl) character sequence into the file. When writing to files, keep in mind that you have to read the data later. You have to use "mirror image" input functions to read data that you output to files.

▶ Random-Access Records

Concept   **What You Will Learn**

You can read and write random-access files that give you the ability to move around in the file (appropriately) randomly.

Sequential file processing can be slow unless you read the entire file into arrays and process them in memory. As explained in the previous section, you have much more disk space than RAM, and some disk files won't fit into RAM because they are simply bigger than the available memory. Therefore, you need a way to quickly read individual pieces of data from a file in any order and process them one at a time.

Definition—A *record* is a structure stored in a disk file.

Definition—A *field* is one or more values in a record that are analogous to a structure member.

You usually read and write files one record at a time. Records contain fields that you read and write to disk. Generally, you store data in structures and write the structures to disk, where they are then called records. When you read a record from disk, you generally read that record into a structure variable and process it with your program.

Unlike with most programming languages, not all disk data for Visual C++ programs must be stored in record format. Typically, you write a stream of characters to a disk file and access that data either sequentially or randomly by reading it into variables and structures.

Using random-access data in a file is simple. Think about the data files of a large credit card organization. When you make a purchase, the store calls the credit card company to receive authorization. Millions of names are in the credit card company's files. There is no quick way that the company can read every record sequentially from the disk that comes before yours. Sequential files do not lend themselves to quick access. It is not feasible, in many situations, to look up individual records in a data file with sequential access.

Use random file access when you must instruct the program to go directly to your record, just as you go directly to a song on a compact disc or a record album. The functions that you use are different from the sequential functions, but the power that results from learning the added functions is worth the effort.

UNIT

24

Storing Data in Files

Your random-access file is like a big array on the disk. You know that with arrays you can add, print, or remove values in any order. You do not have to start with the first array element, sequentially looking at the next one until you get the element you need. You can view your random-access file in the same way, by accessing the data in any order.

Definition—A *fixed-length record file* contains records that are all the same length.

Often, random file records contain fixed-length records. Each record (usually a row in the file) takes the same amount of disk space. Most of the sequential files you read and wrote in the previous unit were variable-length records. When you are reading or writing sequentially, there is no need for fixed-length records because you input each value one character, word, string, or number at a time, and look for the data you want. With fixed-length records, your computer can better calculate where on the disk the desired record is located.

Although you waste some disk space with fixed-length records (because of the spaces that pad some of the fields), the advantages of random file access compensate for the "wasted" disk space (when the data does not actually fill the structure size).

 Tip   Random-access files enable you to read or write records in any order. Even if you want to perform sequential reading or writing of the file, you can use random-access processing and randomly read or write the file sequentially from the first record to the last.

Because all variables of the same structure are the same size, when you read and write structure variables, you are reading and writing fixed-length data values. Working with fixed-length (all the same size) data values gives you the capability to move around in the file, reading and writing any structure in the file. If structure variables (derived from the same structure definition) were variable-length, you would never know how far to move in the file when you wanted to skip ahead five records.

Review   What You Have Learned

Files contain records, which are usually structure variables stored back to back in the file.

 Note   There is no Stop and Type section here due to this section's textual nature.

▶ Opening Random-Access Files

Concept

What You Will Learn

The open function's access mode tells Visual C++ that you want to access a file randomly.

As with sequential files, you must open random-access files before reading or writing to them. You can use any of the read access modes if you are only going to read a file randomly. To update a file, you should use the `fstream` stream. This insists on a mode (from Table 24.1). To update, you would open the file like this:

```
fstream update("update.txt",ios::in | ios::out);
```

The difference between random-access and sequential files is not physical but lies in the method that you use to access them and update them. Suppose that you want to write a program to create a file of the names of your company's top five executives. The following `open()` function call suffices, assuming that `fp` is declared as a file pointer:

```
fp.open("EXECS.DAT", ios::out);
if (!fp)
{ cout << "*** Cannot open file ***";
  return;}   // Exits the program if an error occurs
```

No update `open()` access mode is needed if you are only creating the file. The `!fp` check ensures that the file opened properly. If an error occurred (such as an open disk drive door for a floppy disk file) and the file did not open properly, the program could issue an error message.

However, what if you wanted to create the file, write names to it, and give the user a chance to change any of the names before closing the file? You then would have to open the file like this:

```
fp.open("EXECS.DAT", ios::in | ios::out);
if (!fp)
{ cout << "*** Cannot open file ***";
  return; }   // Exits the program if an error occurs
```

This code enables you to create the file, and then change data you wrote to the file. The `|` symbol is the bitwise OR operator that you saw earlier. Use the bitwise OR operator between two or more of the modes you want Visual C++ to use for `open()`.

As with sequential files, the only difference between using a binary `open()` access mode and a text mode is that the file you create is more compact and saves disk space.

UNIT

24

Storing Data in Files

Note   Remember that you can't open a read-only file for output. You get an error if you try to open a CD-ROM file with `ios::out`. Files on hard disks or diskettes can be set to read-only too.

▶ Jumping with *seekg()*

 Concept ━━━━━━━━━━━━━━━━━━━━━━━ **What You Will Learn**
You can move the random file pointer with `seekg()`.

When you read and write disk files, Visual C++ keeps track of a file pointer. When you first open the file for reading or writing, the file pointer points to the very first byte in the file. When you open the file for appending, the file pointer points to the end of the file (so that you can write to the end of it). You do not always want to begin reading or writing at the location of the file pointer. (If you did, you probably would be using a sequential mode.)

Visual C++ provides the `seekg()` function, which enables you to move the file pointer to a specific point in a random-access data file. The format of `seekg()` is

```
filestream.seekg(longNum, origin);
```

`filestream` is the stream object that you want to access, initialized with an `open()` statement or the constructor. `longNum` is the number of bytes you want to skip in the file. Visual C++ does not read this many bytes, but it literally skips the data by the number of bytes specified in `longNum`. Skipping the bytes on the disk is much faster than reading them. If `longNum` is negative, Visual C++ skips backward in the file (which allows for re-reading of data several times). Because data files can be large, you must declare `longNum` as a long integer to hold a large number of bytes.

`origin` is a value that tells Visual C++ where to begin the skipping of bytes specified by `longNum`. `origin` can be any of the three values shown in Table 24.2.

Table 24.2. Possible origin values.

Visual C++ Name	*Description*
`ios::beg`	Beginning of file
`ios::cur`	Current file position
`ios::end`	End of file

The names `ios::beg`, `ios::cur`, and `ios::end` are defined in the FSTREAM.H header file.

No matter how far into a file you have read, the following seekg() function positions the file pointer at the beginning of a file:

```
fp.seekg(0L, ios::beg);  // Positions file pointer at beginning
```

The constant 0L passes a long integer 0 to the seekg() function. Without the L, C++ passes a regular integer. This does not match the prototype for seekg() that is located in FSTREAM.H. This seekg() function literally reads "Move the file pointer 0 bytes from the beginning of the file."

The following seekg() function positions the file pointer at the 30th byte from the end of the file:

```
filePtr.seekg(-30L, ios::end);    // Positions file pointer
// at the 30th byte
```

This seekg() function literally reads "Move the file pointer 30 bytes from the end of the file."

If you write structures to a file, you can quickly seek any structure in the file using the sizeof() function. Suppose that you want the 123rd occurrence of the structure named Inventory. You would search using the following seekg() function:

```
filestream.seekg((123L * sizeof(Inventory)), ios::beg);
```

You'll see a demonstration of a structure read in the Project 12 program.

 Warning I use the term *structure* carefully. The structure should not have any pointers to other data types because these would not be saved. Also you can't simply create a class by copying data directly into it. The hidden internals will not be set.

To point to the end of a data file, you can use the seekg() function to position the file pointer at the last byte. Subsequent seekg()s should then use a negative longNum value to skip backwards in the file. The following seekg() function makes the file pointer point to the end of the file:

```
filePtr.seekg(0L, ios::end);    // Positions file
// pointer at the end
```

This seekg() function literally reads "Move the file pointer 0 bytes from the end of the file." The file pointer now points to the end-of-file marker, but you can seekg() backwards to find other data in the file.

STOP&TYPE Listing 24.3 contains a program that writes data to a new file and then reads randomly from that file. The program writes the letters of the alphabet to a file called ALPH.TXT. The seekg() function is then used to read and display the ninth and seventeenth letters (I and Q).

Review

Use seekg() to position the file pointer at whatever location you want to read or write next.

▼ **INPUT   LISTING 24.3. USING seekg() TO MOVE THE FILE POINTER.**

```
 1:// Filename: ALPH.CPP
 2:// Stores the alphabet in a file, then reads
 3:// two letters from it
 4:
 5:#include <fstream.h>
 6:#include <stdlib.h>
 7:
 8:
 9:void main()
10:{
11:  char ch;    // Holds A through Z
12:
13:  // Opens in update mode so that you can
14:  // read file after writing to it
15:  fstream fp("alph.txt", ios::in | ios::out);
16:  if (!fp)
17:  {
18:    cout << endl << "*** Error opening file ***";
19:    return;
20:  }
21:
22:  for (ch = 'A'; ch <= 'Z'; ch++)
23:    fp << ch;   // Writes letters
24:
25:  fp.seekg(8L, ios::beg);  // Skips eight letters, points to I
26:  fp >> ch;
27:  cout << "The first character is " << ch << endl;
28:
29:  fp.seekg(16L, ios::beg);   // Skips 16 letters, points to Q
30:  fp >> ch;
31:  cout << "The second character is " << ch << endl;
32:}
```

▼ **OUTPUT**

```
The first character is I
The second character is Q
```

▼ **ANALYSIS**

Line 15's fstream constructor opens the file named ALPH.TXT for both input and output. The if in line 16 ensures that the open worked properly.

The for loop in lines 22 and 23 writes the letters A through Z to the open file. Immediately after writing the data, line 25 repositions the file pointer so that the pointer points to the ninth letter, I. Line 26 then reads a character from the file, at the file pointer's location, so that the I is read into ch.

Line 29 positions the file pointer to the Q, and line 30 reads the Q into ch. The file closes at the program's termination with the destruction of the fstream object.

The preceding program forms the basis of a more complete data file management program. After you master the seekg() functions and become more familiar with disk data files, you'll begin to write programs that store more advanced data structures and access them.

▶ More I/O Functions

Concept
What You Will Learn

There are lots of helpful file I/O functions that you can put in your programming bag of tricks.

Several more disk I/O functions that you might find useful are available. They are mentioned here for completeness. As you perform more powerful disk I/O, you might find a use for many of these functions.

▶ read(*array*, *count*): Reads the data specified by *count* into the array or pointer specified by *array*. read() is called a buffered I/O function. read() enables you to read a large amount of data with a single function call. This function is prototyped in the FSTREAM.H header file. The array pointer is typed as a char * but you can read into any type, including structures, by using a cast such as read((Inventory*)&inventory,sizeof(Inventory));.

▶ write(*array*, *count*): Writes *count* array bytes to the specified file. write() is a buffered I/O function that enables you to write much data in a single function call. Note: The write() function is a perfect complement to the read() function. Try not to mix your I/O routines. If you write to a file using write(), read from it using read(). This function is prototyped in FSTREAM.H.

▶ remove(*filename*): Erases the file named by *filename*. remove() returns a 0 if the file was erased successfully or -1 if an error occurred. This function is prototyped in STDIO.H.

The following function is part of a larger program that receives inventory data in an array of structures from the user. This function is passed the structure. The write() function then writes the structure to the file stream fs.

```
void WriteStructure(Inventory& item) // reference for efficiency
  {
    fs.write((char *)&item, sizeof(inventory));
  }
```

The (char *) typecast operator is required by write(). You must typecast the data being written to a string pointed to by a character pointer as shown here.

> **Note** write() and its mirror image, read(), are extremely powerful. If the
> Inventory parameter is an array that has 1,000 elements, this one-line
> function can still write the entire array to the disk file! You could use the
> read() function to read an entire array of structures from the disk in a
> single function call.

STOP&TYPE Listing 24.4 contains a program that requests a filename from the user and erases the file from the disk using the remove() function.

Review

What You Have Learned

The I/O functions help you work with data files from your program.

▼ INPUT LISTING 24.4. USING THE remove() FUNCTION TO ERASE A FILE.

```
1:// Filename: ERAS.CPP
2:// Erases the file specified by the user
3:
4:#include <stdio.h>
5:#include <iostream.h>
6:
7:void main()
8:{
9:  char filename[255];
10:
11:  cout << "What is the filename you want me to erase? ";
12:  cin >> filename;
13:  if (remove(filename))
14:    cout << "*** I could not remove the file ***";
15:  else
16:    cout << "The file " << filename
17:         << " is now removed";
18:}
```

▼ OUTPUT

```
What is the filename you want me to erase? c:\names.dat
The file c:\names.dat is now removed
```

▼ ANALYSIS

Line 9 defines a 255-element character array to hold the filename that the user wants to delete. The 255 elements give enough room for a pathname if needed. After asking for the name of the file, line 13 attempts to remove the file with the `remove()` function and also checks the return value to see that the deletion worked.

▶ Homework

1. Is there a difference between records and structures? If so, what is it?

2. What is the physical difference between random-access files and sequential files?

3. Can you read a random-access file sequentially?

4. What must you first do before accessing a file?

5. How do you check for errors when opening files?

6. How do you close files?

7. What does the `seekg()` function do?

8. What is the origin in relation to the `seekg()` function?

9. What is the name of the function that erases files?

10. What happens to the file pointer as you read from a file?

11. What is the mirror-image function for `write()`?

12. What are the three origin values possible in the `seekg()` function?

13. True or false: Random file I/O requires that you plan your file's contents more than you must for sequential file access.

14. True or false: You test to see whether there is more data to read sequentially by using the `eof()` member function.

15. True or false: Using `write()`, you can write an entire array of structures in one program statement.

16. True or false: The `read()` that reads `write()`-produced data files usually contains the same arguments as `write()`.

17. True or false: You can't read from a random-access file without first creating it.

18. True or false: You can change the location of the file pointer, making it point to any byte in the file, by using `seekg()`.

Note There is no What's the Output? section for this unit.

UNIT

24

Storing Data in Files

Find the Bug

19. Hubert is having problems. Here is part of his program that attempts to read data from a file. What is wrong with the code?

```
ifstream input(fileName);
if (!fp)
  {
    "Disaster! File not found!";
    return;
  }
while (input.get(inChar))
  cout >> inChar;
```

20. Mary wants her Visual C++ program to erase a file called MYDATA.DAT, which is open and pointed to by the `fileIn` file stream. Help Mary erase the file by fixing this `remove()`:

```
remove(fileIn);
```

21. The following program attempts to perform the same action as Listing 24.3 (ALPH.CPP), with one addition. When the letters I and Q are found, the letter x is written over the I and the Q. Something is wrong, however, in two lines. See whether you can fix the program. To see what the program does when it contains the two bugs, run the program as is and look at the data file it creates (by loading the ALPH.TXT data file into your program editor).

```
// Filename: CHANGBUG.CPP
// Stores the alphabet in a file, reads two letters from it,
// and changes those letters to x

#include <fstream.h>


void main()
{
  char ch;    // Holds A through Z

  // Opens in update mode so that you can
  // read file after writing to it
  fstream fp("alph.txt", ios::in | ios::out);
  if (!fp)
  {
    cout << "*** Error opening file ***";
    return;
  }
  for (ch = 'A'; ch <= 'Z'; ch++)
    { fp << ch; }    // Writes letters
  fp.seekg(8L, ios::beg);  // Skips eight letters, points to I
  fp >> ch;
  // Changes the I to an x
  fp.seekg(-2L, ios::cur);
  fp << 'x';
```

```
    cout << "The first character is " << ch << endl;
    fp.seekg(16L, ios::beg);    // Skips 16 letters, points to Q
    fp >> ch;
    cout << "The second character is " << ch << endl;
    // Changes the Q to an x
    fp.seekg(-2L, ios::cur);
    fp << 'x';
}
```

Write Code That...

22. Write a program that writes a random-access file and then reads that file. Do not use any opens or closes. Use seekg() to reposition the file pointer at the beginning for the reading.

23. Write a program that writes the letters a through z to a random-access file. When it is finished, without closing the file, change the h, p, and t letters in the file to asterisks. Read and print the contents of the file at the end of the program to show that the three changes took place.

Extra Credit

24. Your company wants to reward its top five salespeople for last month. Write a program that asks for a list of the top five salespeople's names. (Assume that no name will be longer than 10 characters.) The program should then write those names to a disk file. Do you see that random-access files are unnecessary in this case?

25. Rewrite the program in question 24 so that it displays every other character in the file of names.

26. Rewrite the program in question 24 so that it displays the file's names backward from the order in which the names are stored.

27. Write a program that reads characters from a file. If the input character is a lowercase letter, change it to uppercase. If the input character is an uppercase letter, change it to lowercase. Do not change other characters in the file.

28. Write a program that displays the number of nonalphabetic characters in a file.

UNIT

24

Storing Data in Files

12

Using Disk Files

STOP&TYPE In this lesson, you learned about libraries of functions and classes, and you saw how to use disks. You have been using files throughout the book to use the screen and the keyboard, but you learned more about the extra techniques for disks. In this lesson, you saw the following:

▶ Character functions
▶ String functions
▶ Numeric functions
▶ Time and date functions
▶ Using class libraries

Project 12 Listing. Using files.

```
1:// File name: PROJCT12.CPP

2:// A simple file maintenance program which

3:// can add or update entries

4://

5:#include <fstream.h>

6:#include <ctype.h>

7:

8:struct PhoneList

9:  {

10:    char name[31];

11:    char phone[21];
```

▶ Sequential and random access

▶ Opening and closing files

▶ Using sequential files

▶ Random-access records

▶ Jumping with seekg()

▶ Helpful file functions

Description

1: Some comments to describe the program.

2: The comments continue.

3: The comments continue.

4: Empty comments can enhance the appearance of your program.

5: Include the file stream header.

5: This header also includes cout and cin, so IOSTREAM.H is not required.

6: Include header for toupper.

7: Blank lines help to make your program more readable.

8: Declare a structure called PhoneList.

9: Structure declarations start with an opening brace.

10: Declare a member to hold the name.

11: Declare a member to hold the number.

continues

Project 12 Listing. continued

```
12: };

13:

14:// Function prototypes

15:void Add(fstream& phone);

16:void Update(fstream& phone);

17:void List(fstream& phone);

18:

19:void main()

20: {

21:    char answer = ' ';

22:    // Declare the stream

23:    fstream phone("phone.lst",ios::in | ios::out);

24:

25:    if (!phone) // If phone file has not been opened

26:     {

27:        cout << "*** Error opening file phone.lst ***";

28:        return;

29:     }
```

Description

12: All structure declarations end with a closing brace and semicolon.

13: Blank lines help to make your program more readable.

14: A comment to describe the workings of the code.

15: Prototype for global function `Add()`.

16: Prototype for global function `Update()`.

17: Prototype for global function `List()`.

18: Blank lines help to make your program more readable.

19: Declare the `main()` routine.

20: All functions start with an opening brace.

21: Declare a variable for receiving the keyboard input.

22: A comment to describe the workings of the code.

23: Declare an `fstream` object to open file `PHONE.LST` in the current working directory.

24: Blank lines help to make your program more readable.

25: If there is a problem with the file...

26: An opening brace marks the start of statements within the `if` block.

27: Give an error message to the user.

28: Exit the program.

29: A closing brace marks the end of statements within the `if` block.

continues

Project 12 Listing. continued

```
30:

31:    while (1) // Do forever

32:      {

33:        cout << endl << "(A)dd, (U)pdate, (L)ist, (Q)uit? ";

34:        cin >> answer;

35:        cin.ignore(80,'\n');

36:        cout << endl;

37:

38:        switch (toupper(answer)) // Allow single test

39:          {

40:            case 'A':

41:              Add(phone);

42:              break;

43:            case 'U':

44:              Update(phone);

45:              break;

46:            case 'L':
```

Description

30: Blank lines help to make your program more readable.

31: Perform the following statements until a break or return is encountered.

32: An opening brace marks the start of statements to be repeated.

33: Prompt the user for input.

34: Get the first character that is typed.

35: Ignore any following characters, including the end of line.

36: Output a blank line to neaten the output.

37: Blank lines help to make your program more readable.

38: Decide which option the user asked for.

39: switch statements start with an opening brace.

40: If the user chose add...

41: Call the Add() function.

42: Continue processing after the switch statement.

43: If the user chose update...

44: Call the Update() function.

45: Continue processing after the switch statement.

46: If the user chose list...

38: toupper makes the lowercase input into uppercase input, saving case statement entries.

continues

Project 12 Listing. continued

```
47:            List(phone);

48:              break;

49:          case 'Q':

50:              return;

51:          }

52:      }

53:   }

54://-----------------------------------------------------------

55:// Add a phone entry

56://

57:void Add(fstream& phone)

58:  {

59:   PhoneList entry = {0};

60:

61:   cout << "What is the name? ";

62:   cin.getline(entry.name,31);

63:   cout << "What is the number? ";
```

Description

47: Call the List() function.

48: Continue processing after the switch statement.

49: If the user chose to quit...

50: return in main() ends the program.

51: This brace ends the switch statement.

52: This brace ends the while loop.

53: This brace ends the main() function.

54: A comment highlights the start of a function definition.

55: A comment to note what the function is for.

56: Empty comments can enhance the appearance of your code.

57: Define a function to add an entry to the phone list.

57: Objects can be passed as parameters. This needs a reference to avoid creating a copy of the file object.

58: All functions start with an opening brace.

59: Declare a PhoneList structure and initialize it to all zeros.

60: Blank lines help to make your program more readable.

61: Ask the user for input.

62: Get a line of input.

63: Ask the user for input.

continues

Project 12 Listing. continued

```
64:    cin.getline(entry.phone,21);

65:

66:    phone.seekg(0,ios::end); // Move to end of file

67:    phone.write((char*)&entry,sizeof(PhoneList));

68: }

69://------------------------------------------------------------

70:// Update a phone entry

71://

72:

73:void Update(fstream& phone)

74: {

75:    PhoneList entry = {0};

76:    const int size = sizeof(PhoneList);

77:    int count = 0;

78:

79:    cout << "Enter entry number :" ;

80:    cin >> count;
```

Description

64: Get a line of input.

65: Blank lines help to make your program more readable.

66: Move to the end of the file.

67: Write out the structure to the end of the file.

68: A function always ends with a closing brace.

69: A comment can be used to help find a function definition.

70: A comment to describe the function.

71: Blank comments can enhance the appearance of your code.

72: Blank lines help to make your program more readable.

73: A function to update the file is defined.

74: All functions start with an opening brace.

75: Declare a PhoneList structure and initialize it to all zeros.

76: A constant is declared to make the code more readable.

77: Declare a variable to record the record number.

78: Blank lines help to make your program more readable.

79: Prompt the user for input.

80: Get the user's response.

continues

Project 12 Listing. continued

```
81:    cin.ignore(80,'\n');

82:    if (count < 1)

83:      {

84:        cout << "Error - not a valid entry" << endl;

85:        return;

86:      }

87:

88:    // Find record

89:    phone.seekg(size*(count - 1),ios::beg); // Find it

90:    phone.read((char*)&entry,size);          // Read it

91:    if (phone.bad() || phone.eof())          // Check for error

92:      {

93:        cout << "Error - not a valid entry" << endl;

94:        phone.clear();                // Clear error flags

95:        return;

96:      }

97:
```

Description

81: Ignore any extra characters.

82: If the input is invalid, reject it.

83: A brace marks the start of the `if` block.

84: Send an error message to the user.

85: Exit the function.

86: A brace marks the end of the `if` block.

87: Blank lines help to make your program more readable.

88: A comment to describe the workings of the code.

89: Find the record by calculating the record length multiplied by the record number.

90: Read the record.

91: If there is a problem reading the record (such as it is off the end of file)...

92: A brace starts the `if` block.

93: Send an error message to the user.

94: Clear the file error flags.

95: Return to the calling function.

96: The brace marks the end of an `if` statement.

97: Blank lines help to make your program more readable.

continues

Project 12 Listing. continued

```
98:    cout << count << ": "           // Confirm entry
99:           << entry.name << '\t'
100:          << entry.phone << endl;
101:   cout << "New name (blank for cancel)? ";
102:   cin.getline(entry.name,31);
103:   if (entry.name[0] == '\0') // Quick zero length test
104:     return;
105:   cout << "New number? ";
106:   cin.getline(entry.phone,21);
107:
108:   phone.seekg(size*(count - 1),ios::beg); // Find it again
109:   phone.write((char*)&entry,size);        // Write it
110: }
111:
112:void List (fstream& phone)
113: {
114:   PhoneList entry;
```

Description

98: Inform the user of the current data.

99: Continue the message.

100: Continue the message.

101: Prompt the user for new data.

102: Get the new name.

103: If the user picked the wrong record, allow the update to be canceled.

104: Leave the update routine.

103: It is good practice to allow users to change their minds after they have had feedback on their choice.

105: Ask for the new phone number.

106: Get the new phone number.

107: Blank lines help to make your program more readable.

108: After the read, the file pointer will have moved; reset it.

109: Write out the data on top of old data.

110: All functions end with a closing brace.

111: Blank lines help to make your program more readable.

112: Define a function to list the entries on the file.

113: All functions start with an opening brace.

114: Declare a PhoneList structure variable.

continues

Project 12 Listing. continued

```cpp
115:    int count = 0;
116:
117:    cout << "Name\tNumber" << endl;
118:    phone.seekg(0,ios::beg); // Set position to beginning
119:    while (!phone.eof())      // While more entries
120:    {
121:      phone.read((char*)&entry,sizeof(PhoneList));
122:      if (phone.eof())        // Eof not set till after end
123:        break;
124:      cout << ++count << ": "
125:           << entry.name << '\t'
126:           << entry.phone << endl;
127:    }
128:    phone.clear();            // Reset eof flag
129: }
```

Description

115: Initialize a count.

116: Blank lines help to make your program more readable.

117: Output a title.

118: Set the file pointer to the start of file.

119: While the end of file is not reported, continue the following processing.

120: The statements repeated are enclosed in braces.

121: Read the file at the current position.

121: read moves the file pointer to after the last character read.

122: If read causes end of file to occur, no more records exist.

123: Leave the while loop.

124: Output the record count.

125: Continue the output with the name.

126: Continue the output with the phone number.

127: The brace marks the end of the while loop.

128: Reset any file flags that might have been set.

129: All functions end with a closing brace.

▼ OUTPUT

```
(A)dd, (U)pdate, (L)ist, (Q)uit? L

Name    Number
1: CompuServe   0121 359 4000
2: Directory Enquiries  192

(A)dd, (U)pdate, (L)ist, (Q)uit? A

What is the name? Operator
What is the number? 100

(A)dd, (U)pdate, (L)ist, (Q)uit? U

Enter entry number :2
2: Directory Enquiries  192
New name (blank for cancel)? International Enquiries
New number? 153

(A)dd, (U)pdate, (L)ist, (Q)uit? L

Name    Number
1: CompuServe   0121 359 4000
2: International Enquiries      153
3: Operator     100

(A)dd, (U)pdate, (L)ist, (Q)uit? q
```

Second run:

```
(A)dd, (U)pdate, (L)ist, (Q)uit? L

Name    Number
1: CompuServe   0121 359 4000
2: International Enquiries      153
3: Operator     100

(A)dd, (U)pdate, (L)ist, (Q)uit? q
```

Appendix ▶

Installing
Microsoft®
Visual C++™ 1.0

Before you can run Visual C++ programs, you must install the Microsoft® Visual C++™ 1.0 compiler that is included with this book. Turn on your computer if it's not already on; start Windows if it is not already started. Locate the book's CD-ROM, and you're ready to begin the installation.

Note   Visual C++ 1.0 is provided through special arrangement with Microsoft Corporation. Visual C++™ 1.0 for Windows® copyright Microsoft Corporation, 1992-1994. All rights reserved. Read the end-user license at the back of this book before using the software.

▶ Minimum System Requirements

Visual C++ 1.0 requires the following minimum configuration:

- ▶ IBM Personal Computer, or 100% compatible, running MS-DOS version 5.0 or later.
- ▶ Microsoft Windows 3.1+, Microsoft Windows for Workgroups 3.1+ (running in enhanced mode), or Windows 95.
- ▶ An 80386 or higher processor.
- ▶ A VGA monitor.
- ▶ 4MB of available memory (8MB recommended).
- ▶ A hard disk with enough disk space to install the options you need. The Setup program lets you select installation options and provides you with the disk-space requirements for the options you select. It then checks to make sure you have enough space before copying files.
- ▶ A CD-ROM drive.

▶ What Will Happen During Installation

The Visual C++ compiler that you get with this book is actually more than just a Visual C++ compiler. It is a complete Windows-based programmer's workbench with many more tools than you'll need to complete this book. It's a Windows 3.1-based product that will also work with Windows for Workgroups and Windows 95.

Note   Visual C++ Version 1.0 does not run under Windows NT.

The name of the compiler is Microsoft Visual C++ 1.0. The version that comes with this book is a complete, fully functional version, except that no printed documentation is included and Microsoft offers no technical support for the product. Be assured that nothing in the Visual C++ language is left out; in fact, the online help provides a wealth of useful information. You get a full implementation of Visual C++. The enclosed compiler supports every command and function in the Visual C++ language.

The installation procedure has two parts:

1. The book's source code files will be copied to your hard drive.

2. The Visual C++ compiler will be installed to your hard drive.

After the compiler is installed, you are ready to begin entering and running Visual C++ programs on your computer. The way that you install is slightly different under Windows 3.1 and Windows for Workgroups than with Windows 95. If you are not familiar with the way Windows works, refer to your Windows documentation to find out how to run the Windows tutorials that Microsoft provides with Windows. These are the best ways to get quickly up to speed with the way Windows works.

▶ Starting the Installation

To install the software, insert the book's disc in your CD-ROM drive and follow these instructions.

Windows 3.1+ users: Choose Run from the Program Manager File menu and type `D:\INSTALL` in the Command Line box. If your CD-ROM drive is not `D`, substitute the proper drive letter in this command. For example, if your CD-ROM is in drive `G`, type `G:\INSTALL`. Click OK to continue.

Windows 95 users: Click the Start button and click on the Run option. Type `D:\INSTALL` in the Open box. If your CD-ROM drive is not `D`, substitute the proper drive letter in this command. For example, if your CD-ROM is in drive `G`, type `G:\INSTALL`. Click OK to continue.

The following installation program will ask you a number of questions. The safest way to install is to do as you are told!

Installation of Book Files

Follow the on-screen instructions in the installation program. The book's source code files will be installed to a directory named `C:\VC12`, unless you changed this name during the install program.

When the source code files have been installed, the setup program for Microsoft Visual C++ 1.0 will automatically begin.

Installation of Visual C++ 1.0

Installing the Visual C++ compiler is pretty easy. The installation program does all the work!

The Setup program prompts you with a dialog box that describes the program and lets you continue or exit. Choose Continue and the Installation Options dialog box appears.

Use this dialog box to configure the installation to fit your system. If you have more than 40MB of free hard drive space, you can simply choose the default installation by clicking on the Continue button.

If you are short of disk space, you need not install all the options. But be sure you at least have the following options:

▶ Microsoft Visual Workbench

▶ Microsoft C/C++ Compiler

▶ Runtime libraries

These will fit into about 10MB of disk space, although you need a few megabytes of free disk space to ensure the correct operation of Windows and the compiler. It is also very useful to have the online help for when you want to explore a little on your own.

You can choose the drive and directory you want to install to, but if you're not totally sure why you want to change this, it's best to stick with the defaults. You change the drive or directories by selecting the Directories button on the selection screen.

Click on the Continue button of the Installation Options dialog box to begin the installation. Note that you can easily rerun the setup program to add options if you missed something important.

After you see the Setup Complete message box, the installation program asks whether to restart your computer. Accept this option to ensure that your computer is properly configured before using Visual C++.

When the Visual C++ installation is complete, it creates a Program Manager group (Windows 3.1+) or Programs folder (Windows 95) for the Visual C++ programs.

▶ Starting Visual C++

Windows 3.1+ Users: To start the Visual C++ compiler, choose the Microsoft Visual C++ Program Manager group. Find the blue icon called Visual C++ and double-click on it. The Visual C++ Workbench starts.

Windows 95 Users: To start the Visual C++ compiler, click the Start button, and choose Programs | Microsoft Visual C++ | Visual C++. The Visual C++ Workbench starts.

Good luck, and enjoy your life as a Visual C++ programmer!

▶ Troubleshooting

The default installation should work fine. If you accidentally change some settings, you should ensure that the following options are set in the Project | Options dialog box of the Workbench program:

- ▶ Project type: QuickWin application (EXE).
- ▶ Uses Microsoft Foundation classes: Not checked.
- ▶ Build mode: Debug.

▶ Support

If you're experiencing problems with the CD-ROM itself, with the book's programs, or with installing Visual C++, you can contact our support department (Macmillan Computer Publishing) for help.

Note   The support department can only offer limited support for Visual C++ 1.0—meaning help with installation and getting started. They can't help you with learning how to program or with problems you might experience while creating programs with Visual C++. Microsoft Corporation does not offer any product support for this special offering of Visual C++ 1.0.

Please be prepared to give a detailed description of the problem you're experiencing, along with information on your computer system.

Internet E-mail
Send a message to support@mcp.com with a detailed description of the problem you're having.

CompuServe
GO SAMS to visit the Macmillan Computer Publishing forum and leave a message in the Programming message area (Section 9).

Phone
(317) 581-3833

Fax

(317) 581-4773

Mail

Macmillan Computer Publishing
Attention: Technical Support
201 West 103rd Street
Indianapolis, IN 46290

B

The ASCII Table

Dec X_{10}	Hex X_{16}	Binary X_2	ASCII (DOS)	ANSI (Windows)	Ctrl	Key
000	00	0000 0000	null	000-032	NUL	^@
001	01	0000 0001	☺	not def.	SOH	^A
002	02	0000 0010	☻		STX	^B
003	03	0000 0011	♥		ETX	^C
004	04	0000 0100	♦		EOT	^D
005	05	0000 0101	♣		ENQ	^E
006	06	0000 0110	♠		ACK	^F
007	07	0000 0111	•		BEL	^G
008	08	0000 1000	◘		BS	^H
009	09	0000 1001	○		HT	^I
010	0A	0000 1010	◙		LF	^J
011	0B	0000 1011	♂		VT	^K
012	0C	0000 1100	♀		FF	^L
013	0D	0000 1101	♪		CR	^M
014	0E	0000 1110	♫		SO	^N
015	0F	0000 1111	☼		SI	^O
016	10	0001 0000	►		DLE	^P
017	11	0001 0001	◄		DC1	^Q
018	12	0001 0010	↕		DC2	^R
019	13	0001 0011	‼		DC3	^S
020	14	0001 0100	¶		DC4	^T
021	15	0001 0101	§		NAK	^U
022	16	0001 0110	▬		SYN	^V
023	17	0001 0111	↨		ETB	^W
024	18	0001 1000	↑		CAN	^X
025	19	0001 1001	↓		EM	^Y
026	1A	0001 1010	→		SUB	^Z

Dec X_{10}	Hex X_{16}	Binary X_2	ASCII (DOS)	ANSI (Windows)	Ctrl	Key
027	1B	0001 1011	←		ESC	^[
028	1C	0001 1100	∟		FS	^\
029	1D	0001 1101	↔		GS	^]
030	1E	0001 1110	▲		RS	^^
031	1F	0001 1111	▼		US	^_
032	20	0010 0000	space			
033	21	0010 0001	!	!		
034	22	0010 0010	"	"		
035	23	0010 0011	#	#		
036	24	0010 0100	$	$		
037	25	0010 0101	%	%		
038	26	0010 0110	&	&		
039	27	0010 0111	'	'		
040	28	0010 1000	(	(		
041	29	0010 1001	)	)		
042	2A	0010 1010	*	*		
043	2B	0010 1011	+	+		
044	2C	0010 1100	,	,		
045	2D	0010 1101	-	-		
046	2E	0010 1110	.	.		
047	2F	0010 1111	/	/		
048	30	0011 0000	0	0		
049	31	0011 0001	1	1		
050	32	0011 0010	2	2		
051	33	0011 0011	3	3		
052	34	0011 0100	4	4		

Dec X_{10}	Hex X_{16}	Binary X_2	ASCII (DOS)	ANSI (Windows)	Ctrl	Key
053	35	0011 0101	5	5		
054	36	0011 0110	6	6		
055	37	0011 0111	7	7		
056	38	0011 1000	8	8		
057	39	0011 1001	9	9		
058	3A	0011 1010	:	:		
059	3B	0011 1011	;	;		
060	3C	0011 1100	<	<		
061	3D	0011 1101	=	=		
062	3E	0011 1110	>	>		
063	3F	0011 1111	?	?		
064	40	0100 0000	@	@		
065	41	0100 0001	A	A		
066	42	0100 0010	B	B		
067	43	0100 0011	C	C		
068	44	0100 0100	D	D		
069	45	0100 0101	E	E		
070	46	0100 0110	F	F		
071	47	0100 0111	G	G		
072	48	0100 1000	H	H		
073	49	0100 1001	I	I		
074	4A	0100 1010	J	J		
075	4B	0100 1011	K	K		
076	4C	0100 1100	L	L		
077	4D	0100 1101	M	M		
078	4E	0100 1110	N	N		

Dec X_{10}	Hex X_{16}	Binary X_2	ASCII (DOS)	ANSI (Windows)	Ctrl	Key
079	4F	0100 1111	O	O		
080	50	0101 0000	P	P		
081	51	0101 0001	Q	Q		
082	52	0101 0010	R	R		
083	53	0101 0011	S	S		
084	54	0101 0100	T	T		
085	55	0101 0101	U	U		
086	56	0101 0110	V	V		
087	57	0101 0111	W	W		
088	58	0101 1000	X	X		
089	59	0101 1001	Y	Y		
090	5A	0101 1010	Z	Z		
091	5B	0101 1011	[	[		
092	5C	0101 1100	\	\		
093	5D	0101 1101	]	]		
094	5E	0101 1110	^	^		
095	5F	0101 1111	–	–		
096	60	0110 0000	`	`		
097	61	0110 0001	a	a		
098	62	0110 0010	b	b		
099	63	0110 0011	c	c		
100	64	0110 0100	d	d		
101	65	0110 0101	e	e		
102	66	0110 0110	f	f		
103	67	0110 0111	g	g		
104	68	0110 1000	h	h		

B

The ASCII Table

Dec X_{10}	Hex X_{16}	Binary X_2	ASCII (DOS)	ANSI (Windows)	Ctrl	Key
105	69	0110 1001	i	i		
106	6A	0110 1010	j	j		
107	6B	0110 1011	k	k		
108	6C	0110 1100	l	l		
109	6D	0110 1101	m	m		
110	6E	0110 1110	n	n		
111	6F	0110 1111	o	o		
112	70	0111 0000	p	p		
113	71	0111 0001	q	q		
114	72	0111 0010	r	r		
115	73	0111 0011	s	s		
116	74	0111 0100	t	t		
117	75	0111 0101	u	u		
118	76	0111 0110	v	v		
119	77	0111 0111	w	w		
120	78	0111 1000	x	x		
121	79	0111 1001	y	y		
122	7A	0111 1010	z	z		
123	7B	0111 1011	{	{		
124	7C	0111 1100	¦	l		
125	7D	0111 1101	}	}		
126	7E	0111 1110	~	~		
127	7F	0111 1111	Δ	□		
128	80	1000 0000	Ç	□		
129	81	1000 0001	ü	□		
130	82	1000 0010	é	‚		

Dec X_{10}	Hex X_{16}	Binary X_2	ASCII (DOS)	ANSI (Windows)	Ctrl	Key
131	83	1000 0011	â	ƒ		
132	84	1000 0100	ä	"		
133	85	1000 0101	à	…		
134	86	1000 0110	å	†		
135	87	1000 0111	ç	‡		
136	88	1000 1000	ê	^		
137	89	1000 1001	ë	‰		
138	8A	1000 1010	è	Š		
139	8B	1000 1011	ï	<		
140	8C	1000 1100	î	Œ		
141	8D	1000 1101	ì	□		
142	8E	1000 1110	Ä	□		
143	8F	1000 1111	Å	□		
144	90	1001 0000	É	□		
145	91	1001 0001	æ	'		
146	92	1001 0010	Æ	'		
147	93	1001 0011	ô	"		
148	94	1001 0100	ö	"		
149	95	1001 0101	ò	•		
150	96	1001 0110	û	–		
151	97	1001 0111	ù	—		
152	98	1001 1000	ÿ	~		
153	99	1001 1001	Ö	™		
154	9A	1001 1010	Ü	š		
155	9B	1001 1011	¢	>		
156	9C	1001 1100	£	œ		
157	9D	1001 1101	¥	□		

B

The ASCII Table

Dec X_{10}	Hex X_{16}	Binary X_2	ASCII (DOS)	ANSI (Windows)	Ctrl	Key
158	9E	1001 1110	₧	□		
159	9F	1001 1111	ƒ	Ÿ		
160	A0	1010 0000	á			
161	A1	1010 0001	í	¡		
162	A2	1010 0010	ó	¢		
163	A3	1010 0011	ú	£		
164	A4	1010 0100	ñ	¤		
165	A5	1010 0101	Ñ	¥		
166	A6	1010 0110	ª	¦		
167	A7	1010 0111	º	»		
168	A8	1010 1000	¿	¨		
169	A9	1010 1001	⌐	©		
170	AA	1010 1010	¬	ª		
171	AB	1010 1011	½	«		
172	AC	1010 1100	¼	¬		
173	AD	1010 1101	¡	-		
174	AE	1010 1110	«	®		
175	AF	1010 1111	»	¯		
176	B0	1011 0000	░	°		
177	B1	1011 0001	▒	±		
178	B2	1011 0010	▓	²		
179	B3	1011 0011	│	³		
180	B4	1011 0100	┤	´		
181	B5	1011 0101	╡	µ		
182	B6	1011 0110	╢	¶		
183	B7	1011 0111	╖	·		
184	B8	1011 1000	╕	¸		

Dec X_{10}	Hex X_{16}	Binary X_2	ASCII (DOS)	ANSI (Windows)	Ctrl	Key
185	B9	1011 1001	╣	¹		
186	BA	1011 1010	║	°		
187	BB	1011 1011	╗	»		
188	BC	1011 1100	╝	¼		
189	BD	1011 1101	╜	½		
190	BE	1011 1110	╛	¾		
191	BF	1011 1111	┐	¿		
192	C0	1100 0000	└	À		
193	C1	1100 0001	┴	Á		
194	C2	1100 0010	┬	Â		
195	C3	1100 0011	├	Ã		
196	C4	1100 0100	─	Ä		
197	C5	1100 0101	+	Å		
198	C6	1100 0110	╞	Æ		
199	C7	1100 0111	╟	Ç		
200	C8	1100 1000	╚	È		
201	C9	1100 1001	╔	É		
202	CA	1100 1010	╩	Ê		
203	CB	1100 1011	╦	Ë		
204	CC	1100 1100	╠	Ì		
205	CD	1100 1101	=	Í		
206	CE	1100 1110	╬	Î		
207	CF	1100 1111	╧	Ï		
208	D0	1101 0000	╨	Ð		
209	D1	1101 0001	╤	Ñ		
210	D2	1101 0010	╥	Ò		
211	D3	1101 0011	╙	Ó		

Dec X_{10}	Hex X_{16}	Binary X_2	ASCII (DOS)	ANSI (Windows)	Ctrl	Key
212	D4	1101 0100	╘	Ô		
213	D5	1101 0101	╒	Õ		
214	D6	1101 0110	╓	Ö		
215	D7	1101 0111	╫	×		
216	D8	1101 1000	╪	Ø		
217	D9	1101 1001	┘	Ù		
218	DA	1101 1010	┌	Ú		
219	DB	1101 1011	█	Û		
220	DC	1101 1100	▄	Ü		
221	DD	1101 1101	▌	Ý		
222	DE	1101 1110	▐	Þ		
223	DF	1101 1111	▀	ß		
224	E0	1110 0000	α	à		
225	E1	1110 0001	β	á		
226	E2	1110 0010	Γ	â		
227	E3	1110 0011	π	ã		
228	E4	1110 0100	Σ	ä		
229	E5	1110 0101	σ	å		
230	E6	1110 0110	μ	æ		
231	E7	1110 0111	γ	ç		
232	E8	1110 1000	Φ	è		
233	E9	1110 1001	θ	é		
234	EA	1110 1010	Ω	ê		
235	EB	1110 1011	δ	ë		
236	EC	1110 1100	∞	ì		
237	ED	1110 1101	ø	í		
238	EE	1110 1110	∈	î		

Dec X_{10}	Hex X_{16}	Binary X_2	ASCII (DOS)	ANSI (Windows)	Ctrl	Key
239	EF	1110 1111	∩	ï		
240	F0	1110 0000	≡	ð		
241	F1	1111 0001	±	ñ		
242	F2	1111 0010	≥	ò		
243	F3	1111 0011	≤	ó		
244	F4	1111 0100	⌠	ô		
245	F5	1111 0101	⌡	õ		
246	F6	1111 0110	÷	ö		
247	F7	1111 0111	≈	÷		
248	F8	1111 1000	°	ø		
249	F9	1111 1001	•	ù		
250	FA	1111 1010	·	ú		
251	FB	1111 1011	√	û		
252	FC	1111 1100	ⁿ	ü		
253	FD	1111 1101	²	ý		
254	FE	1111 1110	■	þ		
255	FF	1111 1111		ÿ		

B

The ASCII Table

Visual C++ Operator Precedence Table

Precedence Level	Symbol	Description	Associativity
1	::	C++ scope access/resolution	Left to right
2	()	Function call	Left to right
	[]	Array subscript	
	->	Visual C++ indirect component selector	
	.	C++ direct component selector	
3 Unary	!	Logical negation	Right to left
	~	Bitwise (1's) complement	
	+	Unary plus	
	-	Unary minus	
	&	Address of	
	*	Indirection	
	sizeof	Returns size of operand in bytes	
	new	Dynamically allocates C++ storage	
	delete	Dynamically deallocates C++ storage	
	type	Typecast	
4 Member Access	.*	C++ dereference	Left to right
	->*	C++ dereference	
	()	Expression parentheses	
5 Multiplicative	*	Multiply	Left to right
	/	Divide	
	%	Remainder (modulus)	

Precedence Level	Symbol	Description	Associativity
6 Additive	+ -	Binary plus Binary minus	Left to right
7 Shift	<< >>	Left shift Right shift	Left to right
8 Relational	< <= > >=	Less than Less than or equal to Greater than Greater than or equal to	Left to right
9 Equality	== !=	Equal to Not equal to	Left to right
10	&	Bitwise AND	Left to right
11	^	Bitwise XOR	Left to right
12	¦	Bitwise OR	Left to right
13	&&	Logical AND	Left to right
14	¦¦	Logical OR	Left to right
15 Ternary	?:	Conditional	Right to left

continues

Precedence Level	Symbol	Description	Associativity
16 Assignment	=	Simple assignment	Right to left
	*=	Compound assign product	
	/=	Compound assign quotient	
	%=	Compound assign remainder	
	+=	Compound assign sum	
	-=	Compound assign difference	
	&=	Compound assign bitwise AND	
	^=	Compound assign bitwise XOR	
	¦=	Compound assign bitwise OR	
	<<=	Compound assign left shift	
	>>=	Compound assign right shift	
17 Comma	,	Sequence point	Left to right

 Note   Because of the confusion in most precedence tables, the postfix ++ and - - and the prefix ++ and - - don't appear here. The postfix operators usually appear in level 2, and the prefix operators appear in level 3. In practice, perform prefix before all other operators except for the scope resolution operator, and perform postfix right before the statement continues to the next executable statement in the program. Visual C++ purists will cringe at this description, but it works 99.9 percent of the time, while the "technically correct" placements of these operators simply confuse programmers 99.9 percent of the time.

Appendix ►

Visual C++
Command
Reference

Note   Here are the primary Visual C++ keywords. You can't give functions or variables the same names as any of these keywords.

The following are keywords in Microsoft C and C++. Names with leading underscores are Microsoft extensions. You can't use any C keywords in a C++ program.

C Language Keywords:

__asm	__fastcall	__self
auto	float	__segment
__based	for	__segname
break	__fortran	short
case	goto	signed
__cdecl	__huge	sizeof
char	if	static
const	__inline	struct
continue	int	switch
default	__interrupt	typedef
do	__loadds	union
double	long	unsigned
else	__near	void
enum	__pascal	volatile
__export	register	while
extern	return	
__far	__saveregs	

C++ Language Keywords:

..catch	operator	try
class	private	virtual
delete	protected	__multiple_inheritance
friend	public	__single_inheritance
inline	this	__virtual_inheritance
new	throw	

The following are not keywords, but they have special meaning in Microsoft C++:

argc	envp	_setenvp
argv	main	_set_new_handler
__emit	_setargv	

 Note   The catch, template, throw, and try keywords are reserved for future versions of C++.

Index

SYMBOLS

P

X-Y-Z

W

Add to Your Sams Library Today with the Best Books for Programming, Operating Systems, and New Technologies

The easiest way to order is to pick up the phone and call

1-800-428-5331

between 9:00 a.m. and 5:00 p.m. EST.

For faster service please have your credit card available.

ISBN	Quantity	Description of Item	Unit Cost	Total Cost
0-672-30663-8		Visual C++ 2 Developer's Guide, 2E (book/disk)	$49.99	
0-672-30471-6		Teach Yourself Advanced C in 21 Days (book/disk)	$34.95	
0-672-30561-5		C Programming: Just the FAQs (book/disk)	$25.00	
0-672-30080-X		Moving From C to C++	$29.95	
0-672-30593-3		Develop a Professional Visual C++ Application in 21 Days (book/CD)	$35.00	
0-672-30487-2		Teach Yourself Object-Oriented Programming with Visual C++ 1.5 in 21 Days	$29.95	
0-672-30364-7		Win32 API Desktop Reference (book/CD)	$49.95	
0-672-30462-7		Teach Yourself Microsoft Foundation Class Library Programming in 21 Days	$29.99	
0-672-30531-3		Teach Yourself Windows 95 Programming in 21 Days, 2E	$35.00	
0-672-30594-1		Programming WinSock (book/disk)	$35.00	
0-672-30717-0		Tricks of the DOOM Programming Gurus (book/CD)	$39.99	
0-672-30562-3		Teach Yourself Game Programming in 21 Days (book/CD)	$39.99	
❏ 3 ½" Disk		Shipping and Handling: See information below.		
❏ 5 ¼" Disk		TOTAL		

Shipping and Handling: $4.00 for the first book, and $1.75 for each additional book. Floppy disk: add $1.75 for shipping and handling. If you need to have it NOW, we can ship product to you in 24 hours for an additional charge of approximately $18.00, and you will receive your item overnight or in two days. Overseas shipping and handling adds $2.00 per book and $8.00 for up to three disks. Prices subject to change. Call for availability and pricing information on latest editions.

201 W. 103rd Street, Indianapolis, Indiana 46290

1-800-428-5331 — Orders   1-800-835-3202 — FAX   1-800-858-7674 — Customer Service

Book ISBN 0-672-30637-9

and those portions of the SOFTWARE which are identified in the documentation as the VBX Controls ("VBX") *provided* that you: (a) distribute the REDISTRIBUTABLES, SAMPLE CODE, MFC, and VBX object code only in conjunction with and as a part of your software application product which adds significant and primary functionality; (b) do not use Microsoft's name, logo, or trademarks to market your software application product; and (c) agree to indemnify, hold harmless, and defend Microsoft from and against any claims or lawsuits, including attorney's fees, that arise or result from the use or distribution of your software application product. You may not distribute the REDISTRIBUTABLES, MFC, or VBX object code as part of any software product that can be used to create other software product(s) which use VBX controls. The SAMPLE CODE is limited to those files which are located in the MSVC\SAMPLES and MSVC\MFC\SAMPLES sub-directories which are created after the SOFTWARE is installed, using the default settings in the setup program, on a hard disk.

7. EXPORT RESTRICTIONS. You agree that neither you nor your customers intends to or will, directly or indirectly, export or transmit (i) the SOFTWARE or related documentation and technical data or (ii) your software product as described in sections 5 and 6 of this License (or any part thereof), or process, or service that is the direct product of the SOFTWARE, to any country to which such export or transmission is restricted by any applicable U.S. regulation or statute, without the prior written consent, if required, of the Bureau of Export Administration of the U.S. Department of Commerce, or such other governmental entity as may have jurisdiction over such export or transmission.

LIMITED WARRANTY

LIMITED WARRANTY. Except with respect to the SAMPLE CODE, MFC, VBX, and REDISTRIBUTABLES, which are provided "as-is", without warranty of any kind, Microsoft warrants that (a) the SOFTWARE will perform substantially in accordance with the accompanying written materials for a period of ninety (90) days from the date of receipt, and (b) any hardware accompanying the SOFTWARE will be free from defects in materials and workmanship under normal use and service for a period of one (1) year from the date of receipt. Any implied warranties on the SOFTWARE and hardware are limited to ninety (90) days and one (1) year, respectively. Some states/jurisdictions do not allow limitations on duration of an implied warranty, so the above limitation may not apply to you.

CUSTOMER REMEDIES. Microsoft's and its suppliers' entire liability and your exclusive remedy shall be, at Microsoft's option, either (a) return of the price paid, or (b) repair or replacement of the SOFTWARE or hardware that does not meet Microsoft's Limited Warranty and which is returned to Microsoft with a copy of your receipt. This Limited Warranty is void if failure of the SOFTWARE or hardware has resulted from accident, abuse, or misapplication. Any replacement SOFTWARE or hardware will be warranted for the remainder of the original warranty period or thirty (30) days, whichever is longer. Outside the United States, these remedies are not available without proof of purchase from an authorized non-U.S. source.

NO OTHER WARRANTIES. To the maximum extent permitted by law, Microsoft and its suppliers disclaim all other warranties, either express or implied, including, but not limited to implied warranties of merchantability and fitness for a particular purpose, with regard to the SOFTWARE, the accompanying written materials, and any accompanying hardware. This limited warranty gives you specific legal rights. You may have others which vary from state/jurisdiction to state/jurisdiction.

NO LIABILITY FOR CONSEQUENTIAL DAMAGES. To the maximum extent permitted by law, in no event shall Microsoft or its suppliers be liable for any damages whatsoever (including without limitation, damages for loss of business profits, business interruption, loss of business information, or any other pecuniary loss) arising out of the use of or inability to use this Microsoft product, even if Microsoft has been advised of the possibility of such damages. Because some states/jurisdictions do not allow the exclusion or limitation of liability for consequential or incidental damages, the above limitation may not apply to you.

U.S. GOVERNMENT RESTRICTED RIGHTS

The SOFTWARE and documentation are provided with RESTRICTED RIGHTS. Use, duplication, or disclosure by the Government is subject to restrictions as set forth in subparagraph (c)(1)(ii) of The Rights in Technical Data and Computer Software clause at DFARS 252.227-7013 or subparagraphs (c)(1) and (2) of the Commercial Computer Software—Restricted Rights 48 CFR 52.227-19, as applicable. Manufacturer is Microsoft Corporation/One Microsoft Way/Redmond, WA 98052-6399.

If you acquired this product in the United States, this Agreement is governed by the laws of the State of Washington.

Should you have any questions concerning this Agreement, or if you desire to contact Microsoft for any reason, please contact your local Microsoft subsidiary or sales office or write: Microsoft Sales and Service/One Microsoft Way/Redmond, WA 98052-6399.

IMPORTANT—READ CAREFULLY BEFORE OPENING SOFTWARE PACKET(S). Unless a separate multilingual license booklet is included in your product package, the following License Agreement applies to you. By opening the sealed packet(s) containing the software, you indicate your acceptance of the following Microsoft License Agreement.

Microsoft ® Visual C++™

(version 1.0)

MICROSOFT LICENSE AGREEMENT

(Single User Products)

This is a legal agreement between you (either an individual or an entity) and Microsoft Corporation. By opening the sealed software packet(s) you are agreeing to be bound by the terms of this agreement. If you do not agree to the terms of this agreement, promptly return the unopened software packet(s) and the accompanying items (including written materials and binders or other containers) to the place you obtained them for a full refund.

MICROSOFT SOFTWARE LICENSE

1. GRANT OF LICENSE. Microsoft grants to you the right to use one copy of the enclosed Microsoft software program (the "SOFTWARE") on a single computer. The SOFTWARE is in "use" on a computer when it is loaded into temporary memory (i.e. RAM) or installed into permanent memory (e.g., hard disk, CD-ROM, or other storage device) of that computer. However, installation on a network server for the sole purpose of distribution to one or more other computer(s) shall not constitute "use" for which a separate license is required.

2. COPYRIGHT. The SOFTWARE is owned by Microsoft or its suppliers and is protected by United States copyright laws and international treaty provisions. Therefore, you must treat the SOFTWARE like any other copyrighted material (e.g., a book or musical recording) *except* that you may either (a) make one copy of the SOFTWARE solely for backup or archival purposes, or (b) transfer the SOFTWARE to a single hard disk provided you keep the original solely for backup or archival purposes. You may not copy the written materials accompanying the SOFTWARE.

3. OTHER RESTRICTIONS. You may not rent or lease the SOFTWARE, but you may transfer the SOFTWARE and accompanying written materials on a permanent basis provided you retain no copies and the recipient agrees to the terms of this Agreement. If the SOFTWARE is an update or has been updated, any transfer must include the most recent update and all prior versions. You may not reverse engineer, decompile, or disassemble the SOFTWARE.

4. DUAL MEDIA SOFTWARE. If the SOFTWARE package contains both 3.5" disks and a CD-ROM disk, then you may use only the disks appropriate for your single-user computer. You may not use the other disks on another computer or loan, rent, lease, or transfer them to another user except as part of the permanent transfer (as provided above) of all SOFTWARE and written materials.

5. LANGUAGE SOFTWARE. You have a royalty-free right to reproduce and distribute executable files created using the SOFTWARE as part of your software application product *provided* that you: (a) do not use Microsoft's name, logo, or trademark to market your software product; (b) include a valid copyright notice on your software product; and (c) agree to indemnify, hold harmless, and defend Microsoft and its suppliers from and against any claims or lawsuits, including attorneys' fees, that arise or result from the use or distribution of your software product. If required in the SOFTWARE documentation, you agree to display the designated patent notices on the packaging and in the README file of your software product.

6. REDISTRIBUTABLE COMPONENTS. Microsoft grants you a non-exclusive royalty-free right to use and modify the source code version of those portions of the SOFTWARE which are identified in the documentation as the Sample Code ("SAMPLE CODE") and the Microsoft Foundation Classes ("MFC"). You may not distribute the SAMPLE CODE or MFC, or any modified version of the SAMPLE CODE or MFC, in source code form. Microsoft grants you a non-exclusive royalty-free right to reproduce and distribute the object code version of those portions of the SOFTWARE designated as grid.vbx, winmem32.dll, winhelp exe, vtd.386, penwin.dll, oemsetup.inf, ddeml.dll, commdlg.spa, commdlg dan, commdlg.dll, commdlg.dut, commdlg.fin, commdlg.frn, commdlg.ger, commdlg.itn, commdlg.nor, commdlg.por , commdlg.swe, dib.drv, expand.exe, lzexpand.dll, mcipionr.drv, olecli.dll, olesvr.dll, regload.exe, shell.dll, smallb.fon, smalle.fon, smallf.fon, stress.dll, toolhelp.dll, ver.dll, inhelp.hlp, markmidi.exe, and mfc200.dll (the "REDISTRIBUTABLES"), the SAMPLE CODE, MFC

continues on preceding page